SAM PECKINPAH'S WEST

Sam Peckinpah's West

NEW PERSPECTIVES

Edited by Leonard Engel

THE UNIVERSITY OF UTAH PRESS

Salt Lake City

© 2003 by The University of Utah Press
All rights reserved
Printed on acid-free paper

 The Defiance House Man colophon is a registered trademark of The University of Utah Press. It is based upon a four-foot-tall Ancient Puebloan pictograph (late PIII) near Glen Canyon, Utah.

08 07 06 05 04 03
5 4 3 2 1

LIBRARY OF CONGRESS CATALOGIN-IN-PUBLICATION DATA

Sam Peckinpah's West : new perspectives / edited by Leonard Engel.
   p.   cm.
Includes bibliographical references and index.
   ISBN 0-87480-772-7 (pbk. : alk. paper)
1. Peckinpah, Sam, 1952–1984—Criticism and interpretation.
 I. Engel, Leonard, 1936–
   PN1993.3P43 S26 2003
   791.43'0223'092—dc21
                                    2003010947

Dedicated to Moira

To Lenny, Tom, Kristin, Missy,

And to Tessa and Toby

CONTENTS

Acknowledgments   viii

Introduction ❖ A Terrible Beauty Is Born: Peckinpah's Vision of the West
   JOHN M. GOURLIE AND LEONARD ENGEL   3

One ❖ Auguries of Redemption:
   Peckinpah's Mythological Critique of American History
   ARMANDO JOSÉ PRATS   19

Two ❖ Comic Elements in Peckinpah's *The Westerner*
   PHILIP J. SKERRY   55

Three ❖ The Double Vision of Tragedy in *Ride the High Country*
   JOHN L. SIMONS   63

Four ❖ "Fall in behind the Major":
   Cultural Border Crossing and Hero Building in *Major Dundee*
   MATT WANAT   87

Five ❖ Peckinpah's Epic Vision:
   The Wild Bunch and *The Ballad of Cable Hogue*
   JOHN M. GOURLIE   115

Six ❖ Divining Peckinpah: Religious Paradigm and Ideology
   in *Convoy* and *The Ballad of Cable Hogue*
   FRANK BURKE   129

Seven ❖ *Junior Bonner:*
 Old West/ New West or the Antinomies of the Father
 RICHARD HUTSON   151

Eight ❖ Don't *Mess* with Texas: Recuperating Masculinity in *The Getaway*
 STEPHEN TATUM   171

Nine ❖ "Who Are You?" "That's a Good Question":
 Shifting Identities in Sam Peckinpah's *Pat Garrett and Billy the Kid*
 LEONARD ENGEL   199

Ten ❖ "We're Always Moving": Sam Peckinpah's Making of *Convoy*
 ELAINE MARSHALL   211

Eleven ❖ Ford, Peckinpah, and the Advantages of Making (Many) Westerns
 ROBERT MERRILL   231

Twelve ❖ *The Killer Elite* and the Critics: A Note on the Art of Interpretation
 LEONARD ENGEL   249

Sam Peckinpah Filmography   255

Contributors   257

Index   261

ACKNOWLEDGMENTS

This book has truly been a labor of love, and I have a number of people to thank for helping me bring it to completion.

My colleague John Gourlie has helped in so many ways; his advice and strong support have made the vision we had a reality. My genuine thanks to all the contributors; their good work and perseverance indicate that studying Peckinpah's films has been a labor of love for them, too. I must mention Richard Hutson, Elaine Marshall, and Steve Tatum; they have been especially helpful. I wish to express my gratitude to Linda Broker and Quinnipiac's Faculty Research and Sabbatical Leave Committees; they provided time and funding for this project. Many thanks to Quinnipiac's excellent library staff, especially June DeGennaro, Linda Hawkes, Richard Kipphut, and Janet Valeski, and to my colleague Jonathan Blake for his help on the Index. Thanks, also, to Dawn Marano at The University of Utah Press, for her wise counsel and patience.

Finally, a special thanks to my wife, Moira, for her understanding and constant support, and to Tessa and Toby, who listened to more talk about Sam than they care to remember.

SAM PECKINPAH'S WEST

INTRODUCTION

JOHN M. GOURLIE AND LEONARD ENGEL

A Terrible Beauty is Born

PECKINPAH'S VISION OF THE WEST[1]

Writing and directing for television in the 1950s, a time when Westerns were at the height of their popularity, Sam Peckinpah embraced the myth of the heroic lawman, a figure embodying the essence of virtue and nobility, that the genre heartily depicted in the 1940s and 1950s. When he began writing and directing feature films in the 1960s, Peckinpah transformed this myth to depict the death of the old ways as a more greedy and crushing social order arose. So in *Ride the High Country* (1962), the high-minded, heroic Steve Judd embodies a dying breed. He illustrates the price one pays to remain true to his values in a world that no longer honors them. At the moment of Judd's death in the film's final scene, Peckinpah identifies the hero with the western wilderness. He depicts an idealized wilderness—a paradise unspoiled, as though frozen forever, like the pastoral scenes on Keats's Grecian urn. For, like Keats, Peckinpah is more deeply concerned with images that probe the heart of truth and beauty than the rough surface of his characters and their actions might lead any casual viewer to suspect.

Essentially the wilderness—the Old West—dies with Judd. In his handling of the scene, Peckinpah mythologizes this moment, framing the death scene so that we see what Judd sees just before he dies: the peace and beauty of the mountains, far above the rabble and lowlife of the towns and mining camps. Judd is perhaps fortunate in that he will not have to watch civilization overtake and finally destroy the wilderness landscape with which he has been identified. Following *Ride the High Country*, Peckinpah's films transform the myth as they place the action in a desert terrain, symbolizing the wasteland world that replaces a more noble past. This desert terrain also expresses the moral condition of the characters who inhabit it. Gone is the lawman—the figure who intrinsically embodies the virtue and nobility of the classic warrior hero.

In Peckinpah's vision, Gil Westrum, Steve Judd's partner, inherits what is left after Judd's "Old West" dies, essentially the wasteland world that follows. Just as Gil is an alternative version of Steve Judd, so most of Peckinpah's succeeding heroes are versions of Gil Westrum. They inherit a Hobbesian world where life is short, nasty, and brutish. In this world it is a given that man's baser nature has full range: his blindness, crudeness, selfishness, greed, and lust for violence. The social contract functions unjustly or has failed altogether. Gil Westrum's heirs survive as rebels or outlaws, the law having lost its meaning with the death of Steve Judd and his world.

In Gil Westrum, Peckinpah significantly suggests that the figure of the outlaw may also be identified with the artist. Westrum's initial appearance in the film as a carnival showman operating a shooting gallery appears to symbolize the filmmaker and the Western genre in their roles as show business and entertainer. So, behind the figure of the outlaw in Peckinpah's films, one might also see the artist, who by his very nature must live and perceive, like the outlaw, beyond the conventions and mores of his society. If this is so, one sees from the beginning how much more profound Peckinpah's Westerns and his explorations of the figure of the outlaw are. Just as Peckinpah shows his outlaw heroes functioning in a world that has lost its traditional values, so as an artist he must function in a world shorn of its myth. But the memory of myth remains. The memory of the classic Western stands like a shadow—the ghost of Steve Judd—behind Peckinpah and his versions of the Western. The tension between the classical shadow world and the present Peckinpah world generates a depth of meaning that reverberates throughout his films. If Peckinpah's films themselves generate a myth, it is a myth of men in transition, caught in a wasteland world between a lost paradise and a devouring future.

If any one of his films generates this myth, it is *The Wild Bunch* (1969). In the beginning of the film, the members of the Bunch appear brutal, murderous, and without redeeming characteristics. Their past is already lost. As Peckinpah has them play "their string out to the end," they smash their lives against the beachhead of the mechanized and murderous modern world to come.

Peckinpah dramatized their actions with such aesthetic power that the release of *The Wild Bunch* in 1969 caused shock waves both in Hollywood and in theaters around the country. Most audiences could not see beyond the blood, violence, and brutality, but a certain number of viewers recognized Peckinpah's artistry. Among them film scholars like Jim Kitses, Garner Simmons, and Paul Seydor penetrated the public controversy over violence.

Responding to the aesthetic quality of the films, they initiated the serious interpretation of Peckinpah's new vision of the Western, to the benefit of all students and critics who follow them.

But whatever notoriety Peckinpah had gained from *The Wild Bunch*, his reputation generally declined in reviews of the films that followed it. By 1983, when he directed his last feature film, *The Osterman Weekend*, most critics did not regard him or his work very highly. After his death the following year, 1984, both he and his films remained almost forgotten by the public for a decade. Yet, when Warner Brothers released the restored version of *The Wild Bunch* for theaters in 1995, things changed dramatically. As Stephen Prince notes, with "glowing reviews [for *The Wild Bunch*] in the popular press, and . . . the publication of [David] Weddle's 1994 biography of Peckinpah, the director reemerged into the spotlight as an authentic . . . voice in the American cinema and one in need of careful critical reassessment" (Prince 1998, 3–4). The years that followed saw a spate of books and articles on Peckinpah and his films, highlighted by the work of Weddle, Michael Bliss, Prince, and a reissue of Paul Seydor's 1980 book, *Peckinpah: The Western Films: A Reconsideration* (1997)[2]

Credit belongs to Paul Seydor for his early and major recognition of Peckinpah's achievement. Significantly, as a means of articulating Peckinpah's achievement, Seydor placed Peckinpah's cinematic narratives in the context of our literary tradition. Likewise, David Weddle relates Peckinpah's "intensely personal vision" to our literary heritage, claiming it was "filled with recurring themes and imagery that have obsessed a long line of American artists" (Weddle 1994, 10). Similarly, in a critical tribute shortly after Peckinpah's death in 1984, Kathleen Murphy summarizes Peckinpah's connection to "Melville, Hawthorne, Twain, Hemingway, Faulkner." "They all fished dark waters," she writes, "from Moby Dick's domain to the Mississippi to the Big Two-Hearted River. . . . Our most native sons are outlaws all, men obsessed by whatever dream is violated or diminished . . . by a white whale or war, by unmanning bureaucracy or changing times—these fractured souls convulse in outrage" (Murphy 1995, 74).

Seydor's book-length study of Peckinpah's Westerns was part of a larger critical reevaluation of film itself as a medium of storytelling. By linking Peckinpah to the classics of American literature, Seydor, like others, attributed to film a status previously reserved for literary work of the highest order. Especially important was Seydor's handling of the Western, a popular genre usually considered lowbrow entertainment, as deserving of such status. He recognized that the popular genre could be used above and beyond its cliches and conventions to present depths of character, thematic profundity, reverberating insights, and compelling drama—all etched in indelible images. Seydor recognized that by using the Western, a genre characterized by mythmaking, Peckinpah was able to address our human condition within its framework of mythic power. Acknowledging the trail Seydor has blazed, the current essays seek to extend and enrich our understanding of Peckinpah's contributions to the realm of myth and storytelling, the realm whose flames illuminate our being, our deeds, and our place in the currents of time.

In the first essay of this collection, "Auguries of Redemption: Peckinpah's Mythological Critique of American History," Armando Prats outlines our cultural traditions as Peckinpah treats them. Prats specifically discusses the relationship between history and the mythic hero, and he places Peckinpah's films, particularly his Westerns, in a historical framework, dramatizing the hero's conflicts with a dehumanizing history. Presenting an overview of Peckinpah's work, Prats's essay provides a map, as it were, to orient the reader while the essays that follow offer a detailed close-up of one or sometimes two of Peckinpah's films.

David Samuel Peckinpah was born on February 21, 1925, in Fresno, California.[3] As a child, he spent long periods of time on a cattle ranch belonging to his grandfather Denver Church in Crane Valley, near Peckinpah Mountain. He later referred to this time as the happiest in his life, like a lost Eden. However, his relationship with the school system in Fresno was stormy, an early sign, perhaps, of the difficulty he would have with authority figures. In his senior year, his parents finally sent him to San Rafael Military Academy, where he earned more demerits than anyone else in the school's history. After a brief stint with the Marines in 1945, he attended Fresno State College, graduating with a B.A. in drama in 1949. Subsequently, he earned a Master's degree from the University of Southern California, writing his thesis on Tennessee Williams.

Peckinpah first entered the film industry with Allied Artists as third assistant casting director for Don Siegel. Working well with Siegel, Peckinpah became his personal assistant on several films, including *Riot in Cell Block 11*, *Invasion of the Body Snatchers*, and *Crime in the Street*. Siegel urged him to write for television, and, following Siegel's advice, Peckinpah wrote ten episodes of the CBS *Gunsmoke* series, produced in 1955–1956. In 1958 he directed his first television film, "The Knife Fighter," for the *Broken Arrow* series. In the same year, he directed "The Sharpshooter," which became the pilot for a popular new series called *The Rifleman*. Peckinpah's concluding experience with the TV Western came in 1959–1960 when he co-wrote and directed several episodes for the NBC series *The Westerner*. This series, argues Philip Skerry in chapter 2 of this collection, "Comic Elements in Peckinpah's *The Westerner*," was crucial to his cinematic development and to the feature films he would eventually direct. Furthermore, these episodes reveal a comic side of Peckinpah that critics have frequently overlooked.

In 1961, Peckinpah directed his first feature film, *The Deadly Companions*. The scope of a feature film gave him greater latitude in thematic development, but he chafed over losing control of the finished product to studio executives. Yet Peckinpah introduces themes here that he later developed in his major films, especially the theme of a world fraught with dangerous discrepancies between appearance and reality in which the protagonist pursues a path of vengeance. The film dramatizes the arduous struggle wherein the central character, Yellowleg, by eventually learning to love, is able to come to terms with his desire for revenge. Such a character, one seeking to avenge a perceived insult or injury, became the model for many subsequent Peckinpah heroes.

This film was closely followed by *Ride the High Country* (1962), shot by Lucien Ballard, the cinematographer who would collaborate with Peckinpah on many of his later features. When Judd dies in the gunfight at the end, he fulfills his personal goal—"To enter my house justified." But the simple virtues of courage, loyalty, and friendship are portrayed as outmoded, and Judd, embodying them, has become an anachronism. In casting the veteran Western actors Joel McCrea and Randolph Scott as the leads, Peckinpah signals that the changes involve not only the West but the Western film itself. In chapter 3, "The Double Vision of Tragedy in *Ride the High Country*," John Simons focuses on this change and argues that Judd becomes "a martyr to the values and meanings of the Old West." His death is a tragic sacrifice in the attempt to redeem the other characters and the land. Simons also shows the extent of Peckinpah's influences by examining Judd's death in the light of Greek tragedy and the Bible.

Unfortunately, the controversy surrounding the film's production and release anticipated difficulties Peckinpah would continue to have with studio executives over control of his films. MGM released *Ride the High Country* as the second half of a double feature, but to the studio's surprise and chagrin, it received good reviews and eventually became one of Peckinpah's most popular films. *Newsweek* called it "the best picture of 1962"; the following year it won several awards in Europe.

Peckinpah's next feature film, *Major Dundee* (1965), also became embroiled in controversy. Believing it too long, the studio cut several important scenes, further damaging its already fragile narrative coherence. The general public and most critics immediately dismissed it. Yet in spite of its failures, *Major Dundee* was far more ambitious in scope than anything Peckinpah had attempted before. Matt Wanat reexamines this flawed but intensely interesting film in chapter 4, "'Fall in behind the Major': Cultural Border Crossing and Hero Building in *Major Dundee*." In his analysis, Wanat argues that Peckinpah explores new territory through the characters of Dundee and Tyreen. Peckinpah's artistic ambitions, while not fully realized in *Major Dundee*, would come to fruition in the bloody conflict between Pike Bishop and Mapache in *The Wild Bunch*, his next major film.[4]

Soon after the critics' rejection of *Dundee*, Peckinpah entered a period of exile. He was fired abruptly from the set of *The Cincinnati Kid* after he had worked for only four days as its director. This disgrace coupled with reports of outrageous behavior during the filming of *Dundee* caused him to be blacklisted by the industry for two years. Returning to television during this time, Peckinpah adapted and directed Katherine Anne Porter's short novel *Noon Wine*. The production was hailed as a major artistic achievement, and its success gave Peckinpah another chance in Hollywood.

Peckinpah began the most productive phase of his career as the director of *The Wild Bunch*. Today, *The Wild Bunch* is clearly recognized as Peckinpah's masterpiece. But upon its release in 1969, a storm of controversy erupted over the graphic depiction of violence and bloodshed. It was often unfavorably compared to Arthur Penn's *Bonnie and Clyde* in their respective depictions of a final bloodbath in which the outlaw protagonists are mowed down in a hail of bullets. However, in technique and style, *The Wild Bunch* goes far beyond the slow-motion finale of *Bonnie and Clyde*. Creating elaborate montage sequences by intercutting violent action with slow-motion footage and various telephoto zooms, Peckinpah made a film that exhilarated a few, provoked many, and disturbed all. Although reviled by many viewers and critics for its extended portrayals of violence—the final battle sequence is seven minutes long—the film focuses more deeply on a complex interplay of ambition, loyalties, lost values, memories, survival, and sacrifice—all played out on the sands of shifting appearances that render truth, reality, and ultimate worth an elusive El Dorado.

Viewer outrage notwithstanding, Peckinpah's depiction of violence did seem to capture an essence of the 1960s. Coming at the end of an extremely violent decade in our history when we were deeply involved in the war in Vietnam, *The Wild Bunch* was generally understood at the time to be either a pro-war allegory or a dark comment on the nature of violence in American life. More recently, Stephen Prince's *Savage Cinema: Sam Peckinpah and the Rise of Ultraviolent Movies* addresses the issue of violence directly as it examines Peckinpah's use of cinema "to inquire into the phenomenon of violence in human life" (Prince 1998, xvi). Prince points out that most of the assessments of Peckinpah's work tend to deemphasize his connection with "the turbulent era of the late 1960s and early 1970s" (1998, 6). But Prince himself argues compellingly that Peckinpah's work during this period, encompassing his best films, cannot be divorced from what was happening in Vietnam or in the streets of our major cities.

In their treatment of violence, Peckinpah's films have an uncanny way of evoking the cultural turmoil of the 1960s and 1970s. This era was comparable in some ways to Peckinpah's vision of the "Old West" as a time when codes failed or were severely tested. The period of the 1960s, especially, was characterized by astounding technical advances, a sea change in race relations, urban riots and upheavals, and brutal assassinations, all in the context of the escalating violence of the Vietnam War. For Peckinpah, the America of the 1960s found its parallel in the America of the "Old West." Each period saw a historical era come to an end. Indeed, in his rendering of the "Old West," Peckinpah raises questions about the meaning of history—be it the 1880s or the 1960s—when violence and cultural turmoil sweep the old verities into oblivion.

When specifically questioned about his portrayal of violence in *The Wild Bunch*, Peckinpah claimed that "it's an anti-violence film because I use violence as it is. It's ugly, brutalizing, and bloody . . . awful. I was trying to tell a simple story about bad men in changing times. I was trying to make a few comments on violence and the people who live by violence" (Farber 1969, 8). Despite Peckinpah's claims, some continue to debate whether he intended "an anti-violence film" or whether he was more interested in a technical wizardry of filmmaking that, ultimately, celebrates violent death. Yet the continuing reexamination of *The Wild Bunch* testifies to the degree that the earlier preoccupation with Peckinpah's violence had obscured a recognition of his major artistic concerns. Such studies as Michael Bliss's *Doing It Right: The Best Criticism on Sam Peckinpah's* The Wild Bunch, Bliss's general study *Justified Lives: Morality and Narrative in the Films of Sam Peckinpah*, David Weddle's critical biography, *"If They Move . . . Kill 'Em": The Life and Times of Sam Peckinpah*, and, more recently, Bill Mesce's *Peckinpah's Women: A Reappraisal of the Portrayal of Women in the Period Westerns of Sam Peckinpah*, acknowledge the portrayal of violence, but focus on the deeper issues enmeshed in the film's rich, multilayered texture.

Following it closely, *The Ballad of Cable Hogue* (1970) extends the mythic possibilities suggested in *The Wild Bunch*. If *The Wild Bunch* dramatizes the tragedy and loss identified with "good" bad men as warrior heroes, then *Ballad* may be seen as one warrior's discovery of love and a home place after being on the road for too long. The vision of the two films taken together bears comparison with Homer's epic vision in *The Iliad* and *The Odyssey*, a parallel closely examined by John Gourlie. In chapter 5, "Peckinpah's Epic Vision: *The Wild Bunch* and *The Ballad of Cable Hogue*," Gourlie explores the conditions of war and peace depicted in the two films, analyzing the choices that help define the self—the search for self-worth, the search for love, and the search for human community.

Ballad did not fare well at the box office nor at the hands of the critics; however, like *The Wild Bunch*, it has experienced a renascence of perceptive critical commentary in recent years. When Cable Hogue, whose character recalls Old Testament figures, finds water in the desert, the film employs New Testament rebirth and resurrection imagery that *The Wild Bunch* had foreshadowed. Peckinpah himself claimed that the film "is about a man who found water where it wasn't . . . it's also about God" (Seydor 1997, 165). Frank Burke explores these spiritual touchstones in chapter 6, "Divining Peckinpah: Religious Paradigm and Ideology in *Convoy* and *The Ballad of Cable Hogue*." In Burke's view, by using different aspects of the Judaeo-Christian tradition, Peckinpah depicts paired opposites—a "positive" and a "negative" of religious aspiration. Burke claims that *Cable Hogue* dramatizes failed spirituality, while *Convoy* later depicts moral development, culminating in transfiguration.

In *Ballad*, Peckinpah again commands the technical mastery demonstrated in *The Wild Bunch*, but in *Ballad* it is used to affirm life and love. Richard Jameson has noted that Peckinpah does "just about anything to break away from conventional notions of linearity. . . . He splits and compartmentalizes the screen, he overlaps images, he speeds up the motion"; he compresses "hours into minutes, and [makes] minutes seem like hours"—all techniques that result in a new "freedom and spontaneity" (Jameson 1981, 39) for the characters. But perhaps even more, Peckinpah's technical mastery—particularly his handling of editing and montage—serves as an objective correlative of the multiple points of view operating simultaneously in his narratives. The collisions—of conflicting interests, of differing codes, of moral ambiguities, of shifting appearances, of past with present, of physical needs with spiritual aspirations—all find technical embodiment in the careful juxtapositions of images arising from Peckinpah's editing.

While *The Ballad of Cable Hogue* suggested a new level of "freedom and spontaneity" in Peckinpah's filmmaking, *Straw Dogs*, released in 1971, intensified the violence controversy, with some critics finding it even more loathsome than *The Wild Bunch*. Pauline Kael, writing in *The New Yorker*, called it the "first American film that is a fascist work of art" (Kael 1972, 84). However, most reviewers saw the film not as an endorsement of violence but as a graphic dramatization of a violence seemingly inherent in human nature.

In theory, Peckinpah's next film should have been a success. *Junior Bonner* (1972) featured two generations of stars: stars who had been popular, Ida Lupino and Robert Preston, and stars who were popular at the time, Steve McQueen, Ben Johnson, and Joe Don Baker. Again dealing with generational change, the film focused on the New West—the annual rodeo in Prescott, Arizona, which had already become one of the Sunbelt's best-kept secrets. Likewise the theme, the protagonist who "goes down his own road," is deeply ingrained in the American character and in our literature. In a reversal of Thomas Wolfe's memorable theme iterated in his novel *You Can't Go Home Again*, Steve McQueen's character *does* go home again and becomes the local hero when he wins the main event.

Although the critics liked it, *Junior Bonner* was not a commercial success. Without major scenes of violence, the film did not generate the controversy that surrounded Peckinpah's earlier works. Yet *Junior Bonner* has a complex thematic structure, which Richard Hutson examines in chapter 7, "*Junior Bonner*: Old West/New West or the Antinomies of the Father." Crucial to the structure are the father-son, brother-brother relationships, and these relationships, Hutson argues, are symbolic of deeper issues in the film. Also, *Junior Bonner* "is as completely resonant with ideas about the meaning of the West as anything Peckinpah ever did." It provides, Hutson concludes, "one of the best dramas of a basic dilemma for Westerners . . . the contradictory impulses to hold unto an identifiable and identifying past and to join the accelerations of historical change."

In addition to *Junior Bonner*, *The Getaway*, appearing in 1972, again starred Steve McQueen as well as members of Peckinpah's repertory company, Ben Johnson and Slim Pickens, among others. Although not a Western in a strict sense, the film is set in the West and has Western-like chases and shoot-outs. It again raises disturbing issues of gender and violence, which Stephen Tatum explores in chapter 8, "Don't *Mess* with Texas: Recuperating Masculinity in *The Getaway*." Tatum concludes that, although Peckinpah's ending ultimately "stabilizes sexual, gender, and class differences" through the character of Doc McCoy, the film's amazing techniques create a prolonged irresolution for the spectator.

In 1973, Peckinpah made his last real Western, *Pat Garrett and Billy the Kid*. Starring James Coburn as Pat Garrett and Kris Kristofferson as Billy, the film reprises Peckinpah's themes of the passing of the West and the decline of its traditional values. Peckinpah dramatized the issues of personal identity that arise for Pat Garrett and Billy the Kid because the West is changing. Garrett articulates his willingness to change when he states, "The times are changing" and "I want to grow old with the country." In effect, Garrett chooses to be part of the new, impersonal corporate society, represented by the Sante Fe Ring, that cannot tolerate the ruthless independence of the Kid. Billy's immediate refusal to change, "Times, maybe . . . not me," sets the stage for the inevitable showdown between the two in the tragic conclusion of the film. In refusing to change or to escape to Mexico, Billy chooses a radical freedom. The choice makes him a hero but it also dooms him, for he knows it is only a matter of time before he will be killed. But when Garrett finally shoots him, Garrett kills a spiritual part of himself as well. The treatment of the issues of personal identity and integrity is discussed in chapter 9, "'Who are you?' 'That's a Good Question': Shifting Identities in Sam Peckinpah's *Pat Garrett and Billy the Kid*."

Before releasing *Pat Garrett and Billy the Kid* to theaters, MGM cut sixteen minutes. Strikingly, these cuts eliminated the framing scenes that constituted the beginning and ending of the film. These scenes show Garrett's death. As Peckinpah conceived it, the entire action of the film occurs as a flashback in Garrett's mind as he lies dying. By conceiving of the film as occurring in the mind of Pat Garrett, Peckinpah internalizes his vision of the West. Indeed, Garrett's death stands as one in a series of deaths throughout Peckinpah's films. By treating the death of his heroes in a special way, Peckinpah allows both the hero and the viewer to take the measure of the hero's life at the very moment of his death. Such deaths would include the death of Steve Judd, the death of Pike Bishop, the death of Cable Hogue, the death of Sheriff Baker, the death of Billy, and the death of Pat Garrett. If one draws a line from the death of Steve Judd to the death of Pat Garrett, one can measure the distance Peckinpah has traveled in the Western. As revealed through Garrett's death, the "Old West" is cast as a dying memory in the hero's mind, even as he himself perishes. The power of this conception is that experience in Peckinpah's Westerns is envisioned not only as external action but as something that registers on the heart and soul of the hero.

In addition, by prolonging the moment of the hero's death, Peckinpah often suggests the transition from one world to another. Doing so, Peckinpah adds immeasurably to the dimensions of his portrayal as he momentarily lifts the hero above the Hobbesian world in which he has had to live. Thus, surprisingly, Peckinpah's vision assumes a spiritual dimension rarely associated with the Western or with Peckinpah himself. Indeed, this spiritual dimension profoundly grounds the religious imagery entwined in much of Peckinpah's work. Moreover, insofar as the Western symbolizes the course of American history in his films, Peckinpah registers not only the temper of his times through the actions of his films but the impact of these times upon the inner being of his heroes. In this conception Peckinpah's hero is modern man himself, caught in the web of time. In choosing the legendary story of Billy the Kid to symbolize the mythic history of the West, Peckinpah symbolically internalizes the whole subject matter of the Western genre itself in *Pat Garrett and Billy the Kid*. In such an artistic role, Peckinpah, like Keats's sylvan historian, frames those images upon the film's urn that immortalize whatever was given to Peckinpah of truth and beauty to create.

About his next film, *Bring Me the Head of Alfredo Garcia* (1974), Peckinpah said, "I did *Alfredo Garcia*, and I did it exactly the way I wanted to. Good or bad, like it or not, that was my film" (Simmons 1982, 208). Most reviewers at the time disliked it, and it was even censored in Sweden and Germany. A nightmarish revenge story, the film dramatizes the gruesome quest of the protagonist, Benny, played by Warren Oates. A honky-tonk piano player, Benny is hired to deliver the head of Alfredo Garcia to a wealthy Mexican named El Jefe. El Jefe avenges his family honor by killing Garcia, who has impregnated El Jefe's daughter.

Although not a Western, *The Killer Elite*, appearing in 1975, is like a Western and is, in some ways, best understood as an allegory of Peckinpah's own personal struggles. It caused strong critical reaction at the time, including a memorable review by Pauline Kael (1976), which is discussed more fully in chapter 12, "*The Killer Elite* and the Critics: A Note on the Art of Interpretation."

Peckinpah's next film, *Cross of Iron* (1977), is set in 1943 on the Eastern Front. Starring James Coburn, Maximilian Schell, and James Mason, the film presents its pacifist message through horrific scenes of warfare. Cut by fifteen minutes for release in this country and barely marketed, it was a commercial failure, but nevertheless it received high critical praise. Terence Butler called it "one of Peckinpah's finest studies of the purging of hatred through violence" (Butler 1979, 105). As he did in *The Wild Bunch*, Peckinpah offers probing insights into the nature of the warrior hero.

Convoy (1978) was called by Derek Malcolm "a Western disguised as a road movie which has great trucks for horses and their drivers as daredevil heroes" (Wakeman 1988, 766). According to Garner Simmons, Peckinpah also "wanted to turn the world of the trucker into a microcosm of modern American society" (Simmons 1982, 234). Offering a different perspective, Elaine Marshall in chapter 10, "'We're Always Moving': Sam Peckinpah's Making of *Convoy*," maintains that Peckinpah saw it "as a story about the movie-making process." His vision makes "this much-maligned movie something worthier of its maker than has been allowed."

After four years without work, Peckinpah directed his last feature film, *The Osterman Weekend* (1983), based on a Robert Ludlum novel with a screenplay by Alan Sharp. It should have been a good opportunity for Peckinpah, but the script had more lapses than the film could overcome. A conspiracy tale that reveals Peckinpah's fascination with electronic surveillance, it has some fine sequences, especially a bloody conclusion that recalls the ending of *The Wild Bunch*. However, most critics saw the film as overly complicated and, at times, verging on the incomprehensible.

Robert Merrill's essay, chapter 11, "Ford, Peckinpah, and the Advantages of Making (Many) Westerns," focuses on Peckinpah's artistry in filmmaking and his relationship with other directors. Comparing Peckinpah's films to those of Ford, Hawks, and Anthony Mann and to filmmakers who have made one well-known Western, such as Zinnemann, Altman, and Stevens, Merrill argues that Peckinpah is able to bring his characters to life while avoiding the more sentimental attachments other directors betray even in their best works. He is, Merrill claims, our best director of Westerns, and he transformed the stereotypes and cliches of the genre into an authentic vision.

Recently, Bill Mesce has broken new ground in his compact study *Peckinpah's Women: A Reappraisal of the Portrayal of Women in the Period Westerns of Sam Peckinpah* (2001). Mesce argues that Peckinpah's portraits of women are much more complicated than he's been given credit for. "The victimization of women in Peckinpah's West is," Mesce writes, "presented not out of a gratuitous or deserving punishment of womanhood, but as a product of . . . the monopoly of power held by men, and also by the failings of men" (Mesce 2001, 167).

From today's perspective, Peckinpah's dramatization of male/female relationships is unlikely to satisfy most women and probably not even most men. Even when he treats significant women characters, Peckinpah's world remains predominantly male. Although Peckinpah's women seem to be depicted in secondary roles where they are interludes, untrustworthy, or not the major game of life, in actuality they are integral to the action. Many may find expressions of Peckinpah's apparent chauvinistic outlook the greatest weakness and limitation of his work. At the same time, this weakness is, as with Hemingway, of one piece with his greatest strength. It is perhaps no accident that his greatest work was done in the Western genre, which easily accommodates a terrain dominated by male interests.

Peckinpah's ability to look more meaningfully at violence than most filmmakers is linked to both his conceptions of manhood and his handling of the Western genre. Perhaps a certain conception of hard-bitten masculinity steeled Peckinpah to look more unremittingly than most at the violence in human life. No doubt he also found such violence within himself, and he dramatized it, in turn, in his films. If this is so, Peckinpah's films are themselves the most severe critique of masculine failure and the male's propensity for violence. For even if their bonds work, the male characters are still circumscribed by their own limiting codes of masculinity. Also, in many ways, the failure of male-female relationships puts more pressure on these male relationships. Thus, when the bonds between males collapse under the pressure of Peckinpah's central issues—greed, betrayal, society's corruption, and changing times—the tragedy is all the more encompassing. But in the end, to the degree that Peckinpah's films raise ultimate questions about life's values, then his best work might be seen to examine a male ethos in a manner that encompasses gender even as it transcends its issues alone.

Peckinpah's best films portray deep emotion with a visual and dramatic intensity that few filmmakers achieve. Significantly, the violence for which Peckinpah is infamous is an intrinsic part of his artistic achievement. As he links his story and its themes to imagery of violence, the real power of Peckinpah's filmmaking becomes visceral. As he dramatizes violence so that it reverberates throughout a film, the violence energizes perception.

Thus Peckinpah's best films are vehicles of perception. But in their violence, they often hit the viscera even before they hit the emotions, and certainly before they register on the mind. But once raised, Peckinpah's issues are raised for both character and viewer alike. And as with the masculine ethos, Peckinpah raises the issues in the Western genre so powerfully that he uses the genre to reach beyond it to a level of universal concern. In doing so Peckinpah portrays a current world of flawed characters, limited actions, and self-serving motivations set against the backdrop of a more heroic and noble past. In the simplest sense, the tragedy he portrays is the unattainability of the heroic virtues of the classic Western. But more complexly, Peckinpah's films often contain an elegy for this lost past and portray the protagonists striking compromises that would allow them to survive in an unsatisfactory world. A more engulfing tragedy arises as the contending forces of Peckinpah's world defeat even these compromises and throw the protagonists into a violent contest for survival or vindication. In all this, Peckinpah's transformation of the Western genre is so masterful that his films support an ongoing search for their meaning. For, in the end, Peckinpah's best films do constitute an artistic endeavor to address the great issues: the trials of self, the quest for meaning, injustices of the social and economic order, and, ultimately, the encounter with the force of time that sweeps all before it. To the degree that Peckinpah's films succeed in this endeavor, we may claim that a terrible beauty is born.

Notes

1. This essay focuses on Peckinpah's Westerns and quasi-Westerns. But in tracing his career, we have included mention of all of his feature films for the sake of completeness. We've done so for several reasons. First, the issues raised in his Westerns often appear in his non-Westerns. Second, what is a quasi-Western or a transposition of the Western into another genre is open to debate. And third, a viewer unfamiliar with his work might benefit from the overview provided here.

2. We are deeply indebted to the work of Paul Seydor, Michael Bliss, David Weddle, and Stephen Prince. They have helped us immeasurably in our own understanding of Peckinpah's films, and we gratefully acknowledge their inspiration.

3. We are indebted to John Wakeman's edition of *World Film Directors*, volume 2, pages 754–67, for its distillation of the biographical and factual information.

4. The actor R. G. Armstrong referred to *Major Dundee* as "Moby Dick on horseback." A more telling comparison might be to Melville's novel *Mardi* (1849), which preceded *Moby Dick* by two years, for *Mardi* provided Melville with the opportunity to test his epic vision, learn something about dramatizing metaphysical quests, and prepare to realize his artistic intent on a grand scale. What *Mardi* was to *Moby Dick* for Melville, *Major Dundee* was to *The Wild Bunch* in Peckinpah's development as an artist.

References

Bliss, Michael. 1993. *Justified Lives: Morality and Narrative in the Films of Sam Peckinpah.* Carbondale: Southern Illinois University Press.

———. 1994. *Doing It Right: The Best Criticism on Sam Peckinpah's* The Wild Bunch. Carbondale: Southern Illinois University Press.

Butler, Terence. 1979. *Crucified Heroes: The Films of Sam Peckinpah.* London: Gordon Fraser.

Farber, Stephen. 1969. "Peckinpah's Return." *Film Quarterly* 23.1 (Fall): 5–11.

Jameson, Richard T. 1981. "The Ballad of Cable Hogue." *Film Comment* 17 (January/February): 38–40.

Kael, Pauline. 1972. "The Current Cinema: Peckinpah's Obsession," *The New Yorker* 47.50 (January 29): 80–85.

Kitses, James. 1969. *Horizons West: Anthony Mann, Budd Boetticher, Sam Peckinpah: Studies of Authorship Within the Western.* Bloomington: Indiana University Press.

Mesce, Bill. 2001. *Peckinpah's Women: A Reappraisal of the Portrayal of Women in the Period Westerns of Sam Peckinpah.* Lanham, Md.: Scarecrow Press.

Murphy, Kathleen. 1985. "Sam Peckinpah: No Bleeding Heart." *Film Comment* 21.2 (March-April): 74–75.

Prince, Stephen. 1998. *Savage Cinema: Sam Peckinpah and the Rise of Ultraviolent Movies.* Austin: University of Texas Press.

Seydor, Paul. 1997. *Peckinpah: The Western Films: A Reconsideration.* Urbana: University of Illinois Press.

Simmons, Garner. 1982. *Peckinpah: A Portrait in Montage.* Austin: University of Texas Press.

Wakeman, John, ed. 1988. *World Film Directors.* Vol. 2. New York: H. W. Wilson Co.

Weddle, David, 1994. *"If They Move . . . Kill 'Em": The Life and Times of Sam Peckinpah.* New York: Grove Press.

ONE

ARMANDO JOSÉ PRATS

Auguries of Redemption

PECKINPAH'S MYTHOLOGICAL CRITIQUE OF AMERICAN HISTORY

AMERICAN POSTMYTHIC: AXIOMS OF THE CLASSIC WESTERN AND OF THE PECKINPAH WESTERN

The American *postmythic*—that eagerly awaited *novus ordo seclorum*—whose coming-to-be in the *classic* Western presupposes the consummation of the heroic deed, enjoys already its pharisaical plenitude when the hero of the Peckinpah Western first appears before us. The opening of the Peckinpah Western—and especially of *Ride the High Country* and *The Wild Bunch*—elaborates upon and extends the classic Western's construction of the postheroic order by locating the hero squarely in such an epoch. Peckinpah's postheroic America zealously promotes itself as the nation complete and integral, its destiny manifestly fulfilled. Subsequent though it is to the heroic age—indeed, *consequent* upon it—this middle and middling America represents itself as the sole source and repository of both the national inheritance and the national hopes, its own *archê* and *telos*. All dialectical processes between mythic and postmythic are thus implicitly circumscribed within the limits of this order that would be both self-archaizing and self-commemorative, both token of time's evolutionary blessings and distinctly, if paradoxically, atemporal.

At the end of the classic Western, the new order of the ages comes into being as much because the hero leaves the scene of heroic action as because he disposes of such threats—bad men, Indians, a hostile land—as a hopeful yet powerless nation has identified for him. Whereas the hero of the classic Western rides *away from* the emerging historical order—Ringo (*Stagecoach*) from Lordsburg, Will and Amy Kane (*High Noon*) from Hadleyville, Shane (*Shane*) from Grafton's saloon, Ethan Edwards (*The Searchers*) from the Jorgensen home—the Peckinpah hero rides *into* a version of that order.[1] At the beginning of the Peckinpah Western, then, the hero finds himself in the midst of—indeed scourged by—something like the very world that his classic-Western counterparts have left behind. That postmythic world, which in Peckinpah has come of age, reveals that its ideals, once so seductively expressed, seem now, in retrospect, to have served but as an ingenious stratagem to enlist the hero in the coming-to-be of the current mediocrity. The would-be nation effectively tempts the hero of the classic Western into coming to its aid: it tenders visions of agrarian empires, proffers the primal Arcady, the delights of the pre-lapsed Eden itself—dream worlds all that impress the hero in the service of their realization. The threat to the Peckinpah hero is accordingly *this new order itself*: though he rides into such a world at the beginning of the action, the Peckinpah hero is no more *of* it than the hero of the classic Western is as he rides out of it.

An America self-defined by the decrees of worldly inheritance and the imperatives of material progress is, as Peckinpah properly revealed it to be, an America once again in need of the redemptive act that none but the Western's hero can bring about. To be sure, the American postmythic would thrive by its studied oblivion of the heroic. Yet the Peckinpah hero engages the postmythic world by reintegrating the mythic deed with the hopes of an ideal national history—with aspirations that at last find themselves justified in the national past. Thus, "revision" in the Peckinpah Western means not so much a reinvention of the genre—a genre reinvented is "only" a genre reenvisioned, and thus reaffirmed—but the recasting of the hero's redemptive deed in relation to an epoch that claims (unlike that of the classic Western) to have no need for heroes.

Peckinpah's postmythic appears before us *not* as a perversion of America's Edenic hope but *as the full measure and utter fulfillment of that hope*. It is not so much an America that has perverted its ideals as an America corrupted *by the realization of its own ideals*. Peckinpah's postmythic America is not—like that of the classic Western—a besieged America awaiting hopefully the fulfillment of those ideals through a heroic deliverance from alien evils, but an America whose banality and venality themselves fulfill squalid dreams. The Edenic hope, articulated and revered in the mythic time, has now in fact come to pass; and we know the backslidden America because it has already come into full possession of its fondest aspirations. "What is this heaven which they expect," asked Thoreau in oracular anticipation of the American postmythic, "if it is no better than they expect?"² The nation's own fall fulfills its hopes. On this point Peckinpah stands unequivocal and uncompromising, and irony here functions at a *moral* level; it is both judgment and sentence on "the American Dream."

To an America that deifies progress and commerce, and that values law and order only as ways of imposing conformity, Peckinpah offers a hero whose deeds *redeem the dream from its fulfillment*. The Peckinpah hero therefore enters this corrupt world not as an instrument of revision but as revision incarnate. His very presence, no less than his actions, enforces the authentic archaeology of American history. "History" therefore functions not as the recorded subversion of myth but as a dialectical component of the action in the Peckinpah Western. It is a false history; false not for being inaccurate or for lacking in discursive objectivity but false, rather, because it betrays the heroic afflatus that made it possible. The true American history, wrought of the hero's resistance to the postmythic, is one that, as we might say with Nietzsche,

> also preserves the memory of the great fighters *against history*, that is to say, against the blind power of the actual, and puts itself in the pillory by exalting precisely these men as the real historical natures who bothered little with the "thus it is" so as to follow the "thus it shall be" with a more cheerful pride. Not to bear their race to the grave, but to found a new generation of this race—that is what impels them ceaselessly forward; and even if they themselves are late-born—there is a way of living which will make them forget it—coming generations will know them only as first-born.³

The Peckinpah hero authenticates American history by binding it over again to its origins in the heroic act. This he does not by proposing that his power for action is the exclusive source of American history but by restoring the efficacy of the heroic deed to a reimagined American ideal. Who knows, then, but that Thoreau, no less than Nietzsche, prefigured Peckinpah:

> To some extent, mythology is only the most ancient history and biography. So far from being false or fabulous in the common sense, it contains only enduring and essential truth, the I and you, the here and there, the now and then, being omitted. Either time or rare wisdom writes it.⁴

In his beginning in the American postmythic the Peckinpah hero already reclaims his proper time, declares his readiness to erase his identity as "late-born," and announce himself "first-born." Revision in Peckinpah accordingly describes a critique, by way of mythic action, not of the classic Western but of the modes of ideal self-definition to which the Western—and by extension America—aspires.

I will limit my elaboration of Peckinpah's mythological critique of American history to *Ride the High Country* and *The Wild Bunch*. These two movies contest the American postmythic by offering the hero as the deliverer of the post-heroic West. In *The Deadly Companions*, it seems to me, Peckinpah had yet to explore the role of American history both as an ideal in the classic Western and as a proper antagonist in any proposed revisions of the genre. By taking on both the conflict of a nation divided and the war against the Indians, *Major Dundee* tends to challenge American history. Eventually, however, these traditional conflicts become subsidiary to the love interest and the war against the French in Mexico. The difficulty was no doubt compounded by the fifty-five minutes that, as Paul Seydor reports, the studio cut from Peckinpah's final cut.[5] In both *The Ballad of Cable Hogue* and *Pat Garrett and Billy the Kid* Peckinpah abandoned the mode of heroic action that he developed in *Ride the High Country* and *The Wild Bunch*. Cable Hogue's demise is more ironic than heroic, though this hardly means that it fails as an indictment of American history. Pat Garrett's murder of Billy the Kid, as sordid as it is historical (and thus anti-mythical), would seem already to foil a possible mythic redemption of American history. As Pat rides out of Pete Maxwell's place, where he has just shot Billy, a little boy runs after him, pelting him with stones. The elemental expression of outrage defines, perhaps, a surrender to the inevitability of historical time: Pat, who acquiesced in the historical ("Times are changing, Kid") and Billy, who challenged it ("Times, maybe, not me"), are now bound each to the other in a dialectic that produces not the bang of heroic action but a whimper of regret. Before elaborating on Peckinpah's mythological critique of American history, I propose a brief overview of the conception of American history in the classic Western. The moment of intersection between classic and revisionist Westerns emphasizes, as I wish to emphasize here, the cultural significance of Peckinpah's revisionist project.

The Classic Western's Theorem of American History

Though often only by indirection and inference, the classic Western offers its own account of America after the mythic deed. Since the days of Fenimore Cooper, John Cawelti writes, the Western articulates "the saga of America in terms of a complex myth of the frontier, which gains much of its richness and complexity from the anti-myth which it contains within itself."[6] Richard Slotkin elaborates on the genre's thematic integrity:

> The different forms in which ideology is voiced have their own special powers and properties, which affect the substance of the ideological communication and the way in which it will be received.
>
> . . .
>
> The logic of myth is the logic of metaphor and narrative. It depends less upon analytical reason than on an instant and intuitive understanding and acceptance of a given meaning. The movement of mythic narrative, like that of any story, implies a theory of cause-and-effect, a theory of history; but these implications are only rarely articulated as objects of criticism, since their operation is marked by the traditional form of the narrative, its conformity to habits of thought, generic conventions, and literary expectations so deeply ingrained that we are unconscious of them.[7]

So considered, the classic Western generates a vision of American history that is only indirectly related to history as a formal discourse. The classic Western presents a mythic, or at least a generic, historiography that confers upon the heroic act virtually all the power to bring about a socio-cultural order at once inchoate and full-formed, an order that has impossibly matured to fruition in the very act of its emergence—an America, therefore, at once young and wise, such as Melville's White Jacket describes in a millennialist rapture: "We are the pioneers of the world; the advance-guard, sent on through the wilderness of untried things, to break a new path in the New World that is ours. In our youth is our strength; in our inexperience, our wisdom. At the period when other nations have but lisped, our deep voice is heard afar."[8]

Would that it were so: an America at once "young" and "wise" and not, as it is so often in the Western's postmythic, simultaneously naïve and overbearing. According to the classic Western, American *history* arises out of mythic *consequence:* whatever follows the *mythic act*—the climactic shootout or the fight with the Indians—begins a different epoch. The mythic act both defines its own proper epoch and declares the advent of America's historical identity. It inscribes, accordingly, the boundaries of two distinct world orders. Mircea Eliade identifies mythic time by means of a distinction familiar to antiquity. The phrase *in illo tempore* ("in *that* time") designates the mythic epoch that claims distinction in the collective memory of "this time" (*in hoc tempore*), or, as we might say, of this *our* (post-heroic) time. "The myth," Eliade writes, "relates a sacred history, that is, a primordial event that took place at the beginning of time, *ab initio*. . . . The myth, then, is the history of what took place *in illo tempore*, the recital of what the gods or the semidivine beings did at the beginning of time."⁹

The immediate aftermath of the mythic deed reveals the complete realization of the ideals articulated in the time (now past) of the hero's essential errand. "Myth," Eliade writes, "narrates a sacred history";

> it relates an event that took place in primordial Time; the fabled time of the "beginnings." In other words, myth tells how, through the deeds of Supernatural Beings, a reality came into existence, be it the whole of reality, the Cosmos, or only a fragment of reality—an island, a species of plant, a particular kind of human behavior, an institution.¹⁰

In the classic Western the order that follows upon the heroic deed is almost always *institutional:* the new epoch is now defined by and devoted to "law and order." Not surprisingly, therefore, the fulfillment of the nation's fondest hopes often indicates an elemental and characteristic intolerance, a pervasive suspicion of the new or the different. Those who had so recently clamored for change are about to be known by their instituted and institutional loathing of change.

A basic construction of the epoch (*in hoc tempore*) that has come to supersede the heroic time (*in illo tempore*) underlies the various forms of the American postmythic. Such an epoch would seem to hold untold possibilities—possibilities for ideal development, which is to say, for increased union in diversity, for those magnanimous forms of inclusion and opportunity that produce the true adventures of cultural evolution. But the selfsame epoch would also encompass the many possible corruptions of such vast potential: the surrender to mediocrity glorifies the dread business of law and order because it mistrusts freedom, favors social seemliness over civic action, sustains, in short, the deadly virtues that drive away the hero of the classic Western and only grudgingly greet the Peckinpah hero. Consistently, however, the middling hopes of the classic Western tend to anticipate such an epoch as though it were an American chiliasm. Edward Said uses Talal Asad's term "synchronic essentialism" in order to identify the representation of an epoch whose temporal amplitude, decided and determined by its paradisal vision, discloses no actual process of development.¹¹ This is history without happenings or without the discourse of happenings; a history, as Said writes, "radically attenuated if not banished. Viewed as a current of development, as a narrative strand, or as a dynamic force unfolding systematically and materially in time and space, human history . . . is subordinated to an essentialist, idealist conception. . . ."¹²

Moreover, we so readily acquiesce in the presumed atemporality of the American postmythic because the classic Western binds it ineluctably to *our* time. The ideals of the classic Western belong to and define our own epoch. The classic Western can be shamelessly self-congratulatory, unctuous even, if only because it elicits our complicity in its essentialist scheme of things. We locate ourselves as witnesses to the birth of the new time, and then return to our own as if it were coeval with it, not an evolution from it but a timeless extension of it. We see ourselves in the unextinguished glow of cultural glory. The postmythic confuses its power to *enroll* the hero in its cause with its power to *bring about* its fondest desires: the hero's absence from the postmythic becomes an occasion for a historical revision that declares his absence from the mythic epoch itself. The postmythic can entertain such a delusion, of course, not only because the hero appears to exist wholly for its sake, but also because the hero is no longer present to deny the new order's historical constructions—its emplotments, so to say. This delusion, whereby the postmythic represents itself as the power to realize its own hopes, enables the classic Western to foreshadow its own mythic revisions—and thus to herald Peckinpah.

Even as the classic Western articulates the hopes of a young nation, it also identifies the coming post-heroic order as the *irony* of America's fulfilled hopes. At the intersection of the mythic and the historical, at the precise moment when history emerges in the form of mythic consequence, the classic Western almost always produces a fissure, perhaps even a distortion: the yearned-for millennial order does in fact come to pass in consequence of the heroic deed, yet this order never quite takes the ideal form of the vision articulated in the time *before* the heroic deed, when the fate of the nation teetered uncertainly. For if the ideal of the historical epoch inspired the hero, it was the mythic time itself that exalted the ideal, which was then clean and innocent and irreproachable.

To be sure, the America that had depended on the hero had also inspired him. In this regard, *Shane* remains unparalleled for its articulation of the vision that moves the hero to action. To a newly arrived Shane, Joe Starrett presents his vision of a Jeffersonian freedom. The blessed life of the yeoman farmer—what Leo Marx identified as "the ideal of the middle landscape"[13]—lies within the grasp of every American: "These old timers," Joe propounds,

> they just can't see it yet, but running cattle on an open range just can't go on forever. It takes too much space for too little results. Those herds [of Ryker's] aren't any good. They're all horns and bone. Now cattle that is bred for meat

and fenced in and fed right—that's the thing. You've got to pick your spot; get your land, your own land. Now a homesteader, he can't run but a few beef, but he can sure grow grain, and cut hay, and what with his garden and the hogs and milk—well, he'll make out all right.

Or consider one of John Ford's many contributions to the same vision. Shortly after Ethan Edwards arrives at the Jorgensen home after his first year in search of his niece Debbie, Mrs. Jorgensen, in explicit contradiction of her husband Lars's virtual surrender before the harsh western land, voices the following reverie:

> Now Lars, it just so happens we be Texicans. Texican is nothing but a human man way out on a limb—this year and next, and maybe for a hundred more. But I don't think it'll be forever. Some day this country's going to be a fine good place to be. Maybe it needs our bones in the ground before that time can come.

These, certainly, are no mean ideals. Had not Whitman himself said, as R. W. B. Lewis reminds us, that the new Adam, having created himself, "must next create a home"?[14] Surely *Shane*'s Joe Starrett finds his supreme vindication in the Jeffersonian attestation that "those who labor in the earth are the chosen people of God, if ever he had a chosen people, whose breasts he has made his peculiar deposit for substantial and genuine virtue."[15] And in *The Searchers* Mrs. Jorgensen's vision of an Edenic America rising triumphantly out of the Great American Desert accords with Henry Nash Smith's observation that "[t]he myth of the garden was contrary to empirical possibility on the plains but it was true to the course of history."[16]

Manifest Destiny, presumably consummated in the immediate aftermath of the mythic deed, sacrifices the hero to the rapacity and venality that thereupon become indicia of the American character. At the end of John Ford's *Stagecoach*, as Ringo and Dallas ride out of Lordsburg to Ringo's ranch across the border, Doc Boone remarks: "Well, they're saved from the blessings of civilization." Doc Boone's censure of the postmythic—which is most likely Ford's own—excepts none but the hero and the heroine, who have already left the boundaries of the city—of the city of God, Lordsburg—or of "the fine good place to be"—of an Eden, in short, sure on the verge of yet one more lapse. In the very instant of their emergence, civilization's blessings become its curses, and the better angels of the nation's nature mutate grotesquely into its demons and its furies.

Almost incessantly in the classic Western, then, the social forces that entrusted their hopes to the hero—and that rejoiced, however secretly, to see those hopes consecrated in gunsmoke and blood—now take comfort in the hero's ride into the sunset. At the end of *Shane*, then, Joey Starrett is to carry these most glad of all tidings to his mother: "Tell her," Shane instructs him, "there are no more guns in the valley." Once Ethan Edwards returns Debbie to civilization, he must turn his back on the newly founded "fine good place to be"; he has no choice, nor do we give him any, if only because we find it unnerving that the hero should have punctuated his sacrifice on behalf of "American" values by taking an Indian scalp.[17] The ride into the sunset thus became the hero's escape from a world that he had fashioned in patent and unequivocal denial of the values on whose behalf he had labored: for the sake of peace and law and order he had shot many men (sometimes in the back), had taken a scalp, even. The *how* of such a world already belied its *what*; its means already subverted its end.

All that the hero leaves behind, however, is a world condemned to "progress," or to its own improbable sense of it. The Western, certainly, shows great concern for such a postmythic world, but it does so even as it anticipates its impenitent meanness. Progress thus signals a curious mode of temporality—not the sort in which the community develops a higher sense of itself—a greater cohesiveness, say, wider sympathies, the blessings of a shared freedom—but one, rather, entirely devoid of growth, unfolding paradoxically as an indefinite duration in which there is no change, except almost certainly change for the worse. Almost certainly the new order shall forsake the virtues of the middle landscape for moral mediocrity. What can possibly await Joey Starrett on the farm after he witnesses the effulgence of Shane's triumph at Grafton's? In the last image of Joe Starrett—barely conscious after his fight with Shane, held in his wife Marian's arms—where now is the agrarian fervor? Did Shane perform his sacrifice that he might deliver America *unto* the garden or Joey *from* it? And what of the "fine good place to be" after Ethan Edwards? What sort of world does Ethan's niece Debbie come "home" to? Can we forget that earlier Laurie Jorgensen, now Martin Pawley's bride-to-be and thus an American Eve of sorts, had condoned Ethan's earlier attempt to shoot Debbie? Had Laurie not argued that Martha, Debbie's mother, herself would have wanted it so? These questions suggest why the ride into the sunset, more moral recourse than generic cliché, reveals the hero's implicit disgust at the new and stern dispensation.

At times, then, it was impossible not to foresee the undisguised viciousness of the coming historical order, as when *High Noon*'s Will Kane, in church seeking to deputize men for a posse, suffers the indignity of Mayor Henderson's specious appeal to "progress." At first, Henderson's praise of

Will Kane seems to guarantee that the people will join him against the Miller gang: "What this town owes Will Kane here, it can never pay with money; and don't ever forget it. He's the best marshal we ever had, maybe the best marshal we'll ever have." Then comes the reversal, though at first subtle, sophistical: "We made this town with our own hands, out of nothing. And if we want to keep it decent, keep it growing, we've got to think mighty clear here today. And we've got to have the courage to do what we think is right, no matter how hard it is." What may have seemed the speech of a civic leader able to move the citizens to righteous self-defense turns instead into shameless grandiloquence masking raw greed:

> Now, the people up North are thinking about this town an awful lot. . . . But if they're going to read about shooting and killing in the streets, what are they going to think then? I'll tell you. They're going to think this is just another wide-open town, and everything we worked for will be wiped out. In one day, this town will be set back five years, and I don't think we can let that happen.

Finally, the conclusion: "Will, I think you better go while there's still time. It's better for you, and it's better for us."

In the classic Western, the pieties of "progress" foretell a mean and contemptible world: the advent of law and order and civilization—though these ideals may compose the full measure of an Edenic America—marks instead the onset of greed and meanness and intolerance. Compromised and compensatory, the dream (or rather the rationalization) of progress takes on a dreadfully familiar tone. In the catalogue of middle-class hopes, this American dream identifies all that life must *not* be sacrificed to.

Now, at the end of *High Noon*, when the historical epoch has come into being, we know the American Dream but by the irony of its having come all too true. That the classic Western consistently identifies such an irony is therefore evident in two tenets of generic closure: the ride into the sunset (whereby the hero escapes the nerveless and uninspired time at hand), and the generic refusal to narrate the story of a time without heroes. Thus Will Kane marks the triumph of devotion, of fidelity, which he alone possesses completely, when he tosses the tin star down in the dusty street. Here, as we see the close-up of Will's boot heel turn for the buggy, where Amy awaits him, we witness, in the absolute concision of the gesture, the general rule whereby the classic Western sunders the hero from the world that he makes possible. Will takes with him all heroic virtue when he and Amy ride out of Hadleyville. Except perhaps for the boy Johnny, there remain behind only the faithless, perhaps lying in uneasy wait for a hero—not a hero to deliver them from themselves, however, but one whom they may yet again sacrifice to their ideal America.

On Entering the Spaces of the American Postmythic

The heroes of *Ride the High Country* and *The Wild Bunch* make their first appearance in the very world to which the classic Western refuses a story. Lewis has correctly noted that the hero of American fiction, beginning with Natty Bumppo, "seems to take his start outside time, or on the very edges of it," and that the hero's "initial habitat is space as spaciousness, as the unbounded, the area of total possibility."[18] And to be sure, the Peckinpah hero rides into the site of the postmythic from an outside; yet the postmythic itself, inasmuch as it claims that outside for its own, has so *circumscribed* the imaginative spaces of that ahistorical region that the hero has no choice but to ride into the deadly postmythic. Consider the two openings.

In *Ride the High Country* the preposterous and preposterously named Samsons—father Luther and son Abner—owners of the Bank of Hornitos, define, in their own implausibly assertive figures, the postmythic as the lapsed. Peckinpah allows the Samsons to recite the creed of mediocrity that guides the new order. When Steve Judd expresses dismay that he will not be guarding $250,000 in gold, as Luther's letter said, but only $20,000 (in time, Steve and Gil will leave Coarsegold with only $11,000), Abner responds: "Our original estimate was overly enthusiastic. The strike is not a mother lode, but it is productive—slow and steady, and we intend to get our share." Then Luther chimes in: "The days of the forty-niners are past, and the days of the steady businessman have arrived."

In *The Wild Bunch* Pike Bishop and the Bunch ride into San Rafael, Texas, dressed in Pershing-era cavalry uniforms, and an unsuspecting Mayor Wainscoat addresses the South Texas Temperance Union in a tent meeting. His texts are Leviticus 10:9 (so that the words that mark the entrance of the Bunch identify the post-heroic by the ethics of prohibition: "Do not . . .") and Proverbs 23:30–31. Then follows the sermon—this even as the children, shown in cuts away from the tent (and therefore unattended), already stage the cruel sacrifice of the scorpions to the red army ants, enact, therefore, all the wanton fiendishness that a grave and abstemious nation can summon in the righteous cause of social respectability: "Now, folks," Wainscoat continues, "that's from the Good Book. But in this here town, it's five cents a glass. Five cents a glass! Does anyone really think that that is the price of a drink?" Shortly thereafter the Temperance Union parades its zeal through the streets of San Rafael, only to be caught in the deadly crossfire between the Bunch and the bounty hunters.

In the aftermath of the San Rafael massacre, however, we learn of an even more malignant incarnation of the postmythic: Harrigan—merely Harrigan, the "P. L." of his first and middle names appears only under the wanted posters of the Bunch—arrogant and heartless, now stands, unmoved and unrepentant, among the casualties resulting from his failed attempt to capture Pike and the Bunch. Harrigan, who carries out the imperial decrees of the Pecos and South Texas Railroad, has deliberately kept his plans from Mayor Wainscoat and the Temperance Union, choosing rather to put them in harm's way than to risk the opportunity to kill the Bunch for warning the citizenry of the impending firefight. When Benson, a city official, says to Harrigan that the city holds him responsible for the carnage, Harrigan balefully snarls: "We represent the law!" Law, therefore, and of course order, and commerce and progress and business and prosperity—all the world's bromides, then—assert themselves, even *define* themselves explicitly, as antiheroic. If the hero is to resist the historical epoch, he must learn to acknowledge its immense power, one derivative of which is its power of seduction. When the Bunch, back in camp, realize that they have risked their lives not for gold but for metal washers, Pike, frustrated, exclaims: "They set it up!" Then Lyle Gorch, puzzled, asks: "'They'? Who in the hell is 'they'?" Here Old Man Sykes, seemingly irascible yet fairly bursting with sardonic laughter, explains it to him, and to us, in a felicitous tautology:

> "They"? Why, "they" is just plain and fancy "they." That's who "they" is. Caught you, didn't "they"? Tied a tin can to your tail, led you in, and waltzed you out again. Oh, my, what a Bunch! Big, tough one, eh? Here you are, with a handful of holes, a thumb up your ass, and a big grin to pass the time of day with. "They"! Who the hell is "they"?

"They"—unrenowned yet prominent, at once distant and ubiquitous—the monolithic "they," then, with claims on flesh and blood and soul, derives its power from the heroic individual yet now turns it against him. It has been said often, indeed as if in an incantation, that the Peckinpah hero is a man out of his time. And no doubt he is; but the assertion merely refers us to one side of the basic relation that identifies the Peckinpah hero. The other side defines the postmythic West as itself the time out of joint. The West—the West not as region but *as America*—sheds its Edenic status only to be refigured—at the beginning—as but the latest account of the fallen nation.

If the heroic action of the classic Western makes possible the historical epoch, then in the Peckinpah Western it erases that selfsame epoch, and thus invests it anew with the hopes of the whole nation. The mythic now follows upon the postmythic, but by so doing it reorganizes the epochal structures of the national identity. This implied reversion of the classic Western's temporality—which as I have suggested defines the nature and scope of revision in the two Peckinpah Westerns under consideration—explains the peculiar relation between the hero and the world in which he inaugurates his deliverance of the post-heroic order. To be sure, then, the Peckinpah hero is a man out of his time, for he is through and through the creature of history. But such an identity, precisely because *history* confers it upon him, means (if all too paradoxically) that he is a *forgotten* man: the collective memory exists as such precisely because it fails to remember him.

In a way, of course, the American postmythic *does* recognize the hero: the Samsons have hired Steve Judd, and Harrigan's hellhounds lie in wait for Pike and the Bunch. But the hero is now a power to be co-opted (enrolled in the cause of "the steady businessman"); or else to be hunted down as if he were a rabid dog—all in the name of "the law." The special case of Deke Thornton in *The Wild Bunch* exemplifies the status of the hero as both co-opted and persecuted. Though he pays for his freedom from Yuma prison in the coin of bondage to the railroad, Deke still manages to identify the degeneracy that animates the new historical order. In the aftermath of the massacre at San Rafael, Deke properly characterizes the post-heroic by identifying its controlling fetish—namely, law and order—with the impulse toward domination for rapacity's sake: "Tell me, Mr. Harrigan: how does it feel, getting paid for it? Getting paid to sit back and hire your killings with the law's arms around you? How does it feel to be so goddamned right?" As clearly as Deke articulates the power of the postmythic, however, Harrigan renders it more powerful still. Without one jot of remorse, Harrigan replies: "Good." In Harrigan, Peckinpah enables us to see that American history was primarily, was perhaps only, a quest for dominion—that the ideal inheritance whereby the nation would come into possession of the Garden was all along the unremitting animus against the land, against the native inhabitants, against the individual—the shrill and furious drive for empire over the human soul itself. In such a world the hero must accordingly claim presence—must perhaps seek refuge—at the very margins. For that world implicitly ordains his absence as a fundamental condition of its continuity. Here in the postmythic, heroism would be recognized only in the forms that render it subsidiary, capable of being controlled, and thus devalued. The definition of "myth" as falsehood originates always in the postmythic. It is the sign of the postmythic.

History, as I have just now noted, forgets the hero: both Gil Westrum in *Ride the High Country* and Pike Bishop in *The Wild Bunch* appear in disguise when we first meet them. Their disguises confirm their resignation to the passing of the mythic epoch. Hardly can there be an irony greater than that Gil should run a crooked shooting gallery as "The Oregon Kid." Having to *pose* as the hero that he in truth *has been,* Gil appears before us as "the envy" (or so he tells Steve Judd) "of every small-minded ribbon clerk and shirttail towhead from here to Pocatello." Nothing therefore so cruelly enforces the irony that defines him as does this condition whereby his very presence as *showman* (indeed, as Buffalo Bill epigone) betokens the oblivion to which the historical epoch consigns his heroic deeds. A kindred irony explains how Pike Bishop comes to wear the uniform of the same army that, supported and transported by the railroad, hounds him across the Mexican border and beyond.

The American postmythic likewise enforces that initial condition in which the hero appears as if condemned to a crushing mediocrity. Steve Judd shows up in Hornitos to guard the Samsons' gold—this one but the latest in a long string of equally ignominious jobs—"bartender, stick man, bouncer, what have you—not much to brag on," as he later tells Gil—jobs that all betoken his own acquiescence in the passing of the mythic epoch. Steve wears no disguise, of course, but his threadbare appearance, spitefully noted by Abner Samson, as well as his age, noted with surprise by, of all people, the positively Pleistocene Luther, place him out of his heroic heyday. But if Steve's identity is in question, so is the town's own. Progress and respectability have come to the town of Hornitos, and it wears them as tokens of its corruption. (*Hornitos*: little furnaces; Hell's little toehold in the pinchbeck Eden.) Thus, the gas lamps and the cars and the helmeted, baton-wielding policemen—these palpable tokens of improvement and prosperity, of decency and authority—function inevitably as correlatives of the belly dancer that entices the two curious boys, of Gil's rigged shooting gallery, of Heck Longtree's crooked camel-and-horse race. Yet the corruption of the post-heroic is perhaps in greatest evidence in this, that the world can fool the hero into believing that it welcomes him when all that it means to do (now that it has to admit that it still needs him) is to exploit him. So Steve rides into Hornitos believing that the crowd cheers his advent, only to be ignominiously shoved aside by a uniformed policeman: "Get away from there! Watch out! Get out of the way, old man! Can't you hear? Can't you see you're in the way? Get out of here!" And he is indeed in the way—not so much of the onrushing camel and horses but of the postmythic's smug self-delusion.

If not wiser than *Ride the High Country* in the ways of the postmythic, then at least warier toward them, *The Wild Bunch* greatly intensifies the deadliness that the post-heroic town marshals against the hero. The socially respectable folk of *Ride the High Country* have been now transformed into Mayor Wainscoat's ascetic legion, and the force of law embodied in Hornitos's uniformed policemen have become the spluttering, raging demons—T. C. and Coffer and Jesse and the rest—that lie in wait, barely able to restrain their bloodlust, on the rooftops of San Rafael. (By way of exempting Deke Thornton from the general vice, Peckinpah first shows him asleep.) And the somber and severe band under Wainscoat and the socio-cultural refuse under Harrigan come both to find their single expression in the cuts away to the well-scrubbed children—white and Hispanic alike—whose angelic faces gaze rapturously at the writhing scorpions and then, as the long opening sequence comes to a close, at the flames that consume scorpions and ants alike. Caught in the crossfire of cruelty and sanctimony, the heroes must withdraw.

We have only to look at Hornitos and San Rafael to see them for what they are. There is no hidden corruption, no secret sin to expose, no hypocrisy to unmask. The very conspicuousness of the postmythic's fall contributes to Peckinpah's identification of the hero. If such a world summons the energies of its own corruption against the hero—if it drives him to dissemble (as Gil Westrum does) or seeks to co-opt him (as it does Steve Judd) or hounds him to the ends of the earth (as it does to Pike and the Bunch)—then it must be that *humanity* is already conferred, as perhaps it has ever been, only on these who form the object of so relentless a persecution. The other, the complementary, source of Peckinpah's critique of the American postmythic is therefore *the humanity of the hero*. In its beginning, the classic Western had almost always declared the need for a superhuman hero. Almost insurmountable forces, such as the Plummer brothers or the Rykers or the Miller gang, had called upon the Western to produce a hero whose dexterity with the gun had to be nothing short of miraculous: on the streets of Lordsburg Ringo kills the three Plummer brothers with his last three cartridges; at Grafton's, Shane beats the deadly Jack Wilson to the draw and then kills the two Rykers. By contrast, the Peckinpah Western presents a hero known first and last by his humanity, for such is the form of heroism that the American postmythic requires—which means, then, that the post-heroic itself is no less deadly an antagonist than Jack Wilson or Frank Miller for so fairly brimming with propriety and civility.

The Narration of Heroic Humanity

Driven by historical forces either to conceal his identity or to surrender his mythic freedom, how shall the Peckinpah hero affirm his readiness to undertake the mythic deed? In a world where respectable mediocrity masks a frenzied avarice, where law sanctions not social order but cruelty and rapacity in the name of social order, what are the possible signs whereby we might come to know the Peckinpah hero's power to act? It is a feature of these two Westerns, seldom noted, that Peckinpah entrusts the identification of the hero's humanity to the tormented and the contemned, to the meek of the homily, then. No sooner does Elsa Knudsen see Steve, Gil, and Heck just outside her father Joshua's farm than she hurtles out of the barn (where she labored downcast, in heavy boots and coarse cloth) and into the house, to emerge in delicate pink, Eve resplendent, envisioning, in the advent of the heroes, her deliverance from her father's lapsed garden. Abused by the severe righteousness of her father, she recognizes not only Heck as her potential mate, but Steve and Gil as the true fathers come to rescue her from Joshua.

Angel's village, ravaged and tyrannized by Mapache, has come miraculously alive following the arrival of the Bunch;[19] and now Pike, Old Sykes, and Don José (the village patriarch) look on in fascination as the churlish Gorch brothers become suddenly inoffensive, even gentle, in a game of cat's cradle with Rocío, a young girl from the village:

> *Pike.* Now *that* I find hard to believe.
>
> *Don José.* It's not so hard. We all dream of being a child again—even the worst of us. Perhaps the worst most of all.
>
> *Pike.* You know what we are, then.
>
> *Don José.* Just so, the both of you.

Though he knows them to be outlaws, he knows them as well by the elemental sign of their humanity, which in this abiding moment is vested in the longing to regain innocence. When the fiesta concludes and the Bunch ride out of the village, all the people join in the traditional Mexican song *La Golondrina* ("The Swallow"). The song functions as the choric plaint confirming the humanity—now characterized as frailty and mutability by way of the shelterless and flightless bird—with which Don José has already anointed the Bunch (here transcribed as it is sung in the scene):

> ¿Adonde irá, veloz y fatigada,
> La golondrina que de aquí se vá?
> ¿Adonde irà?

> Buscando abrigo y no lo encontrará.
> ¡Oh, cielo santo! y sin poder volar!
> Junto a mi lecho le pondré yo su nido,
> En donde pueda la estación pasar.
> También yo estoy en la region perdido
> ¡Oh, cielo santo, y sin poder volar!

("Where will it go, swift yet spent / The swallow that now takes its leave? / Where will it go? / Seeking shelter yet it shall find none, / Oh, holy heaven! And unable to fly. / Next to my bed I shall place its nest, / Where it shall spend the season. / I, too, am lost in this land, / Oh, holy heaven! And unable to fly!")

Peckinpah gives us no more certain affinity between the human and the heroic than he does at the end of the movie, when he repeats this farewell, except that the earlier celebration of a tragic humanity at the ending is transfigured into the apotheosis of the Bunch, thus allowing the meek celebrants themselves to be exalted by their earlier benediction of the outlaws.

We know, furthermore, if only by an appeal to convention, that in the classic Western the code of heroic identity designates the hero by the iconic six-gun. The gun that betokens mythic being has its source in the fabulous shooting matches of Fenimore Cooper's *Leatherstocking Tales*. We find the equation between the gun and the heroic reiterated in Westerns as different in tone and texture as *Destry Rides Again* (Marshall, 1939), *My Darling Clementine* (Ford, 1946), *Red River* (Hawks, 1947), and *The Tin Star* (Mann, 1957). And we find it in its unalloyed purity in *Shane:* when Shane leaves the dinner table to hack at the stubborn stump on the Starrett farm, Joey thinks that he has left for good. Joe dispels the boy's concern by pointing to the gun belt slung on the back of Shane's chair: "Oh, he's not going, Joey. He wouldn't go without taking that."

In Peckinpah the hero never moves with such poise, with such easeful grace, in the aura of the six-gun. Pike Bishop, for one, learns early the way in which history abrogates the power of the six-gun. In the aftermath of the failed robbery in San Rafael, amid the uncertainty of the Bunch's plans, one fact emerges clear and incontestable, and it is Pike who states it: "We've got to start thinking beyond our guns. Those days are closing fast." Toward the end of *Ride the High Country*, Steve Judd, mortally wounded in the exchange of gunfire with the Hammond brothers, emboldens Gil Westrum to the last triumphant moment by invoking the impulse of old: "Let's meet them head-on—half-way, just like always." He affirms his heroic lineage, claims his close kinship with the six-gun and the redemptive shoot-out. And yet, with the revealing exception of "The Oregon Kid's" crooked shooting gallery (he wins by shooting at his targets with buckshot), neither Steve nor Gil gives any early displays of prowess with the gun. More relic than icon, the six-gun, if only through the fundamental irony of its own enfeebled presence, reveals the extent to which the Peckinpah hero must revitalize the postmythic even without recourse to the once-indispensable and unchallenged force. In *The Wild Bunch*, new and far deadlier "icons"—the Colt's .45 ACP (1911) semi-automatic pistol of Pike's and the .30mm Browning machine gun—mock the six-gun's woefully diminished firepower, proclaim its obsolescence (yet these new icons also determine how much greater is the firepower needed to counter the correspondingly greater iniquity in the Peckinpah postmythic). Following the shoot-out at Mapache's village, Peckinpah confirms his earlier demystification of the six-gun, this time far more concisely than when Pike counseled thinking beyond the gun: a point-of-view shot of Deke Thornton cuts to a zoom-in on the holstered—that is to say, then, useless—Colt's revolver of the dead Pike Bishop.

That in Peckinpah the six-gun—or at least its "mystique"—only imperfectly defines the hero suggests that the mythological critique partially consists of the *narrated search* for alternative modes of heroic identification. This given release of the Peckinpah hero from the classic code of generic identity must not imply that he is thereby deprived of potentialities for a redemptive mythic deed. In a postmythic world, a world no less dehumanized by the "norm"—Hornitos, San Rafael, the Samsons, the Temperance Union, the railroad—as by the perversions of the norm—Joshua Knudsen, the Hammonds, the bounty hunters, Harrigan, Mapache—a clear sign of humanity is a portent of greatness to come, an augury of redemption. Humanity is not the Peckinpah hero's disguise—the borrowed garb in which, like Odysseus returned to Ithaca, he patiently bides his time. He does wear his disguises, as we have seen, but he does this so that he may move more or less freely in the middle landscape. His humanity, however, is his own intrinsically, and he owes it to no one. It is his own to proffer, even in the midst of the post-heroic, as the surety of his mythic power. His heroism emerges from this humanity, then, as much to assert it as to transcend it. The hero's humanity—and we may know it plainly, as by his age or his mortality; or in its meaner forms, as rancor and regret; or by its more exalted ones, as resignation and fidelity and self-sacrifice—defines the postmythic itself even as it articulates his own possibilities for heroic action—for the transcendence of the merely complaisant and comfortably human, then. Thus the American postmythic functions as both the *contrast* to and the *context* of that humanity. The hero challenges history's complacent millennialism, its assumption that it enjoys the full blessings of the earthly paradise.

But humanity in the two Westerns under consideration is more than the resistance to a post-heroic age; more, even, than the affirmation of a heroic identity before the conformist multitude: it is the bond of faith in an act pure and integral; it is the deed itself begotten of an "overwhelming hankering for a little old-time activity," as Gil Westrum puts it early in *Ride the High Country*. At times, to be sure, the hero's own unchecked rancor threatens his humanity. Gil, whose initial motive for riding with Steve Judd is to rob him of the gold (or to wheedle it out of him), is perhaps the most cynical of these heroes. On the way to Coarsegold, he updates Steve on the fate of Old Doc Franklin, whom they both knew in younger days:

> [Franklin] gave thirty years of his life to make the West safe for decent people. You'd 've wept to see the way they turned out to pay tribute to him—all three of them: the mortician, the grave digger, and me. . . . I was commenting on the fairest flower that grows within the human heart—gratitude.

With the possible exception of Pat Garrett, whose surrender to the historical seems so abject, no hero of a Peckinpah Western has a more compromised career than Gil Westrum. Almost to the end he nurtures the bitterness that seems at times to corrode his soul: Gil helps us to identify the antiheroic animus more by embodying the various vices of the postmythic than by performing a deed or expressing a sentiment that stands in clear contrast to it. This resentment of Gil's is all the more contemptible when we recall that he is not even expressing a felt conviction about a perverted America but insidiously attempting to corrupt Steve's resolve to return to Hornitos with the gold and spitefully enlisting the young Heck Longtree as his accomplice by infecting him with greed. In this context, even Gil's career as "The Oregon Kid" seems not only a way of earning a meager livelihood in the new order of things but a sort of vindictiveness against the postmythic powers: he exacts his petty revenge on Hornitos not only by operating a crooked shooting gallery but also by pretending to embody that heroic essence which he knows all too well the respectable citizens would not recognize were it to appear before them stripped of all disguises. Yet if Gil is of all these heroes the most degraded, his eventual transformation overcomes the greatest obstacle. Gil's rancor becomes in fact the outward sign of a humanity *honored* in the very instant that his heroic act *transcends* it. At the end, as Steve lies dying, we receive confirmation that Gil's very bitterness prefigured his heroic deed. Gil, who has come to Steve's rescue, assures him that he will take care of Heck and Elsa, "just like you would've." Steve responds, "Hell, I know that. I always did. You just forgot it for a while, that's all."

Thus the heroic emerges out of shattered dreams. The American Dream, at least as the postmythic understands it, has long since passed by Steve Judd. Incapable though he is of responding to the historical with a rancor to match Gil's own, he does voice his many regrets. He could have married Sarah Truesdale, but as Gil, who also knew her, reminds him—and as Steve himself all too certainly knows—"What woman wants to sit around waiting for her husband to be brought home with his head shot off?" We have seen Pike bemoan the string of menial jobs that he has held of late. He also regrets his age and the holes in his boots, his two-dollar watch, his indifferent horse, and the unforgiving saddle. Most of all, however, Steve regrets that his humanity, in the form of his irreducible mortality, brought him nothing but penury and anonymity. Keeper of moral tallies that he is, moreover, he has figured what his worth would be if the "decent folks" had paid him in kind for his sweat and his blood:

> *Steve.* When I became a lawman, the world lost a first-class bookkeeper. So, just to pass the time one day, I sort of calculated what it was worth getting shot at. I figured it at about $100 a shot.
> *Gil.* You'd 've earned quite a sum by now.
> *Steve.* Getting hit—I figure that's worth anywhere from a thousand on up.
> *Gil.* That's three thousand dollars I know you've got coming.
> *Steve.* Four brings it up to date. And when you tally up all those fights and bushwhackings and coal camps—that time in Lincoln County—five weeks in the hospital, six months out of work. You add them all up, and I figure I was owed about all the gold we could carry out of these mountains. That's something to dream about.

Steve's regrets bind him to the form of the American Dream that the postmythic itself dreams, so that he seems, here at least, only too glad to exchange flesh and blood, perhaps even soul, for Caesar's coin. But Steve was just, after all, passing the time of day by appealing to the fantastic alchemy that would transform blood and violence into money; and so his musings may well account for the full extent of his regret. But the same fantasies mark only the surface of Gil's deep-seated rancor.[20] Much later, on the trail back to Hornitos, we see clearly the difference between the two:

> *Steve.* Now I'm getting back a little respect for myself, and I intend to keep it, with the help of you and that boy [Heck] back there. Good to be working again, Gil.

> *Gil.* Yeah, partner. You know what's on the back of a poor man when he dies? The clothes of pride, and they're not a bit warmer to him dead than they were when he was alive. Is that all you want, Steve?
>
> *Steve.* All I want is to enter my house justified.

The temptation duly spurned, Steve already overcomes the regret that had seemed to define his own humanity. If the revisionist Western narrates the story of loss—of youth and vigor and righteousness, of the very forces, then, that may have once prefigured America itself as *the high country*—then Steve's affirmation stands as that forfeiture already reclaimed. As he lies mortally wounded in the shallow trench, just after the shoot-out with the Hammond brothers, Steve tells a now chastened Gil: "How did we figure—a thousand dollars a shot? . . . Those boys sure made me a lot of money. They put 'em all in one spot." The reference to the exchange rate now carries none of Gil's mean cynicism. Instead, this irony *justifies* Steve as he stands at the threshold of his "house"; it certifies the balance of his life's account: in dying without the money he dies in full possession of his soul. Perhaps despite its deserts, the historical shall emerge redeemed, and regret shall turn, as if by mythic alchemy, to hope recovered.

Yet we should hardly think that Gil survives only to usher—or rather, to use Steve's preferred term, "transport"—Elsa and Heck into a new version of the postmythic. The farm, that noble Jeffersonian dream, has been defiled by Joshua Knudsen, who may have, for all we know, killed his own wife (perhaps named in the screenplay to evoke Hawthorne's famous heroine) in a fit of self-righteousness; for her grave marker reads: "Hester / wife of Joshua Knudsen / 1845–85 / Wherefore, O harlot hear the / Word of the Lord: / I will judge thee as women / That break wedlock and shed / Blood are judged: I will give / Thee blood in fury and in jealousy" [Ezek. 16:35, 38]. And the very presence of the depraved Hammonds in the farmhouse, during the climactic shoot-out, would seem but yet another reason to eliminate the farm as a possible Eden. Indeed, though the climactic shoot-out takes place within Joshua's fences, we see Gil, Heck, and Elsa walking away from them, seeking a world beyond them. Nor does it seem likely that Gil shall usher the Edenless couple to Hornitos or some such respectable outpost of progress, and the reformed Heck has long since given up tempting Elsa with dreams of San Francisco. Heck and Elsa now share no brighter prospects than Ringo and Dallas do at the end of *Stagecoach*. Like Doc Boone, Gil may pronounce them "saved from the blessings of civilization," but it is up to them, no less than it is for Ringo and Dallas, to discover, or rather, to create, the high country.

That the hero should now be not an individual but a *Bunch*; that here, moreover, beset and bedeviled by the American cult of the self, his elemental humanity should take the form of togetherness, and should by time and rage and blood come to be annealed into the bond of heroic identity—this surely stands as a milestone of generic revision, yet far more so as a hallmark of the possible forms of heroic action in post-heroic times.[21] To Mayor Wainscoat's first words, words that snarl the ethics of prohibition ("Do not . . ."), Pike Bishop's first words, antiphonal and assertive, are: "Let's fall in." Theirs the call not to social cohesiveness for progress's or safety's sake; theirs rather the exhortation—continual, impassioned, and thus thematically dominant—to loyalty as both the sign and aspiration of the human. "The code of the Bunch—" writes J. Douglas Canfield, "the code of the West, loyalty, fidelity to the Bunch, would seem to be the one positive among all the machismo, the one positive aspect of male bonding."[22] Fidelity consecrates their humanity, bestows upon it its benediction as a power for action. It is, in the end, the great source of strength in *The Wild Bunch*. And yet it is devotion without goal or purpose or mission: it is devotion, rather, fully and freely lavished, almost at times squandered, in the very teeth of a senseless world—fidelity, then, which produces an act that redeems both agent and object, that invests meaninglessness itself with an essential nobility.

In Joseph Conrad's *Heart of Darkness*, Charlie Marlow voices the value of the sort of fidelity that I am trying to express. Surrounded by a natural world from which all the comforting markers of Western civilization have vanished, and traveling in the company of white men who gild their grasping with the pretense of virtuous surrender to a civilizing mission—beset, then, not only by a menacing land but also by the teeming emptiness of Europe's moral failure, Marlow grounds his elemental humanity in devotion. In the "mournful gloom" that envelops Gravesend and the Thames, he enlightens his friends aboard the *Nellie*:

> The earth for us is a place to live in, where we must put up with sights, with sounds, with smells, too, by Jove!—breathe dead hippo, so to speak, and not be contaminated. And there, don't you see? your strength comes in, the faith in your ability for the digging of unostentatious holes to bury the stuff in—your power of devotion, not to yourself, but to an obscure, back-breaking business. And that's difficult enough.[23]

Devotion, so conceived of, answers to no external compulsion. It is, in its surrender to something beyond the Self, as much an exercise of moral freedom as can be had in a world awash with injustice. Fame and renown, which have been known to follow upon it, are but its dregs, the vestiges out of which the postmythic would co-opt and corrupt the transformative deed. Nor is it to be confused with manias or teleologies: Pike Bishop is no Ahab, and the Bunch have not yielded up their freedom to a mad purpose, as does the crew of the *Pequod* (minus Ishmael, of course, who knows enough of devotion). Fidelity implicitly subverts classes and hierarchies: the action that it empowers at once creates and honors difference, Otherness, novelty, possibilities: meet the bad guys "head-on—half-way, just like always," though the deed shall cost you your life; risk your life for worthless steel washers and then make sure that you can laugh about it. Devotion never acts for the sake of identity. And yet it is their fidelity that distinguishes the Bunch. Devotion, so conceived of, is the moral life *in extremis*, affirming not an ethic or an end but a renewal of life itself. It may be no more than Sisyphus hard at work for the work's own sake, and therefore free from the gods' dire decree.

The Wild Bunch abounds with instances of fidelity. The young Crazy Lee, shotgun in hand, exuberantly leading terrified clerks and matrons in a far more rousing version of "Gather at the River" than the Temperance Union's earlier one, stands his ground, on Pike's orders, long after the rest ride out of San Rafael. He becomes thereby the first to die for loyalty's sake. Crazy Lee pledges to guard the terror-stricken burghers, "Till hell freezes over or you [Pike] say different." The rallying cry of the Bunch is Pike's repeated "Let's go!"—a rallying cry at times prodding, at others inspiring, but ever the exhortation to action, even when, as in the climactic scene, action means certain death. Because fidelity comes to be life itself, Pike's counsels carry with them a desperate urgency. For example, on their way to Agua Verde by way of the desert, horses and riders together tumble headlong down sand dunes, and the Bunch, as they have done since the debacle at San Rafael, fall once again to bickering. The Gorches blame Old Man Sykes for this latest fiasco, and Tector Gorch pulls his pistol on the old man. Pike's angry intervention establishes the difference between the Bunch and the common groups: "We're gonna stick together!" Pike shouts, "Just like it used to be! When you side with a man, you stay with him, and if you can't do that, you're like some animal. You're finished! We're finished! All of us!"[24]

Yet let us not over-praise the Bunch's fidelity, each to the other, as if it were a divine gift rather than, as it is, a wisdom learned. In the melee at San Rafael, the Bunch forget Crazy Lee, and the lawmen shoot him dead. Much later, when Mapache detains Angel, Dutch, who has ridden into Agua Verde with him, does nothing to save his friend, all but ignoring his pleading looks.

Mapache then asks Dutch what he should do with Angel. "He's a thief," Dutch says, full of high sentence. "You take him," and rides away with the gold. For his part, Deke pursues the Bunch because he himself was once left behind, and there are a good number of moments—some lighthearted (like the passing of the communal whiskey bottle that deliberately yet playfully excludes Lyle Gorch), others potentially deadly (as when Tector tosses a lit stick of dynamite at Sykes, who is enjoying a private moment), and others still (say, the one given in the flashback to Deke's arrest) that suggest the extent to which fidelity in *The Wild Bunch* needs to be learned before it can be fully deployed as a source of action.

Pike, of course, is guilty of a failure of loyalty. Because of him Deke Thornton is in jail, hounded by Harrigan that he may in turn hound Pike (so that in a terrifying irony Harrigan enforces Pike's remorse). In this way, the historical claims him—and this by his own doing: by his guilt as much as by the failure of loyalty itself, he stands condemned to the postmythic, and thus requires a deliverance of his own. Yet here, in the lapse as in its consequent remorse, we readily find a conspicuous token of Pike's humanity. His is after all the oldest kind of lapse, and therefore the one that shapes the origin of our own humanity. His ideal of loyalty, however compromised, constitutes therefore the highest human aspiration—namely, that an ideal, even one wrought of remorse and regret, shall find complete expression in the action that liberates the sinner even as it indemnifies the sinned-against. Pike's guilt, to be sure, has another source. The basic relation whereby Pike affirms his humanity consists of a triad: Pike, Deke, and Dutch. These three together, in the intersections of their moral failures and hopes, at once define and enact the ideal of loyalty prerequisite to heroic action. In the development of this relation my emphasis tends toward Dutch, for he seems to define—though more by word than by deed—the code of loyalty to which the Bunch must in the end answer if they are to transcend the condition that ranks the human as no better than the flawed. Dutch, however, is no more important to the relation than Pike or Deke. Nor is he more human than these other two, nor, in the final reckoning, more loyal. Dutch's is the voice of a righteous, if earth-bound, humanity; and although he never articulates anything so noble as Steve Judd's depth of moral ambition—the longing "to enter my house justified"—or Pike Bishop's fervent ideal of devotion, his gift still reminds us that the struggle between mythic and postmythic emerges in the form of a conflict between the human and the *anti-* heroic.

Following the pandemonium in San Rafael, the Bunch, seated at an open-air table, witness the debauchery of Mapache and his fellow Sodomites, all of whom have taken their high seat on the veranda of a ruined house. Dutch complains that he is down to his last "twenty in silver." In the banter that follows, Pike becomes a mischievous mock-apologist for the degenerate post-mythic, and while his humor gets the better of Dutch, it also plays the foil to the distinctive humanity of the Bunch:

> *Pike.* With the way the generalissimo's cleaned out this part of the country, you ought to have a lot to spare.
>
> *Dutch.* Ah, generalissimo, hell! He's just another bandit grabbing all he can for himself.
>
> *Pike.* Like some others I could mention?
>
> *Dutch.* [*Over the general laughter of the table*] Not so as you'd notice, Mr. Bishop. We ain't nothing like him! We don't hang nobody. I hope some day these people here kick him and the rest of that scum like him right into their graves.

Amid such epidemic wickedness, this sudden eruption of Calvinistic righteousness anticipates the apocalyptic shoot-out and designates the Bunch themselves as agents of the *new* post-heroic order. More important, Dutch helps to clarify the moral context for the rescue of Deke Thornton from Harrigan, and in doing so he helps restore Pike Bishop's own lapsed soul. At night, in the hideout, following the disaster at San Rafael, as the Bunch get ready for much-needed sleep, Pike tells us that he abandoned Deke; and in a flashback, we see Pike and Deke in a whorehouse.[25] When the Pinkertons show up at the door, Pike runs out the back, while Deke is shot and captured.

By narrating the event, Pike accounts to Dutch for Deke's imprisonment, even as, by confessing, he atones for his failure of trust. It is, however, the *structure* of the sequence, of which the flashback is only a part, that discloses Dutch's moral authority. Just before the flashback to the whorehouse, Dutch asks Pike whether he has anything "lined up." When Pike suggests that they steal the payrolls of army garrisons, Dutch replies, "They'll be waiting for us," and Pike responds, "I wouldn't have it any other way." It is here that Peckinpah, by way of a ripple dissolve, shifts the action to the whorehouse scene. That he cuts to it at this moment would seem to suggest that he tests Pike's present defiance—"I wouldn't have it any other way"—by measuring it against a past deed, when loyalty yielded before the impulse for self-preservation. Yet the moment also identifies his humanity, and this in two distinct ways: first, of course, it points up Pike's frailty; second, however, it attests his capacity to beget an ideal of action—"I wouldn't have it any other way"—out of the guilt-ridden recollection of his lapse. At the end of the sequence Dutch consecrates both senses of that humanity. But let us return to the flashback.

Deke, "all caught up," as he puts it, is ready to go, but Pike wants to stay longer. "They're not going to look for us in our own back yard," Pike reassures him, and when Deke asks how he knows this, Pike answers, "Being sure is my business." Even as one of the prostitutes is letting the Pinkertons in, Pike is insisting that the knock on the door is only a hotel clerk's. At that instant, Peckinpah returns to the scene at the hideout, amidst the mocking echoes of Pike's hollow certainty: "Being sure is my business." Cutting back to the whorehouse scene, Peckinpah enacts the foreshadowed calamity: the Pinkertons shoot Deke and capture him; Pike escapes.

At the end of this flashback sequence, the action returns to the hideout. Dutch, his saddle for a pillow, turns over on the dirt floor to go to sleep, saying, "Pike, I wouldn't have it any other way, either." Peckinpah's sternest moralist absolves Pike by declaring him worthy of the faith that Pike failed to keep with Deke. Peckinpah has defined Pike's elemental humanity by the *failure* of fidelity, yet Dutch declares his absolute loyalty to this same humanity, compromised though it may be. Moreover, the implied absolution makes possible Dutch's own eventual judgment of Deke Thornton, in a later scene. For Dutch already understands, as Pike, burdened with remorse, does not, that Deke, though aggrieved and abused, has nonetheless sold his soul to Harrigan. He may have done so reluctantly, under protest and in the face of threats, and he may have subverted the conditions of the bargain by passing up the several chances to shoot Pike (from the San Rafael rooftop and from the bridge across the Rio Grande), but Dutch's moral code will let none of this argue for Deke's exoneration.

Long after the whorehouse-scene flashback, as Pike and Dutch watch from afar, Coffer, first lieutenant in Deke's "gutter trash" army, shoots Old Man Sykes, wounding him in the thigh. Pike and Dutch watch with binoculars:

> *Pike.* They got Freddy [i.e., Sykes]. Looks like he's hit pretty bad.
> *Dutch.* Damn that Deke Thornton to hell!
> *Pike.* What would you do in his place? He gave his word.
> *Dutch.* Gave his word to a railroad!
> *Pike.* [*Enraged*] It's his word!
> *Dutch.* [*Equally enraged*] That ain't what counts! It's who you give it to!

Dutch allows Pike to understand that Deke is an accomplice in his own fate, and as guilty of his own breach of faith as he is a victim of the furies that Harrigan sets after him. And yet, what does Dutch's severe judgment establish most clearly if not Deke's own humanity (even, perhaps, as it determines the limits of Dutch's own morality)? And by the implied claim of an elemental bond with the human, does the same judgment not thereby reaffirm Pike's own humanity as well? Is the angry exchange between Pike and Dutch not the means whereby Peckinpah prepares—indeed anoints—Deke for the "work" that is yet to be done even after the death of the Bunch? Let us also keep in mind that, at this point, Dutch himself has just returned from Agua Verde, where he betrays—or at least abandons—Angel,[26] so that the moralizing against Deke ("Gave his word to a railroad!") and against Pike ("It's who you give it to" that counts!), taken in their immediate context, smacks of the transparent dodge whereby the guilty upbraid their own misdeeds by the swagger of their most boisterous condemnations. There is none of the Bunch left who has not failed, none left who has not given proof of his humanity, and thus of his fitness for heroic action.

HAVING IT NO OTHER WAY

After all the declarations of fidelity and all the avowals and moral refinements, the *doing* still lies before them. One crucial moment seems requisite, however, for such a doing—an unequivocal gesture—indeed, more than that, an insight—to mark the readiness for action.[27] I am referring to Pike's vision of the infant child in the whorehouse, in the scene immediately before the climactic shoot-out. The context of this vision seems proper; it balances things out: if the failure of Pike's fidelity was set in a whorehouse, perhaps the reaffirmation of it should take place in a similar setting. At this point, recall, Angel is already a prisoner of Mapache. Shortly after Dutch arrives back at the mountain hideout with his share of the gold, the Bunch, perched up high on a mountain, see Coffer shoot and wound Old Man Sykes (hence Dutch's invectives against Deke and the railroad, above). The Bunch have to abandon their mountain hideout because they are running out of water; they cannot "make a run for the border," as Dutch suggests, because Deke and the bounty hunters, Pike assures him, would "follow us every step of the way." Besides, Pike is "tired of being hunted." They will go back to Agua Verde and Mapache's camp. Mapache, Pike tells Lyle, is "so tickled with those guns he'll be celebrating for a week and happy to do us a favor. Thornton's not gonna follow us there."

No sooner do they arrive before the portals of Mapache's Sodom than they witness the barbarous spectacle of Angel, limp and half dead, dragged behind Mapache's car—some latter-day Hector but that the profanation of his body precedes his death, and that neither rage nor grief nor even vengeance but debauched and wanton cruelty drives the engine of torture. It is especially painful to see the children ride on Angel's back: the imps of San Rafael reappear to wreak their inhumanity not on ants and scorpions but on an angel. Already the Bunch's anger is at white heat, and Pike offers to buy Angel with half his (Pike's own) share of the gold. Mapache refuses. What is gold to the delight he takes in torturing Angel? Then Zamorra, one of Mapache's lackeys, tells Pike and the Bunch, "Why don't you go get a drink? Enjoy yourselves. There's women everywhere—*muchas, bonitas!* Don't be foolish and change his [Mapache's festive] mood." The inevitable pimp appears (he was one of the passengers in Mapache's car) and offers to procure the women for the Bunch. Their sense of right foiled, perhaps cowed, by Mapache's refusal to release Angel and by the firepower at his disposal, the Bunch retreat to familiar haunts.

Pike has at last consummated his attraction for the young woman (is it really necessary to call her a whore?) with whom he has been exchanging amorous glances ever since the Bunch first sought refuge in Mapache's camp. As the woman, her camisole down below her shoulders, dabs herself gently with a wet cloth, Pike sits on the edge of the cot to put on his boots. We hear a baby cry, and Pike turns around, surprised. The camera zooms in on the infant and then cuts back to Pike, who casts a disbelieving look at the woman, still dabbing herself, unapologetic, impassive. Perhaps, having seen the baby, he sees her differently; or perhaps he sees himself differently. Maybe he is merely surprised that she is a mother. And maybe he sees here all that is good and true and elemental—the child whose essential innocence redeems the perversities of the urchins in both San Rafael and Agua Verde, and especially those of the uniformed boy who will shoot Pike with his rifle from a balcony. He sees also the woman whose youth and beauty and quiet dignity—whose innocence, really—amply compensate for Teresa's betrayal of Angel and offset the images of postmythic womanhood that we derive from the San Rafael crones and the Agua Verde harpies, and in particular from the Madonna of the Bandolier, who greeted us as the first image of Agua Verde—the sullen woman who nurses her babe while wearing an ammunition belt, who raises that child, then, for whom violence is as mother's milk—and from that other woman, another of Mapache's whores, whom Pike spares after he shoots the man hiding behind the mirror only to have her shoot him once he turns his back on her.

Still sitting on the cot, Pike reaches for a bottle and drinks its last drops dry. He now tosses and turns the bottle gently in his hand, as if pondering a purpose, then looks again at the woman, who goes on with her gentle ablutions, now and then looking back at him with only a faint curiosity. From the next room, Pike hears the wails and drones of the Gorches' prostitute: *"Doce es más que dos"* ("Twelve is more than two"), she whines repeatedly. Pike appears at their door, looks Lyle in the eye, and simply says, "Let's go." Lyle, perhaps for the first time fully of a mind with Pike, responds, "Why not?" Pike returns to his room only to give the woman an amount of money far greater than her services would call for—"doubtless, all he has," Canfield writes.[28] She looks up at him from the money in her hand—wide-eyed yet composed, glad to have the money yet not one whit the less dignified for it, silent yet vaguely oracular. Outside the whorehouse, Dutch sits with his back to the wall, whittling contentedly. Pike has only to look at him, and Dutch up at him: Dutch now declares the fullness of loyalty not by conscientious moralizing or uncompromising indignation but with silence and a smile.

Clearly Pike's vision of the child and the mother qualifies all that remains of the Bunch's life. No one seriously disputes the importance of the moment. Yet what has the Bunch decided here? And how have they come by that decision? The rescue of Angel—if this should indeed be (as many assert) the aim of their action—remains no less desperate, no less impossible. If they have decided to rescue Angel—if they propose to do now what they failed to do at least twice before—it can hardly be because they now know that the odds are better, let alone because they expect to escape from Agua Verde and enjoy their gold. (Did not San Rafael show them already that they did well to escape with their hides "and a big grin to pass the time of day with"?) No more plausible does it seem that Pike's vision should reveal to him, as if in a Quixotic epiphany, his life's purpose—that is to say, the rescue of mother and child from the general iniquity of Agua Verde. Such a rescue would be, at best, a derivative consequence of the Bunch's action, hardly, then, the impetus for it. Besides, what do the Gorches and Dutch know of the mother and the child? They never see them. And yet they wholeheartedly assent to Pike's exhortation.

Pike converts the vision of the child into action ("Let's go"). The vision, instant, unexpected, unmediated, enlivens in him the glory of that longing given at once in the danger and the daring—in that knowing audacity that raises the human to the level of (dare one say) the angels: "They'll be waiting for us," counsels caution. "I wouldn't have it any other way," the heroic responds. Before he had this vision, Pike was willing to part with but half his share of the gold as ransom for Angel. Now, by giving the woman all that he has left, he renounces gold itself as the measure of a life—and so of his *own* life, which earlier he seems to have surrendered to Mammon (for example, when he said to Angel, "Ten thousand cuts an awful lot of family ties"). The heroic, even by the most pedestrian understanding of it, cancels all exchange rates; recklessly magnanimous, its doings are always out of all proportion to any and all measurements. The child, then, I would like to suggest, functions as a correlative of Pike's commitment to action. It does not so much inspire it as it clarifies it. The child, then, or rather the vision of it, properly honored, carries no symbolic meaning—no significance beyond itself—because it is all *value*—all intrinsic and inherent worth. Therein its power: in the absolute integrity of its presence, it invigorates the moral imagination of the hero. The child is accordingly not so much an innocence to be protected from the postmythic as it is a moral distillation from which to draw life's own breath, the power to act in free yet faithful compact with life itself, even if life should be no more, in the end, than "an obscure, back-breaking business."

I would, moreover, complicate the Bunch's dying deed by way of a suggestion that controverts much of what is asserted about the climactic shoot-out in *The Wild Bunch*—namely, that the Bunch die for an *identity*, that in the end they receive, for their pain and sacrifice, the great Existentialist benediction—selfhood.[29] The action, I would say, rather *erases* identity—not only the labels and stamps that the postmythic imposes on the Bunch, but those that the Bunch impose on themselves. Let Dutch rail and vent that "we ain't nothing like" Mapache and his minions. Even if they had not so willingly enlisted in Mapache's service, there was a point in their lives when they had no identity except the Otherness that they voiced in opposition to the various forms of the postmythic. It is not, then, identity that they find in the last desperate yet pure act; it is identity that they *lose* in and through it. They become, they *are*, the act; and should sophistry insist that *being* the act is *who* they are, then we will let it explain how it came to subordinate the very deed that made "identity" possible. Let us recall, moreover, that identity has notoriously claimed to abide in the midst of life's multifariousness; and the Bunch, I submit, comes to focus all their lives through the prism of that one last act. Identity is at best a by-product of action. At worst, it is the idol-worship with which the postmythic, ever ready with its platitudes and shibboleths, debases the heroic act. The Bunch dream of identity no more than they dream of metal washers; and if, like Steve Judd, they, too, should enter their house justified (as the concluding montage, reprising the ride out of Angel's village, seems to suggest) it is not, as it is in Steve's case, for being but for doing—for meeting "them head-on—half-way, just like always." Pike's business of "being sure" has no longer to do with the mere evasion of capture. It reveals itself as the fidelity which, both tendered and received, can be the only certainty in the faithless postmythic. Theirs, then, the commitment not to death but to *dying*, not the act of despair—the suicidal deed animated by the straitened hope of easeful slumber—but the surrender to the act that, for holding so fearful a consummation, cannot but be integral and pure, the last, the most profound, affirmation of fidelity to life. If, as many assert, the Bunch die in an act of complete solidarity with each other, still that solidarity comes to be expressed, first and last, as an act of devotion to action, not to the persons who share in it. Theirs is loyalty to the deed and the doing.

So consider: Mapache slices Angel's throat, and every one of the Bunch fires on Mapache, killing him instantly; yet none of Mapache's minions fires back. Instead there follows a silence, thick with tension, a silence broken first by Dutch's impish giggle, and then by Pike, who now whirls about, focuses on Mohr (the German military adviser) and shoots him dead. This is the shot that *initiates* the superabundant shoot-out—the shoot-out that for its extravagance of scale alone can be explained not by invoking directorial self-indulgence or even the Vietnam allusiveness that the shoot-out is often, and a bit preciously, held to signify,[30] but the grotesque extent of the postmythic's viciousness, and so the concomitant extent of the violence requisite for its eradication. Yet the shot that Pike fires at Mohr signals something even more fundamental: the shoot-out unfolds freely, not out of necessity; Pike instigates it *against all instinct for survival, against all hope of an escape from Agua Verde*. It is therefore the act of supreme freedom lived in the duration of the dying, the unprovoked and disinterested surrender to a pure moment, the clutch at immortality. The noblest product of action is not identity but the power for action. It is the living of life, as Hemingway's Jake Barnes might have said of the Bunch as much as of bullfighters, "all the way up."

The shoot-out at Agua Verde produces no new postmythic order. No respectable citizenry emerges to engage in the business of America or to babble the fury of its parsimonious ethics. Yet one gesture attests the power of the Bunch's deed: as Deke's "gutter trash" bounty hunters mingle with the other vultures (human and avian), Deke walks up to where Pike lies dead, still clutching the trigger-handle of the Browning machine gun. A point-of-view shot shows Pike's holstered Colt's six-shooter, the weapon rendered useless by the sheer prodigality of the firepower deployed in the climactic shoot-out. The camera now zooms in on the six-gun, and then we see Deke's hand reaching for it. As the hand is unholstering the gun, a cut to a long shot shows Deke examining the gun curiously, perhaps noting that it has not been fired. Even as he continues to do this, the camera zooms in on him, so that we see him in medium close-up as he now registers his revulsion at the ravening glee of the bounty hunters, who idiotically shout their recognition of Pike and the Bunch. The camera turns to them, and when it follows them as they move across Deke, we note that Deke has just finished putting Pike's gun in his belt. Of this sublime gesture of Deke's, Paul Seydor eloquently writes: "In a quiet moment that seems to set a seal of benediction on all that has happened, Thornton walks up to Pike's body and takes his friend's pistol, a gesture that signals the fulfillment of his word to Harrigan and pays tribute to his dead comrade, who was killed paying some old debts of his own."[31]

Yet the gesture—especially as it comes to be extended by the cut to the medium shot of Deke and the subsequent zoom-in—also signals the first moment of Deke's new freedom: he draws it—the gun, his freedom—from the old friend who has consummated his act of devotion and who thus lies released of his debt to Deke. In this way Deke does not quite settle with Harrigan (you never settle with those who want your soul, even when they have it) as much as he claims freedom from that dreadfully compromised loyalty—from the *who*, if we may recall Dutch's earlier outburst, that he gave his word *to*. When the "gutter trash," loaded with their "bounty," leave Agua Verde, they find Deke sitting outside on the ground, his back to the adobe buttress of the ruined walls, his horse's reins in his hand. "You ain't comin'," Coffer notes. "No," Deke replies simply and sees them ride away (only to snicker at the shots, in the far distance, that signal their death at the hands of Old Man Sykes and the new Bunch).[32] Deke remains there, sole witness to the devastation and to the slow exodus of the survivors from the general pollution of the land.

No, no new postmythic emerges out of the apocalyptic purge. For it was the postmythic itself that needed purging—that yet *needs* purging: when Old Man Sykes approaches the gates of Agua Verde with his new Bunch (which includes Don José, from Angel's village, as well as a young boy, just about as old as the one who shot Pike moments earlier). Only now that Sykes approaches Deke does the full significance of drawing and keeping Pike's gun become evident. Deke has no better plan, as he tells Sykes, than to "Drift around down here [and] try to stay out of jail." But Sykes, who already binds the original Bunch to the new one, offers Deke a new freedom, not the freedom *from*, the one that he has already earned—the freedom from Harrigan and from having to ride with "gutter trash" and from his own lapsed loyalty to Pike—but a bolder form of freedom, a freedom *to*: "Well, me and the boys here, we've got some work to do. You want to come along? It ain't like it used to be, but it'll do." Deke looks up at Sykes and smiles. Sykes blurts out an endearing chuckle that soon becomes knee-slapping, uproarious laughter, the laughter that only the free laugh. Deke laughs for the first time in the movie. Even before he mounts up, the opening strains of "La Golondrina" begin to play, and the camera cranes up above the ramparts of Agua Verde and witnesses the ride of the new Bunch, even as the image of the riders dissolves continually with those of Pike's Bunch, themselves laughing.

And so they ride on, sure in their wisdom of only one thing: that wherever they undertake their "work," some form of the postmythic or another "will be waiting" to destroy them, yet just as assured that they will "have it no other way," and armed with a Colt's six-shooter that at once acknowledges and defies the dreadful odds against them in a world of machine guns and semi-automatic weapons and automobiles and aeroplanes. The six-gun, however useless its firepower may have been rendered, binds Deke (and us) to the mythic and the mythic deed—not so much as a deadly weapon or as a relic of some past out of the classic Western, but as a sort of badge authorizing him for the new work ahead, which is never really so unlike the one that "used to be." Indeed, the six-gun's very obsolescence as a weapon certifies the moral efficacy of the work yet to be done: it betokens Deke and the new Bunch's uncompromising fidelity to action, despite its tragic consequences. In the foretokened doom they shall find their freedom; in their vision of an imminent dying they shall consecrate a way of life.

Notes

1. For a development of these generalizations, see, for example, A. Carl Bredahl Jr., "After Words: The Western Movies of John Ford and Sam Peckinpah," in *Seeing Beyond: Movies, Visions, and Values: 26 Essays by William R. Robinson and Friends,* edited by Richard P. Sugg (New York: Golden String Press, 2001), 281–302; Armando José Prats, "A New Geography of Paradise: George Stevens's *Shane* as Trans-Edenic Vision: A Meditation in the Spirit of and Dedicated to W. R. Robinson," in *Seeing Beyond*, 248–80; and Armando José Prats, *Invisible Natives: Myth and Identity in the American Western* (Ithaca: Cornell University Press, 2002), especially 278–87, on *The Searchers*.

2. Henry David Thoreau, *A Week on the Concord and Merrimack Rivers* (1849; New York: Library of America, 1985), 308.

3. Friedrich Nietzsche, "On the Uses and Disadvantages of History for Life," in *Untimely Meditations,* translated by R. J. Hollingdale (Cambridge: Cambridge University Press, 1983), 106–7.

4. Thoreau, *A Week,* 49.

5. Paul Seydor, *Peckinpah: The Western Films* (Urbana: University of Illinois Press, 1980), 55.

6. John G. Cawelti, *The Six-Gun Mystique Sequel* (Bowling Green, Ohio: Bowling Green State University Popular Press, 1999), 60.

7. Richard Slotkin, *The Fatal Environment: The Myth of the Frontier in the Age of Industrialization, 1800–1890* (Middletown: Wesleyan University Press, 1985), 22.

8. Herman Melville, *White Jacket, or the World in a Man-of-War*, edited by Harrison Hayford, Hershel Parker, and G. Thomas Tanselle, vol. 5 of *The Writings of Herman Melville* (Evanston and Chicago: Northwestern University Press and Newberry Library, 1970), 151.

9. Mircea Eliade, *The Sacred and the Profane: The Nature of Religion*, translated by Willard R. Trask (New York: Harcourt Brace; New York: Harvest Books, 1957), 95. For another elaboration of this idea in the Western, see Armando José Prats, "Back from the Sunset: The Western, the Eastwood Hero, and *Unforgiven*," *The Journal of Film and Video* 47: 1–3 (Spring-Fall 1995), 106–23.

10. Mircea Eliade, *Myth and Reality*, translated by Willard R. Trask (New York: Harper & Row; New York: Harper Torchbooks, 1963), 5–6.

11. Edward Said, *Orientalism* (New York: Random House, 1978), 240.

12. Ibid., 246.

13. Leo Marx, *The Machine in the Garden: Technology and the Pastoral Ideal in America* (New York: Oxford University Press, 1964). See, for example, 113–22.

14. R. W. B. Lewis, *The American Adam: Innocence, Tragedy, and Tradition in the Nineteenth Century* (1955; Chicago: University of Chicago Press, 1984), 50.

15. Thomas Jefferson, *Notes on the State of Virginia*, edited by William Peden (New York: W. W. Norton, 1982), 164–65.

16. Henry Nash Smith, *Virgin Land: The American West as Symbol and Myth* (Cambridge: Harvard University Press, 1950), 180.

17. For a critique of this moment in *The Searchers*, see Prats, *Invisible Natives*, 58–70.

18. Lewis, *American Adam*, 9.

19. Recall that the first image of Angel's village, which has the Bunch riding in from the background, shows a starving dog in the foreground.

20. Gil, Paul Seydor writes, "misses the irony of Steve's calculations, of how inadequate money is to measure a person's worth, which is why Steve insists that all any man has a right to expect is the sum his contract calls for." *Peckinpah: The Western Films*, 36.

21. *The Magnificent Seven* (1960), of course, features an earlier bunch. But that bunch went to Mexico not, like Pike's own, to flee the postmythic but to create it out of that elemental conflict, so dear to the classic Western, between the defenseless farming community and the ravening outlaws led by Calvera, played by Eli Wallach.

22. J. Douglas Canfield, *Mavericks on the Border: The Early Southwest in Historical Fiction and Film* (Lexington: University Press of Kentucky, 2001), 131.

23. Joseph Conrad, *Heart of Darkness*, edited by Robert Kimbrough, 2nd ed. (New York: W. W. Norton, 1971), 50.

24. For a similar reading of the same scene, see Canfield, *Mavericks on the Border*, 131.

25. I am trying to clarify the function of a crucial gesture of Dutch's in the context of the flashback, but we should not forget that the flashback begins as a dissolve from Deke Thornton to Pike. Coffer (the Strother Martin character) asks Deke what kind of man the bounty hunters are up against in Pike. "The best," Deke responds. "He never got caught." It is here that we see a dissolve from a close-up of Deke to a close-up of

Pike, and thus note the ironic bond that ties the men each to the other as a preface to the story of failed loyalty.

26. Some will no doubt rebuke me for what may seem a harsh judgment of Dutch, reminding me that the odds are all against him in a rescue effort. What? Any more significantly so, really, than they are against the Bunch later, during the climactic scene? And did he really have to identify Angel as a thief, and do it with such contempt? Consider, also, that, moments later, in the mountain hideout, while the four members of the Bunch (Pike, Dutch, Lyle, Tector) reflect on Angel's fate as they wait for Sykes and the horses, it is Dutch who says: "He played his string right out to the end." Is Dutch invoking his severe Calvinism in order to mask his own failure of loyalty? Note Pike's glance at Dutch: a look of disbelief, perhaps, that Dutch can be so unfeeling. Later, returning to Mapache's camp, they see Angel being dragged behind Mapache's car. Says Pike in disgust: "God, I hate to see that." Replies Dutch: "No more than I do." Is he not yet again justifying himself?

27. As I lay the groundwork for my discussion of the climactic shoot-out in *The Wild Bunch*, a clarification seems to be in order, if only here. I treat Mapache's Agua Verde as a version of the postmythic. Historically and politically, of course, Agua Verde and Mapache and the German advisers and the references to Huerta and Villa all identify a Mexico that has more in common with the conditions prevailing in the classic Western before the arrival of the hero than with the postmythic that greets the Peckinpah hero. But Peckinpah does not seem to me to make the political history of Mexico hold ascendancy over the moral concerns that the postmythic raises, even from our first encounters with it, in San Rafael. Thus Agua Verde, with its grotesque parodies of postmythic progress—the automobile and (if only in reference) the aeroplane and the machine gun—functions as both an extension and a corruption of the postmythic in San Rafael.

28. *Mavericks on the Border,* 134.

29. The most recent exponent of this view of *The Wild Bunch* is J. Douglas Canfield, with whom to disagree is to court error. See *Mavericks,* 138.

30. For an account of the relation between the Vietnam War and *The Wild Bunch,* see Stephen Prince, *Savage Cinema: Sam Peckinpah and the Rise of Ultraviolent Movies* (Austin: University of Texas Press, 1998), 25–45.

31. *Peckinpah: The Western Films,* 136.

32. Thus no postmythic order converts the Bunch into the reward money that Harrigan offers for them.

TWO

PHILIP J. SKERRY

Comic Elements in Peckinpah's *The Westerner*

In 1995, Lincoln Center featured the first major retrospective of Sam Peckinpah's work. The three-week-long tribute featured all fourteen of Peckinpah's films, as well as a sampling of his work for television. In his review of the retrospective in *The New Yorker*, Terrence Rafferty claims, "If you look at Peckinpah whole, you can see where he came from and where he ended up."[1] I first started to look at Peckinpah "whole" when I wrote a paper on *The Westerner* for the 1996 Popular Culture conference in Las Vegas. My purpose then was to place the extraordinary series *The Westerner* within the context of Peckinpah's complete works and thus to ". . . look at Peckinpah whole . . .," as Rafferty states. In this study, I'd like to continue that purpose, only this time I should like to focus on one aspect of Peckinpah that critics seem to have ignored and that is encapsulated in the episodes of *The Westerner*: Peckinpah's comic vision of the West.

It is perhaps surprising to think of Peckinpah's Western vision as comic, especially when we consider the pervasive violence in almost all of his films and the major theme of betrayal that characterizes his major works. But Peckinpah is more than a master of mayhem and cynicism; in order to see him whole, we must discover the other side of Peckinpah, the side not so easy to see. Garner Simmons sees this other side in his perceptive essay in *Film Heritage*, "Sam Peckinpah's Television Work." Speaking of the three episodes from *The Westerner*—"Brown," "The Courting of Libby," and "The Painting"—Simmons says:

> Extremely funny, these episodes reveal a side of Peckinpah's directorial abilities seldom considered by his critics, despite the recurrence of comic elements in his

features.... In light of this, the criticism that Peckinpah's talents are limited to violence-related drama alone seems to be more dependent upon the individual critic's inability to look beyond the most obvious than upon any short-coming in Peckinpah.[2]

Simmons's article was written in 1975, when Peckinpah's "... life and art spiraled into a nihilistic abyss . . ." as Peckinpah biographer David Weddle puts it. In the 1980s, though, according to Weddle, "the great Peckinpah revival started,"[3] and as a result we are better able to see Peckinpah's work with perspective and balance. Yet most critics and reviewers still consider the Peckinpah of *The Wild Bunch* as the essential Peckinpah. However, the Peckinpah of *The Ballad of Cable Hogue* is also the essential Peckinpah, and I believe that *The Westerner* bears this out.

Peckinpah's extraordinary television series—Paul Seydor praises "... its high quality, almost unprecedented for a television series at the time ..."[4]—came at the crest of popularity of the television Western. In 1959, one year before the series aired, there were twenty-eight Westerns on network television. As J. Fred MacDonald points out in his book *Who Shot the Sheriff*, "If October 3–9, 1959, was a typical week on American television, viewers in Minneapolis, St. Paul—served by six commercial stations with no overnight programming—had eighty-one Western programs available for viewing, including adult and juvenile series, syndicated shows, and feature films."[5] Sam Peckinpah was one of the seminal figures in the evolution of the television Western, having written for *Gunsmoke, Broken Arrow, Tales of Wells Fargo, Have Gun—Will Travel, Tombstone Territory*, and many others. Yet while Peckinpah's film output is easily available on videocassettes and on cable and network television, no such availability exists for the television work.

Gary Yoggy has written a landmark study of the television Western, *Riding the Video Range*, that has helped to remedy the situation. But the fact remains that an extremely important aspect of Peckinpah's development as a Western director is simply not available for general viewing. Thus, if we judge only by the feature films, it is easy to miss the comic side of Peckinpah's Western vision. Paul Seydor says about the lack of available copies of the series, "*The Westerner* in particular deserves a far better fate than the one to which it remains consigned. This work as a whole reveals a young artist, soon to be a master, discovering fairly early his themes and materials and working in conventional forms that he was already beginning to manipulate in fresh and original ways."[6]

Peckinpah had been discovering "his themes and materials" from 1955 through 1958, writing numerous television Westerns. It was in 1958, though, that Peckinpah experienced his watershed year, for not only did he begin directing Westerns, he also began his association with Dick Powell's *Zane Grey Theater*, where he both wrote and directed episodes of *The Rifleman*. After leaving the series because of creative differences with the show's producers, Peckinpah set up an office and staff at Dick Powell's *Zane Grey Theater* to produce pilots. At 4-Star, Powell's studio, Peckinpah was commissioned to write and direct a half-hour pilot that, if successful, would become a regular series. Because 4-Star had been successful with series built around gimmicks like Lucas McCain's notch-levered, rapid-fire rifle, Powell came up with the idea of a Winchester rifle, specially equipped with an eight-power, cross-haired scope, and bored to fire a larger-than-average bullet. In Powell's commission, Peckinpah would be given a free hand to write and direct the pilot as he saw fit. Peckinpah at last had achieved a measure of artistic freedom, and he took full advantage to create a show built not around a gimmick, but rather around, as Weddle puts it, ". . . the West as it really was, a show about a saddle tramp instead of a gunman, a painfully human drifter moving from one cattle outfit to the next."[7]

The series that Peckinpah created for Powell is the essence of comedy, but comedy taken in its most general sense as dealing with, as one critic puts it, ". . . man in his human state, restrained and often made ridiculous by his limitations, his faults, his bodily functions, and his animal nature. . . . Comedy has always viewed man more realistically than tragedy, and drawn its laughter . . . from the spectacle of human weakness or failure. Hence its tendency to juxtapose appearance and reality, to deflate pretense, and to mock excess. The judgement made by comedy is almost always critical."[8]

Seen in this light, the thirteen episodes that Peckinpah completed for 4-Star are comic in tone, although several episodes are not funny in the accepted sense of that term. Peckinpah built his series around a quintessentially human character, Dave Blassingame, a decidedly unheroic character who wanders through the Western landscape with his faithful canine companion, Brown, and observes the folly, stupidity, greed, lust, and violence of his fellow Westerners. Blassingame's picaresque adventures are meant to expose the discrepancy between appearance and reality and to hold the Western legend up to a very critical light.

Even the darker episodes of *The Westerner* reveal Peckinpah's essentially comic vision. In "Going Home," for example, Peckinpah peels away the veneer of glamour that had come to be associated with the outlaw hero of the *Shane* mode. The wounded outlaw Little Bick, as he is called, is being transported in a makeshift cart by his mother and his wife, Suzy, away from the vicious bounty hunters vying for the $2,000 reward. Dave Blassingame comes upon the pathetic trio after they have been attacked by a renegade bounty hunter, who has betrayed his partners and set off to get the $2,000 reward himself. The bounty hunter is killed by the already wounded Little Bick, who is again shot, this time mortally. Dave witnesses his death and vows to help the mother bring Bick home to bury him. Suzy, the "bereaved" wife, had other plans, though. Before he died, Little Bick had convinced Suzy to turn in his body for the $2,000 reward, "dead or alive." Suzy tries to convince Dave to help her get the money by turning in Bick's body. In a pastoral lull in the action, Suzy and Dave look out over an idyllic valley. Suzy tries to appeal to Dave's self-interest by convincing him to help her in securing the reward money. Dave claims, though, that he is ". . . a stranger to ambition" and that he will help the mother bury Bick. Eventually, the remaining bounty hunters attack the trio, and Dave kills them, but Suzy is shot. Her dying words act as a subversion of the pastoral note created earlier: "I never did want to be in the middle of nowhere in a big empty prairie in the middle of nothing."

The comic vision of "Going Home" exemplifies the fifth comic structure in Gerald Mast's study of film comedy, *The Comic Mind: Comedy and the Movies*. According to Mast, the comic structure illustrated in "Going Home" ". . . is unified by the central figure of the film's action. The film follows him around, examining his response and reactions to various situations. This is the familiar journey of the picaresque hero—Don Quixote, Huck Finn, Augie March—whose function is to bounce off the people and events around him, often in the process revealing the superiority of his comic bouncing to the social and human walls he hits."[9] In "Going Home," the "walls" are the outlaw hero and the pastoral vision of the West, both soundly critiqued and debunked through the experiences of the *Pícaro*, Dave Blassingame.

In this sense, then, *The Westerner* represents one of the fictive modes that Northrop Frye describes in his seminal work *Anatomy of Criticism*. Frye identifies five modes—myth, romance, high mimetic (epic and tragedy), low mimetic (comedy and the novel), and ironic—based on the hero's stature in relation to other characters and to his environment. In the low mimetic, the hero is decidedly not superior to his environment or to other characters.[10] Peckinpah was deliberate in creating such a low-mimetic character. He says of the controlling viewpoint of his main character, Dave Blassingame: "I wanted to create a truly realistic saddle bum of the West. I wanted to make him as honest and real as I could do it. I drew him unlettered—most of these guys couldn't read or write. Not too bright. Certainly unheroic. . . . That's what David Blassingame is—a saddletramp."[11] Yet, in creating such an unheroic character, Peckinpah also presents a character true to himself, even though that self is not heroic in the traditional sense. In episode after episode, Dave Blassingame witnesses the folly of human greed, violence, and lust; and although he, himself, is fallen, he has enough integrity to ride on after each episode, avoiding the entanglements that maim and kill the other characters. The existential motto of Dave Blassingame is contained in his response to the frustrated wife in "Mrs. Kennedy," Margie Lee, who wants Dave to stay with her after Dave has killed her jealous husband in self-defense: "You had somebody built up in your mind before I came here—something I ain't, never was, can't be." That sense of himself and his own limitations is what prevents Dave from keeping the gold that he knows is stolen in "Dos Piños." That same integrity helps him realize the futility of trying to rescue the prostitute from her corrupt life in the episode entitled "Jeff."

In creating such a character, Peckinpah was going against the grain, for in 1959–1960, the Western was in a high mimetic mode—that is, the prevailing character was emphatically heroic. In fact, the Western genre had assumed epic dimensions and had become a modern morality play. The conflict between good and evil was played out in the context of a national epic: the trek West and the defining of a national identity.[12] Peckinpah created a series, though, that undercut the epic dimension of the West and that muddied the distinction between good and evil. Peckinpah's main character, Dave Blassingame, is not above adultery, drunkenness, brawling, and lying. In his comic humanity, he foreshadows characters such as Gil Westrum and Cable Hogue.

The full thrust of Peckinpah's comic vision is best seen in the three shows that feature Dave Blassingame's nemesis, Burgundy Smith, one of the most finely drawn portraits of the con-man ever seen on television. Burgundy, beautifully played by John Dehner, is the apotheosis of Melville's Confidence Man—he is never what he seems, and at the same time he gives his victims what they want: self-gratifying illusions. He is neither a villain nor a hero. Along with Melville's Confidence Man, Burgundy Smith is akin to Mark Twain's scoundrels and frauds, the Duke and the King, in *The Adventures of Huckleberry Finn*. Like Twain's rapscallions, Burgundy Smith allows Peckinpah to highlight the comic foibles of his characters.

The three shows featuring Burgundy Smith—"Brown," "The Painting," and "The Courting of Libby"—were all written by Bruce Geller, and all three were directed by Peckinpah himself. As Garner Simmons points out in his piece on Peckinpah's television work, Peckinpah directed five of the thirteen shows in the short-lived series, and three of them were the comedies featuring Burgundy Smith, who was the brainchild of writer Bruce Geller.[13] The fact that the majority of Peckinpah's creative energies went toward the creation of these three comic episodes is significant. The plot thread that holds the three shows together is Burgundy Smith's machinations in attempting to get Blassingame's dog Brown. The importance of Brown to Blassingame is summed up in his statement to Smith in the show entitled "The Painting"—"A man don't need nothing but a horse, a gun, and a dog"—which could be the comic credo of the whole series.

Peckinpah and Geller create, in the duo of Burgundy Smith and Dave Blassingame, a comic polarity: Dave, unsophisticated, unlettered, and naïve; and Burgundy, literate, cultured, and totally unscrupulous. Together, they explode the myths of the Western genre. In "Brown," Dave and Burgundy take part in the drunken brawl that masquerades for the Fourth of July celebration in the typical western town. So much for patriotic celebration. In "The Painting," Burgundy disguises himself as Count Francois de Bergerac in order to seduce and then create a scandalous portrait of the sexy cattle baroness Carla. So much for the culture and civilization of western life. In "The Courting of Libby," Burgundy Smith has become the wealthy "avocado king" in order to woo the voluptuous Libby. Of course, the unsophisticated Dave also falls for Libby. Both Dave's and Burgundy's nuptial plans are blasted, though, by Libby playing both ends against the middle and marrying the richest man in town. So much for true love and the sanctity of marriage.

The critical response to the show was somewhat mixed, but on the whole favorable. However, the series was cancelled. The NBC censors objected to the "excessive drunkenness, sex, rough language, and brutality," and NBC president Robert Kintner did not like the show. The show's time slot did not help its ratings. It was scheduled on Friday evening at 8:30 p.m., which was unofficially designated as the children's hour, and it appeared opposite a new animated show by the name of *The Flintstones*. Many creative people protested the show's cancellation, and Peckinpah even had a chance to save the show if he promised to make changes that would in effect dilute the series' "adult" tone. Both he and Brian Keith refused, telling the NBC execs to take their offer and "shove it up their ass," in Peckinpah's words.[14]

The Westerner came at a transitional time in the evolution of the Western. After 1960, the Western would veer in the direction of what Northrop Frye calls the "Ironic" fictive mode and what critics call the "adult" or revisionist Western. Peckinpah would certainly take part in this new type of Western filmmaking, but his short-lived series *The Westerner* is testimony to a "kinder, gentler" side of "Bloody Sam."

Notes

1. Terrence Rafferty, "Artist of Death: *The Wild Bunch* directed by Sam Peckinpah," *The New Yorker*, March 6, 1995: 127.

2. Garner Simmons, "Sam Peckinpah's Television Work," *Film Heritage* 10.2 (Winter 1974–75): 6–7.

3. David Weddle, "*If They Move . . . Kill 'Em*": *The Life and Times of Sam Peckinpah* (New York: Grove Press, 1994), 8.

4. Paul Seydor, *Peckinpah: The Western Films: A Reconsideration* (Urbana: University of Illinois Press, 1997), 27.

5. J. Fred MacDonald, *Who Shot the Sheriff? The Rise and Fall of the Television Western* (New York: Praeger, 1987), 56.

6. Seydor, 31.

7. Weddle, 169.

8. C. Hugh Holman, *A Handbook to Literature*, 3rd ed. (New York: The Odyssey Press, 1972), 108.

9. Gerald Mast, *The Comic Mind: Comedy and the Movies*, 2nd ed. (Chicago: University of Chicago Press, 1979), 7.

10. Northrop Frye, *Anatomy of Criticism: Four Essays* (Princeton: Princeton University Press, 1957), 34.

11. Seydor, 11.

12. Philip J. Skerry and Brenda Berstler, "You Are What You Wear: The Role of Western Costume in Film," in *Beyond the Stars III: The Material World in American Popular Film*, edited by Paul Loukides and Linda Fuller (Bowling Green, Ohio: Bowling Greeen State University Popular Press, 1993), 78.

13. Simmons, 6.

14. Weddle, 182.

References

Frye, Northrop. 1957. *Anatomy of Criticism: Four Essays*. Princeton: Princeton University Press.

Holman, C. Hugh. 1972. *A Handbook to Literature*. 3rd ed. New York: The Odyssey Press.

Kirkley, David H. Jr. 1979. *A Descriptive Study of the Network Television Western During the Seasons 1955-56–1962-63*. New York: Arno Press.

MacDonald, J. Fred. 1987. *Who Shot the Sheriff? The Rise and Fall of the Television Western*. New York: Praeger.

Mast, Gerald. 1979. *The Comic Mind: Comedy and the Movies.* 2nd ed. Chicago: University of Chicago Press.

Rafferty, Terrence. 1995. "Artist of Death: *The Wild Bunch* directed by Sam Peckinpah." *The New Yorker*, March 6, 1995: 127–29.

Seydor, Paul. 1997. *Peckinpah—The Western Films: A Reconsideration.* Urbana: University of Illinois Press.

Simmons, Garner. 1974–75. "Sam Peckinpah's Television Work." *Film Heritage* (Winter): 1–16.

Skerry, Philip J., and Brenda Berstler. 1993. "You Are What You Wear: The Role of Western Costume in Film." In *Beyond the Stars III: The Material World in American Popular Film,* edited by Paul Loukides and Linda Fuller, 77–86. Bowling Green, Ohio: Bowling Green State University Popular Press, 1993.

Weddle, David. 1994. *"If They Move . . . Kill 'Em": The Life and Times of Sam Peckinpah.* New York: Grove Press.

Yoggy, Gary. 1995. *Riding the Video Range: The Rise and Fall of the Western on Television.* Jefferson, N.C.: McFarland and Company.

THREE

JOHN L. SIMONS

The Double Vision of Tragedy in *Ride the High Country*

> Tragedy is born in the West each time the pendulum of civilization is halfway between a sacred society and a society built around man.
> —Albert Camus

> In the last day, that great day of the feast, Jesus stood and cried, saying, "If any man thirst, let him come unto me, and drink. He that believeth in me, as the scripture hath said, out of his belly shall flow rivers of living water.
> —The Gospel According to St. John

> [California] is a tragic country—like Palestine, like every promised land.
> —Christopher Isherwood

I.

Sam Peckinpah has described *Ride the High Country* (1962) as a film about the "salvation and loneliness" of its solitary hero, Marshal Stephen Judd (Murray 1972, 74). At another, though related, level this classic Western centers on the concept of tragic sacrifice, and an equally tragic theme, the threatened death of the American West. In an act of sacrificial surrender, Steve Judd (Joel McCrea) dies so that a blighted land may be redeemed, restored to new life symbolized by Judd's regenerated friendship with his old partner, Gil Westrum (Randolph Scott), and the imminent union of two young people, Elsa Knudsen (Mariette Hartley) and Heck Longtree (Ron Starr).

Although a tragedy, *Ride the High Country* demurs, in at least one aspect, in conforming to the classic Aristotelian definition because Steve Judd, while imperfect, lacks the requisite "tragic flaw" that leads to his undoing and eventual death. But as Northrop Frye points out in *Anatomy of Criticism*, in his chapter "The Mythos of Autumn: Tragedy," it is a reductivist fallacy to assume that all tragic actions are based on a rebellious hero's "violation of moral law," or that "Aristotle's 'flaw' must connect with sin or wrongdoing" (Frye 1957, 210). Instead Frye adduces various kinds of tragic actions, among these the disputed genre of "Christian tragedy." In spite of its apparently anti-tragic denial of the Greek—and Shakespearean—notion of the shadowy complicity of good and evil, and the even more resolutely untragic Christian promise of eternal life, this particular dramatic form, mutatis mutandis, remains tragic for Frye because of its focus upon the life-pattern of its protagonist. Specifically, Frye (1957, 22) argues that Christian tragedies are those that symbolize "the Passion, as do all tragedies in which the hero is any way related to or a prototype of Christ." Additionally, these tragedies emphasize "the success or completeness of the hero's achievement," that moment of "full rich serenity" which is "often a sequel to a previous tragic or heroic action, and [which] comes at the end of a heroic life" (Frye 1957, 221). By choosing to emphasize the Christ-like sacrificial nature of the protagonist over the central Christian paradox of death and resurrection, a theme that is taken seriously but is left open-ended and ambiguous at the end of *Ride the High Country*, Frye avoids one of the key sticking points in the debate over the possibility of Christian tragedy.[1] Frye's tragic model, then, informs the archetypal design of the life, death, and eventual "salvation," to use Sam Peckinpah's word, of Stephen Judd.

That Sam Peckinpah should employ the literary model of Christian tragedy to depict Stephen Judd's life and death should surprise no one who knows anything about Peckinpah's childhood growing up in Fresno, a youth dominated by questions of law (his late father [prototype of Steve Judd], uncles, and brother were all lawyers and judges), and "a Bible which was very big in our family" (Whitehall 1969, 73). Peckinpah, a lifelong student of the Bible, eventually rebelled against the rigid strictures of his religious upbringing (his mother, about whom Peckinpah had very mixed feelings, was a fervent Christian Scientist), but this does not preclude his absorbing—and remembering—the Bible's stories, parables, and miracles that he had heard as a boy, while subsequently making them his own. Peckinpah's actual religious beliefs at any particular time seem far less important than his persistent use of the Bible as an organizing frame of reference for his writing and for the visual iconography of his films. Finally, what makes Peckinpah's relationship to Christianity, and to Christian tragedy, interesting is not, as W. H. Auden has written, that artists like Peckinpah "necessarily believe the Christian dogmas, but that their conception of man's nature is, historically, derived from them" (Corrigan 1981, 164).

Contrastingly, if one were to read *Ride the High Country* within a more traditional definition of the tragic flaw, and view it once again from the prism of Sam Peckinpah's personal past, then I believe the hamartia "figure" would be an America whose all-too-human fall from grace and whose tragic history Peckinpah depicts at a time of turbulent national change. Steve Judd, and the Old West—its mythic men, its legendary land—that he so venerates, function as victims of America's westward expansion, its simultaneous betrayal both of its people's deepest dreams and of its magnificent natural resources. Rapacious yet repressive, acquisitive yet nihilistic, the turn-of-the-century West we witness in *Ride the High Country* effectively seeks out the ruin and death of men like Stephen Judd, men whose commitment to law and justice (the name "Judd" echoes the legal word "judicious"), to community, and to the sanctity of nature renders them useless and anachronistic.

Sam Peckinpah's films nostalgically—and often bitterly—rue the near extinction of the pastoral West, especially the California Peckinpah knew as a child, a California of small farms and ranches, of mountain hunting trips (there is a Peckinpah Mountain near the former family ranch outside of Fresno), of solitary and unsullied high-country lakes and forests, now almost obliterated by an advancing "civilization." In an interview Peckinpah laments his riven childhood, regrets the passing of an older, better world, and decries the changes: "Today the [family] ranch is gone. There are motels. It's all gone" (Whitehall 1969, 174). The "all goneness" of Peckinpah's past will function as a crucial metaphor in *Ride the High Country*'s dialectic between presence and absence, climaxing in the double disappearance (dead and "gone") of Stephen Judd at film's end. Likewise for Peckinpah, enduring human values, "[o]utdated codes like loyalty, friendship, grace under pressure, all the simple virtues . . . have become cliches . . ." (Murray 1972, 72). If people practice those virtues in Peckinpah's romantic-pessimistic world, they must, like Stephen Judd, die for them, but die in such a way as to keep their values alive in others.

To summarize, what makes *Ride the High Country* so rhetorically and artistically satisfying lies in its shifting back and forth between the double discourses of Christian and Aristotelian—more particularly, historical—tragedy. Never choosing one over the other, but rather opting to represent both of them at once, and often in conflict, the film brings each to rich and complex expression. Thus it is a mistake to opt for one vision of the West over another, as Peckinpah biographer David Weddle does when he writes of a Western "mythology that Sam Peckinpah and his generation could no longer believe in, no matter how much they might have yearned to"(Weddle 1994, 221). Both Wests are present in *Ride the High Country*. In this respect it resembles a number of early 1960s Western films—*The Misfits*, *The Man Who Shot Liberty Valance*, *Lonely Are The Brave*, *Monte Walsh*—all of which lament the passing of a heroic way of life. Like these other films, *Ride the High Country* mixes praise-song and threnody, faith and fact, preserving in its tortured oppositions a complex, multifarious vision of tragic experience. Like F. Scott Fitzgerald, Peckinpah fulfills the "test of a first-rate intelligence" in his "ability to hold two opposed ideas in the mind at the same time, and still retain the ability to function" (Fitzgerald 1945, 69). That we are dealing here with contrasting definitions of the tragic genre makes Peckinpah's achievement in *Ride the High Country* all the more aesthetically impressive.

Finally, more than any director of Westerns other than John Ford,[2] Sam Peckinpah refashions the biblical Fall in the Garden of Eden, itself the originary tale in any definition of Christian tragedy, as the historical fall of the American West. In so doing he recasts the heroic attempt to redeem the dying West as an imitation of Christ's sacrificial death upon the cross.[3] In what follows I propose to explore Peckinpah's binocular vision of tragedy by tracing it through the iconic figure of Stephen Judd in his tragic confrontation with a ruthlessly secularizing, ardently modernizing America.

II.

Ride the High Country is shot through with biblical language and imagery. At the same time the film is highly critical of its most putatively religious figure, Swedish farmer Joshua Knudsen (R. G. Armstrong), the smugly self-righteous and sanctimoniously overbearing father of an innocent young daughter, Elsa. The Knudsen farm, nevertheless, looms as the film's geographical, structural, and symbolic focal point. Like the Garden of Eden, and so many other mythic visions of paradise, it lies "at the 'center of the world'" (Eliade 1978, 166) of *Ride the High Country*. The farm, ablaze with autumn colors— the seasonal colors of tragedy in Northrop Frye's theory—is ringed by golden trees and adjoined by majestic mountains. Almost allegorically, it is situated between two contrasting locations: the foothills town of Hornitos, with its contrasting corrupt carnivals and pinched and puritanical society, typified by two balding, effetely wizened bankers, a father and son ironically and incongruously named "Samson," and the physically devastated mountain mining camp of Coarsegold, a virtual Sodom and Gomorrah of drunkenness and sexual excess.[4] In its purest essence, the farm, mediating between nature and society, embodies that classically American version of a pastoral Eden that Leo Marx defines as "a mythic idea, an all-encompassing vision that converts the ethic of the middle link into the 'true and only' philosophy for Americans" (Marx 1967, 112).

But the Knudsen farm is not what it seems to be from a distance. It first appears up-close on screen as grim and foreboding, photographed from deep within a dark and dirty barn where Elsa Knudsen, figuratively buried alive, and dressed like a man, barely gendered as a woman, bends and toils over mounds of filthy hay. Her father, gloomy and Plutonic, tyrannous and authoritarian, jealously harbors repressed incestuous desires for his daughter. Knudsen's wife, Elsa's mother, is named Hester, a name that must surely be no accident, though Peckinpah has acknowledged that he was less conscious of the Hawthornian connection than of the rather strained biblical connection to the book of Esther until it was pointed out to him by friends (Seydor 1980, 32). Five years ago Hester was driven from the farm by her sin-crazed, sex-obsessed husband's rigid, authoritarian ways. Whether she entered the harlot's trade, as the inscription on her grave, placed there by her husband, indicates, or whether her escape from the farm has been perversely interpreted in that manner by her husband, we cannot tell. We do know that a similarly grim fate awaits Hester's daughter who, though independent and strong-willed, cannot alone save herself. She needs help, and only Steve Judd, a surrogate father-figure, will be willing to give it to her. In a series of intricate symbolic dissolves, which are the key interpretive focus of this essay, Peckinpah will make it clear that Elsa's hope for a new life, and the concomitant restoration of lost natural and human harmony to the Knudsen farm,[5] rest with the salvific figure of Stephen Judd.

Accompanied by his friend and former deputy, Gil Westrum, his last name a bibulous corruption of the words "Western" and "rummy," as well as by Heck Longtree, Westrum's partner in carnival con games, Steve Judd has contracted with the banker Samsons of Hornitos to transport gold down from the Coarsegold mining camp to the bank. Too old to hold down a regular marshal's job, and fallen on impecunious and threadbare times, Judd hopes to win back some of his former "self-respect" by performing his duties with integrity and professionalism. Westrum and Longtree, on the other hand, intend to entice Judd with their scheme to steal the gold. Failing this, they imply that they will kill him for it if he refuses to accede to their plans. As many critics have pointed out, Gil Westrum functions as a Mephistophelean figure to tempt Steve Judd away from an ethical commitment to honor his contract with the bank. Gil wears suitably—and comically—Satanic red long-johns and remarks to Heck that even if "the Lord's bounty is not for sale, the devil's is." The first time he encounters Steve in the film, Gil, looking like a grotesquely comic version of buffalo-slaying Bill Cody, expresses his surprise by saying, tellingly, "I'll be damned!" An older man like Steve, Gil too has fallen on ragged times. But Steve refuses, in spite of his reduced situation, to compromise his principles, while Gil is only too willing to compromise all of his. Twice they journey through the Knudsen farm on their way to and from Coarsegold. In languaage that underscores the double nature of tragedy in this essay, Paul Seydor describes that journey as "a kind of passage—moral, ecological [and] mythical" (Seydor 1980, 33). It is also a journey that leads to the film's deepest tragic revelations.

Gil Westrum's role is to tempt Steve Judd as they ride through the at once realistic as well as allegorically charged High Sierras. He assails Judd's lack of resources after so many years of loyal service in bringing law and justice to the West. He also remarks on Judd's loneliness in the absence of his one true love, a woman with the suitably pastoral name Sara Truesdale, whom Judd knew years ago, but who, fearing Judd's dangerous profession, rejected his proposal of marriage when he refused to abandon the law. When Gil makes a comparison between Sara's smile and general demeanor in relation to Elsa, Steve, clearly affected, attempts to brush aside the comparison. But it has left its mark on the solitary old man, who has no money, no home, no spouse, no children or grandchildren, unlike Sara Truesdale, now living on a ranch in Idaho where she and her husband raise, as Gil tells him, "*blooded* horses" (italics mine).

While moved by memories of Sara, Judd also seems to intuit Gil's darker intentions. He communicates with his old friend in such a way as to make it evident that he has pierced Gil's verbal and physical disguises, and that through suggestive language and parable-like actions he intends to return Gil to spiritual health.

Critics conditioned to discuss Peckinpah's films as works of an insidiously ironic, angry, and apocalyptic iconoclast may miss the manner in which *Ride the High Country*, though suffused with its creator's inveterate sense of irony, paradox, and self-awareness, affirms at the same time basic Christian values. This paradox within a paradox becomes apparent in the following close analysis of these two key scenes in *Ride the High Country*, scenes that anticipate the extraordinarily inventive montage sequences of Peckinpah's later, more technically innovative films.

On the night before the Judd party leaves the Knudsen farm during its first visit there, Joshua Knudsen quarrels bitterly with his daughter Elsa over Heck Longtree's amorous attentions toward her. Knudsen catches the two of them taking in the night air by a hay wagon in the barnyard and angrily sends Elsa into the house. There the father, furious at Elsa for implying that he wants her all to himself, strikes her violently. Confused, Joshua goes to his knees before Elsa, begging her forgiveness, then retreats to his own bedroom. Angry and rebellious, her hands covering her face, Elsa sinks to her knees on the floor, vowing that this is the last time her father will ever hit her. Next follows a remarkable dissolve, in which technically "two images blend in such a way that their union constitutes a symbolic equation" (Dick 1990, 61): the stricken figure of Elsa slowly fuses with and is briefly juxtaposed over a shot of her mother's grave. Then in a moment of Poe-esque terror, Elsa sinks, literally dissolves, and finally disappears into that same grave, its daunting wooden cross inscribed, as was traditional in ancient crucifixions, with her sin-obsessed father's biblical injunction against his "fallen" wife: "Wherefore, O Harlot, hear the word of the Lord. I will judge thee as women that break the wedlock and shed blood are judged. I will give thee blood in fury and in jealousy." Ultimately, Joshua Knudsen will pay for destroying Hester in the very "blood and fury" to which he has sentenced her. For now the camera indicates his guilty complicity in that death when it slowly dollies back and simultaneously pans, left to right, to reveal the cause of Hester Knudsen's early death: the kneeling figure of Joshua, hands tensely clasped and seeming to form a large fist, silently praying, eyes closed, beside his wife's grave. These tightly framed, weakly lit images, static in their depiction of a blindly fixed and obdurate soul, suggest not the prayer of forgiveness or trust in divine mercy, but rather the "fury" of judgment and retribution. For this is the twisted misreading of Old Testament patriarchal law favored by a so-called Christian, but decidedly uncharitable, father.[6] Joshua Knudsen is a latter-day Roger Chillingworth, who has sentenced *his* Hester to eternal damnation. The scene horrifies because it foreshadows Elsa's fate. On account of the father's cruel actions, driving both mother and daughter away from what is no longer a "home" to either of them, Elsa may be doomed to repeat the apparent "sins" of Hester Knudsen. This cinematographical burial scene also can be linked to the Elsa we first encounter *buried*, entombed deep inside her father's barn.

If the brutal confrontation in the Knudsen house, as well as the image of the praying father's face (fittingly, he will die this way, eyes open, seeing nothing, bent over a fence beside his wife's grave, a bullet through his forehead) offer no hope, then a second dissolve, which completes the montage, stands radically opposed to the preceding scene of enclosure, terminus, and death. As the figure of Joshua Knudsen begins to vanish, the screen fades into a close-up of two feet, Steve Judd's as we come to learn, soaking in a rapidly moving clear mountain stream. Peckinpah prepares for this transition by, in the previous, graveyard shot, moving the Judd party, in deep space left to right, through a sunlit avenue of trees, out beyond the praying Knudsen. As they cross the film frame, they pass by the ranch's windmill and trough and seem to emerge in the distance from the crude wooden cross, seen in close-up, above Hester's grave. This draws the viewer's eye into the following dissolve, prepares him/her for the cinematic transition that occurs, and adumbrates, as we shall see, the theme of life coming out of death that is key to this entire sequence, and to *Ride the High Country* as a whole.

In a moment of ironic daring typical of Sam Peckinpah, the former scene, so sanctimoniously reverential in the apparent image of the grieving husband praying beside his wife's grave, represents at bottom a perverse adherence to the fundamentalist letter of biblical law. But why then in the subsequent shot does the camera focus in close-up (from a medium high angle), upon those soaking feet? On a story level, Peckinpah obviously intends his audience to respond to the naked humanity of his aging hero, Stephen Judd, who welcomes such casual comforts as cooling his trail-sore feet in a mountain stream. But on a discursive level, and as part of an intricate montage sequence, those feet will come to symbolize a larger, potentially tragic action, more specifically the Christian "mimesis of sacrifice" (Frye 1957, 214) at work in the film.

As the camera dollies outward and pans slightly to the right (a camera movement parallel to Knudsen at his wife's graveside), it reveals the entire figure of Steve Judd, gazing at his feet in the flowing water and obviously enjoying the sensation. This is one of several important moments in the film where the man of law, Stephen Judd, also expresses an abiding attachment to the western landscape. It is also one of those moments where the tragic man and the tragic land are seen in relation to each other. The director then cuts, perhaps rhetorically emphasizing a thematic separation, to something—and someone—quite different, a smirking young man, Heck Longtree, fully clad and sitting on the bank beside the sliding stream. Judd looks over and remarks, "In about thirty years you'll like the feel of it too!" Heck is sizing Judd up, preparing for the moment in which, serpent-like, he and Gil Westrum will strike, seizing the gold from the seemingly helpless older man. Heck interprets Steve's actions as signs of weakness. He then pulls a sandwich from his saddle bag, unwraps it, and tosses the wrapper away. "Pick that up," commands Judd, "these mountains don't need your trash!" Once again the film emphasizes that Steve Judd's ethical and spiritual being is allied with his veneration for nature.

At a literal level the stream interlude, written and filmed unobtrusively so as not to draw attention to its symbolic artifice, unfolds as a serio-comic didactic moment along the trail, articulating certain differences in values between Steve Judd and Heck Longtree. But a more complicated interpretation arises from this scene of instruction when the sage older man attempts, indirectly, to impart knowledge and wisdom to a reluctant young disciple. Foolishly, Heck refuses to comprehend Steve's actions and words. Bearing in mind that this moment cinematically mirrors Joshua Knudsen's grim vigil at his wife's grave, then Joshua's spiritual blindness and Heck's related failure to see what Steve is teaching him directly complement each other. Reading more deeply into this crucial moment, it becomes apparent that the lesson Steve Judd wants to teach Heck Longtree, and subsequently Gil Westrum, bears a close resemblance to a pivotal event in the New Testament Gospel according to John, the scene in which a humble Christ startles his disciples by endeavoring to wash their feet (John 13). Michael Bliss indicates as much when he relates Steve Judd's foot-washing to a "pleasurable self-baptism" (Bliss 1993, 47) Thus a seemingly mundane event expands into biblical meaning through the conversion of lush foothill terrain into a moral and religious landscape. In Breughelesque fashion, the trees of Eden and the Jordan River suddenly manifest themselves in the indigenous California mountains. This form of symbolically charged realism produces what Leo Braudy describes, in reference to several contemporary Roman Catholic directors (Peckinpah in fact briefly converted to Catholicism during the 1960s), as a kind of "incantatory moment, a mode of suprarealistic perception that I would like to call a sacramentalizing of the real, not so that it be worshipped but so that its spiritual essence . . . inflect[s] what is otherwise a discrete collection of objects in space" (Braudy 1986, 18). Surely this "sacramentalizing of the real" is what Peckinpah intends in an iconographically rich montage sequence, foreshadowed in its religious implications the night before at the Knudsen dinner table where Steve Judd and Joshua Knudsen engage in a contest of duelling biblical quotations.

The New Testament passage to which I refer occurs at the time "when Jesus knew that his hour was come that he should depart out of this world unto the Father," that "having loved his own which were in the world, he loved them unto the end" (John 13:1). In a related manner Steve Judd knows, and has probably suspected from the beginning, that Heck and Gil intend to betray him. Imitating Jesus with his disciples, Judd never completely loses faith in them.

In John the most sincere, and at times most prosaic, of Christ's disciples, Simon Peter, cannot understand why Christ should commit such a humble and self-abasing act as washing the feet of his followers. But Peter, ever impetuous and headstrong, misunderstands as usual. Like Heck Longtree, he interprets Jesus's actions on a superficial level. Christ replies, in language that echoes Steve Judd's advice to Heck: "What I am doing you do not know now, but afterward you will understand" (John 13:7). In time Peter will comprehend Christ's actions, and so too will Heck Longtree, significantly by another waterside, a mountain lake where he is forced to choose allegiances between Gil and Steve.

In the gospel Peter goes so far as to tell Christ that his "hands and head" also require washing. He is baffled by Jesus, who replies, "He who has bathed does not need to wash, except for his feet, but he is clean all over, and you are clean, but not every one of you" (John 13:10). This may explain why Peckinpah frames a close-up of Steve Judd's feet in the water for the initial shot of this concluding scene of the montage. Those talismanic feet give the lie to the hypocritical picture of Joshua Knudsen's praying hands. Like Heck Longtree and Gil Westrum, Knudsen is unclean in his spiritual being, unwilling to allow the Bible's genuine message of faith and forgiveness to wash over him.

Steve Judd must, of course, gather at his own river and cleanse his own feet, for no one joins him in the sacred western stream, though symbolically he intends through his homely example to "cleanse," to purify the spirit of young Heck Longtree. But Heck has, unwittingly, chosen another biblical path to follow. As Gil Westrum's corrupt companion, he ignores Steve's exhortations. We have already seen the manner in which Peckinpah depicts the smooth-talking seducer Gil as the devil incarnate. If that is so, then Heck Longtree, the youthful betrayer, fulfills the role of young Judas, reflecting similar events from the Book of John. This is probably why Peckinpah depicts Heck in the act of eating. John locates the story of Christ's betrayal in the Last Supper, just prior to the Feast of the Passover, "the devil having now put into the heart of Judas Iscariot, Simon's son, to betray him" (John 13:2).

The stream, as indicated above, carries baptismal implications as well, were Heck to allow himself to enter its revivifying waters and be cleansed/

saved. This should surprise no one conscious of the life and films of Sam Peckinpah, Westerner and inveterate hydrophile, who invariably, as Kathleen Murphy writes in her obituary to Peckinpah, "found baptisms where he could, in tacky hotel showers, in the free flow of wine and tequila, in momentarily Thoreauvian ponds [and streams, one might add], and always in the blood of his much fallen and fragmented heroes" (Murphy 1985, 74). Water runs through all of Peckinpah's films, and its presence is always noteworthy.[7] When, for instance, Elsa Knudsen first observes the Judd party riding through the trees toward her father's farm, dominating the foreground of the film frame stands a horse trough, symbolically analogous to the windmill and trough noted earlier in the graveyard scene. Peckinpah uses this homely domestic association to link Elsa and Steve through the practical and unobtrusive watering trough. The relationship between mutable water and renewed life for this young girl imprisoned, buried beneath her father's stifling control, alerts us to her potential rescue by Steve Judd.

No less important, the first strains of genuine feeling between Elsa and Heck occur that evening after dinner when Heck, standing outside the kitchen window, offers to dry the dishes that Elsa, pumping water beside him, has been washing. Here Heck, though only temporarily, seems less the aggressive Lothario than an attentive and affectionate young man. Similarly, when Heck and Elsa first exchange a tender kiss up in the high mountains, the kiss takes place beside a cerulean blue lake. There, once again, Heck's sexual demons (one notes both Freudian and religious—as in Judas's suicide—connotations in the name "Long-tree") seize him and he attempts to force Elsa down to the ground. Thus it is little wonder why the crudest member of the odious Hammond brothers, Henry (Warren Oates), whose character failings—as well as first name—parallel Heck's, refuses to bathe before his brother Billy's wedding to Elsa.

Baptism in the Christian church symbolizes a spiritual cleansing, the remission of sins and the promise of eternal life through Christ. Its meaning centers on death and death overcome. In that sense it parallels the sacrament of Holy Communion. Kathleen Murphy suggests the connection between these two most important Christian rituals in her comparison of baptismal water to the sacrificial blood of Peckinpah's heroes. It is not by chance that Steve Judd dries his feet with a blood/wine-red, though slightly faded, indigenously western bandanna, thus linking baptism and Holy Communion.[8] As the Johannine exegete in the *Harper's Bible Commentary* writes, "many interpreters believe that John deliberately replaced the Lord's [Last] Supper with his distinctive portrayal of Jesus's washing the disciples' feet," since "the words of the [eucharistic] institution interpret Jesus's death, just as the foot washing does" (Mays 1988, 1066). Heck Longtree, a Judas figure and devil's disciple, affirms only the value of money and the sensual pleasures of the body. His is a material soul, given over to his appetites and wholly resistant to the spiritual blandishments of Stephen Judd. Baptism and Holy Communion thus act as two related sacraments promising redemption and new life. Heck cannot understand this, and instead prefers to litter the venerable high-country mountains with unclean "trash," a word that once again links him to the "white-trash" Hammond brothers.

Heck's crude act of mastication, a clutter of crumbs strewing his shirt front, parallels, as I have argued, the Johannine text. In John 13, after he has bathed the disciples' feet, Christ figuratively conflates the foot-washing with the eating of bread, saying, "He that eateth bread with me hath lifted up his heel against me." Not knowing of whom Jesus speaks, the disciples ask him to name his betrayer and Jesus replies, "He it is to whom I shall give a sop [morsel] when I have dipped it." John continues: "And when he had dipped the sop, he gave it to Judas Iscariot, the son of Simon." Then after Judas eats the morsel, Satan enters into him, "so that the eucharistic bread appears in a demonic inversion [paralleling the same sacred/profane inversion in the Knudsen-praying/Judd-washing scenes], and Satan, the Opponent/Helper, is incorporated into the human agent" (Kermode 1979, 92). Life becomes death, salvation damnation, through Judas/Heck's violation of the sacraments.

The sandwich (bread) Heck eats vulgarly parodies and crudely blasphemes the Eucharist, itself a complex symbolic mimesis of Christ's death on the cross and resurrection from the grave. Indeed, Steve Judd, aware of Gil's and Heck's imminent betrayal, will soon die to save them both. There in a lush grove of willows, beside a flowing stream, betrayal and death loom. But a counter-action unfolds as well: the Christian ritual of acceptance of sacrificial death, and the promise, through baptism, of new life, enacted by Stephen Judd before two resistant, unwitting disciples.

At this point in the film Sam Peckinpah, as he has done throughout *Ride the High Country*, most recently with Heck and his discarded wrapper, joins the theme of the tragic betrayal of the human spirit to the tragic abuse of the land, and particularly the self-betrayal of America as a nation. Gil Westrum, returning to the streamside, pauses to lift one of Steve's boots, within the sole of which he finds a gaping hole. Unaware that he too, like Heck, is enacting a greater biblical drama, Gil ironically mimics John the Baptist. Responding to the Pharisees when they question his authority to baptize, John, who has not yet encountered Christ, responds, "He it is who coming after me is preferred before me, *whose shoe's latchet* [sandal] *I am not worthy to unloose*" (John 1:27, italics mine).

Gil Westrum, of course, sees only the literal boot (confusing sole with soul), which enables him to comment sardonically on the historical theme of contemporary society's ingratitude toward those who have suffered and sacrificed to settle the West. Thinking of footwear, Gil invokes the memory of a mutual acquaintance of theirs, "old Doc Franklin," who wore fancy-toed boots he ordered from Boston. Now dead and forgotten, Doc, who "gave thirty years of his life to make the West safe for decent people," could attract only three people to his funeral, says Gil: "The mortician, the grave digger, and me." Historically self-conscious, *Ride the High Country* is filled with references to a forgotten or fallen America. The film begins with the travesty of a (John) Fordian patriotic celebration that culminates in a rigged horse and camel race that mocks an authentic national hero, Stephen Judd.[9] In a film so concerned with true and false fathers, it is possible to infer that "old Doc Franklin," like most names in the Peckinpah canon, has not been chosen randomly. Rather it is onomastically intended to evoke one of our nation's genuinely iconic figures and founding fathers, an inventor who also helped to "invent" America, Benjamin Franklin. Though not literally a medical man, Franklin was in his later years known by the honorific "Doctor." Born, as we know, in Boston, where Doc Franklin purchased his boots, Ben Franklin helped write the U.S. Constitution, was an ambassador to France, and at his death was the most famous and revered American in the world. Gil Westrum's Doc Franklin, on the other hand, has died in obscurity, having given, like Steve Judd, "thirty years of his life" to an ungrateful West. As with Doc Franklin, Steve too will be buried by only three people, Gil, Elsa, and Heck.

In a film so richly suffused with biblical references it is difficult to ignore the multiple uses of the number three in the text. Earlier Steve tells Heck that in "about thirty years" the boy will appreciate the soothing comforts of water on his aching feet. Then, more relevantly, we learn that Doc Franklin, like Steve Judd, labored "thirty years" to make the West a better place to live. Finally, Gil, who has been teaching young Heck his duplicitous trade for "better than three years," tells Steve that only "three people" were there to attend Doc's funeral. Even those who are relatively unfamiliar with the Bible know enough to associate the number thirty with the "thirty pieces of silver" Judas was given to betray Christ, or that Christ was age thirty when he began his mission. Peckinpah prepares the viewer to make this connection earlier when, in a brilliantly ironic stroke, he has the covetous and essentially materialist Joshua Knudsen, twisting and perverting the Bible, instruct his daughter, whom he has just struck, to "Receive my instruction and *not silver,* knowledge rather than choice gold" (emphases mine). And at the dinner table that night, Steve Judd, responding to Joshua's accusation that he is "trafficking" in gold, replies that he is "transporting," not "trafficking," and that, quoting the Bible himself, "A good name is rather to be chosen than great riches, a loving favor rather than *silver* or gold" (emphasis mine). Finally, of course, the number "three" is even more loaded in its biblical range of reference: to the triune nature of the Godhead, to Christ's crucifixion on Golgotha between two thieves,[10] and to Christ's resurrection on the third day after his death. Such biblical parallels can hardly be accidental coming from a director-writer as steeped in Old and New Testament texts as Sam Peckinpah, who makes a film the text and subtexts of which are rife with biblical quotation and allusions.

In that same exchange about Doc Franklin, Peckinpah's irony reaches its climax as Gil, the most Cain-like of friends, employs a pastoral metaphor to entice Steve into casting off his deepest principles. Of the public's repudiation of Doc Franklin, Gil comments on their lack of "gratitude, the *fairest flower* that grows within the human heart" (emphases mine). Throughout *Ride the High Country*, Peckinpah demonstrates that the betrayal of the human world and the violation of the natural world (Coarsegold is the crucial example) are the same, that Steve Judd and the film's eponymous "high country" are finally the same redemptive entity, and that each is being desecrated on the altar of greed and corruption, all in the contradictory name of "progress."

While Steve Judd's own life bears striking parallels with Doc Franklin's, Gil's story of Franklin's sad fate fits also into the secondary pattern of historical tragedy that parallels its Christian counterpart. That a country so dedicated to the ideals propounded by its Founding Fathers should at the same time betray those very ideals helps make *Ride the High Country* a genuinely indigenous tragedy.

The Judd group depart this Edenic oasis and resume their allegorical journey up the mountainside to the physically brutalized—and spiritually brutalizing—mining camp of Coarsegold. Steve leads the way with Gil and Heck following. Peckinpah chooses to film their departure from behind and above in an overhead shot, employing a Chapman crane to create an arresting effect. About this important moment in the film Garner Simmons writes:

> Of the many memorable shots involving the Chapman there is one that begins at a river bank by a stand of aspen [*sic*] trees as Steve Judd mounts his horse and

rides on ahead, leaving Heck and Gil to exchange comments on the likelihood of Steve joining them to steal the gold. As Heck and Gil mount up, the camera begins to crane some thirty feet into the air allowing us to look beyond the aspens [sic] golden in the autumn sunlight, to where Steve is joined by his companions. Uniquely coupled with the beauty of this shot is its impact from the way it visually parallels the relationship between these three men: Steve rides ahead, alone and pointing the way, while Gil and Heck must pass the same ground to reach him. (Simmons 1982, 45)

Simmons's language seems strikingly Bunyanesque, especially in its reference to Judd's "pointing the way," as in Christ's charge to his disciples to "Follow me." Gil and Heck, two lost pilgrims, climb a Calvary of conscience, and ultimately consciousness. With Judd, they number, once again, a biblical trio, two thieves and a guiltless man. Add to this the spectator's visual sensation, through the use of the ascending crane, of rising above the spatio-temporal continuum into a God's-eye view of the events below, thus imparting a kind of omniscient perspective to the shot. Some higher force stands outside and above the immediate action and guides the film's subsequent events.

In a like manner George Bassman's musical score reflects the contest between earthly—or material—wills and a divine—or numinal—perspective. Initially, as the crane begins its ascent, the music becomes brooding and sinister; Gil and Heck ride behind Steve, and we already know they intend to do him harm if he refuses to help them steal the gold. But as the camera boom concludes its movement above the stream, the willow trees, and the three riders, its lens comes to rest upon the resplendent high mountains off in the distance. At this point the film's dominant "high country" nature theme, its only memorable musical motif, and one we also associate with Stephen Judd, reasserts itself, overlapping and then engulfing the previous musical motif. Here too we find a biblical parallel. On the day Christ comes to John to be baptized, the heavens open and a spirit like a dove descends upon Christ (Mark 1:10; John 1:27).

Ride the High Country's most celebrated moment, which represents a completion and culmination of the scene beside the mountain stream, centers on the emotionally charged and cathartic death of the old marshal, Stephen Judd, at film's end. There, having been reconciled to his friend, Gil Westrum, and assured of the safety of Heck and Elsa, Steve Judd at last, to use his own chosen biblical phrase, one often used by Sam Peckinpah's father, David, enters his human and heavenly house "justified." Judd dies to rise, falling down below the film frame to enter the seasons of the earth, yet leaving a towering mountain, traditional symbol of spiritual transcendence, in his place. So entwined with the Christian themes of death and resurrection, but also of a more temporal and elegiac "sense of loss, [the] feeling that an era has ended" (Skerry 1990, 14), this moment climaxes the double vision of tragedy in *Ride the High Country*. It is possible, therefore, to experience *both* a permanent sense of loss *and* the spiritual ascendance of Stephen Judd, enduring beyond the grave. Thus, depending on one's own mytho-religious predilections, *Ride the High Country* ends with either the paradoxical, and overtly Christian (though certainly with a pagan element added), triumph of life emerging out of death, or the tragic finality of death alone, and with it the imminent vanishing of the Old West. I would suggest that Sam Peckinpah, inveterately ambivalent, wants us to experience *both* emotions. We remember once again that Peckinpah described his film as about "salvation and loneliness," terms that equate perfectly with the Christian and historical views of tragedy presented in the film.

Finally, I would argue that although no single interpretation is adequate to explain the ending of the film, Stephen Judd's death does clarify and expand upon certain symbolic meanings implicit in the events that occur earlier at the Knudsen farm as well as the encounter beside the mountain stream. Regardless of how we feel about Judd's death, that death changes the three (that sacred number) lives of Gil Westrum, Heck Longtree, and Elsa Knudsen, and those changes are achieved through the spiritualization of natural images.

Gil Westrum has already begun his regenerative process when, after deserting the Judd party the night before, he comes charging into the Knudsen farm in order to save Steve and the two young people from the horrible Hammonds. In the printed script we learn that Judd, in attempting to rescue gunshot Heck, is wounded, "much more seriously, in his side" (script note, 104), having been "*nailed* . . . good" (script note, 190) by Elder Hammond (John Anderson). Both of these details seem crucial to me, because they bear close relationships to the story of Christ's crucifixion. The crucifixional reference to "nailing" Steve Judd is obvious. Less apparent in the idea that Steve is shot in the side, and that in the ensuing shoot-out the Hammonds manage to put all their bullets "in the same spot" (or "in one place," as the earlier draft indicates). The script describes Steve as holding on to his "midsection," but clearly in the film Peckinpah changes it to his left side where Steve is mortally wounded.[11] One is impelled, especially within the context of significant symbolic wounds in such important future films as *The Wild Bunch* and *Pat Garrett and Billy the Kid*, to read the placing of Steve's wound as an oblique reference to St. John's description of the expired Christ on the cross. In John 19:34 a Roman centurion, attempting to determine whether Jesus has died, "pierced his side, and immediately there came out blood and water." In the First Epistle of John, 5:6, the writer describes Christ as "the son of God, who came through water and blood." Allegorically, John conflates Christ's death and the centurion's action with the promise of new life as envisioned in the ceremony of baptism as well as in the ritual of Holy Communion. I have earlier argued how these two rites are intertwined in the mountain-stream scene. Here in the last moments of *Ride the High Country* Sam Peckinpah reprises one of the film's crucial moments. Again, in the First Letter of John, verses 5–8, we are told that Christ is "he who came by water and blood . . . not with the water only but with the water and blood. And the Spirit is the witness because the Spirit is the Truth. These are three witnesses, the Spirit, and the water, and the blood; and these three agree." Reading for "Spirit" the distant mountain toward which Steve, his body transfigured by light, gazes just before he turns to the earth to die; and for "water" the barnyard windmill and watering trough that appear in the immediate distance in Judd's place as he sinks to the bottom of the frame; and for "blood" that which pours forth into the ground from that one central wound of humanity, it is not difficult to understand why this is a memorable death, why Seth Cagin and Philip Dray point out that the violence in *Ride the High Country* is so "pointedly cathartic and even sacred" (Cagin and Dray 1974, 17).

To Cagin and Dray's tragic and religious terms, "cathartic" and "sacred," I would also add "sacrificial." For Steve Judd dies not just for an idea of himself, but also for his friend, Gil Westrum, and for the future of the West as embodied in Elsa and Heck. As Gil bends over his fallen comrade, he tells him not to "worry about anything," that he will get the gold to the bank in Hornitos. Steve replies in language the newly repentant Gil will surely understand, "Hell, I know that. I always did. You just forgot about it for awhile, that's all."

Steve "always" knew who the real Gil Westrum was, which is why he was so hard on him when Gil forgot. Their last words to each other, Steve's "So long, partner," Gil's "I'll see ya later," are among the most emotionally rending in this or any other film. And doubly so because when Gil says "I'll see ya later," at some deeper transcendental level he means it. For as he rises from the dying Steve, who would prefer to "go it alone," behind Gil, and absorbing his body at the center of the screen, stands a soaring cottonwood tree, the midafternoon sun dappling through its leaves and branches and illuminating the outline of Gil's body almost as if it were a medieval painting. The

Tree of Death becomes the Tree of Life through the redemptive power of Steve's sacrificial surrender. While Gil glows in the late-afternoon autumn sun, Steve lies prone, as Jim Kitses writes, "an old man in the shadow of [that] great tree in the yard" (Kitses 1970, 158).

Steve Judd dies so that his friend might achieve new life. The same result is achieved for Heck and Elsa. Since sight is such a crucial metaphor in *Ride the High Country*, as well as the New Testament, the mortally wounded Steve's comment to Gil, "I don't want them to see this. I'll go it alone," hardly seems unusual. But it is sight or, more specifically, vision, vital to all cinematic experience, and especially so here, that is so metaphorically important (Bliss 1993, 35). Earlier, in the graveyard scene, we watched Elsa disappear, in that disturbing dissolve, into her mother's grave. Now we witness Steve Judd's disappearance from the film frame, with only the rumpled ridge of his buckskin jacket—analogous perhaps to the high-country mountains with which we identify his spirit—barely rising above the bottom of the frame. Is it not possible that cinematically we are witnessing a sacrificial death, i.e., that in this humble barnyard epiphany Steve Judd substitutes his body for Elsa's in the earlier graveyard montage, and dies so that Elsa and the genuine West that she stands for might live? But that is only one part of the final equation in this highly charged, remarkably complex scene. As Steve speaks his last words to Gil, between them, in mid-to-deep space, stands that same romantic hay wagon where Elsa and Heck, though Heck barely knew it, began their courtship in earnest. In the earlier tableau Peckinpah photographs the two potential lovers in close-up, haloed by the surrounding hay from the wagon. It is a scene out of rural, pastoral romance, or a painting by Constable, which reaches its culmination through the rustic hay wagon, recast as symbol of their unity and imminent marriage, heralding once again new and fertile life emerging from the tragic but redemptive death of Stephen Judd.

At the end of *Ride the High Country* Sam Peckinpah chooses to frame Steve Judd's last solitary moment within a superimposed golden border, a frame within the film frame, which to some viewers may look almost tacky and phony, while to others it may indicate just how desperate Sam Peckinpah is to *contain* Steve Judd's death within some mode of overtly deliberate artistic control. For whatever reasons he has chosen to end his film in this manner, it nevertheless enables him to establish a symbolic link to the illuminated body of Gil Westrum, the festive aureole of hay that, crown-like, surrounds Elsa and Heck, and the overall "mythos of autumn" which for Northrop Frye describes tragic actions. Now Stephen Judd, a martyr to the virtues and meanings of the Old West, as land, as idea, dies his hero's death, and as his body touches the ground, the words THE END, in gold, flash suddenly, abruptly, upon the screen. As Frank Kermode has written in *The Sense of an Ending*, "THE END" is a figure for death (Kermode 1968, 7). Here that figure seems doubled, for both the hero and the film die before us. Does this apparent finality indicate that Sam Peckinpah intends for us to experience the complete disappearance of the true Western hero at film's end? This hardly seems the case. Steve Judd's legacy to both the characters in the film and to the audience of the film is too lasting, too *enduring*, for that to be the case.

Lastly, it seems that for Sam Peckinpah Steve Judd's death places the burden of the future, and maybe *that* is why the doubled, or tripled, sense of an ending in *Ride the High Country* seems so emphatic, if ambiguously so, upon those who would profit from an act of tragic sacrifice and those who would not, upon those who would care about what was for Sam Peckinpah, ever paradoxical, the *real*, as in *mythic*, West, and those who would not. We know, from our perspective in the latter part of the twentieth century, that the world Steve Judd stands for no longer exists, that it will never return. *Ride the High Country* ends as it began, unwilling, unable to resolve the double vision of tragedy that the personally triumphant—and historically traumatic—disappearance of Stephen Judd so brilliantly limns.

Notes

1. It is beyond the scope and purpose of this essay to engage the many reasons why the notion of "Christian tragedy" represents for many critics and theologians a contradiction in terms. Frye's useful definition enables me to situate *Ride the High Country* within the somewhat hybrid ranks of works of literature and film that are both Christian and tragic. For a well-reasoned refutation of the subgenre "Christian tragedy," see D. D. Raphael, *The Paradox of Tragedy*, 37–67. For a spirited defense of the same idea, see Nathan Scott, ed., *The Tragic Vision and Christian Faith*.

2. In 1962 also John Ford directed his last great Western, *The Man Who Shot Liberty Valance*, a film that in many ways resembles *Ride the High Country*. Ford's central symbol, the cactus rose, holds a similar significance when compared with Peckinpah's trees, streams, and mountains. Each film stars an aging hero (John Wayne/Joel McCrea) who dies in order to preserve a certain idea about the meaning of the West, but who simultaneously makes possible the very change that leads to his destruction. As Tom Doniphon, John Wayne first "appears" in *Liberty Valance* as a dead man lying in a pauper's pine box, a Western film moment no less surprising than Steve Judd's disappearing, like an extinct species, from the film frame at the end of *High Country*. For more on the connection between these two films see Skerry, "The Western Film: A Sense of an Ending."

3. In *West of Everything*, Jane Tompkins's controversial reading of the masculinist tradition of Western novel writing in America at the turn of the twentieth century, Tompkins contends that the male-centered Westerns of writers like Owen Wister and Zane Grey arose out of a defensive reaction against the popular tradition of the highly Christianized feminine romance of the latter half of the nineteenth century. *West of Everything* is full of contradictions, not the least of which concern the notion of Christian sacrifice. In spite of her argument for the anti-religious masculine "materialism" of Westerns, Tompkins writes near the end of her book that at the repressed core of the Western stands "the hero, who offers himself as a savior of his people, sacrificing his heart so that they can live, [which] replicates the Christian ideal of behavior, giving the self for others, but in a manner that is distorted and disguised so that we do not recognize it" (1992, 220). Tompkins even concludes that the Western hero hides but cannot completely conceal that "feminine part of himself" that enables him to die for others: "[I]nwardly the hero has performed a sacrifice—an ironic and tragic sacrifice—for the very thing he offers up, his heart, his love, his feelings, are what Christ in the trinitarian division of labor has come to represent" (220). By describing someone who could easily be Steve Judd as well as numerous other Western heroes, Tompkins seems to be refuting her own central thesis. In addition, she overstates the case through her contention that Christian sacrifice is presented in such a "distorted and disguised" manner that it is unrecognizable to most viewers and critics. The spontaneity and freshness Tompkins achieves in *West of Everything* are gained at the price of her almost total exclusion of the considerable body of scholarship devoted to the Western, including its relationship to the Bible. Tompkins fails, for instance, even to mention Michael Marsden's important essay, "Savior in the Saddle: The Sagebrush Testament." Marsden and the critics he discusses in his essay have aided my own understanding of the biblical element, especially the relationship between the Old and New Testaments, in Peckinpah's film.

4. It is clear that Sam Peckinpah depicts the monstrously pocked and hideously denatured lunar orefields of Coarsegold as a modern Eliotic wasteland. It is less apparent that he intends a similar purpose with the more conventional town of Hornitos. But the effect is the same: their relationship, as Paul Seydor points out (1980, 34), is symbiotic. Each serves the other, and both feed the money machine. This is most tellingly represented in Hornitos by the name given to the camel Heck rides against the local horses: "The Phantom of the *Desert*" (my emphasis). What better way to depict the blasted landscape of the heart and of the land through rapacious exploitation than with a Middle Eastern desert animal, the camel, especially when we consider Peckinpah's attention to biblical references throughout *High Country*? Here I refer to the Book of Matthew, chapter 19, verse 24: "It is easier for a camel to go through the eye of a needle, than for a rich man to enter the kingdom of God."

5. Like Annette Kolodny in her important study *The Lay of the Land*, Peckinpah connects the rape of the land with the rape of the female. For Kolodny, as for Peckinpah, at the center of the "uniquely American 'pastoral impulse'" lies the "desire to respond to the landscape as feminine" (Kolodny 1975, 8). Therefore Peckinpah associates the rescue of Elsa from the dreadful Hammond brothers with the regeneration of the

Knudsen ranch. Their de facto incestuous desire for Elsa duplicates her father's own barely concealed lust for her. For a more critical and suspicious reading of the way in which the "feminization" of the land can work against women's interests and their actual historical lives, inasmuch as they are excluded from cultural, masculine, and political power, see, for example, Lawrence Buell's *The Environmental Imagination*, especially his chapter 1, "Pastoral Ideology." Buell's comments on Leo Marx's refusal to view nature as nature and not some "anti-urban" antidote, though highly qualified, to industrial expansionism, are important correctives to Marx's seeming disinterest in nature as representing a system of values within itself (Buell 1995, 13–14).

6. In his 1955 essay "The Garden of Eden and the Deacon's Meadow" (reprinted in *A Sense of History: The Best Writing from the Pages of "American History"*), Perry Miller argues that of American artists and writers of the early nineteenth century "the biblical vision out of which these particular examples come was so predominantly, almost exclusively confined to the Old Testament," that "there were hundreds of Edens, Josephs, Elijahs for every rare Cruficixion or still more rare re-creation of the Manger, while Madonnas are, of course, nonexistent" (Miller 1985, 113–14). Joshua Knudsen, named after one of the great warrior generals of the Old Testament, fits Miller's description perfectly. His wilderness pioneer's sense of the world and of the western frontier derives almost exclusively from his often mistaken and perversely narrow readings of the Old Testament, which he quotes liberally while virtually ignoring the New Testament. Steve Judd, on the other hand, draws generously from both books of the Bible. But his spiritual credo derives from the New Testament, specifically Christ's parable of the Pharisee and the tax collector. Steve, paraphrasing the passage from Luke 18, and reflecting this favorite quotation of Sam Peckinpah's father, says, in opposition to Gil Westrum's materialism, "All I want is to enter my house justified." The name "Judd" and the word "justified" both share similar Latin roots (jus/justice; judex/judge). Scripturally "justified" means "accepted by God," or "right with God" (May and Metzger 1973, 1272). The heavenly "house" Judd enters when he dies at the end of the film is presided over by a high mountain, traditionally associated with the spiritual world. Earlier, when the Judd party arrive at the Knudsen ranch and request a night's lodging, Joshua's response, "There's *room in the house* [inn]. I have no objections if you want to spend the night in the barn [manger]" (my emphasis), implies, though unknown to Joshua, some form of rebirth for the Knudsen ranch. Steve Judd becomes the source of new life. Stephen, Judd's "Christian" name, also indicates a New Testament connection. St. Stephen, who spoke against the law of the Sanhedrin, was stoned to death for his adherence to his faith and was subsequently known as the "First Christian martyr." One might argue that Stephen Judd dies a martyr to his faith in an old and vanishing West.

7. The stream in which Steve bathes his feet is also an ambivalent symbol, exemplifying both the Christian and historical versions of tragedy employed by Sam Peckinpah in *Ride the High Country*. On the one hand the flowing water "signifies fertility and the progressive irrigation of the soil; and on the other hand it stands for the irreversible passage of time and, in consequence, for a sense of loss and oblivion" (Cirlot 1971, 274). Thus in addition to its baptismal implications, the stream also indicates the tragic movement of time, the Heraclitean flux that leads ultimately to death. Both Steve Judd

and the West he venerates are doomed unless some miraculous transformation takes place, a transformation for which Sam Peckinpah holds only tentative hope.

8. That Peckinpah, and not a costumer, deliberately chose the common *red* bandanna may seem far-fetched to some readers, but he was a director obsessed with loading complex meanings into the smallest details: "[Lucien] Ballard reflects that Peckinpah's attention to the ambience of his films is an integral part of his technique. He remarked that, for example, while making *Ride the High Country* Peckinpah selected virtually *every piece of clothing the actors were to wear*, a practice he carried over through each of his projects" (Reisner and Kane 1970, 25, emphases mine). Thus it hardly seems hyperbolic to suggest that Elsa Knudsen's auburn hair color almost perfectly matches the color of Steve Judd's horse, building an analogy between Elsa and nature and Steve Judd that is underscored, ironically, at her ill-fated wedding ceremony with Billy Hammond, when old Judge Tolliver refers to a "good marriage" as being like "*a rare animal*, hard to find, almost impossible to keep" (italics mine). On another occasion Peckinpah insisted that an actor playing a villain change the color (brown) of his shoe laces to a darker shade during the filming of *The Getaway*. Stories like this abound. In *High Country* the color red has already taken on religious significance in the context of Gil Westrum's long-johns and also a red shirt Heck Longtree wears at the beginning of the film. Red may have many different symbolic meanings, depending upon the specific cinematic and/or historical context in which it is used. At any rate, in this film it produces a complex catachresis of interpretive possibilities.

9. An important shot centers on Steve Judd, atop his horse, pausing for a moment when he first rides into Hornitos. Over his head the word "America" is inscribed on a city sign, while flanking his figure, with Judd placed exactly at the center of the film frame, are two rows of red, white, and blue American-flag bunting. But the effect created by the bunting is ironic, for Hornitos ignores Judd as a national hero, and treats him as a forgotten figure from an abandoned past. The real source of power here rests with a strapping young policeman who, when he orders Judd off the street, does so in a low angle shot, a large looming phallic flagpole, the American flag flowing beneath it, jutting above his imposing form. The old order has passed, and this "patriotic" celebration does not exist to honor history's giants, men like Steve Judd. His arrival in Hornitos more closely parallels the mocked and derided Christ's entrance into Jerusalem on Palm Sunday than it does some hero's welcome.

Viewers familiar, as doubtless Sam Peckinpah was, with John Ford's classic film, *Young Mr. Lincoln* (1939), may be reminded of fledgling lawyer Abe Lincoln's allegorical arrival in Springfield, Illinois, where he begins his fabled law practice. Although no celebration is in progress, it is clear that Lincoln, riding a mule (in imitation of Christ's sacrificial ride into Jerusalem, on the back of an ass/donkey), makes a comically understated but no less iconic entrance into the town he is so richly associated with in American history, bringing with him, as it were, the law for which he is so justly famous. The theme of "the Law" also seals Lincoln's relationship with man of law, Stephen Judd.

10. In one of the film's most explicitly Christian-allegorical moments the camera focuses on Steve Judd the morning after he has taken Gil prisoner for attempting to steal

the Hornitos bank's money. He stands shaving, his face lathered with soap, a straight-edged razor in his hand. Behind him lies a dull, sluggish-looking mountain lake, with patches of green algae adorning the shore and numerous fallen or stripped trees rising or collapsing languidly from its shallow depths. Most important, Judd is filmed within this Cinemascope shot so that he stands directly in the middle of the frame between two tall dead trees, creating a Golgotha-like effect, just as he learns from Heck that Gil, his prisoner, has betrayed him again and escaped. The crucifixional implications of Gil's treachery, coupled with the sacrificial aspect of that straight-edged razor, serve to deepen the Christ-like nature of Steve Judd in this scene.

11. Within the traditions of medieval and Renaissance western art, Christ's redemptive wound is always depicted as being on his right side. The Book of John does not indicate upon which side the centurion's wound is inflicted. But since the right side is associated with "righteousness," the left with duplicity, or something "sinister," it is interesting to speculate why Sam Peckinpah, no doubt aware of these associations and of the traditions of western painting, locates Steve's wound on his left side. I would suggest that it resides in Peckinpah's own ambivalence about Judd's *human* capacity to redeem a doomed American West, that finally nothing and no one is strong enough, virtuous enough to make that possible. The wound's location may then be another indication of Peckinpah's pessimism about the West as dream or ideal, a pessimism that plunges toward much darker depths in such films as *Major Dundee*, *The Wild Bunch*, and his most despairing Western, *Pat Garrett and Billy the Kid*. The fault lies not with Stephen Judd, but with the historically represented America that Peckinpah depicts in all of his Western films.

References

Bachelard, Gaston. 1983. *Water and Dreams*. Translated by Edith R. Farrell. Dallas: Pegasus Foundation.

Bliss, Michael. 1993. *Justified Lives: Morality and Narrative in the Films of Sam Peckinpah*. Carbondale: Southern Illinois University Press.

Braudy, Leo. 1986. "The Sacraments of Genre: Coppola, DePalma, Scorsese." *Film Quarterly* 39 (Spring): 17–28.

Buell, Lawrence. 1995. *The Environmental Imagination: Thoreau, Nature Writing, and the Formation of American Culture*. Cambridge: The Belknap Press of Harvard University Press.

Cagin, Seth, and Philip Dray. 1974. *Hollywood Films of the Seventies*. New York: Harper & Row.

Cirlot, J. E. 1971. *A Dictionary of Symbols*. 2nd ed. Translated from the Spanish by Jack Sage. New York: Philosophical Library.

Corrigan, Robert W. 1981. *Tragedy: Vision and Form*. 2nd ed. New York: Harper & Row.

Dick, Bernard F. 1990. *Anatomy of Film*. 2nd ed. New York: St. Martin's Press.

Dukore, Bernard F. 1999. *Sam Peckinpah's Feature Films*. Urbana and Chicago: The University of Illinois Press.

Eliade, Mircea. 1978. *A History of Religious Ideas*. Vol. 1. Chicago: University of Chicago Press.

Fine, Marshall. 1991. *Bloody Sam: The Life and Films of Sam Peckinpah*. New York: Donald I. Fine.

Fitzgerald, F. Scott. 1945. *The Crack-up*. Edited by Edmund Wilson. New York: New Directions.

Frye, Northrop. 1957. *Anatomy of Criticism: Four Essays*. New York: Atheneum.

Guerin, Wilfred L., Earl G. Labor, Lee Morgan, and John R. Willingham. 1979. *A Handbook of Critical Approaches to Literature*. 2nd ed. New York: Harper & Row.

Kermode, Frank. 1968. *The Sense of an Ending: Studies in the Theory of Fiction*. New York: Oxford University Press.

———. 1979. *The Genesis of Secrecy: On the Interpretation of Narrative*. Cambridge: Harvard University Press.

Kitses, Jim. 1970. *Horizons West: Anthony Mann, Budd Boetticher, Sam Peckinpah: Studies of Authorship within the Western*. Bloomington: University of Indiana Press.

Kolodny, Annette. 1975. *The Lay of the Land: Metaphor as Experience and History in American Life and Letters*. Chapel Hill: University of North Carolina Press.

Marsden, Michael T. 1974. "Savior in the Saddle: The Sagebrush Testament." In *Focus on the Western*, edited by Jack Nachbar. Englewood Cliffs, N.J.: Prentice-Hall.

Marx, Leo. 1967. *The Machine in the Garden*. New York: Oxford University Press.

May, Herbert G., and Bruce M. Metzger. 1973. *The New Oxford Annotated Bible with the Apocrypha*. New York: Oxford University Press.

Mays, James L., general editor. 1988. *Harper's Bible Commentary*. San Francisco: Harper & Row.

Miller, Perry. 1985. "The Garden of Eden and the Deacon's Meadow." In *A Sense of History: The Best Writing from the Pages of American History*. Boston: Houghton Mifflin.

Murray, William. 1972. "*Playboy* Interview: Sam Peckinpah." *Playboy* 19.8 (August): 65–74, 192.

Murphy, Kathleen. 1985. "Sam Peckinpah: No Bleeding Heart." *Film Comment* 21.2 (March-April): 74–75.

Paglia, Camille. 1991. *Sexual Personae: Art and Decadence from Nefertiti to Emily Dickinson*. New York: Vintage.

Raphael, D. D. 1960. *The Paradox of Tragedy*. Bloomington: Indiana University Press.

Reisner, Joel, and Bruce Kane. 1970. "Sam Peckinpah." *Action: Directors Guild of America* 5.3 (May-June): 24–27.

Scott, Nathan, ed. 1957. *The Tragic Vision and Christian Faith*. New York: Haddam House.

Seydor, Paul. 1980. *Peckinpah: The Western Films*. Urbana: University of Illinois Press.

Simmons, Garner. 1982. *Peckinpah: A Portrait in Montage*. Austin: University of Texas Press.

Skerry, Philip J. 1990. "The Western Film: A Sense of an Ending." *New Orleans Review* 17.3 (Fall): 13–17.

Tompkins, Jane. 1992. *West of Everything: The Inner Life of Westerns*. New York, London: Oxford University Press.

Weddle, David. 1994. *"If They Move . . . Kill 'Em": The Life and Times of Sam Peckinpah*. New York: Grove Press.

Whitehall, Richard. 1969. "Talking with Peckinpah." *Sight and Sound* 38.4 (Autumn): 172–75.

Williams, Raymond. 1966. *Modern Tragedy*. Palo Alto: Stanford University Press.

FOUR

MATT WANAT

"Fall in behind the Major"

CULTURAL BORDER CROSSING AND HERO BUILDING IN *MAJOR DUNDEE*

For all the talk about the radical or revisionist nature of Sam Peckinpah's Westerns, the Peckinpah hero represents white, male interests. The choices faced by Peckinpah's heroes are not primarily between white interests and the interests of people of color. Rather, Peckinpah's heroes must choose between self-interest and sociopolitical commitment to something larger than themselves, and the sociopolitical option in Peckinpah's films usually comes in the form of political underdogs. Peckinpah's heroes are often running away from something, but they end up running into heroic glory, and Peckinpah's films draw attention to their heroes' evasions of responsibility to the degree that these heroes' final heroic acts are often ironic or even superficial. In this essay I concentrate on Peckinpah's *Major Dundee* (1965) as an example of the Peckinpah hero's evasion of responsibility and the Peckinpah film's cynicism about the sociopolitical potential of the hero. *Major Dundee*, with all its flaws, is a perfect place to start a discussion of Peckinpah's western heroes, his self-reflexive strategies for exploring the failures of western heroism, and his 1960s image as an outlaw hero of the cinema. Moreover, because of its interests in cultural border crossings, especially into Mexico, *Major Dundee* lays the groundwork for future Peckinpah excursions into his favorite setting for sociopolitical revolution and heroic retreat.

Major Dundee is among the cinema's most interesting and disturbing examples of cultural border relationships. *Major Dundee* borrows from John Ford's *Rio Grande* (1950) the premise of a river connoting cultural borders beyond geography. The Rio Grande in Ford's film divides the United States and Mexico, of course, but it also symbolizes postbellum divisions between

North and South, divisions that are reconciled in the film when North and South unite against a common Apache enemy. *Major Dundee* borrows this premise but uses it to explore a particularly sinister model of cross-cultural understanding.

The following essay, first and foremost, explores Peckinpah's politics through some of *Major Dundee*'s cultural border crossings, which are symbolized by river crossings in the film. Specifically, I am interested in these border crossings for the twisted version of a multicultural education they afford the hero, Dundee (Charlton Heston). These border crossings are in fact simulations of perceived traits from cultural groups outside Dundee's understanding, and Dundee's simulations help force the assimilation of the groups he simulates while the hero consistently evades sociopolitical responsibility. Secondly, this essay asks questions about the potential and limitations of *Major Dundee*'s self-consciousness regarding border crossing and hero building. But first a few words on the contentious production and convoluted plot of *Major Dundee*.

Sorting through the Mess of *Major Dundee*

"Sam Peckinpah's" *Major Dundee* is a narrative and sociopolitical mess of a movie. I am most concerned with the sociopolitical mess, but the movie is analytically impenetrable without some discussion of the narrative mess as well, which is partly attributable to the film's contentious production. According to Paul Seydor, the shooting length and budget of the film were cut by "fifteen days and about a million dollars," one third of the original budget, just two days before shooting began.[1] These cuts contributed to tensions between Peckinpah and producer Jerry Bresler from which the filmmakers and film never recovered. Additionally, Columbia bypassed advance screenings to avoid honoring Peckinpah's final cut of the film, and in all "fifty-five minutes of material that Peckinpah considered essential" was deleted or not included.[2] The director was promised a three-hour road-show epic by the studio and created an original director's cut that ran two hours and forty-one minutes. But he was forced to settle for an original-release print that, according to Doug McKinney, ran two hours and fourteen minutes, and his vision is now represented by two hours and two minutes on video.[3]

However, *Major Dundee* fails for reasons beyond loggerheaded infighting between Peckinpah and his financiers. The film's concept of a motley band of outsiders chasing redemption, self-definition, and Apaches into Mexico belongs on a short list of the most convoluted plots in film history. As Harry

Julian Fink was attempting to adapt his own story to the screen, his draft of the script "stopped after 163 pages and covered only about a third of the story," prompting angry intervention and rewriting by Peckinpah.[4] Moreover, Charlton Heston, who played Major Amos Dundee, admits that it was never entirely clear what the film was to be about, anyway.[5]

The intentional fallacies awaiting analysis of a project as uncertain as *Major Dundee* should be enough to send critics running faster than producers away from Peckinpah's vision. But the care *Major Dundee* demands of any close reading is worth the effort, since part of the film's failure is born of its ambition. On one hand, the film seeks to reconcile issues of race, region, nation, and, less obviously, gender by using the mid-1860s to dramatize a variety of sociopolitical crises of the mid-1960s. On the other hand, the film reveals the failure of an individual vision when it comes to accommodating myriad sociopolitical interests, and by doing so Peckinpah's film draws attention to the limitations of models of western heroism deeply ingrained in the genre. *Major Dundee*'s fiascoes are not simply problems of narrative structure. Rather, *Major Dundee* fails most interestingly in its cultural border crossings, its attempts to reconcile Amos Dundee's personal obsessions with his heroic potential as unifier of a volatile national microcosm and liberator of oppressed people.

PLOT SUMMARY

Major Dundee begins after the Apache warrior Charriba (Michael Pate) has defeated an entire company of the Fifth Cavalry at the Rostes ranch. Bugler Ryan (Michael Anderson Jr.) has recorded the incident in his 1864–1865 Journal and will serve as the film's narrator. Dundee, a Union officer sent to run a prison as punishment for trying to fight his own war at Gettysburg, seizes the opportunity to redeem himself. Without any orders to do so, the major sets out to capture or kill Charriba and return the abducted Rostes children. To this end he enlists the help of African American guards, Southern prisoners, and an assorted band of outsiders and misfits. Most important to Dundee's mission is a former friend, Benjamin Tyreen (Richard Harris). Tyreen is an Irish immigrant and Southern gentleman, while Dundee is a Virginian devoted to the North.

Dundee orders Lieutenant Graham (Jim Hutton) to steal supplies from a Union train, and the cavalry sets out for Mexico, where Charriba has fled. On the trail, Ryan bugles a tune, the Confederates sing "Dixie," the Union soldiers sing "The Battle Hymn of the Republic," and the civilians sing "My

Darling Clementine" in a cacophony of chauvinism recalling a famous scene in *Casablanca* (1942) and intimating internal conflicts to come over racial tensions, regional tensions, and Dundee's egomaniacal quest.

The Rostes children are soon returned. Nonetheless, Dundee plans a sneak attack, but he is drawn into a trap set by Charriba, who counterattacks and defeats the major. In dire need of food after losing 70 percent of the group's stores at the bottom of the river, Dundee orders the attack of a French garrison. The French lancers, under Maximilian I, have seized a town sympathetic with the Juaristas, and Dundee's raid inadvertently renders him a revolutionary hero to the Mexican villagers, though he has violated international treaties in the process and has found a new enemy in the French. In the village, Dundee and Tyreen fight over Teresa Santiago (Senta Berger), a German woman whose husband was killed for supporting Juarez. Dundee allows the lancers to escape the village in order to draw in more French supplies, eventually ambushing and again defeating the French, who exact revenge by brutally killing all of the village except Teresa and some children.

Meanwhile, the Rebel O. W. Hadley (Warren Oates) is caught deserting, and, after Dundee orders a firing squad, Tyreen shoots O. W. himself. Following this incident, Tyreen threatens to kill Dundee once the "Apache are taken or destroyed." Dundee seeks solace beside a river in the arms of Teresa, is wounded in the leg by an Apache arrow, and is saved by the Southerners. Forced to recover in Durango, Dundee betrays Teresa with a prostitute and goes on a drunk, wallowing in self-pity until Tyreen and the others rescue him from French spies. He regains his command and tricks Charriba into entering his picket lines for a night raid. Dundee's men ambush the Apache, and Bugler Ryan kills Charriba. The Apache beaten, Tyreen and Dundee prepare for a fatal contest but are interrupted by attacking French lancers who run them to the Rio Grande, where the African American Aesop (Brock Peters), the Southern Irishman Tyreen, and many others die protecting "the colors" of the American flag and Dundee's mission. Suffering heavy casualties, Dundee's remaining men enter Texas and Ryan strikes up a tune.

The Southern Hero: Heroic Modeling and Assimilation

The conflict between Dundee and Tyreen mirrors the larger conflicts within Dundee's makeshift cavalry, conflicts Dundee needs Tyreen to help him resolve. From the very beginning, Dundee's potential for uniting his divided command is dubious. For example, at one point in the prison Dundee establishes his authority by walking directly through an angry Southern mob, but this assertion of power is a self-conscious joke on the part of the filmmakers. Heston, the actor who once parted the Red Sea and united masses as Moses in *The Ten Commandments* (1956), is reduced to parting a sea of Southerners and further dividing his command in *Major Dundee*. This moment of division comes after Dundee has called for volunteers from "you thieves, renegades, deserters, you gentlemen of the South," and Tyreen has drawn applause from the Southerners with his response, "It is not my country, Major Dundee. I damn its flag and I damn you and I would rather hang than serve."

Tyreen and his Southern men are eventually coerced into Dundee's ranks by threats of execution, but Tyreen is still presented as the leader that Dundee is not, primarily because Tyreen possesses a cross-cultural understanding that escapes the major. This cross-cultural understanding is perhaps best expressed in Tyreen's growing association with the African American troops, an association that begins early in the film when Tyreen calls the particularly racist Southerner Benteen (John Davis Chandler) a "redneck peckerwood." Tyreen's appropriation of the epithet "peckerwood," a term for white people typically used by African Americans, foreshadows his later attempt to break up a fight between Benteen and the African American Sergeant Aesop. Tyreen intervenes in this fight by complimenting the black troops on their "river crossing" at the Rio Grande, "river crossing" symbolizing the border crossing of Aesop's men from jail workers to respected soldiers. Like Aesop, Tyreen also has crossed a border, dissociating himself from Southern racism as his Southern honor brings unity to Dundee's command that Dundee cannot.

Tyreen's border crossing is a personal victory for the character, and the association of the Southerner with racism reflects tensions of the 1950s and 1960s, when Northerners routinely intervened with Southern black leaders in the segregationist South. However, within the thematic context of *Major Dundee*, the tension between Tyreen and Dundee is not simply a tension between Southern honor and Northern law, or between Southern racism and Northern enlightenment. Rather, Tyreen's model of honorable tolerance claims Southern autonomy but also exemplifies Tyreen's dissociation from the Southerner Benteen's bigotry, and this dissociation partly represents the film's watering-down of the racism underlying the Southern gentleman for an era of civil rights. This watering-down of the Southerner is ideologically necessary for Tyreen to remain a noble Southern hero in the eyes of a 1960s audience, and it also seems necessary in order for Tyreen to model leadership to Dundee, who fails to intervene in the racial turmoil of his own unit.

At the Rio Grande, Tyreen is presented with the opportunity to summon a nearby group of Confederate soldiers, but he keeps his word to Dundee, crossing the river and literally leaving behind the American South. Tyreen's assimilation back into the Union is necessitated not only by his word but also by the cultural border crossing he offers Dundee. Tyreen's ability to make connections across racial borders and his assimilation back into the Union are intertwined. He simultaneously mends divisions in Dundee's command, models heroic border crossing, and abandons a particularly racist definition of the South. However, by mending divisions Tyreen is always in danger of abandoning his men, and by modeling heroic border crossing Tyreen is further dissociated from his men, who become scapegoats for racism. Moreover, while Tyreen models nobility and accountability for Dundee, Dundee never really learns to simulate this behavior so much as he exploits Tyreen to accomplish the mission.

This relationship between Dundee, Tyreen, and the men is particularly clear when O. W. Hadley deserts Dundee's cavalry at the river. Hadley, played brilliantly by Peckinpah regular Warren Oates, seems withdrawn from the other Southerners as they swim in the river. Then, he disappears but is caught and brought back to Dundee.[6] When Dundee calls for a firing squad, Tyreen suddenly shoots Hadley himself. By shooting Hadley, Tyreen reasserts Southern self-control and articulates his own secret leadership of Dundee's cavalry. This is another moment of assimilation by Tyreen, drawing some opposition from the Southern troops, but it is assimilation complicated by the fact that the gesture asserts Tyreen's control over his assimilationist border crossing. Fittingly, this shooting occurs during one of the film's longest river scenes.

Conversely, Hadley's growing friendship with Aesop suggests cross-cultural alternatives to Tyreen's border crossings. Preceding Hadley's desertion and execution, Hadley and Aesop share binoculars and a moment of solidarity when they watch the French from a safe distance. Aesop brags: "My boys can take that outfit with one hand tied behind our backs, the walking ones anyway," laughing with Hadley about how the French are soft because they are not from the South. Aesop is specifically referring to black soldiers in the French army, and, while the scene reconciles Hadley and Aesop by finding their common Southernness, this is another obvious moment of assimilation for Aesop. Aesop dissociates himself from the plight of the black Frenchmen, who, like African Americans, are victims of European imperialism. His segregation of his duties to fighting within his race taints whatever is positive in this scene. Still more, when Aesop uses the phrase "one hand tied behind our backs" he associates his six men with the one-armed, half-

Indian Potts (James Coburn), who earlier wrestles the Indian scout Riago (José Carlos Ruiz) with only one arm and is a model of assimilation in *Major Dundee.*

For all of these reasons, Aesop's growing friendship with Hadley has a specifically assimilationist tenor for the African American. Nonetheless, Hadley's ability to admire Aesop strikes through the classist apology for Southern racism offered by Tyreen earlier in the movie. Hadley dissociates himself from his Southern peers, including his own brother, and his desertion can also be read as a penance for his own racism outside the sociopolitical microcosm of Dundee's cavalry. Hadley is redeemed, then, not by the violence of Dundee's mission but by attempting to understand Aesop. Therefore, Tyreen's shooting Hadley himself, while this action reasserts Southern self-control and simultaneously articulates the importance of Tyreen to Dundee's project, is also a destruction of an alternate model of Southern rebellion, one that finds absolution for the legacy of racism not through classist reliance on European aristocracy or a common imperialistic mission but through human understanding.

Most important to Tyreen's attempt to retain control by shooting Hadley is his promise that follows: to kill Dundee once Charriba has been taken or destroyed. This promise recalls the duel of honor that got Tyreen cashiered out of the Union army, and if Dundee accepts he will be reclaiming his Southernness by respecting the Southern tradition of the honorable duel. Significantly, after Charriba is defeated and killed, Tyreen and Dundee prepare for the duel only to be interrupted by the French lancers who finally attack the cavalry at the Rio Grande. Aesop dies bearing the "colors," and the racial symbolism of this term for the flag should be obvious. When Aesop falls, Tyreen picks up the flag mid-river, screams like some absurd hero dying to prove an existential point, and mounts a suicidal, one-man attack against the French on the Mexican side. Tyreen's men watch his death, proud of their leader, and the emphasis on their point of view rearticulates the notion that the Southerner is at the core, both symbolically and literally, of Dundee's unit. But Tyreen dies saving the Union flag, and this bit of assimilation is accompanied by the fact that the Southern hero dies fleeing Confederate Texas for the Mexican side of the Rio Grande.

The importance of the Southerner is a key to understanding much of the assimilation and heroic modeling at the heart of *Major Dundee.* As civil rights gave way to black power, Peckinpah's Western, like so much Hollywood product, failed to center the African American, opting instead for the Southern white as dominant heroic agent, but *Major Dundee* foregrounds assimilation and the complex relationship between region, race, nation, and class at almost every turn. While Dundee is offered a model to imitate with Tyreen, he spends more time using Tyreen for selfish ends. Nevertheless, the possibility of simulation lurks in the relationship between the two men, requiring other heroic models to articulate the importance of modeling. Perhaps most significant in this network of simulation and assimilation is "playing Indian," a phenomenon I will explore in the next section.

"Playing Indian," Killing Indians: Simulation and Extermination

Philip J. Deloria writes, "Playing Indian, then, reflects one final paradox. The self-defining pairing of American truth with American freedom rests on the ability to wield power against Indians—social, military, economic, and political—while simultaneously drawing power from them. Indianness may have existed primarily as a cultural artifact in American society, but it has helped *create* these other forms of power, which have then been turned back on native people."[7] Deloria explores the notion of playing Indian from before the Boston Tea Party through social movements beginning in the 1960s and 1970s. He focuses on everything from Tea Party "Indians" to Girl Scouts to Deadheads. While Deloria's interests are not primarily in cinema, his notion of the importance of Indianness to white self-definition is useful for reading images of American Indians in film. *Major Dundee* exemplifies the notion of playing Indian, as Amos Dundee struggles to understand and, therefore, defeat Sierra Charriba. The "final paradox" in the film, like that described by Deloria, is that Dundee's appropriation of perceived Indian characteristics enables the defeat of the Indian. This is only an apparent paradox, of course, since the border crossing at the heart of Dundee's cultural project has precious little to do with a Native point of view; rather, Dundee must learn from the enemy in the way military leaders always have, and the goal is still racist extermination.[8]

With regard to its interest in learning from the enemy, *Major Dundee* borrows heavily from John Ford's *Fort Apache* (1948).[9] Phil Hardy calls *Fort Apache* a "remounting of the Custer myth."[10] Hardy no doubt makes such a comparison because the film involves an officer, played by Henry Fonda, who fails to take seriously the military savvy of the Indians he is fighting. Fonda's character is green, obsessed with protocol, and unable to adapt to social change or change in the battlefield. Though warned by his second-in-command (John Wayne), he fails to take seriously the demands or intelligence of the Apaches, and he leads his men straight into an ambush where he dies bravely but stupidly. The optimism of Ford's ending, where Wayne's character honors the bravery of his former commander without mention of his failures, is as ironic as Ford's later film about historical cover-up, *The Man Who Shot Liberty Valance* (1962). Ford's ending in *Fort Apache* is eager to bury its critique of a white soldier's hubris in heavy-handed patriotism, but it must have been laughable, even to a 1948 audience, to watch a cavalry officer disparage Cochise and Geronimo to their faces, as Fonda's character does in one scene. Ford's *Fort Apache* shows the bravery of its tragic hero, but John Wayne's character is finally the heroic center of the film, warning against the dangers of underestimating the enemy but also remaining loyal to the cavalry. Captain Tyreen, *Major Dundee*'s equivalent to Wayne's character, models not so much loyalty to the cavalry but rather the importance of cultural border crossing to heroic leadership.

A running theme in a number of Westerns between *Fort Apache* and *Major Dundee* involves white people's attempts to better understand American Indians. The benevolent versions of this theme, from Delmer Daves's *Broken Arrow* (1950) to John Ford's *Cheyenne Autumn* (1964), are almost always patronizing race-relations movies that, like their postwar equivalents in the genres of war film and melodrama, are finally Eurocentric affairs with frequently flat characters of color. Unscrupulous Indian agents and "renegade" Indians become frequent scapegoats for racial tensions, often implying that U.S. imperialism supported by military force existed only to save ambushed coaches and ranches in skirmishes caused by uncooperative individuals. In other versions of this trend, e.g., Charles Marquis Warren's *Arrowhead* (1953) and Ford's *The Searchers* (1956), racist representatives of white power fuse an anthropological knowledge of Indian customs with an imperialistic and frequently bloodthirsty quest to "subdue" Native Americans. In *The Searchers*, for example, Ethan Edwards (John Wayne) shoots out an Indian's eyes, explaining to the others that he has done so to force the dead man to wander blind in the spirit world.

In *Major Dundee*, understanding the Apaches or, rather, playing Indian becomes a key to defeating the Apaches. The most significant early moment of playing Indian, or Dundee's failure to play Indian, is the major's first defeat by Charriba, during which Tyreen models cross-cultural understanding beyond relations between black and white. Attempting a surprise attack, Dundee is beaten by Charriba. Significantly, the defeat is made less severe by Tyreen's cunning at border crossing. Before the surprise attack, an old Apache (Francisco Reyguaera) delivers the Rostes children, and Dundee's Sergeant Gomez (Mario Adorf) translates that the man is tired of fighting but that he fought because "It's their land, all of it." Gomez pauses mysteriously after he translates, his translation mixing what is supposed to be the old man's words with a third-person reference to the Apache. The sergeant's pause is telling. Gomez is a perfect Union soldier, but he is also a liminal figure since, according to Jim Kitses's research on Peckinpah's original intentions, Gomez "had been stolen by the Apaches and had ridden with them for two years against his fellow Mexicans."[11] Gomez's pause as the old Apache talks reveals mystery in this otherwise loyal character, even to the point of implying his empathy with the Apache enemy.

Dundee is as oblivious to Gomez's potential empathy as he is to almost every racial tension in his unit. He sends the children to safety with Gomez, a strange decision since, if the major questions Gomez's loyalties at all, the Mexican sergeant is the last person he should let out of his sight before a surprise attack. Therefore, Dundee's sending Gomez away with the children is a potential tactical mistake. Since the Rostes children are, significantly, dressed like Indians, Dundee's sending away the cross-cultural sergeant and the children, all of whom have mastered the art of playing Indian, is a symbolic mistake as well. Fittingly, the attack is a total failure. The Apaches wait for the cavalry and ambush.

Tyreen, a better equipped leader for border crossing, leads the first men across the river, and Tyreen is the first to note that it is a trap. When some Apaches approach dressed as Union soldiers, Tyreen whistles "Dixie," and they betray their identity by not responding angrily. Tyreen's acute understanding of the North/South tension of Dundee's cavalry informs his ability to spot the Apaches' disguises. The attack as a whole, however, is a failed border crossing, a flawed attempt to get across the river, Apache lines, and a border of cultural understanding.

Balanced against the fiasco at the river are two later altercations that involve playing Indian: (1) the cavalry's attack on the sleeping French after Hadley and Aesop have watched them enter a canyon; and (2) the cavalry's attack and defeat of Charriba in another canyon. The first of these battles is actually training for the second. After Dundee's men liberate the Mexican village, they deliberately allow the French to escape. Later, the French give chase but are tricked into passing the bulk of Dundee's men as Aesop and Hadley watch and laugh at their frivolous European incompetence. Aesop brags that his men could take the African French troops with one hand behind their backs, a boast I have shown to reveal Aesop's assimilation by segregating his duties along racial lines, symbolically connecting him to the one-armed Potts. Dundee's men attack the sleeping French with the Indians

Potts and Riago leading the raid. Significantly, the attack begins with Potts strangling a black picket, one of the African soldiers in charge of night watch. This sneak attack not only locates the success of the raid with Potts's Indianness but also punctuates the assimilationist connection between Potts, Aesop, and the black French soldiers. Second in the night attack is the Apache scout Riago, who shoots into French tents, followed by a cry from Reverend Dahlstrom (R. G. Armstrong): "Mighty is the arm of the Lord." This combination of characterization and battle, a tightly edited fusion of exposition and action that would later become Peckinpah's trademark, re-affirms the assimilation of Riago, a self-proclaimed "praying Indian," by aligning his position in the sneak attack with the bloodthirsty Christianity of Dahlstrom. Therefore, the night attack on the French lancers models the importance of Indianness to successful strategy by privileging the prowess of Potts and Riago, but the attack is also marked by constant nods to the assimilation of Potts, Riago, and, by association with the previous scene, the African French and African American soldiers.

Playing Southern distinguishes Aesop's men from the black French troops, but both Aesop's men and the black French eventually suffer. Likewise, playing Indian is at the core of the attack's success, even though this border crossing is accompanied by Potts's and Riago's loss of a Native identity. Indianness is explored and performed by Dundee's cavalry, a model of heroic success, but the Indian is simultaneously subject to Christian and European hegemony insofar as Dahlstrom defines the attack as a Christian undertaking, and the whole affair is accompanied by the assimilation of characters of color.

Finally, Dundee defeats the Apaches by using the strategy the Apaches used to defeat him. Ryan's voice-over comments: "We ran from the Apaches and the French, then circled and headed for the river and home. The men were angry, wanting to continue our pursuit, and then suddenly we knew we weren't running away from anything. We were running toward the end of our search." In these lines there is a reflexive attention to the end of the movie, looming like the Rio Grande in the distance, just two battles away. Moreover, the words "our search" validate Jim Kitses's claim that the cavalry's struggle, like Marlow's in the imperialist/impressionist novel *Heart of Darkness* (1902), is partly internal.[12] But the internal "search" motif in Peckinpah's movie is about more than an imperialist ideology of the evolution away from and return to "savagery." While this European racist mainstay operates in the film, it is also important that the men's running mirrors the Apache's strategy at the river. Potts tells Dundee, "This is as good a place as any to do what you have in mind," again noting the internal nature of Dundee's struggle but articulating this struggle along lines of strategy, here a strategy Dundee borrows from Charriba. Dundee's men enter a canyon, and Dundee orders that the pickets, represented by the culturally liminal characters Gomez and Potts, allow the Apache to enter the cavalry's lines, where the Apache are ambushed by Dundee's men. During the fight that ensues, the Apache are vanquished, and Bugler Ryan kills Charriba. The idea of drawing the Apache into the ambush is an appropriation of Charriba's earlier strategy and as such indicates that Dundee has learned something about playing Indian. Charriba's band is literally taken within the cavalry's ranks, entering through the gatekeepers Potts and Gomez, who both are forced to skirmish at the picket lines and are nearly killed by Dundee's plan. The absorption of Charriba's strategy, i.e., playing Indian, allows for the literal absorption of Charriba's Apache warriors, and the film's most violent scene of assimilation follows as the Apache Indians are destroyed by Dundee's supposed Indianness.

Just as Dundee relies on the Southern hero Tyreen, eventually assimilating his old friend and Aesop as flag bearers destroyed by the major's quest for glory, Dundee relies on a notion of Indianness to destroy the Indians. This is not a new pattern in American film, for the supposedly Indian-like Indian killer is at the heart of racist fantasies from Cooper to films like *Rio Grande*, *Arrowhead*, and *The Searchers*. However, the attention to the assimilationist aspects of these appropriations of Southern and Indian Otherness speaks to a cynicism in Peckinpah's vision, born in the absurdity of *Major Dundee*'s attempts to reconcile contentious cross-cultural relationships with a common mission, a mission that is itself motivated by selfishness. Doug McKinney and Richard Slotkin note that Ford's *Rio Grande* (1950) reconciles North and South as the cavalry chases Apaches into Mexico.[13] *Major Dundee* borrows this project, but adds layer upon convoluted layer of national, racial, regional, international, interracial, and interregional identities into a filmic model of cultural border crossing that is at once oriented toward appropriations of Southern and Indian Otherness and aimed at assimilating the models for this Otherness. In *Major Dundee* the primary purpose of border crossing is to serve Dundee's egomaniacal mission, but the goals of Dundee's personal mission have obvious social consequences: (1) the assimilation of African Americans (i.e., Aesop and his men), Mexican Americans (i.e., Gomez), Native Americans (i.e., Gomez, Potts, and Riago), and Southerners (i.e., Tyreen and his men); (2) the destruction of renegade Indians (i.e., Charriba) and Southerners (i.e., Tyreen and Hadley). These are social goals accomplished through Dundee's personal obsessions. However, Dundee's social accomplishments are marked by fraudulence. This is especially true of Dundee's liberation of Juarista Mexicans from the French, and Mexico is the third of the cultural borders we must explore.

¡Viva Dundee! "Revolutionary" Heroism at Mexico's Expense

Interestingly, Dundee finally learns the value of simulation somewhat indirectly, not by simulating Tyreen's Southernness or Charriba's Indianness but rather by playing the Mexican revolutionary. However, this too stems partly from his relationship with Tyreen. Tyreen's ties to Mexico through the Mexican American War are contradictory, and *Major Dundee* does very little to account for Tyreen's oppositional past relationship with Mexico, concentrating instead on Tyreen's ability to speak Spanish and, therefore, his ability to cross cultural borders more fluidly than the major can. If anything is reconciled for Tyreen in Mexico, it is his European past with his Southern present. Tyreen's suicidal attack on French lancers at the end of the movie, an act of crazy bravery observed by his proud Southern men, qualifies his earlier use of European identity to separate himself from the "ignorant" South. Tyreen conveniently serves as a model hero for Dundee's mission by disowning a stereotype of Southernness while still heroically realigning himself with his Southern men and the Mexican underdog. This is a neat ideological trick of *Major Dundee*, which struggles to maintain the nobility of the Southern gentlemen amidst a disavowal of the racism at the heart of this image. This disavowal is achieved through Tyreen's deference early in the plot to classism and Eurocentric sources of Southern nobility, but finally, because Europe, in the form of the French, represents spoiled tyranny, Tyreen the potential tyrant must fight against the French. Tyreen is, therefore, Southern but not racist, European but not privileged, a hero both noble and answering to the downtrodden. This cultural border crossing is a testament to Tyreen's adaptability, which Dundee lacks, at least until he defeats the Apaches.

Nowhere is Dundee's jealousy of Tyreen's ability to cross borders more prevalent than in the men's struggle for the love of Teresa Santiago. Teresa herself is a model of successful border crossing; like Tyreen she reconciles her European ancestry with her devotion to underdogs: the Juarista villagers. Born German, Teresa apparently acquired her Spanish name, "Santiago," from her husband, a doctor murdered for his support of Juarez's attempts to rid 1860s Mexico of French control. The Spanish first name "Teresa" and her Spanish accent are never adequately explained by the film, indicating that her supposed German origins might simply be a ridiculous attempt by filmmakers to avoid an interracial coupling between Teresa and Dundee. However, this explanation is dubious, at least where Peckinpah's interests are concerned; Peckinpah married Mexican actress Begonia Palacios, who played a bit part in the film, after falling for her on the set. Moreover, given the film's interest in border crossing and characters of mixed cultural alliances, it is hard to imagine this singular attempt at segregation in an otherwise multicultural film, though Hollywood's racism has produced stranger decisions based on segregationist paranoia.[14] Most plausibly, Teresa is created German to identify her with Tyreen and with sympathetic European intervention in Mexico, balanced against the tyranny of the French.

In fact, sympathetic intervention in Mexico is an important theme of *Major Dundee* and Peckinpah's other Mexico Westerns. Dundee arrives to rob the French garrison and finds the French are locked behind closed doors, a starving dog greeting the cavalry as they enter the village. Teresa tells Dundee that there are neither women nor food and supplies in the village, assuming that Dundee enters without "flying the colors" because he intends to rape and pillage. She is correct in assuming that Dundee intends to steal food—he hides the colors to avoid an international incident—and she is at least symbolically correct that he seeks women, since Dundee's relationship with Mexico will consistently be mediated through Teresa. As if to prove his intentions are truer than they actually are and alleviate his guilt, Dundee abruptly orders his men to fire at the French, even before Teresa finishes describing the suffering of the village. The major struggles to dissociate himself from the French, especially after Teresa equates the cavalry with common thieves hiding behind phony causes: "We've been attacked by Apaches, by local bandits, by freebooters from Texas, and liberated by the French, and now United States Cavalry." She uses the term "liberated" with clear sarcasm, equating the U.S. Army with the French oppressors, and pointing out the euphemisms used by European and European-American powers to justify imperialism.

Unable to charm Teresa with Spanish, as Tyreen does when he first meets her, Dundee aims his efforts at liberating the villagers, and following the distribution of French stores to the remaining women and children, Dundee poses on a crumbling wall with graffiti reading, "Viva Dundee." But neither Dundee nor Tyreen is wholly redeemed by the cavalry's act of heroism. When Dundee tells Tyreen, "You look like quite the gentleman," Tyreen replies, "After the war, Amos, the Tyreens of County Claire become the landed gentry of Virginia." Tyreen still fantasizes about being "landed gentry," Eurocentrism undermining his intentions regarding the peons of the village, and Tyreen questions Dundee's motives as well when he says, "You haven't got the temperament to be a liberator, Amos." Therefore, on the surface, Dundee and Tyreen redeem themselves by fighting for the revolutionary cause, but both men are, in reality, motivated by selfishness. Upset that Teresa enjoys Tyreen's gentlemanly demeanor, Dundee says, "He is corrupt, but I will save him." Constantly pointing to the "charade" of Tyreen's behavior, reducing Tyreen's nobility to a "style" in the eyes of Teresa in order to win her love, Dundee is himself a false liberator as well. He sits upon a crumbling wall, labeled with a political slogan proclaiming his revolutionary heroism, and, later, he looks from the crumbling arches of the village entrance across a river into the distance, imagining that he has finally crossed a border. But he lacks the patience to be a sincere revolutionary. He soon looks at his watch, worried that the fiesta following the liberation has run too long and that Charriba continues to elude him, and he orders that the French be allowed to escape.

The Mexican village becomes, for Dundee, an idyllic fantasy and a feminized space that, like the home of Circe, keeps him from his mission. But the village also offers Dundee the chance to be a real hero for the sociopolitically oppressed, an offer he eventually refuses after initially exploiting it to build his heroic image. Once the French have escaped, Dundee's cavalry practices its ambush skills on the lancers, but his refusal to follow through with his commitment to the villagers and Teresa allows the French to again raid the village, this time murdering everyone but Teresa and a couple of children who end up in the cavalry's care. Describing the massacre, Potts says, "Them boys in the pretty hats make the Apaches look like missionaries." Tyreen adds, "Never underestimate the value of a European education." Potts's sympathies for the Apaches turn the Europeans into the film's most grotesque monsters, but it does not appear that Potts or anyone else gets the irony of equating missionaries with goodness in a cavalry where the holy man is the murderous Reverend Dahlstrom. Furthermore, Tyreen's joke reaffirms Potts's claim that the Apache massacre pales in comparison to white Europeans' penchant for torture, but Tyreen's joke also serves as a possible commentary on his own claims to European nobility, claims made by an Irishman no less, certainly aware of the evils of empire.

Increasingly, Teresa becomes devoted to Dundee despite the fraudulence of his revolutionary heroism, but her devotion rings as falsely as his revolutionary commitment. This may be flawed character development, perhaps unsurprising given Peckinpah's lousy track record with female characters and given the inordinate number of characters in the film, or this may be an indication that she, like Tyreen and Dundee, is playing at caring. I think the falsity of her devotion is a little of both. Potts and Tyreen return Teresa to the cavalry only minutes before the execution of O. W. Hadley. When Tyreen shoots Hadley, Teresa covers the eyes of a Mexican child and turns her head, unwilling to let the child or herself see the violence of their liberators. Even though Tyreen does the shooting, the overwhelming tone of the scene is that Dundee has made a mistake by executing Hadley, dividing a command that was finally beginning to come together. Hadley claims that he ran off because he was "hankering for a woman" back at the Mexican village, and this too foreshadows Dundee's failure as a leader as the film cuts to Teresa's face, hinting at Dundee's hypocrisy to come when he will withdraw with Teresa outside the pickets, deserting his men and eventually drawing fire from Apaches.

Outside the pickets, Dundee and Teresa swim together and embrace in a scene that, by comparison to the film's stark desert and canyon imagery, is softly composed, lush with greenery, Edenic. Dundee is purified by the water and by Teresa's love, absolved for the death of Hadley, but the moment at the river is illusory. Teresa confides, "I've seen too much dying. I wanted so desperately to feel alive. For both of us to feel alive." Then, after he asks if she has thought of living in the United States and she says she has not, an Apache arrow strikes deeply into his leg. Suddenly, they are attacked, but the Southern troops are there to rescue them, and Tyreen points out that Dundee is a hypocrite, deserting his lines for a woman "of rather doubtful virtue."

Tyreen speaks as one wounded by unrequited love, but his reference to Dundee's hypocrisy and Teresa's questionable virtue points to the illusoriness of their moment at the river. It is fitting that the river is where they both struggle to feel alive, because this scene is also a failed border crossing for Dundee. The major tries to bring Teresa, like everything else on his journey, back to America, only to be reminded of division by an Apache arrow. Forced to recover in Durango, Dundee slips into drunkenness. Like a dream the Durango sequence seems to operate outside of conscious time, as Teresa enters a room to find a bearded, long-drunk Dundee with a prostitute. The prostitute asks in Spanish if Dundee is Teresa's man: "¿Era tu hombre?" Teresa replies, "No." The moment is brief but devastating, punctuating the illusoriness of their bond but also affirming Dundee's real relationship with Mexico, Peckinpah's heroic, revolutionary fantasy but also his perpetual "whore." Later, Tyreen the border crosser leads a rescue of Dundee from his drunkenness and French spies. Looking at Dundee, a bearded, failed Moses in a poncho, Tyreen comments, "You make an unlikely looking Mexican."[15]

This failed attempt to adopt another cultural identity exemplifies Dundee's failed border crossings all along.

Major Dundee's journey is one of border crossings not only into Mexico but also into images of Southernness, renegade Indianness, and Mexican revolutionary heroism. These border crossings are personal, even solipsistic. But Dundee's solipsism yields political consequences: temporary liberation of Mexican Juaristas and forced assimilation of several cultural groups. *Major Dundee* explores the tensions between Dundee's selfish quest for heroic regeneration and its consequences, as the hero exploits and/or simulates what amount to heroic stereotypes: the Southern gentleman, the renegade Indian, the Mexican revolutionary. But if Peckinpah's film is driven by these stereotypes, the film also consistently makes an issue of the disparity between Dundee's supposed heroism and the path of destruction it leaves. Some of the trickiest business of reading, especially reading through the lens of cultural studies, involves negotiating the difference between what ideologies a text advocates and what ideologies a text reveals. *Major Dundee* is a particularly difficult film for the critic in this respect because it seems often to advocate and reveal at the same time. *Major Dundee* is a phallocentric and Eurocentric film insofar as its central obsession is Dundee's search for heroism, but the film repeatedly undermines the certainty of Dundee's goals, let alone the success of his search, by suggesting that these goals mask assimilation and destruction for the very models of heroism Dundee summons to his aid.

Nowhere is the undermining of Dundee's heroic goals clearer than in his indifference to the Juaristas. Both Dundee's domestic bliss with Teresa and the liberation are illusory, and Dundee's search for heroism pollutes Mexico, his relationship with Teresa, and almost everyone he touches. At the river, Teresa says, "Oh, it's lovely here." Dundee replies, "I don't spoil it?" She says that he does not, but he actually spoils everything. It is fitting that in the film's last battle, at the Rio Grande, Tyreen and Aesop die protecting the colors, just as the villagers die playing extras for Dundee's revolutionary pose, because Dundee's search for heroic validation almost always destroys the very heroic underdogs from whom he might learn. Even putting aside the culturally destructive nature of his heroic goals, Dundee makes a poor hero. In fact, the cavalry's border crossing back into Texas is really a thinly veiled retreat. The French, not allowed to follow into the United States, obey the border, and Dundee exploits the border, just as he exploits border crossing, to insulate himself from a series of accomplishments in Mexico that are really pretty unflattering. Aside from the rescue of the Rostes children, who seem to have been just fine playing Indian with the Apaches, Dundee's mission accomplishes next to nothing besides destruction.

But the challenge of reading *Major Dundee*, as I note at the beginning of my reading, is also complicated by the film's contentious authorship, particularly by Peckinpah's struggles with Jerry Bresler and Columbia. Peckinpah spent much of the production playing renegade director by flaunting his ability to shoot over budget, and with these details in mind, it is nearly impossible to know the circus that was the production of the film without seeing that circus partly reflected in the film's plot about an egomaniacal leader running amok in another country. David Weddle recounts the odd feeling the cast and crew had of being immersed in Peckinpah's own egomaniacal mission:

> The rivers, the Tehuixtla and Rio Balsas, were cooler, but so polluted with sewage the actors and stuntmen had to have their ears and noses flushed out by nurses after taking falls in the water. And there were the bugs: thousands of welt-inflicting gnats and mosquitoes as big as vampire bats. Only the Yaqui Indian extras and Peckinpah seemed oblivious to the bloodsuckers.
>
> Little by little, the movie and reality were becoming eerily intertwined. The company was no longer playing the parts of cavalry soldiers; it *was* those soldiers. And just like the characters in the film, one by one the crew began to crack under the strain of this journey without end.[16]

Biographers love this stuff: Huston and Hepburn big-game hunting during the production of *The African Queen* (1951), Werner Herzog consumed by the Peruvian jungle while shooting his tale of obsession *Fitzcarraldo* (1982), Francis Coppola's own personal and financial heart of darkness during the making of *Apocalypse Now* (1978).[17] Lost in the loop of art and life, the critic and film historian are perhaps always in danger of attributing false causation to textual features. Weddle, for example, helps Peckinpah play Indian by equating the director's endurance with that of the Yaqui Indians. But is this a flaw of Weddle's account or a reflection of Peckinpah's own attraction/repulsion to border crossing, wallowing in those rivers hour after hour to film the perfect image of a defeated major?

In order to approach textual answers to the questions surrounding the film's back story, the relationship between Peckinpah's and Dundee's obsessions, and the politics of border crossing in the film, we must finally engage directly with the first borders crossed in *Major Dundee*, formal metaborders central to the tone of the film: point of view and narration.

Who Made Major Dundee?
Point of View, Narration, and the Borders of Creation

The first borders crossed in *Major Dundee*, borders crucial to understanding the sociopolitics of subjectivity that govern cultural border relationships in the film, are the interrelated borders of point of view and narration. The film opens with a shot of Ryan's 1864–1865 Journal, the "Foreword" page of which is narrated by a voice other than Ryan's. The voice claims that Ryan, described in third person, is the "sole survivor" of the Rostes massacre and his journal "the only existing record of this tragedy and the campaign that followed." Surprisingly, Michael Bliss is one of the only critics to give the first-person narration that follows the "Foreword" much attention, when he notes, "we need to determine how reliable a chronicler Ryan is, since his reliability will determine how much validity we assign to the events that he relates."[18] One reason critics have given insufficient attention to this device may be a result of auteur theory run amok, since David Weddle suggests that the narrative device was an afterthought inserted by the butcher Bresler, rather than by Peckinpah, after the producer's cut failed to make sense: "Even Bresler recognized that he'd ripped holes the size of sound stages in the narrative, and he tried to plug them up by adding a narration track. Reverting to Harry Julian Fink's initial concept that the story would unfold as a series of diary entries, trooper Ryan became the audience's guide through the twisted wreckage of *Dundee*. The device was pitifully inadequate."[19] For Bliss the narration is important to understanding the tone of the film, while Weddle characterizes it as an failed cosmetic afterthought, their varying approaches reviving a critical controversy about film authorship, interpretation, intention, and accident. However, the inadequacy of the narration need not be the exclusive product of either intention or accident. Even if a narrator was included for continuity, unreliable narration is a common enough device to suggest that a cosmetic Band-aid became a source of irony at the heart of the film's themes of heroism.

There is, for instance, a great deal of potential self-consciousness about narration and subjectivity in the collusion of Ryan's journal with the titles at the film's opening. Peckinpah's title sequences, like the title sequences and cameos of Hitchcock, are almost always calculated to comment on themes in his films.[20] Whether the product of Bresler or Peckinpah, the titles in *Major Dundee* are among the most telling in the director's body of work, and they operate in conjunction with the presentation of Ryan's journal. As the "Foreword" is narrated, the page bursts into flames from the center out, revealing the carnage of the Rostes ranch. This is both a cheesy device reminiscent of the burning map in the credits of *Bonanza* and a more subtle employment of the iris shot commonly tied to point of view in the silent cinema and in self-consciously historical and reflexive movements like the French New Wave. The outward-burning flames create an iris-out, ostensibly tying the image of the massacre to Ryan's point of view through a didactic, visual trick, as if burning away the unidentified editor's "Foreword" to reveal Ryan's story. But the use of fire for the iris shot is ambiguous insofar as the actual fire of the incident either grows from Ryan's account or, more ironically, interrupts his account.

The latter possibility, that of interruption, is plausible when we consider that, at the point that the "Foreword" bursts into flames, revealing the massacre, the frame is already beginning what appears to be a dissolve to another frame, this one of horsemen riding. The dissolve, then, is quite literally interrupted by the iris flame, actually putting two filmic devices for connecting print and non-print image in competition. One way to read this is to equate the dissolve with the source of the "Foreword" and the flaming iris with Ryan, therefore allowing Ryan's narration to burst through the outer narrative frame of the "Foreword" writer. This reading, however, is doubtful, since Ryan's voice-over does not actually start until after the introduction not only of Dundee's visual point of view but also Sierra Charriba's. A more likely reading is that the flames of massacre interrupt the dissolve, which is associated with Ryan's point of view. The flames of massacre, if tied to anyone's point of view at all, are tied to Charriba, who almost immediately stares down and taunts the tortured Lieutenant Brannon.

The potential irony of this flaming iris, suggesting alternatives to Ryan's narration, becomes clearer when accompanied by other characteristics of the scene. First, as noted above, among the burning embers of the Rostes ranch Charriba approaches the dying Lieutenant Brannon and shouts with no small dose of histrionics, "Pony soldier, I am Sierra Charriba! Who will you send against me now?" Charriba's use of "pony soldier" instead of "horse soldier" belittles the cavalry and Brannon, but the statement also anticipates the caption "Major Dundee," which suddenly flashes upon the screen in response to Charriba's question. Charriba's use of English, when elsewhere in the film, save for a few key scenes, non-English speakers speak in non-English tongues, is realistic insofar as he is speaking to Brannon. But the line is forced, almost ridiculous, again raising questions of intention. Is the line the product of Michael Pate's acting ability? Is the line attributable to the genre's consistently racist stereotyping of American Indians? Or is this nonsense the product of Ryan's fantasy?

All three are plausible readings, but it is noteworthy that nothing in the scene attempts to tie this grand proclamation to Ryan's point of view during the aftermath of the massacre. Is Ryan retelling something he actually saw or just something that sounds exciting? Or is Charriba the narrative source of this scene, interrupting Ryan's narration even before it begins? We will never really know, partly because of the clumsiness and inconsistency of the narration throughout the movie. However, there does seem to be a degree of self-consciousness about the limitations of Ryan's vision, since following Dundee's appearance at the massacre a telephoto shot from the top of a hill reveals Charriba watching the cavalry, who are ostensibly unaware of his presence as they approach the carnage. Moreover, this shot of Charriba is repeated as Dundee, Ryan, and Dundee's relief group leave the camp where Ryan's voice-over is first employed, suggesting that Charriba's point of view may even frame Ryan's in an ironic twist of perspective. This point-of-view shot is a double interruption into Ryan's dominant narrative and spectatorial power. First, Charriba's point of view as Ryan and Dundee approach the camp is abrupt and unexpected, accompanied by a dissonant sound effect that interrupts the ridiculous "Major Dundee March" that Mitch Mitchell's Sing Along Gang performs throughout the credits.[21] Secondly, even if we read this shot as Ryan's racist image of the silent menace of Charriba—always, Ryan fears, watching the cavalry—this point-of-view shot interrupts Ryan's narrative by abruptly articulating the absence of Charriba's true perspective from the narrative.

My reading of this convoluted play of point of view is as follows:

(1) The outermost narrative layer is what I will provisionally call "*Major Dundee*";

(2) the image of the "Foreword" page reveals that between Ryan and *Major Dundee* some other narrator, perhaps editor, mediates information;

(3) Ryan's narration, i.e., the pages behind the "Foreword," begin to bleed through the "Foreword," a narrative action visually represented by a dissolve to either Charriba's riders, Brannon's cavalry, or Dundee's cavalry, all three of which are supposedly contained by Ryan's "sole" account of events;

(4) the flaming iris interrupts the dissolve, temporarily subverting Ryan's narrative point of view to show Charriba's visual point of view and proclamation to the dying Brannon (if the dominant point of view here is in fact Charriba's, his hyperbolic bragging may indicate his hubris, but if this is Ryan's fantasy of Charriba, then we are faced with the prospect of the space between Ryan's ideology and the film's);

(5) the words "Major Dundee" violently appear to answer Charriba's question, and Mitch Mitchell's Sing Along Gang begins the "Major Dundee March," suggesting that at the *Major Dundee* layer there is an ideological identification or an ironic ideological identification with the hero Dundee;

(6) an image of Charriba looking down at Dundee's relief patrol re-situates looking with Charriba as the "Major Dundee March" stops, but this too is easily an identification with Dundee and/or Ryan at the outer narrative layer, since this is a typical intrusion in the Western genre, a genre that is inarguably racist in nearly every one of its treatments of American Indians.

One central question of point of view in *Major Dundee* then becomes whether the limits of Ryan's point of view are an accident of flawed production or a self-conscious source of irony. Complicating this first question even further, however, is the limited Native point of view. Is this limitation a further source of irony or just the product of Hollywood racism?

In order to answer this last question it is worth considering that *Major Dundee* was released after fifteen years of Hollywood Westerns that made half-hearted attempts to revise their treatment of Native Americans. On one hand, the hyperbolic nature of Charriba's bragging must have seemed pretty ridiculous to Western fans at the time, well aware of the "noble," though no less racist, treatment of chiefs like Cochise and Geronimo in films of the 1950s and early 1960s, even in John Ford's *Fort Apache* (1948). On the other hand, it is hard to be positive that this hyperbolic acting is intended on the part of the filmmakers to be the product of Ryan's vision. Rather, as I have already noted, this seems to be presented as an intrusion of Charriba's point of view into Ryan's supposedly authoritative narrative space. Assuming that this line is a bit over the top and not the product of my own misreading or bad acting, it is still hard to determine if hyperbole here is meant to be noticed as hyperbole or just more of an unselfconscious stereotype, since this fifteen-year period of the Western produced, in addition to well-meaning but limited revisionism, some of the most explicitly racist Westerns of all time, e.g., *Arrowhead*. The one thing of which I am sure is that *Major Dundee* as a movie is the flawed result of competing visions and that *Major Dundee* is, to some degree, self-consciously about competing visions. Therefore, the failures and the thematic goals of the film leave it both rich with potential self-reflection but also a testament to the dangers of analysis.

The "Foreword" describes Ryan as the "sole survivor" of the massacre, even though only moments later Ryan tells us that the cavalry scout Riago also survived. Ryan is suspicious that Riago has betrayed the cavalry but obviously feels no need to account for the mysterious circumstances of his own survival. Therefore, Ryan's account is suspicious at best. But, as I have tried to ask, what constitutes Ryan's account? What constitutes Charriba's? What constitutes the account of the "Foreword"? And what constitutes the film as a whole? In order to answer the last of these questions it is necessary to admit the ambiguous circumstances of the film's production and the ambivalence at the heart of its sociopolitics while still recognizing the importance of questions about what *Major Dundee* finally does with the politics of race, region, nation, and gender.

I read these questions of point of view at the beginning of *Major Dundee* as a self-reflexive device foregrounding competing visions. This self-reflexivity is born partly in accidents of production brought about by the actual competing visions behind the film, but it is also exploited by the filmmakers to allow the narrative use of point of view to function as a commentary on the competing interests so haphazardly handled by Dundee himself. During the title sequence, the first medium shot of a burning building is superimposed by the names "Mario Adorf," "Brock Peters," and "Warren Oates," the actors playing Gomez, Aesop, and O. W. Hadley. It is fitting that the Mexican American, African American, and Southern characters are together superimposed on the burning house, which offers up an image of cross-cultural assimilation mixed with an image of destruction, walls coming down but excited by and exciting the flames of cross-cultural conflict.

Over all of this imagery of destruction is the "Major Dundee March," performed by Mitch Mitchell's Sing Along Gang and added, according to Paul Seydor, by the studio.[22] The song is an absurdly optimistic soundtrack for the carnage of the massacre and one of the film's sources of greatest irony:

> Though your heart be with the North,
> Or your heart be with the South,
> The coat of blue or gray,
> It's no nevermind.
> Won't be long 'til we'll be home
> Raining kisses on the mouth
> Of the girl we left behind.
>
> Fall in behind the major,
> And we'll all get home again.

The last refrain of the chorus, promising that the major will return everyone safely home, is accompanied by a burning house superimposed with: "Produced by Jerry Bresler." Suddenly, "Directed by Sam Peckinpah" intrudes into the titles as the burning house collapses! Whose joke is this?

The contest of visions behind the film is at the heart of the film's reflexivity and also at the heart of the film's treatment of point of view and Dundee's heroism. Almost none of the men "get home again" alive, though many are assimilated into the big hegemonic reservation known as America. However, America for Dundee means nothing compared to his personal quest for heroic validation, so the fantasy of reconciliation in the song, articulated in terms of North and South to the exclusion of the multiple cultural and cross-cultural categories explored in the film, is ultimately subsumed in an egomaniacal quest for heroism. Dundee's solipsistic heroism, assimilating as it borrows for personal gain, is a source of hegemonic unification, but *Major Dundee* is so deeply cynical compared with, say, *Fort Apache* that it is hard to believe that anything has been resolved.

Ultimately, aligning point of view in the title sequence solely with Charriba, Ryan, or some reductive sense of the larger ideological project of the film misses part of the point, which is that these points of view are in competition. In the opening sequence, Charriba's point of view escapes Ryan, just as Dundee fails so often to penetrate cultural borders in the film, but Charriba's point of view is also Ryan's and Hollywood's imagined Indian menace. When Aesop and Hadley observe the French from a hill, temporarily reconciling their differences through Aesop's assimilation to a Southern identity, their border crossing seizes the balcony point of view "owned" by Charriba earlier in the film. This seizure of visual power prefaces the cavalry's Indian-style attack on the French, since playing Indian is itself a cultural seizure of point of view. And the appropriation of Charriba's point of view by Aesop and Hadley is part of a hegemonic spiral wherein the South appropriates Aesop's point of view, the cavalry's mission appropriates Charriba's, and Dundee assimilates all points of view with the help of his chronicler and heroic initiate Ryan. Therefore, the larger national project of assimilation is mediated through the central egomaniacs of *Major Dundee*: narrator Ryan, Amos Dundee, and "Sam Peckinpah."

Michael Bliss notes how "improbably" Ryan kills Charriba in the last battle between the cavalry and the Indians, stating that this killing "seems to settle the score against Charriba rather too neatly, suggesting that Ryan the storyteller has altered the facts and cast himself in the role of successful avenger simply because it pleased him to do so."[23] Ryan kills Charriba as the

Apache warrior looks down at the battle from the top of the canyon, recalling the hill from which Charriba watches the cavalry at the ranch earlier and, therefore, seizing the point of view or imagined point of view Charriba has used to challenge Ryan's narrative authority and Dundee's heroism all along. As Dundee kicks the dead Charriba into the canyon, Ryan says, "He looks so small now," referencing the smallness of even the most formidable adversaries in death, but doubly drawing attention to point of view: (1) Charriba looks small because his corpse is below Dundee and Ryan in the mise en scene; (2) Charriba "looks" small because his point of view or imagined point of view has been thoroughly appropriated. Ryan's narration, and his narrative point of view, like Dundee's heroism, is the product of coercion. And Ryan's narrative function is directly tied to Dundee's search for heroic validation in the film's last frames, when, apparently retreating from the French, Dundee asks for the militaristic euphemism of Ryan's patriotic bugle: "Play us a tune, son." Southern Sergeant Chillum (Ben Johnson) bears one flag and an African American trooper bears another, but Ryan and Dundee conspire to bear heroic and narrative control of the mission, as Mitch Mitchell again sings: "Fall in behind the major, / And we'll all get home again."

In conclusion, *Major Dundee* belongs to an argument, not just about length, but about tone and continuity, and about a generic attempt at border crossing finally too ambitious for the visions of its creators. *Major Dundee* is neither a successful narrative film nor a radical sociopolitical film. Rather, it is the sort of mess that can occur only when idealistic notions of heroism at the heart of the Western strain to accommodate and reconcile cultural divisions and interactions so explicitly complex they resist containment at all. The movie is formally self-reflexive, full of ironies at the level of plot and character, and a self-referential nod to its production and its director, but the movie defies definitions of revisionism that suggest a repair of old generic problems and related sociopolitical problems. In fact, *Major Dundee* is partly in a state of ill repair because it is born in the collision of revolutionary forces, struggling to speak in old ways and new ways simultaneously and finding those ways incompatible. *Major Dundee* is a mess, but how could so pure a representation of division and the failures of hegemonic models of unification be anything but?

Even without a narrator-initiate twisting the details of the story to fit his own coming of heroic age by destroying Charriba, *Major Dundee* is a story of heroic simulation-without-representation wherein the protagonist redefines his heroism through an array of Others he eventually destroys. The inclusion of the narrator Ryan foregrounds the need for critical viewing to the point of excess, but the title sequence and the egomaniacal motivations of Dundee's character are enough to illustrate that the film came together partly as a reflection of a director's own egomaniacal struggle below the border. The artistic agency behind this production is dispersed among writers, actors, financiers, and the director himself, but *Major Dundee* reveals a directorial persona that would continue through Peckinpah's masterpiece *The Wild Bunch*, always immersed in the sociopolitics of hero-making yet always uncertain about the potential of these heroes or the heroic auteur to make the right choice.

Notes

1. Paul Seydor, *Peckinpah: The Western Films: A Reconsideration* (Urbana: University of Illinois Press, 1997), 69.

2. Ibid., 72

3. Doug McKinney, *Sam Peckinpah* (Boston: Twayne, 1979), 64.

4. Seydor, *Peckinpah*, 68.

5. Marshall Fine, *Bloody Sam* (New York: Donald I. Fine, 1991), 84–92.

6. See Seydor, *Peckinpah*, 75. Seydor notes that Hadley's desertion and execution recall the execution sequence in Howard Hawks's *Red River* (1948), in which Tom Dunson (John Wayne) refuses to look up at the deserter, who is on a horse. *Major Dundee* borrows this idea and Wayne's lines, as Dundee says, "I don't want to look up at him."

7. Philip J. Deloria, *Playing Indian* (New Haven, Conn.: Yale University Press, 1998), 191.

8. For more on the relationship between American Indians and white masculinity, see David Anthony Tyeeme Clark and Joane Nagel, "White Men, Red Masks: Appropriations of 'Indian' Manhood in Imagined Wests," in Matthew Basso, Lauren McCall, and Dee Garceau, *Across the Great Divide: Cultures of Manhood in the American West* (New York: Routledge, 2001), 116. Clark and Nagel describe the late nineteenth-century "contradictory situation in which some American reformers were busy 'civilizing' indigenous people in efforts to turn them into whites, while at the same time other Americans concerned with manhood were busy emulating, or more accurately, *simulating* Indian men in an effort to revitalize Anglo masculinity." This combined simulation and forced assimilation is also at the heart of Major Dundee, including not only the film's treatment of Apaches but also that of Southern whites, African Americans, and Mexicans.

9. For further discussion of the film's connections to *Fort Apache* see Jim Kitses, *Horizons West: Anthony Mann, Budd Boetticher, Sam Peckinpah: Studies of Authorship within the Western* (London: Thames and Hudson, 1969), 146; Seydor, *Peckinpah*, 75; Michael Bliss, *Justified Lives: Morality and Narrative in the Films of Sam Peckinpah* (Carbondale: Southern Illinois Press, 1993), 60; McKinney, *Sam Peckinpah*, 63; and

Richard Slotkin, *Gunfighter Nation: The Myth of the Frontier in Twentieth-Century America* (New York: Atheneum, 1992), 562–67.

10. Phil Hardy, *The Overlook Encyclopedia: The Western* (Woodstock: Overlook Press, 1995), 167.

11. Kitses, *Horizons West,* 140.

12. Ibid., 149. Kitses reads the Indian attire of the Rostes children in terms of a "savage direction open to all menùan interior potential" where civilization masks savagery at its core. There is much in the film to support Kitses's reading of an "interior potential" for savagery, a reading that gives Peckinpah's film far more racist implications than Kitses allows. All of this said, however, I still believe the Rostes children playing Indian makes clearer Dundee's failure to play Indian himself.

13. McKinney, *Sam Peckinpah,* 63; Slotkin, *Gunfighter Nation,* 562–67.

14. According to Ephraim Katz, *The Film Encyclopedia* (New York: Harper, 1994), 116, Berger herself was born in Vienna and cut her teeth in German-language films. But this need not necessitate any mention of German origins for her character, since Caucasians routinely play people from all varieties of ethnic and racial backgrounds in Hollywood cinema.

15. Charlton Heston plays a Mexican policeman in Orson Welles's noir classic *Touch of Evil* (1958), a movie that also explores Heston's Moses image. In *Touch of Evil* Heston makes an "unlikely looking Mexican," a fact that Welles foregrounds with some success.

16. David Weddle, *"If They Move . . . Kill 'Em!": The Life and Times of Sam Peckinpah* (New York: Grove, 1994), 241–42.

17. Huston's Africa, Herzog's Peru, and Coppola's Philippines are chronicled, respectively, in the fiction film *White Hunter Black Heart* (1990), the documentary *Burden of Dreams* (1983), and the documentary *Hearts of Darkness: A Filmmaker's Apocalypse* (1991). These films and numerous written accounts attest to the continuing critical and popular fascination with life mirroring art on the set. That each of these films, and the films about them, explore imperialism is not particularly shocking, since filmmaking in another country is a form of imperialism itself, an exploitation of the land and people, harvested as an image and used for profit.

18. Bliss, *Justified Lives,* 58.

19. Weddle, *The Life and Times,* 252.

20. See Richard Gentnen and Diane Birdsall, "Peckinpah: Cutter," *Film Comment* 17.1 (1981): 35. Gentnen and Birdsall note the self-reflexive use of titles in Peckinpah's *Bring Me the Head of Alfredo Garcia.*

21. It is important to note, however, that sound frequently interrupts alongside the hilltop presence of Indians in Westerns; often, as made famous in John Ford Westerns, the sound is a stereotypical drum cadence tied to the appearance of Indians in all their typical Hollywood accouterments.

22. Seydor, *Peckinpah,* 73.

23. Bliss, *Justified Lives,* 59.

FIVE

JOHN M. GOURLIE

Peckinpah's Epic Vision

THE WILD BUNCH AND THE BALLAD OF CABLE HOGUE

In *The Wild Bunch* and *The Battle of Cable Hogue*, Sam Peckinpah explores issues and values central to our existence with such intensity and depth that the two films create what might be recognized as an epic vision of human experience. These two films constitute Peckinpah's *Iliad* and *Odyssey*. Indeed, Peckinpah's achievement in the two films—and as a filmmaker—can be more fully appreciated by comparing them to Homer's work. Like Achilleus's shield, which displays a city of war and a city of peace, Peckinpah's two films depict the fundamental conditions of war and peace, and, in so doing, explore the underlying choices and possibilities.[1]

Just as *The Iliad* and *The Odyssey* might be seen as creating an overarching structure, so too *The Wild Bunch* and *The Ballad of Cable Hogue* may be seen as forming a larger pattern. Throughout this extended pattern, Peckinpah portrays a heroic grappling with the issues of violent action and—ultimately more important—the heroic choices that underlie such action. These are the choices that define the self: the search for self-worth, the search for love, and the search for human solidarity.

Like *The Iliad*, *The Wild Bunch* explores the question of self-sacrifice. What, in the end, is worth dying for? To the Bunch, the booty of the town bank and perhaps the glory of the exploit initially seem worth the risk. Finally, loyalty to their comrade Angel and, by extension, the values of the village life he embodies seem to make the expending of their own lives meaningful. The Bunch do not appear able to choose the village values for themselves, but they can make them more viable for Angel's people by destroying Mapache's army. The battle on behalf of the village values endows the Bunch with a heroic stature—ennobling men of baser character and instincts, restoring the essential nobility of the leaders. Like Achilleus's fiery vengeance across the plains of Troy, the film's climactic blood bath presents violence of such visual and visceral power as to take the measure of the choice for battle in a way few films—or works of any kind—ever have.

The Ballad of Cable Hogue balances *The Wild Bunch* much as *The Odyssey* does *The Iliad*. In *The Ballad of Cable Hogue*, Peckinpah reworks elements of *The Wild Bunch* to explore the values of life. What makes life in all its trials, agonies, and losses worth living? The values attained by Hogue in his love for Hildy constitute the fruit of Peckinpah's exploration. Vanquishing the interior villainy of the baser self as well as the exterior villains, Hogue survives a corrosive quest for vengeance, a false pride, and a mean-spirited treatment of others. In the end, he gains an expansive sense of self-worth as love flowers in its many forms—love of Hildy, love of friends, love of former enemies, love of one's own desert home—the village values triumphant. With Hogue's death, Peckinpah tests these values further. As Odysseus is the hero of those values rooted in the home, so too is Hogue, whether he lives to enjoy them or not. Like Odysseus, Hogue ultimately sustains these values more by his choosing them than by his living them out.

Peckinpah's unifying vision has not been readily apparent. While many critics admire *The Ballad of Cable Hogue*, its low-key drama has not bedazzled them as has the explosive action of *The Wild Bunch*. As a result, *The Ballad of Cable Hogue* has often been neglected or even dismissed. But to ignore *The Ballad of Cable Hogue* is also to diminish *The Wild Bunch*. It is to overlook the larger vision both films together create. In this vision, *The Ballad of Cable Hogue* enhances the significance of *The Wild Bunch* by exploring another realm of life's meaning. Like the second half of Achilleus's shield, *The Ballad of Cable Hogue* explores the possibilities of love, of friendship, and of peaceful living. In doing so, it explores those possibilities of human existence that are either lost or are simply unattainable in the violent world of *The Wild Bunch*. When taken together, however, *The Wild Bunch* and *The Ballad of Cable Hogue* delineate the larger scope of Peckinpah's epic vision of life.

Indeed, the making of *The Wild Bunch* and *The Ballad of Cable Hogue* stem from a peak period of creative endeavor. Peckinpah began to shoot *The Ballad of Cable Hogue* while he was still editing *The Wild Bunch* in late 1968. Lou Lombardo, Peckinpah's chief editor, would travel to Nevada on weekends to see Peckinpah while he was filming *Ballad* to gain approval of the week's editing of *The Wild Bunch*. In addition, an early version of *The Wild Bunch* was screened for the cast and crew of *Ballad* in Phoenix.[2] So Peckinpah's work on *The Wild Bunch* and *The Ballad of Cable Hogue* really overlapped; one might even say that his work on the one film was intercut with his work on the other. During this period, Peckinpah was at the height of his powers and he enjoyed the greatest artistic control of his films. We should not be surprised, then, that a larger vision informs both *The Wild Bunch* and *The Ballad of Cable Hogue*—and unites them.

In this larger vision, it is clearer that *The Wild Bunch* is not merely preoccupied with violence, but that much of the film depicts the characters' search for perception, direction, and understanding. In the aftermath of the abortive bank robbery, Pike Bishop and Dutch discuss what the holdup meant to them. Pike confesses that he wanted to make one big score and then "back off." Dutch raises the telling and unanswered question, "Back off to what?" Pike's uneasy silence indicates that he does not have an alternative plan for his life. The world of *Ballad* is probably what Pike would like to back off to. Pike's inability to answer Dutch's question, though, seems to indicate not so much that Pike has not planned but that this whole world is no longer a possibility for him. The Bunch's only real option is to carry on as they have been.

The Wild Bunch has an amazing power, and much of the discussion of the film focuses on the violence of its action. While the violence is undeniable, might I suggest that the enduring power of the film resides in the quest for meaning that Pike Bishop embodies. Pike's search for meaning provides an underlying structure to the film and a context for its violence. The Bunch's commitment through Pike to a goal of high worth at the end of the film raises them from the failures and unfulfilling actions they have spent most of the film enduring. And this goal gives the violence a significance in *The Wild Bunch* that it does not have in many later films that imitate the outward pyrotechnics of its gore but fail to capture its depth of narrative purpose.

Throughout most of the film, the Bunch exist as fallen men in a fallen world. While the film makes this point in many ways, the early image of the children first watching scorpions writhe atop an enclosed anthill, then burning them, suggests the fate of the Bunch in a world of tormenting gods and a host of lesser assailants. The ensuing carnage in the town of Starbuck seems to lend vivid credence to this image and its symbolic implications.

Much of the trouble, however, is inherent in the gang and its members. The trouble can be seen in terms of the "code" Pike Bishop asserts they should live by: "We're gonna stick together, just like it used to be. When you side with a man you stay with him! If you can't do that you're like some animal—you're finished—we're finished—all of us!"[3] But the film presents a series of abandonments where, for one reason or another, members of the gang have been left behind. Crazy Lee seems to be left in Starbuck not only to hold the hostages in the bank but to save the gang from an undesirable member. A wounded member of the gang is shot by Pike when he can no longer stay in his saddle. Old Sykes is left to fend for himself when the bounty hunters wound him. We learn that Pike has left a wounded Deke Thornton behind, an action that led to Deke's imprisonment. Finally, Mapache twice takes Angel prisoner, torturing and killing him the second time. The further breakdown of the code seems to be embodied in Deke's implacable pursuit of the Bunch into Mexico as part of Harrigan's efforts to exterminate them. The gang returns only for Angel, and that return precipitates the climactic battle of the film.

The world the Bunch inhabit is a complex and dangerous place, and it does not lend itself to the easy fulfillment of even such a basic code as Pike articulates. It is full of ambush, false appearance, strategy and counter-strategy. In the bank robbery, for instance, the Bunch are disguised as an army unit. But they ride into an ambush, engineered by Harrigan and led by Deke Thornton. The townspeople are ignorant of both schemes, and in an innocent parade of temperance advocates, they march down a street that soon erupts in gunfire. Differing perceptions clearly belong to each group. Part of the drama is the Bunch's discovery that the bounty hunters are waiting on the roof to shoot them, and that Deke Thornton is among them. Of the bounty hunters, Deke alone seems appalled to find the temperance marchers walking squarely into the ambush. The stunned marchers are helplessly transformed into human shields by the escaping members of the Bunch. The two children clutching each other in the midst of the chaotic violence exploding around them symbolize, perhaps, the naïveté of all perceptions, as well as a more general innocence under siege. The further discovery after the melee is that the Bunch have stolen worthless washers rather than gold or silver. The issues expand beyond the simple lapses in following a code. And a central issue becomes how to function in a world of false appearances and illusive reality.

The gang's ride into Mexico is also a ride into deeper self-awareness and perception. The gang's dialogue upon reaching the Texas-Mexico border is revealing:

> Angel: Mexico lindo.
> Gang member: I don't see nothing so lindo about it.
> Other Gang member: Just looks like more Texas, far as I'm concerned.
> Angel: Ah, you have no eyes.

Mexico is "lindo," or beautiful, to Angel, for he is heading home. The other gang members are merely "on the road," rootless drifters; they perceive no beauty. This division between the road and home is fundamental in Peckinpah's vision, and it underlies the gang's dilemmas throughout the film. Perhaps David Weddle's observation about the significance of Mexico to Peckinpah is also relevant here, for Mexico is an artistic "home" for Peckinpah: "Though it would be layered with authentic details to bring it vividly to life on film, Peckinpah's vision of Mexico was not realistic at all, but mythic."[4] So the land we need eyes to see is Peckinpah's mythic land, for the discoveries of self take place in this mythic realm.

Memories have much to do with developing the depth of character; they also delineate significant elements of Peckinpah's mythic land. A series of flashbacks illuminate Pike's character and establish a history of loss tied to failures of perception. One flashback, for example, shows how Deke was shot and captured in a brothel while Pike escaped out the window. Pike failed to heed Deke's fears about the knock at the door because of his blind self-confidence: "It's my job to be certain." Another flashback depicts the death of Aurora, Pike's lost love. Again, Pike and Aurora are surprised by her husband, who unexpectedly bursts through the bedroom door to shoot Aurora dead and to wound Pike in the leg—an injury Pike nurses throughout the film. Unfortunately cut out of standard theatrical releases of the film, these flashbacks (now restored) do much to deepen Pike's character and the story as a whole. The flashbacks further reveal that behind the violence and failed actions of the Bunch stands the tragedy of failed perceptions.

In the flashbacks—and in the film as a whole—the bedroom becomes a place of danger rather than romance. We see love—the major countervailing value to violence—placed outside of Pike's reach. The flashbacks express the inner pressure such events have placed on his life and the stakes riding on his actions in the film. The flashbacks also align the film's characters—Pike, Deke, and Angel—in a complex but significant set of parallels.

Aligned with love, Angel's village becomes one of the central elements on the road of discovery Pike travels. The village comes to symbolize all that Pike would wish to "back off to." It symbolizes love, acceptance, and community. Although the village has been recently attacked, the villagers welcome the Bunch with genuine warmth and hospitality—the only such welcome they experience in the film. In the village embrace, all members of the gang seem to enjoy the possibility of self-renewal and innocence. The most striking example is the game of cat's cradle the Gorch brothers play with a teenage girl. As the village leader comments to Pike's amazement over the scene, "We all long to be children again. . . . The worst of us most of all." The feasting, dancing, and bathing create an enchantment that endows the Bunch with a more complex identity, a link to values and possibilities we have not associated them with. Nowhere is this expressed more lyrically and beautifully than in the Bunch's ride out of the village to the plaintive strains of "La Golondrina" (The Swallow). But while tantalizingly close, such village life is essentially beyond the reach of the Bunch—rendered so by their lifetime of defiant choices and violent actions.

Angel is the Bunch's link to the village, and through Angel, their commitment to the village is ultimately made. Initially, we might see Angel as the son that Pike or Dutch do not have. But even more, Angel is one of them in that his love is betrayed by Theresa. In his agony over this loss, Angel kills Theresa. Killing Theresa literally and figuratively places Angel beyond love's easy embrace. The loss of Theresa aligns Angel with men like Pike and Deke, who are also exiled from love. Theresa's being shot by Angel echoes Aurora's being shot by her jealous husband. Like Deke, Angel is captured and tortured. But in seeking to reclaim Angel from Mapache, the Bunch make their commitment to the code of sticking together and, by extension, to the village.

Significantly, the final stage of Pike's decision to rescue Angel occurs in a bedroom. Through glances and facial expressions, Pike takes his leave of the young Mexican woman and her child. He has just slept with her, and in leaving her, he seems to realize that sustaining ties to woman, hearth, and home can never be his. The sorrow of all such loss plays across Pike's face. The loss of the village values is, perhaps, further symbolized in the small bird tied on a string that one of the Gorch brothers (played by Ben Johnson) abandons, seemingly injured by his play, on the dirt floor. We are reminded of "La Golondrina"—the swallow—the song that accompanies the Bunch as they depart from the village. The village life—evoked initially by "The Swallow" music and here by the bird on a string—is being left behind like a dying bird in the dust as the gang assemble for their confrontation with Mapache. Pike commits himself and the others to action in the first words he speaks in the scene, "Let's go," a refrain Pike uses throughout the film to launch the Bunch into action. Later, after Angel and Mapache have both been killed, the gang might still have "backed off." But the commitment to a larger scale of retaliation occurs even more spontaneously as Pike fires upon the German advisers and initiates the final bloodbath. The famous climactic battle then ensues.

Peckinpah uses the tale of the Bunch to capture a vision of men caught in the web of time. The Bunch are condemned by more than Mapache's army.

The very presence of an automobile and a machine gun symbolizes the passing of a way of life the gang embodies. Their "wildness" is doomed by historical time. As with all humankind, the passage of time that sweeps an older order away sentences the Bunch. In this sense, their fate is the fate of all, however unlike us the Bunch might otherwise seem to be.

Peckinpah perhaps thought of himself as a storyteller in the Homeric mode: "I don't make documentaries.... The facts about the siege of Troy, of the duel between Hector and Achilleus and all the rest of it, are a hell of a lot less interesting to me than what Homer makes of it all. And the mere facts tend to obscure the truth anyway.... I'm basically a storyteller.... The Western is a universal frame within which it is possible to comment."[5] Like the epic breadth of Homer, the scope of *The Wild Bunch* extends from the personal to the universal. Much of Sam Peckinpah himself was in the film. Bill Holden carried out the implications of Peckinpah's insistence that he wear a thin mustache very like Peckinpah's own:

> It wasn't just the thin mustache that Sam had insisted he wear; Holden had begun to take on the vocal qualities and mannerisms of his director. Lou Lombardo recalls: "I told Holden one day after dailies, 'I got you figured, you're doing Sam.' He was running that Wild Bunch just like Sam was running the movie."[6]

So in the failed loves of the film—especially those of Pike Bishop—Peckinpah projects his own failures in marriage to his wives and children. These are poignantly visualized in Pike's wordless leave-taking of the young Mexican woman before the final battle. Perhaps one can also see Peckinpah's alcoholism, his failures in Hollywood, the burdens of his male codes of behavior, and his personal inner turmoil poured into the film. When Pike is shot in the final battle, significantly, he is shot by a woman in a bedroom, and then by a young boy seemingly from the window of the same bedroom. It is not a long stretch to see Peckinpah's own failed marriages and relationships behind such images. At the same time, Pike is gunned down by those who symbolize the procreative capacities of succeeding generations, another indication of time's onslaught if that is not too universal a meaning to attach to these violent images.

Cinematically, we could also suggest that Peckinpah was working in an epic mode. Peckinpah's original version of *The Wild Bunch* contained over 3,600 cuts, while the average American film of that day contained around 600 cuts. The opening gunfight was compressed from twenty-one minutes in its original form to five minutes in its finished form. For such battles, Peckinpah and Lombardo "devised the most creative use of montage since Sergei Eisenstein's *Battleship Potemkin*."[7] The intercutting of fast and slow footage created a rhythm of violent action that surpassed even Kurosawa's work. Over one hundred different gunshot sound effects were used to distinguish the various weapons being fired. Here as elsewhere, one can see an epic reach to Peckinpah's endeavors.[8]

But Peckinpah's epic vision is most evident in his creation of an epic structure in the pairing of *The Ballad of Cable Hogue* with *The Wild Bunch*. In *Ballad*, Peckinpah reworks the issues of *The Wild Bunch* to affirm the choice for life and love rather than their tragic loss. *Ballad* thus responds to *The Wild Bunch* as the other half of human experience. The opening of *Ballad* is especially interesting in that it, like *The Wild Bunch*, shows the code of partnership failing as Taggart and Bowen abandon their partner Hogue in the desert, presumably to die without water. Hogue's honor is also impeached, for Taggart and Bowen accuse him of cowardice. These opening insults impel Hogue on a quest for vengeance. Ultimately, the film depicts Hogue's discovery that the pursuit of vengeance is hollow. More important, Hogue discovers a superior "code" in his love for Hildy. The code of love enables him to surrender the path of vengeance, to transcend the limiting meanness in his own being, and to embrace life fully. If the Bunch are ennobled by the sacrifice of their lives, then Hogue is elevated in the free and loving acceptance of his life.

The Ballad of Cable Hogue depicts the flowering of life at Cable Springs in what might be viewed as the triumph of the village values, those values of peaceful community that were denied the Wild Bunch but that are attained by Hogue in as full a measure as any Peckinpah character is likely to enjoy. Perhaps the easy camaraderie with stagehands Ben and Webb, the hearty backing of the banker Cushing, and the begrudging respect from Quittner, the head of the stage company, best indicate the wider community in which Hogue finds both a place and affectionate acceptance. The deep friendship with Josh and the even deeper love for Hildy complete a circle of blessed human ties that provide the alternative to Hogue's masculine code of honor and its demand for vengeance. Hogue's inner growth is echoed in an increasingly abundant natural world and in intimations of divinity's presence. The fullness of existence celebrated in *The Ballad of Cable Hogue* constitutes a "comic" vision of life's possibilities, one that balances the tragic vision of life in *The Wild Bunch*. Thus, Peckinpah creates his larger vision—an epic vision—in which the comic and the tragic are embraced in the larger structure formed by *The Wild Bunch* and *The Ballad of Cable Hogue* together.

Peckinpah develops the comic perspective of *Ballad* by honoring its own integrity as a story rather than by refuting or balancing *The Wild Bunch* on a point-by-point basis. Nonetheless, *Ballad* does respond to the dilemmas of *The Wild Bunch*. The opening of *Ballad* indicates that we are in a world that contains the same hostilities, betrayals, ambushes, and false appearances that *The Wild Bunch* does. The opening image of the Gila Monster symbolizes the intrinsic dangers of the badlands, and as the lizard explodes from gunfire, even greater human dangers are indicated. The camera reveals in succession first the lizard, then Hogue, then Taggart and Bowen—stalker beyond stalker. Each is initially hidden by the camera—in ambush, as it were—suggesting the same sense of violence and false appearance that we meet in *The Wild Bunch*. Like the Bunch riding to Mexico, Hogue treks through the desert to a new destiny. But Hogue emerges in a world far different from the Bunch's Mexico. Indeed, Peckinpah portrays Hogue's entrance into a mythic world of new possibilities through the doorway of what appears to be divine miracle. After four days of wandering in the desert uttering a variety of prayers, Hogue finds water "where it wasn't" in a moment of total surrender, "You call it, Lord. I'm done in."

In the unfolding world of blessings, Hogue's romance with Hildy most clearly reverses the conditions of the Bunch's domain where love is lost or unsuccessful. The course of Hogue and Hildy's love may not always run smoothly, but it runs true, surviving quarrels and periods of separation. Ultimately, this love redeems Hogue and Hildy from lesser states of being, enabling them to transcend the limitations of their baser selves and to emerge as more fully realized human beings. This transformation is depicted in several scenes at the springs when Hildy visits Hogue in her flight from Dead Dog. On the first night, Hildy and Hogue are both shown bathed in a golden glow as they prepare to meet one another. Hogue acknowledges Hildy's humanity: "Well, what the hell are you? A human being." Hildy appears radiant in a white gown and the renewed innocence and purity of her being. In dialogue, Hogue affirms her elevated status:

> Hogue: Now that is a picture.
> Hildy: You've seen it before, Hogue.
> Hogue: Lady, nobody's ever seen you before.

Hogue and Hildy's love transforms their world into a true "cactus Eden." The beautiful montage scene of cascading water, hens running loose, and Hogue's gift to Hildy of a purple wildflower express their overflowing emotions. The scene ends with Hogue bathing Hildy outdoors in a big wooden tub. The lyrical mood of these beautiful images is sustained by the accompanying song, "Butterfly Mornings," played initially by a guitar, then mounting to a duet between Hogue and Hildy.

The unfulfilled promises and excluded possibilities of *The Wild Bunch* world are realized and explored in the scenes detailing Hogue and Hildy's love. The bedroom is not the scene of death, capture, and loss as it is in *The Wild Bunch*. Rather, in *Ballad* the bedroom is a locale of union and the enhancement of life energies. All that is suggested but unattainable in the Bunch's visit to Angel's village, all that is being destroyed in the flashbacks of Pike's memory is presented in *The Ballad of Cable Hogue* as gifts of life within Hogue's reach. Indeed, Hildy and Hogue's love stands as the central reality and symbol of life's benevolence.

Perhaps equally important is the sense of divinity and miracle, which Peckinpah handles deliberately but delicately. While Hogue's discovery of water "where it isn't" is miraculous indeed, the presentation of divinity through the character of the preacher Joshua Duncan Sloane is more complex. Josh's mixture of lascivious behavior and poetic statement casts a net of irony over the issue of divinity, or at least divinity's spokesman. But Josh is a cut above the tent preacher inveighing against bicycles and booze in town. Even Josh's open sexuality has a celebratory side to it in his admiration of God's artistry in the design of woman. Moreover, Josh's insights, compassion, and poetic language survive much of the ironic undercutting. So it is Josh who suggests that Hogue has found a cactus Eden, who indicates to Hogue that he truly loves Hildy, and who warns Hogue about the corrosive effects of pursuing revenge against Taggart and Bowen. On the whole, Josh adds to the lyrical celebration of existence. Without doctrinal obligations, he sounds the grace notes that celebrate divinity's presence in the arrangements of life. The most telling moment of Josh's eloquence is the funeral eulogy for Hogue. Hogue more clearly becomes an "everyman" in Josh's portrayal:

> Some said he was ruthless, but you could do worse, Lord, than take to your bosom Cable Hogue. He wasn't really a good man, he wasn't a bad man. But, Lord, he was a man![9]

As spokesman for the divine, Josh's words wing us all heavenward at the close of the film.

The closing images of both *The Ballad of Cable Hogue* and *The Wild Bunch* deserve examination, particularly since Peckinpah does not leave us with images of death in either film. In *The Wild Bunch*, the Bunch are reprised laughing, and they are shown primarily in their most joyous moments in the village setting, associated with the song "La Golondrina" ("The Swallow"). The reprise of the "swallow" scenes and music has the effect of transcending the image of the dead (or dying) bird one of the Gorch brothers leaves expiring in the dust just before the Bunch go to their death. Likewise in *The Ballad of Cable Hogue*, a coyote laps water from the well at Cable Springs. The coyote is especially interesting because it evokes several echoes. One is the town name of "Dead Dog." The other is the image in *The Wild Bunch* of an emaciated dog encountered by the gang as they ride into Angel's village. A completion of sorts exists here. Peckinpah's closing image is a healthy, wild coyote rather than a starving or "dead" dog. The important point is that both films close with vibrant images portraying life and vitality. The implication of such images is that Peckinpah embraces the forces of life, suggesting that they carry on whatever death may have transpired. In *The Wild Bunch* reprise of the Bunch and in the closing eulogy of *Ballad*, moreover, there is at least a hint of transcendence in the imagery and the words. As with Homer's poet in *The Odyssey*, the ways of life are on Peckinpah's lips and in his imagery.

The comparison to Homer and his epic vision suggests a perspective on the violence Peckinpah is famous for. First, Homer is one of the few artists to equal Peckinpah in the brutally graphic portrayal of violent death. We might cite the death of almost any of the warriors in *The Iliad*.[10] But just as no one feels such violence is an end in itself in Homer, so we should recognize that it is not the final point in Peckinpah either. Yet so powerful is the presentation of violence in *The Wild Bunch* and so closed off are the Bunch's options that it is hard to see Peckinpah's more life-affirming vision in *The Wild Bunch* alone. *The Ballad of Cable Hogue* makes the larger vision of life-sustaining possibilities clearer. To understand Peckinpah at his artistic best, the violence of *The Wild Bunch* needs to be seen in the larger context *The Ballad of Cable Hogue* provides. Perhaps this vision might be stated thus: violence, while inherent in mankind, violates life's true values. For one's existence to attain satisfying meaning, it must be spent sustaining one's self, one's beloved, one's friends, and one's community in love.

Unfortunately, this vision did not emerge as forcefully as it might have at the time. *The Ballad of Cable Hogue* was for all practical purposes dumped in its theatrical release. Peckinpah's next film, *Straw Dogs*, did much to convince audiences that Peckinpah was indeed obsessed with violence of the most sordid kind. As Peckinpah's own life slid further into a morass of alcohol, drugs, and failed relationships, the brutality and violence in his own personality became a more insurmountable presence. As with Pike Bishop, Peckinpah's personal and career options increasingly closed themselves off.

To appreciate Peckinpah at his greatest, we need to align *The Ballad of Cable Hogue* with *The Wild Bunch*. For in these films, Peckinpah transformed his own personal failures into cinematic art, and in the mythic realm of the Western he created an extraordinarily powerful depiction of life's heroic options. While few might ever consider Peckinpah the equal of Homer, it is instructive to consider that he raised questions similar to those Homer raised. And, I would maintain, he created an epic vision in response to these issues that makes him a worthy successor to Homer—and probably the greatest director to employ the Western as the frame for his storytelling.

Notes

1. I would like to acknowledge my thorough indebtedness to the understanding of Peckinpah's films achieved by Paul Seydor in *Peckinpah: The Western Films* (Urbana: University of Illinois Press, 1980). I am also particularly indebted to David Weddle's biographical and critical work in *"If They Move . . . Kill 'Em": The Life and Times of Sam Peckinpah* (New York: Grove Press, 1994), although I respectfully disagree with his assessment of *The Ballad of Cable Hogue*.
2. Weddle, *Life and Times*, 358.
3. Ibid., 315.
4. Ibid., 316.
5. Ibid., 316–17.
6. Ibid., 336.
7. Ibid., 356.
8. See Weddle's discussion in *Life and Times*, 334–62.
9. Seydor, 156.
10. One example of Homer's gory descriptions of death:

> Idomeneus stabbed Erymas in the mouth with the pitiless bronze, so that the brazen spearhead smashed its way clean through below the brain in an upward stroke, and the white bones splintered, and the teeth were shaken out with the stroke and both eyes filled up with blood, and gaping he blew a spray of blood through the nostrils and through his mouth, and death in a dark mist closed in about him.

The example is from Book Sixteen, and it precedes the deaths of the noted heroes Sarpedon and Patroklos. Richard Lattimore, trans., *The Iliad of Homer* (Chicago: University of Chicago Press, 1951), 339.

The previous reference to Homer's poet is to Demodokos, the blind poet who appears in Book Eight of *The Odyssey*. Odysseus acknowledges him, saying:

> All men owe honor to the poets—honor
> and awe, for they are dearest to the Muse
> who puts upon their lips the ways of life.

Robert Fitzgerald, trans., *The Odyssey of Homer* (New York: Anchor/Doubleday, 1961), 139. In both *The Iliad* and *The Odyssey* Homer associates imagery, often animal imagery, with the death of heroes or other significant elements of the action, the famed "epic similes." The similes serve to associate these actions with the wider concerns and values of the tale. So too in Peckinpah; his animal imagery is not merely naturalistic symbolism but a means of suggesting the larger play of values implicated in the action of his two films.

References

Bliss, Michael. 1993. *Justified Lives: Morality and Narrative in the Films of Sam Peckinpah*. Carbondale: Southern Illinois University Press.

Seydor, Paul. 1980. *Peckinpah: The Western Films*. Urbana: University of Illinois Press.

Simmons, Garner. 1982. *Peckinpah: A Portrait in Montage*. Austin: University of Texas Press.

Weddle, David. 1994. *"If They Move. . .Kill 'Em": The Life and Times of Sam Peckinpah*. New York: Grove Press.

"All I want is to enter my house justified." Steve Judd (Joel McCrea) and Gil Westrum (Randolph Scott), *Ride the High Country*, 1962, Metro-Goldwyn-Mayer. Courtesy of the George Eastman House.

"Back off to what?" Dutch Engstrom (Ernest Borgnine) and Pike Bishop (William Holden), *The Wild Bunch*, 1969, Warner Bros. Courtesy of Photofest.

"He wasn't really a good man, he wasn't a bad man. But, Lord, he was a man!" Cable Hogue (Jason Robards), Hildy (Stella Stevens), Bowen (Strother Martin) and, standing, Joshua (David Warner), *The Ballad of Cable Hogue*, 1970, Warner Bros. Courtesy of the George Eastman House.

"¿Quién es?" Billy (Kris Kristofferson), *Pat Garrett and Billy the Kid*, 1973, Metro-Goldwyn-Mayer. Courtesy of Photofest.

"Fall in behind the major." Amos Dundee (Charlton Heston) and Benjamin Tyreen (Richard Harris), *Major Dundee*, 1965, Columbia Pictures Corp. Courtesy of the Academy of Motion Picture Arts and Sciences.

"Let's go!" Tector Gorch (Ben Johnson), Lyle Gorch (Warren Oates), Pike Bishop (William Holden), and Dutch Engstrom (Ernest Borgnine), *The Wild Bunch*, 1969, Warner Bros. Courtesy of The Museum of Modern Art/Film Stills Archive.

"Bitch!" Pike Bishop (William Holden), *The Wild Bunch*, 1969, Warner Bros. Courtesy of Photofest.

Cable: "We all got our own ways of living." Hildy: "And loving?" Cable Hogue (Jason Robards), Hildy (Stella Stevens), and, standing, Joshua (David Warner), *The Ballad of Cable Hogue*, 1970, Warner Bros. Courtesy of Photofest.

"Stay cowboy." Junior Bonner (Steve McQueen) and Ace Bonner (Robert Preston), *Junior Bonner*, 1972, ABC Pictures Corp. Courtesy of Photofest.

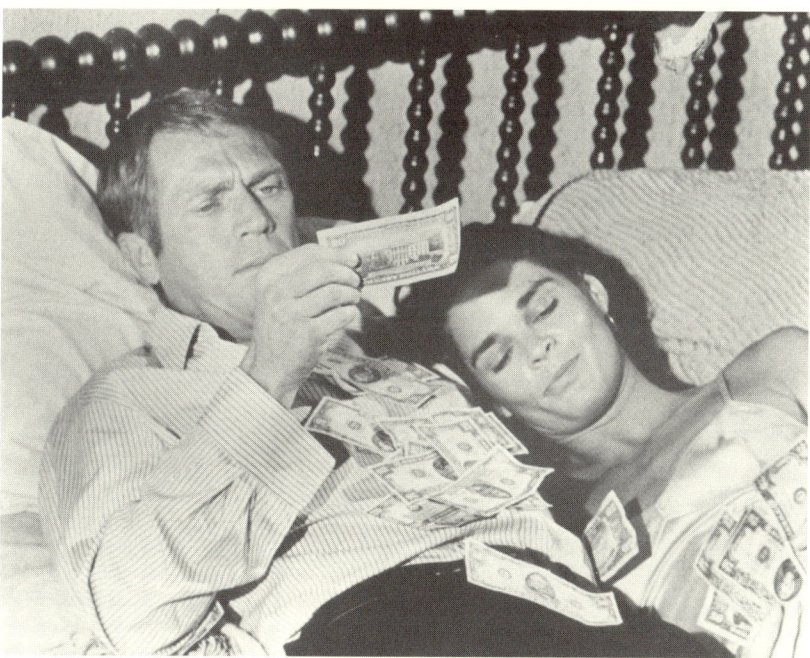

"In God We Trust." Doc McCoy (Steve McQueen) and Carol McCoy (Ali McGraw), *The Getaway*, 1972, Solar/Foster-Bower production for First Artists Production Co. Courtesy of the Academy of Motion Picture Arts and Sciences.

Pat: "It feels like times have changed." Billy: "Times, maybe, but not me." Billy (Kris Kristofferson) and Pat (James Coburn), *Pat Garrett and Billy the Kid*, 1973, Metro-Goldwyn-Mayer. Courtesy of the Academy of Motion Picture Arts and Sciences.

Alias: "Mexico won't be so bad for a few months." Billy: "I guess that depends on who you are." Billy (Kris Kristofferson) and Alias (Bob Dylan), *Pat Garrett and Billy the Kid*, 1973, Metro-Goldwyn-Mayer. Courtesy of the Academy of Motion Picture Arts and Sciences.

"We're always moving." *Convoy,* 1978, United Artists. Courtesy of the Academy of Motion Picture Arts and Sciences.

SIX

FRANK BURKE

Divining Peckinpah

RELIGIOUS PARADIGM AND IDEOLOGY IN
CONVOY AND *THE BALLAD OF CABLE HOGUE*

I—Prefatory Notes

I first wrote this essay following the release of *Convoy* (1978). At that point, there was virtually no sustained academic criticism of Peckinpah, and much of the popular press response to his work was negative. My interest was in establishing the moral seriousness of Peckinpah's two films and their relationship (especially in the case of *Convoy*) to the American literary tradition. Largely because *Convoy* was considered an insignificant film, and a context of Peckinpah criticism had not yet developed, there was little interest in my essay, and I shelved it until I was given the opportunity to rework it for this collection.

Since I first drafted the essay, much has happened. Serious academic criticism has appeared, sparked largely by the appearance in 1980 of Paul Seydor's *Peckinpah: The Western Films*, which masterfully demonstrated, in the light of Peckinpah's entire career to that point, both his seriousness and his importance as an American artist. However, at virtually the same moment, film criticism, working largely on models derived from France, then Britain, veered away from auteurist appreciation and into ideological critique, often directed at Hollywood (American) film.[1] Moreover, auteurism itself came to be seen as (among other things) a representation of Western individualism that masked the social and political workings of films in favor of blindly celebrating artistic genius. And, with the rise of feminism, the tradition of American literature within which Peckinpah is so fruitfully examined came under scrutiny for its perpetuation of masculinist mythologies and modes of thought. In other words, Peckinpah could not have been "discovered" as an auteur and American artist at a worse moment, an irony that very much befits his difficulty earning appreciation throughout his career—from producers, reviewers, and the public.

The result has been that Peckinpah criticism has evolved largely outside canonical film criticism from the 1970s onward, as the latter has considered his work unworthy of attention. This is a shame, because, as Christopher Sharrett's essay "Peckinpah the Radical: The Politics of *The Wild Bunch*," makes clear, Peckinpah's work is not just a mindless reproduction of masculinist, individualist ideology. At its best, it also encourages powerful and complex critiques of the very ideologies of which it is accused, while also providing insight into the dysfunctionality of American society. (The best criticism of Seydor and others addresses the latter but sometimes in a way that lionizes Peckinpah and neglects or explains away some of the more problematic aspects of his work, particularly his representation of women.)

In reconsidering my essay after two decades, I was faced with somewhat of a dilemma. As originally written, the essay was consistent with the tradition of Peckinpah criticism that has followed upon Seydor's groundbreaking work. And, I felt it still offered original insight into the complexity of Peckinpah's two films. So, to my mind, it had its place within a collection devoted to Peckinpah. However, I also value much of the ideological and feminist work that has, unfortunately, marginalized Peckinpah within film criticism, and I did not want to just disregard problematic implications in the two films, especially in *Convoy*. I contemplated an entire rewrite, but that would have eviscerated the original. So I decided to retain the argument, but conclude by addressing certain ideological issues in a way that, while not fundamentally reorienting the essay, at least resituates Peckinpah's work within a critical context from which it has been all too often missing.

A brief note on structure. Since the essay was written upon the release of *Convoy*, it initiated its analysis with that film, and then worked back to the older, and at the time largely neglected, *The Ballad of Cable Hogue*. The currency of *Convoy* made the chronological reversal "natural" at the time. It may seem less natural now, but since the analysis is paradigmatic rather than chronological, comparing New Testament with Old Testament models of behavior, and since the distinctions work quite well moving from the more recent film to the older one, I saw no need to reverse the order. Certainly there is no intent to imply that *Convoy* represents the completion or achievement of something lacking in *The Ballad of Cable Hogue* and is, therefore, a superior film.

II—Religious Thematics

It is well known that Peckinpah had intimate knowledge of the Bible and that religious and biblical references abound in his work.[2] And Peckinpah scholars have noted the distinction in his work between spiritual and material concerns.[3] A spiritual imperative is implied in the evocative title of the very first film that can truly be considered his own, *Ride the High Country*, and I would argue that the ability or (more frequently) inability of his characters to "ride the high country" constitutes the fundamental moral drama of film after Peckinpah film.

Religious and biblical reference serves as a principal means by which Peckinpah highlights the moral dilemmas and capabilities of his characters in *Convoy* and *The Ballad of Cable Hogue*. They are his most overtly religious films. The former has a hero with a strikingly Christ-like appearance who undergoes a death and resurrection near the film's end and whose rebirth takes place in the bus of a Jesus-freak preacher, the Reverend Joshua Duncan Sloane. The latter begins with the death and resurrection of Cable Hogue, who is provided with an apparent "miracle" by the Lord to whom he has been crying out in the desert. Following that, the film details Hogue's evolution into a god who transforms two acres of land into an empire over which he rules supreme. The film's religious dimension is kept constantly before us by a self-proclaimed "man of God," also named the Reverend Joshua Duncan Sloane, who with great rhetorical flourish insists on drawing biblical parallels to Cable's (as well as his own) actions.[4]

Although *Convoy* and *Cable Hogue* are similar in their emphasis on religious patterns and allusions, they are also to a large extent paired opposites—a narrative "positive" and "negative" of spiritual aspiration. *Convoy* seeks to tell a tale of genuine moral development culminating in transfiguration. *Cable Hogue* instead tells a story of materialist stasis culminating in death. Peckinpah conveys the radical opposition by exploiting different aspects of the Judaeo-Christian religious tradition in each.

III—Convoy

> "To know the universe itself as a road, as many roads, as roads for traveling souls"
> —Walt Whitman, "Song of the Open Road"

> "Life itself is a spiritual event"
> —The Reverend Joshua Duncan Sloane

Apologia

There are a number of reasons why it is risky to try to write seriously about *Convoy*. Both the characters, with their CB handles like "Rubber Duck," and the action seem more comic book than real. Moreover, the characters tend to vacillate between cartoon figures and commentators on political and social problems who, we must assume, are to be taken seriously. This creates significant problems of tone, compounded by the acting, which, especially on the part of Kris Kristofferson and Ali McGraw, is pretty dreadful. However, my concern with the film is not dramatic but conceptual, so for reasons that will become apparent, I will ask the reader to suspend disbelief and consider issues other than tone, acting, and dramatic impact.

It also seems risky to take the film seriously because (a) it was a troubled project at a moment when Peckinpah was in crisis; (b) he himself commented negatively on his level of involvement ("I haven't done one good day's work on this picture"—Weddle 1994, 517); and (c) final editing was taken out of his hands. In short, both Peckinpah and the project were, in many ways, out of control. However, this is more characteristic than not of a Peckinpah production, since he was almost always an alcoholic working over budget and in conflict with producers. And even when his substance abuse escalated from alcohol to cocaine during the making of *Bring Me the Head of Alfredo Garcia* (1974), he demonstrated an uncanny ability to produce coherent work.[5] Moreover, while on the one hand demeaning his work on *Convoy*, Peckinpah also said, on the basis of the shoot, "... I thought it had the chance of being one of my best movies" (Fine 1991, 318). And while the final editing was indeed taken over by the studio, this was true of the majority of his films. Moreover, as supervising editor Graeme Clifford said, "The fact that the film was taken away was ... really a nonevent. Sam was still involved.... We were in communication throughout. I was trying to cut according to his wishes. It was pretty well finished by the time he left" (Fine 1991, 319). All things considered, then, and despite the film's dramatic failings, I do not feel it justifiable to dismiss *Convoy* out of hand as unworthy of serious consideration. In fact, a close look at the film tells us a great deal about the director's work and world view and, even more important, about the shaping influences for each.

Convoy and American Tradition

As the root meaning of its title suggests, *Convoy* is a film about "moving together." It conspires to ever greater harmony as disparate truckers fuse into an ever larger and more cohesive and powerful social unit, largely on the open road, that ultimately comes to involve, via the media and politicians, all American society. This vision of ever expanding, transcending harmony is realized through two basic processes: the transformation of law or external control into self-direction and the evolution of mere physical motion into moral and spiritual action.

As my reference to the open road is meant to suggest, *Convoy* clearly situates itself within American literary tradition. As noted above, Seydor (1980, chaps. 6 and 7; 1997, chaps. 7 and 8) links all Peckinpah's work to this tradition, noting the director's familiarity and ideological compatibility with a range of writers from the American Transcendentalists (Emerson, Whitman, Thoreau) to those of the twentieth century (most obviously Hemingway). In terms of the former and apropos of *Convoy*, Seydor (1997, 363) notes that "the ... idea of transcendence ... is never far from [Peckinpah's] concerns." Also apropos of *Convoy*, Seydor cites the expansionist tendency at the heart of American writing: "Emerson's central idea ... is ever to continue to get outside a limited frame of reference to a wider frame of reference, and every American writer after him took it up in one way or another" (1997, 315). While Seydor generally gives precedence to Emerson in his discussion of Peckinpah, I am inclined, at least with *Convoy*, to emphasize Whitman, partly because of the "open road," but also because of the film's emphasis on the common man; the "rude tongue" of its CB "poetics"; its loving, hyperbolic embrace of prosaic subject matter;[6] and its vision of America as an irresistible, unitive, spiritual, democratic force—a becoming-one-with-everything in radical equality and harmony.

It is this last quality that links *Convoy* most directly to Whitman as self-proclaimed poet of the American dream. One of Whitman's editions of *Leaves of Grass* appeared in 1876 partly, as he himself put it, "to celebrate ... the first Centennial of our New World Nationality [i.e., the United States]" (Whitman 1973, 747). A fact that I have never seen addressed in Peckinpah criticism is that *Convoy* was conceived as a project in 1976, the year of the American Bicentennial. And though it took two years for the film to be completed and released, it is clearly made in the shadow of this major historical moment. With its revisiting of important issues and images from contemporaneous American history: Vietnam and Watergate (topics referred or alluded to by various truckers); Kent State (reprised in the calling out of the National Guard in the film); Woodstock and Monterey (the festival atmosphere of the campsite outside Albuquerque); the oil crisis and recession (the "double nickel" or 55-mile-an-hour speed limit), *Convoy*—like the Bicentennial itself—was an attempt to recover and extol the American dream, to resurrect Whitman's America, as it were, following years of turmoil, paralysis, and shame.

From Law to Self-Direction

The transformation of external control (the law in all its repressive negativity) into self-motivation, internalized order, can be seen in the changing relation of Sheriff Lyle Wallace and other authority figures to the convoy. At the beginning, Lyle is in total control. By the end of the Arizona phase he has been temporarily neutralized by a rebellion of truckers. Then in New Mexico he is replaced by two embodiments of authority—Chief Stacy *Love* and Governor *Has-kins*—whose last names reflect an emergent law of community and interrelation rather than of domination. Under their lenient rule, the convoy begins to develop initiative, particularly through the emergence of a leader of its own: Rubber Duck. By the end of the New Mexico phase, Duck and his companions have begun to make crucial decisions without regard for legal implications, and as they move into Texas, they take the law into their own hands. They engage in revolution (versus mere rebellion in Arizona) in the town of Alvarez, whose name evokes the memory of Juan Alvarez, a lifelong revolutionary who sought to keep Mexico free of the foreign rule of Spain, the United States, and France. At Alvarez, they overthrow Lyle and free a fellow trucker, Spider Mike, from Lyle's authority. Immediately after, the convoy proves able to function not only free of the law but free of Duck's authority. En route to Mexico, they are separated from him and become involved in a potentially explosive incident when Love Machine's truck nearly hits several schoolchildren. Although police officers abound at the scene, the truckers resolve the problem without their interference, exhibiting a coolness and self-restraint that had earlier been lacking. (Authority is not merely irrelevant, it's positively dangerous in this scene; the near accident is caused not by Love Machine but by an adult supervisor dressed in a khaki uniform.) In the final bridge confrontation in Texas, though Lyle has reappeared as a menacing force, he functions only as a means to Duck's own end. Duck uses him as an occasion for "martyrdom," through whom he can save the other convoyers[7] and, simultaneously, radically transform or "save" himself. Now Lyle functions as merely the necessary external reflection of Duck's inner powers of self-direction. Finally, back in New Mexico, Lyle is, effectively, united with the convoy. Not only does he join with it in a memorial service for Duck, he becomes fully bound in spirit when he responds not with aggression but with uproarious laughter to Duck's sudden reappearance.

The transformation and assimilation of external authority (law) is reflected in the growth of Rubber Duck. In Arizona, he is nearly as dissociated and controlling as Lyle. However, as he becomes involved with both the convoy and Melissa, he becomes increasingly open and self-sacrificing. He agrees to represent the convoy to Governor Haskins, then he risks his freedom to save Mike. Most important, when he martyrs himself at the bridge to Mexico, he deliberately allows all remnants of his former authoritarian self to be destroyed. In effect, he kills himself off as "Rubber Duck"—his *persona* as a self-protective, macho loner. This is clear from the fact that in confronting Lyle and certain death, he ritualistically adopts his Rubber Duck role—donning his dark glasses, expelling Melissa from the cab, and playing the stereotypical Western hero en route to the final showdown. It's even clearer when he reappears, completely transformed, in New Mexico. Gone is his rig—the locus and symbol throughout of his masculine power—and gone also are his dark clothing, his sunglasses, and his forbidding distance.

The gradual integration of Rubber Duck can be traced through his changing physical relation to the other truckers. At the beginning, he is entirely on his own. Rather quickly, he establishes CB contact with Love Machine and Spider Mike, then at the end of the Arizona phase he is at the head of the growing convoy. Having become fully engaged in New Mexico, he lines up not at the head but rather with truckers on either side as he prepares to overthrow Lyle in Texas.[8] When he reappears in New Mexico in the final sequence, he is completely assimilated—seated in the bus of the Reverend Joshua Duncan Sloane, which has come to serve as the convoy's spiritual center.

From Body or Matter to Spirit

The process of spiritualization in *Convoy* derives not only from Peckinpah's intimate engagement with the Bible and Christian religious tradition. It is linked, I would suggest, to his assimilation of literary models as well. Within Christianity, the movement beyond body or matter to spirit has historically been dualistic, Manichean, requiring the rejection of the former as evil in favor of the latter as the only route to salvation. However, European Romanticism and its heir (in many ways), American Transcendentalism, reject the dualistic aspects of Christian spirituality, seeing the route to spiritualization as a matter of transformation with and through the physical rather than in denial of it. The material world is not abandoned but remade through the agency of the imagination into a spiritual or symbolic as well as physical "real." (The image, in opposition to the thing or the fact, is a principal tool of the imagination in this enterprise.) The real thus becomes "enlightened" both in terms of illumination and in terms of casting off the heaviness of matter. Particularly within American thought, motion and, ultimately, speed, become fundamental to this, as both imply lightness, spirit, the defeat of gravity. This obviously is central to the vision of *Convoy*. I would also note that, since both the image and motion are effective tools for "spiritualizing" the "real," the moving image, or film, is an ideal medium for communicating this process, something Peckinpah tries to accentuate by aligning the movement of the convoy with the movement of his cinematic imagination.

("Spiritual," as should be clear above, is interchangeable with "imaginative." However, I will emphasize the former in discussing *Convoy* because of the religious symbolism, resurrection in particular, and because of the aptness, within the film's moral economy, of the Reverend Joshua Duncan Sloane's pronouncement "Life itself is a spiritual event.")

As with virtually everything else in *Convoy*, the process of spiritualization can be charted through the characters' movement from state to state. In Arizona, life is almost solely physical. Sex (between Duck and Violet) and violence (the truck-stop rebellion) predominate, and the formation of the convoy is little more than the physical aggregation of bodies and trucks. In New Mexico, mental activity begins to dominate. (As the truckers cross into New Mexico, a billboard designates it the "Land of Enchantment.") Here physical motion actually comes to a stop as the convoy becomes the object of curiosity, inquiry, debate. More than that, it becomes a symbol. Society sees it as an embodiment of freedom and self-expression, and for that reason Governor Haskins sees it as a means of furthering his political ambitions. The truckers themselves begin to analyze the significance of the convoy, speculating as to the motives and "injustices" that gave rise to it. (Duck himself becomes noticeably contemplative in discussions with Melissa and Love Machine as they are camped outside Albuquerque.) Decision-making replaces mere blind reaction, and the truckers too begin to relate symbolically: turning the liberation of Spider Mike, whom most of them have never seen or met, into a unifying cause. Now the convoy is joined not just in body but in spirit, as is emphasized when several truckers reach the same decision (to renounce amnesty and free Mike) independently, rather than in a group.

In Texas, physical and mental activity are united as moral action through the revolution in Alvarez (a "peaceful" revolution, significantly, in which no one is killed or seriously wounded). Moreover, moral action, which is initially directed at the world, becomes directed at the self (transformation becomes self-transformation). This occurs both when the convoyers become autonomous for the first time following the near accident and when Duck undergoes radical change through martyrdom at the hands of Lyle.

Finally, back in New Mexico, moral action and self-transformation give way to miraculous creation, creation *ex nihilo*. Life becomes "divine" and love—"convoying" or "moving together" in the richest possible sense—is fully realized. To see this, we must recognize three subtle yet crucial points. First, in sacrificing himself at the bridge, Duck has become a lover (i.e., self-transcendent) in the most profound of ways. Second, in commemorating Duck's life and death, his world (composed of the convoyers, Governor Haskins, and society at large) has assimilated Duck's spirit as its own motive force. Third, so powerful is the urge to recreate Duck through commemoration that the world not only memorializes him, it resurrects him. Born out of the festivities (there is no evidence or even remote possibility that Duck has escaped at the bridge and no suggestion that he existed at the beginning of the memorial service) is the miracle of Duck's centered image. As Duck is reborn and as *Convoy* draws to a close, words spoken earlier by the Reverend Joshua Duncan Sloane become a prophecy fulfilled. "Life itself is a spiritual event." And, in the context of their own changed relation to life, as the truckers head back at film's end to the open road the highway has become, to revise the title of Peckinpah's first landmark film, "high way."

The Religious Model

The nature of moral and spiritual development in *Convoy* virtually assures that its religious dimension be rooted in the New Testament. The film's vision is particularly in tune with that of St. Paul, the most profoundly theological of the New Testament authors. Paul asserted that Christ's death freed man from both the law and the flesh and enabled him to be reborn in love, in spirit, and in freedom. He saw the life of Christ as a call to individuation—challenging man to free himself from the authority embodied by an Old Testament God and Law for self-redemption through personal growth. Thus he saw the life of Christ as a model for moral revolution. Finally, he saw Christ's mission as transforming the Old Testament quest for a kingdom on earth (the establishment of a Jewish nation) into a quest to establish a kingdom of the spirit.

Clearly, as *Convoy* internalizes law as self-direction, supplants authority with revolution and individuation, and evolves from mere physical community to a union of minds and souls, the film comes to fulfill the Pauline, New Testament vision of moral possibility. More obviously, the film derives its principal religious pattern—death and rebirth—from the New Testament. This pattern occurs not only in Duck's experience, but in every major facet of characterization. The fact that the truckers are defined not by given names but by created CB handles suggests a world of death-and-resurrection from the start. "Old Iguana" provides explicit and comic impetus to the theme when he responds to the question "Where were you born?" with his own question: "Originally?" Then we see Lyle Wallace undergo a series of deaths and rebirths. He is knocked unconscious in Arizona and quickly ("miraculously") recovers. He disappears as a physical presence in New Mexico and reemerges as a symbol of repression in the minds of the truckers. He is freed of that identity through the revolution in Texas and is reborn at the bridge as an agent of transformation. Likewise, Spider Mike dies off as a physical presence in order to become a cause and symbol of liberation. In short, Rubber Duck's death and resurrection is only the culminative and most striking example in a film whose structure and meaning are built on this New Testament motif.

IV—*The Ballad of Cable Hogue*

> "All my life I've been scared of . . . livin.'"
> —Cable Hogue

The Story

Once we enter the world of Cable Hogue, we encounter a radically different moral climate. The basic problems that limit Cable and eventually do him in are established in the opening minutes. He is betrayed and left to die in the desert by his partners Taggart and Bowen. Reduced to a state of utter need, he prays to the Lord for water, submits to Him when none seems forthcoming, miraculously "receives" water at the moment of surrender, then—having gulped his fill—collapses into unconsciousness. His partners' acts destroy all natural relation between Cable and his world. (He was, with appropriate respect for the creature, about to kill a Gila monster to share for supper with his friends when he was betrayed.) In addition, both their acts and those of a tyrannical God who must strip Cable to abject dependence before granting water[9] breed humiliation and loss of self-respect. (During Cable's "trial," the

Lord is associated not with generosity but with absolute and arbitrary authority.) As a result, Cable loses his capacity for trust and love, his confidence in the rightness of things. Gone is the life-affirming faith that is essential to the spirit of adventure and that allows one to feel that he or she can be self-determining while at the same time remaining open. Instead he is left with an instinctive passion for self-protection. When he awakens, he is consumed (unawares) with a desire never to be victimized or made helpless again, and he sets out on a career of control, possession, and isolation. Having lost the ability to see life organically, as the fluid interaction between man and a responsive world, he comes to view it imperialistically, as the domination of an alien environment. He develops, as will become clear, a God complex. He turns the water hole he has discovered into a "secured claim" (a phrase used in the film to describe Cable's land), then he turns his claim into a commercial enterprise, "Cable Springs," where no one is allowed water without payment. For the final two-thirds of the movie, he never ventures beyond his one-man kingdom.

Possessed by his need for self-preservation and protection, Cable resists all temptations to become vulnerable and loving. Though he is strongly attracted to Hildy, he places barriers between himself and her. The first is Cable Springs itself. When he is first about to make love to her, he suddenly rushes away, announcing quite tellingly: "I've got to mark my boundaries." Here he is not so much avoiding Hildy (he hasn't really fallen for her yet) as revealing his predisposition to put boundaries ahead of self-exposure. Later, when he comes to love Hildy—and when Josh confronts him with the fact—Cable *does* begin avoiding her. We never again see him away from his "kingdom," and the last two times he and Hildy are together she must come to him.

The second and more subtle barrier is the revenge code he develops and that keeps him at Cable Springs when Hildy goes off to San Francisco. The notion of revenge originates in the opening scene, when Cable tells Taggart and Bowen that he will live to repay their treachery. However, at this point it is much more an instinctive reaction to the moment than the expression of a deep-seated intention. Moreover, as Cable discovers water and begins to create his kingdom, there is no suggestion that revenge has a particularly strong hold on him. In fact it is never mentioned. It is reintroduced—and becomes a serious motive—only when Cable is confronted and threatened by the fact that he loves Hildy.[10]

Cable's scheme to get back at Taggart and Bowen is much more than a mere excuse for staying at the Springs. In fact I would argue (in contrast to all other interpretations of the film that I have read) that it emerges from a need to dominate that grows in direct proportion to Cable's vulnerability to Hildy. The more he senses a loss of control through involvement with her, the more he must create a means of reasserting that control elsewhere. Revenge becomes a ritual or game (Cable's version of the Hemingway bullring) whereby he can prove his manhood and restore his sense of power and self-possession. Eventually, of course, revenge wins out over romance, "war" over intimacy, masculine aggression over feminine connection. Hildy goes off to San Francisco, Cable kills Taggart and makes Bowen his lackey, and by the time Hildy returns it's too late for their love—a fact emphasized by the swift inevitability of Cable's death upon Hildy's reappearance, as he is run over by a car. In fact, the role Hildy plays in Cable's death serves as a kind of ironic justification for his elaborate and subtle avoidance of involvement.

As all the above would suggest, unlike Rubber Duck, Cable never learns to get beyond egoism or a sense of self based on possession and control. This may seem, initially, to be contradicted by the fact that he spares Bowen and cedes Cable Springs to him upon Hildy's return. However, the conditions under which his "generosity" emerges undercut the purity of the latter, a point that becomes clear through a comparison of turning points in *Convoy* and *The Ballad of Cable Hogue*. Whereas Duck is spiritually liberated through willingly surrendering to death (ritualistically and sacrificially killing off the "Rubber Duck" persona in all its alienated egoism at the bridge), Cable is "freed" only at the moment in which he can exert total control over Taggart and Bowen. He traps them, terrorizes them with snakes, and kills the taunting and resistant Taggart.

Of course there are other symbolic explanations for Cable's death, as well: e.g., he has outlived his time and cannot exist in a world of urbanization and industrialization symbolized by Hildy and the car. And his death reflects Peckinpah's thoroughly ironic vision of an irrational world in which a man is killed (a) at the moment in which he has seemingly changed his ways, (b) by trying to save the life of someone who has tried to kill him (he pushes Bowen out of the way of the oncoming auto, only to get hit by it himself), and (c) by his own hand (he himself has accidentally released the hand brake). And all this after having seemed to have been "chosen" by God or destiny in the opening scene for extra-special salvation. However, this multiplicity of meanings, as Cable's death signifies in many ways simultaneously, points only to the complexity of Peckinpah's moral rendering, not to the sole validity of any single interpretation.

Cable's failure to let go of power as the basis of identity is also a failure to let go of possessions, i.e., those things (including Taggart and Bowen) over which he must exercise power. (In this light, even his ceding of Cable Springs functions, somewhat paradoxically, as continuing self-identification through possessions.) In other words, he fails to let go of the material world and undergo the kind of process of spiritualization that occurs in *Convoy*. He remains trapped in a principally physical existence. Not only does he stay tied to a single geographical place, his life becomes characterized by physical acts: providing water (and later food), killing Taggart, getting hit by a car, dying. The extent to which Cable is fundamentally "stuck" is clearly expressed by his relationship to motion (in obvious contrast to the truckers in *Convoy*, whose fundamental purpose, as Duck notes at one point, is "to keep moving").[11] He is not only tied to his water hole, using revenge as an excuse not to budge, but he makes money out of having other people stop there. And, most graphically, he is killed off by the newest instrument of motion in his world. Related to his stasis is his inability (again in contrast to the truckers) to become self-generating—a fault he seems to have acknowledged by responding with such wonder to the fact that Hildy's car "move[s] all by itself."

The Religious Model

In moving (paradigmatically, not chronologically), from a story of love (*Convoy*) to one of control and power (*The Ballad of Cable Hogue*), from revolution to domination, from violence that liberates to eye-for-eye vengeance, from the creation of a spiritual community to the staking out of a kingdom solely of this earth, we substitute an "old testament" for the "new." Accordingly, the religious imagery, patterns, and characterization of *Cable Hogue* are primarily derived from the Old Testament. Cable's initial trial in the desert is distinctly Jobian.[12] His water hole is described by Josh as a "cactus Eden," and he himself is called a "prophet of old" in Josh's funeral oration.

Most important, the notion of the divine in the film is distinctively Old Testament. We have no suggestion of a Christ-like presence within the world. Instead, the Lord is an omnipotent force outside the characters from whom they must beg assistance and salvation. This is clear at the beginning in Cable's entreaties for water, and it's clear at the end in the funeral sermon—addressed entirely to an absent, external authority. It's most significantly evident when Cable, seeking, as Rubber Duck did, to become divine, aspires not to the qualities of Christ but to those of an Old Testament deity.

Basically, Cable tries to become the figure to whom he initially prays (part of his quest never to be dependent again). When he awakens, he immediately takes upon himself the principal role previously played by the Lord:

dispenser of water. And, having assumed the Lord's powers, he never again feels called upon to pray to Him. As master of the water hole and, later, as supreme architect of revenge, he is clearly and pointedly defined by two Old Testament quotations voiced by other characters in the film: "The Lord giveth and the Lord taketh away," and "Vengeance is mine saith the Lord." Eventually, he becomes so godlike that people kneel before him begging to be saved: Josh from a cuckolded husband, Bowen from Cable himself (Seydor 1997, 228). During the revenge scene he is omnipresent yet invisible, all-knowing, and all-powerful, with absolute authority over life and death. He even visits a plague of snakes upon Taggart and Bowen.

Consistent with the Old Testament trajectory of *The Ballad of Cable Hogue,* suggestions of resurrection, though not absent, diminish in frequency and quality as the film progresses. The only potentially genuine death and rebirth occurs at the very beginning, and the self-protective identity with which Cable is "reborn" is the very thing that precludes real redemption. The next suggestion of recreation occurs when "Cable Hogue" becomes "Cable Springs" through Josh's naming of Cable's cactus Eden. Here, in a sense, Cable is transformed, yet the transformation is from person to place, from individual to business enterprise. The third instance of renewal is the absurd "Revival Meeting" that is in progress during Cable's first trip to town. It ends abruptly when Cable collapses the tent, and though the tent is restored by the same evening, the revival itself is not. After that, rebirth and renewal are replaced by revenge as Cable seeks to redeem the past not through self-creation but through violence done to others. As this occurs, burial (emphasizing death without new life) takes on increased importance. Cable digs the grave of a traveler who has refused to pay for water. He threatens to bury Josh if *he* drinks without paying. He then buries his money as a means of trapping Taggart and Bowen, then orders Bowen to bury the dead Taggart. The conclusive burial, of course, becomes that of Cable himself.

There is one ironic form of resurrection near the film's end: Josh's funeral sermon, which serves, in a sense, as the "Ballad of Cable Hogue." However, it serves merely to recreate Cable as a false identity (something Josh had done earlier in transforming "Cable Hogue" into "Cable Springs"), killing Cable off, once and for all, as genuine figure. The sermon's inauthenticity becomes clear the moment Hogue's death is revealed, when Josh switches suddenly from a relatively accurate accounting of his life to blatant exaggeration.

As Josh's sermon suggests and Cable's death confirms, Cable has failed to become *truly* divine. Tied to an earthly kingdom and to an ethic of possessiveness and control, he has remained all too human. This is borne out in the last words of both Josh and the movie: "Take him, Lord, but knowing Cable, I suggest you do not take him lightly." With the kind of subtlety that often characterizes Peckinpah dialogue, we are informed that, unlike Rubber Duck, Cable has not become "light." Heavy and dark with mortality, he has fallen victim to mere bodily death, without chance of resurrection.

It is important to note that the tone of *The Ballad of Cable Hogue* is not as gloomy as the above discussion might suggest. In focusing on Cable's limitations and demise, I have of necessity emphasized the film's tragic dimension. For the most part, *Cable Hogue* is a comic movie, made with much of the same exuberant love as was *Convoy*. Moreover, its comic spirit is related directly to its religious content and, in particular, to the two distinct Old Testament components of Cable's character. First of all, as Job-like he is at the mercy of external forces, hopelessly incompetent when confronted both by the world at large and by his own emotional vulnerability. Secondly, when he tries to resolve his Jobian predicament by becoming a god, he is at best a petty tyrant whose attempts at control, especially early in the film, are as comic as his ineptitude. (Actually, they become part of it.) Both as man and as god, he is a foolish, albeit winning, figure.

Ultimately, of course, the comic spirit of *Cable Hogue* is dissolved. The sudden shift in lighting, tone, and emphasis that accompanies Cable's death makes the final moments quite sad. Having laughed with and at Cable, we now mourn his loss. More than that, we are forced by the film's abruptly downbeat ending to determine why, for all his endearing qualities, Cable had to end as he did. Thus, as Terence Butler puts it: "For all its warmth and lyricism, *The Ballad of Cable Hogue* remains as much an open wound as any of Sam Peckinpah's other movies" (Butler 1979, 68).

V—Politics and Ideology

While the above will, I hope, contribute to ongoing revaluation of the conceptual sophistication and seriousness of Peckinpah's work, I would like to conclude by addressing certain political and ideological aspects of the two films, within the contexts I have established above, thus engaging with areas of contemporary criticism that have, for the most part, avoided significant discussion of Peckinpah's work.

First of all, a note on Peckinpah's films in the light of feminism. I find his films generally problematic in their representation of women. I don't, unlike Seydor (1997, 224–25) find that *The Ballad of Cable Hogue* redeems Peckinpah from accusations of misogyny. And Peckinpah has done himself no favors with his intentionally outrageous and provocative comments about women in various interviews. (See especially Murray 1972.) However, I find some of his films—*The Ballad of Cable Hogue* included—among the most extraordinary representations, and oftentimes critiques, of masculinity in American film (and literature). For this reason alone I find them worthy of serious attention.

But rather than concentrate on gender (except for a brief moment later in conjunction with *Convoy*), I would like to address the cultural and political critique of America within *The Ballad of Cable Hogue* and the ideological limitations of *Convoy* as an affirmation of an ideal America.

It has been noted that *The Ballad of Cable Hogue* functions, in part, as a critique of capitalism. For example, Bliss says: "The film makes it quite plain that materialism's greatest incarnation, capitalism, is an obsessive disease that compels the practitioner to treat virtually all things, whether goods or people, as commodities" (Bliss 1993, 130). The centrality of capitalism to America, the importance of the American flag in the film,[13] and the movie's rendering of the passing of the West (a definitive moment in American history, especially on the level of symbol and myth) make it inevitable that the film be perceived, at least in part, as commentary on the United States. In fact, in addition to its critique of capitalism, the film offers an extraordinary mirror of certain American traits:

—a blend of isolationism and expansionism (living in the desert but also taking part of it over) that seems contradictory until one notes that both derive from a desire for complete control over one's world;
—paranoia and a desire for revenge deriving from some originary wound (a commonplace in American literature and film, hence in American self-representation);
—obsession with private property.

Because of this, it is possible to employ the film and its tragic ending as a vehicle for addressing the profound moral failure of America itself. For the America Peckinpah portrays in *Cable Hogue* is founded not on a passion for discovery, adventure, and change (the proselytizing myth of America) but on the need to found an empire (politically a nation, psychologically the private bounded self), to hide within it, and to respond to everything from outside as a threat and with violence. Add in the wound-based paranoia that gets projected onto the outside, and the result is a need for total domination in any encounter with the other. Cable, for the most part, embodies American inwardness. We need to include a figure such as David Sumner (*Straw Dogs*

1971) to flesh out the portrait with an isolationist turned inside out. In conjunction, they point with remarkable accuracy to the vacillation between isolationism and imperialism, protectionism and global market domination, that has characterized America in the twentieth century. They may well explain Peckinpah's take on American involvement in Vietnam, the use of the National Guard at Kent State, Nixon's paranoia and aggression, Reagan's cowboy imperialism, and a host of other things that clearly provide the backdrop for much of Peckinpah's work.

When we turn to *Convoy*, we have quite a different situation. Its end result is not a critique of America. Rather, as I noted earlier, *Convoy* seeks, in the light of the Bicentennial, to envision an America that fulfills both Peckinpah's and Whitman's notion of an ideal democracy. And while I sought to present a rather seamless view of how, via its New Testament vision of ego-transcendence and rebirth, it achieves this, I would now like to open the film and my reading of it to certain ideological concerns, related to the film's incarnation of Christianity and of Whitman and, more broadly, the American literary tradition. First and most obviously, there is the issue of masculinity. In its reworking of both New Testament and Whitmanesque models of spiritual transformation, *Convoy* remains firmly centered in the Western, American, and Hollywood tradition of the male hero. Linked to this, of course, is its lingering emphasis on the individual, because, though alienated individualism is presumably jettisoned via Duck's death at the bridge, the film's pilgrim's progress is articulated principally in terms of a single character and leader rather than in terms of "the people" (in contrast to, for example, the Soviet cinema of the 1920s).

In the light of recent discussions of politics, gender, Hollywood, and Western culture, what I have just said is fairly obvious. However, there is a more subtle ideological issue at work in *Convoy*, linked to its Transcendentalist ethos of becoming one with the universe. As commentators on American literature have begun to note, while the dissolving of the self into the other seems to offer an ideal of social and spiritual connectedness, there is a very thin line between dissolving into and becoming the other, between selflessness and appropriation.[14] Addressing the relationship of self and other in the work of Emerson, Whitman, and Henry James and taking us back, in a sense, to my discussion of *The Ballad of Cable Hogue*, Quentin Anderson notes that such writers resort to an "absolutism of the self" (Anderson 1971, ix): "This absolutism involves an extreme passivity [e.g., the dissolution of the self into other], which is complemented by, must be complemented by, the claim of the imperial self to mastery of what has almost overwhelmed it" (ix–x). Related to this, in my mind, is the ease with which openness in someone like Whitman so easily turns into conquest. "I see the cities of the earth and make myself at random a part of them" (Whitman 1973, 144) can readily become "the east and the west are mine, and the north and the south are mine" (Whitman 1973, 151).[15]

This fine line between surrender or openness and the desire to dominate becomes exacerbated when stories of adventure are, as so often happens in American literature and film, myths of foundation: i.e., representing the establishment of a new society. Here (and this is a recurrent issue in the Western) the urge for discovery can quickly transmogrify into the need to occupy, define, and control space. "Walt" (as Whitman persona) or, for that matter, Rubber Duck, can swiftly become Cable Hogue. Ultimately, then, differences between Old Testament and New, between *Convoy* and *The Ballad of Cable Hogue*, may not ultimately be all that firm, particularly if the myth of dying to the self and being reborn as other is just an act of self-deception masking the same old will to power that underlies more obvious acts of expansion and conquest. What form of megalomania might underlie the will to be or to feel at one with the universe? Is it possible to read the empowerment of Duck and the truckers in their collective experience of death and rebirth not as a lessening of aggression but as its apotheosis in "divine" mastery?[16] The imperialist histories of the two sources from which Peckinpah's salvific vision emanates, Christianity and the United States, do not offer strong reassurances to the contrary.

At the same time, it is important to note that analyses of imperialist psychology in nineteenth-century American literature involve a good deal of reading into the past what has happened in the present. And they may well ignore important historical issues, such as the fact that Emerson and Whitman were still very much writing as post-colonialists, seeking to articulate the independence and self-determination of a society once ruled by Britain. The "absolutism of the self" had its unique political and psychological role and perhaps even justification within this cultural enterprise. Moreover, to simply hitch Peckinpah on to American Transcendentalism is to ignore *his* post-colonial moment, in which he is trying to imagine his society free of an imperialist heritage most recently evident in Vietnam.

Clearly, an adequate examination of the issues I have noted here would require a different essay, or perhaps a monograph. I hope that in raising them I have succeeded in opening out Peckinpah's work to a kind of analysis it receives infrequently and usually in a negative light. His films are anything but simple or reductive. They deserve serious ideological attention because of the problems they raise and, even more, because of the way in which they raise them. Even a film such as *Convoy*, while less satisfying aesthetically than a *Wild Bunch* or *Cable Hogue*, can prove immensely satisfying as a tool for examining masculinity and Christian mythmaking, American Transcendentalism and foundation stories, American post-colonial representations past and present, the United States as myth and mystification—in short, a host of issues that remain fundamental to understanding not just one director's films but the vast cultural and intellectual environments that they help chart.

Notes

1. See Nichols (1976 and 1985) for a comprehensive anthology of film criticism and theory, focusing largely on post-1968 developments, including the ideological critique of American film auteurs such as John Ford. See also Casetti (1999), Easthope (1994), and Cook and Bernink (1999).

2. Seydor (1997, 345) notes: "He could hold his own in a scholarly discussion of the Bible, which he read all the way through, committing parts of it to memory."

3. For example, Bliss: "Just as money and monetary references function in [*The Ballad of Cable Hogue*] as major examples of life's material aspects, emotional and sexual longings, when they are allied with genuine tenderness, stand in for the truly spiritual aspects of existence" (1993, 132).

4. Bliss (1993, 127 ff.) and Seydor (1997, 215 ff.), among others, have identified with great precision the religious dimension of *The Ballad of Cable Hogue*.

5. Although *Bring Me the Head of Alfredo Garcia* was not well received by the critics, it has recently undergone well-deserved reconsideration (Fine 1991, 274; Bliss 1993, 251 ff.). Interestingly, and cocaine aside, Peckinpah has affirmed his complete satisfaction with the filmmaking process—i.e., his level of authorial control: "I did it exactly the way I wanted to. Good or bad, like it or not, that was my film" (Simmons 1982, 208).

6. Whitman is better able to celebrate rudeness and prosaicness because of the distancing effects of language. They are acceptable as concepts communicated "at one remove" through words. However, when they become immediate realities, thrust directly in our face via the concrete imagery of film, they are more threatening and more readily susceptible to being easily dismissed as trivial—hence part of the "unappeal," to critics and to the public, of *Convoy*.

7. Lyle has made it clear all along that he is not interested in conquering the convoy as a whole—just Duck—and implicit in Duck's actions is his own sense that in sacrificing himself to Lyle he will free other truckers from Lyle's vengeful pursuit.

8. The temporary physical separation of Duck from the others in Texas might seem to suggest a breakdown in the process of integration. However, such is not the case. The crucial thing here is that, though Duck and the convoyers are separated in body, they are more unified than ever in spirit. This is accentuated by the nature of the CB contact between them and by the convoyers' response to what they intuit as Duck's death at the river.

9. Unlike Seydor, I do not believe there is a God actually at work in Hogue's world, just Cable's notion of a power to whom he can pray and so be granted a miracle. Nonetheless, this perception of an all-powerful, tyrannical deity *is* at work, dictating not only Cable's response to his "trial," but his later actions in the film.

10. Another indication that Cable is not overly concerned with revenge early on is the fact that Josh, not Cable, reintroduces the subject.

11. Duck's comment is a bit flippant at the time but it does, nonetheless, underline a crucial dimension of his story of spiritualization. Peckinpah's "morality of motion" is, of course, clearly expressed in the famous line from *The Wild Bunch*—"If they move, kill 'em"—which underscores the negative and ultimately tragic climate of that film.

12. Seydor (1980 and 1997) and Bliss both note this.

13. The use of the flag is, I think, even more complex than has generally been noted, especially in the scene in which it is given to Hogue to display at Cable Springs. Critics generally see this as a moment of pure patriotism on Peckinpah's part, because when Cable asks, "What's it gonna cost me?" and the answer is "Nothing," it seems to imply a moment beyond capitalism. However, the flag is given to Cable only because he has established the material worth and usefulness of his land. Hence it has already cost him plenty. So I think we need to distinguish between Cable's innocent and naïve response to the moment and the more complex moral climate (i.e., the film itself) into which it is inserted.

14. This revision of American literature originates in large part with Anderson (1971) and has been carried on in Bercovitch and Jehlen (1986) and Fisher (1992).

15. I realize that in jumping from one poem to another and extracting lines from different moments within a poem's process I am playing a bit fast and loose with Whitman's poetry, but I do believe my quotations here are a true indication of the kind of contradictoriness or paradox that runs throughout his work in terms of openness to versus ownership of experience.

16. Another limitation to *Convoy* is suggested by Myra Jehlen in her discussion of the American "New World epic," a phrase that could be applied to the film. She notes the tendency of this literary form, and more particularly its authors, to end up in political and ideological tautology: "Having adopted their culture's *controlling* metaphor—"America" as synonym for human possibility—and having made this the ground of radical dissent, they effectually redefine radicalism as an affirmation of [America]. For the metaphor . . . does not transcend ideology. It portrays the American ideology, as all ideology yearns to be portrayed, in the transcendent colors of utopia. . . . Thus Whitman (in one view of *Democratic Vistas*) identifies the American future as utopia, and utopia, therefore, as the essence and telos of the American Way" (Bercovitch and Jehlen 1986, 434–35). In other words, if America is the solution to America the problem, where, after all, is the problem?

References

Anderson, Quentin. 1971. *The Imperial Self: An Essay in American Literary and Cultural History*. New York: Vintage Books.

Bercovitch, Sacvan, and Myra Jehlen, eds. 1986. *Ideology and Classic American Literature*. New York: Cambridge University Press.

Bliss, Michael. 1993. *Justified Lives: Morality and Narrative in the Films of Sam Peckinpah*. Carbondale: Southern Illinois University Press.

Butler, Terence. 1979. *Crucified Heroes: The Films of Sam Peckinpah*. London: Gordon Fraser.

Casetti, Francesco. 1999. *Theories of Cinema, 1945–1995*. Translated by Francesca Chiostri and Elizabeth Gard Bartolini-Salimbeni, with Thomas Kelso. Austin.: University of Texas Press.

Caughie, John, ed. 1981. *Theories of Authorship: A Reader*. London: Routledge.

Cook, Pam, and Mieke Bernink, eds. 1999. *The Cinema Book*. 2nd ed. London: BFI.

Easthope, Anthony. 1994. *Contemporary Film Theory*. London: Longmans.

Fine, Marshall. 1991. *Bloody Sam: The Life and Films of Sam Peckinpah*. New York: Donald I. Fine, Inc.

Fisher, Philip. 1992. "American Literary and Cultural Studies Since the Civil War." In *Redrawing the Boundaries: The Transformation of English and American Literary Studies*, edited by Stephen Goldblatt and Giles Gunn. New York: Modern Language Association of America.

Jehlen, Myra. 1986. "Afterword." In *Ideology and Classic American Literature*, edited by Sacvan Bercovitch and Myra Jehlen, 418–42. New York: Cambridge University Press.

Murray, William. 1972. "*Playboy* Interview: Sam Peckinpah." *Playboy* 19.8 (August): 72.

Nichols, Bill, ed. 1976, 1985. *Movies and Methods, An Anthology*. 2 vols. Berkeley: University of California Press.

Seydor, Paul. 1997. *Peckinpah: The Western Films: A Reconsideration*. Urbana: University of Illinois Press.

Sharrett, Christopher. 1999. "Peckinpah the Radical: The Politics of *The Wild Bunch*." In *Sam Peckinpah's* The Wild Bunch, edited by Stephen Prince. New York: Cambridge University Press.

Showalter, Elaine, ed. 1985. *New Feminist Literary Criticism: Essays on Women, Literature, and Society*. New York: Pantheon.

Simmons, Garner. 1982. *Peckinpah, a Portrait in Montage*. Austin: University of Texas Press.

Stimpson, Catharine R. 1977. *Sex, Gender, and American Culture*. New York: Praeger.

Warren, Joyce W., and Margaret Dickie, eds. 2000. *Challenging Boundaries: Gender and Periodization*. Athens: University of Georgia Press.

Weddle, David. 1994. *"If They Move—Kill 'Em!": The Life and Times of Sam Peckinpah*. New York: Grove Press.

Whitman, Walt. 1973. *Leaves of Grass*. A Norton Critical Edition, edited by Sculley Bradley and Harold W. Blodgett. New York: W. W. Norton & Company, Inc.

SEVEN

RICHARD HUTSON

Junior Bonner

OLD WEST/NEW WEST OR
THE ANTINOMIES OF THE FATHER

Sons, we say, are repetitions of their father. But we also note the inevitable differences between the brothers as well as between the brothers and the father. Not only repetition but also difference is at stake. How is difference possible? Only within the repetition of the same. One son goes one way, and the other son goes another way, but both are definitely sons of their father. One son repeats the father, with a difference, and the other son repeats the father, with a difference, and the two sons differ from each other, although their differences have a family resemblance, derivative, as they are, from the father. Perhaps this is to say that the father is an unstable figure who differs from himself.

We might want to claim that one brother is better than the other, that he is better because he repeats the father more faithfully or because he differs more markedly from the father as he rejects some embarrassing or outmoded features of his inheritance. There are good repetitions and bad repetitions. Or we expect the sons to be rivals to the father as well as rivals to each other, true or false claimants of the father. Such issues and problems constitute the narrative of *Junior Bonner*. What makes for the brilliance of such a narrative is its simplicity. The possible filiations between the father and his two sons have the near clarity of a logical exercise. A spectator may watch in awe before the narrative working out of such simplicity with an unfathomable depth. Such a narrative gathers a great many themes in the meaning of the West, as of 1972.

Vladimir Propp, the Russian folklorist, mentions "tales in which the heroes [brothers] part at a road marker" so that "each brother's fate may form a completely separate tale."¹ If Peckinpah, or his screen writer Jeb Rosebrook, who has to be given major credit for the complexities of this narrative,² was working from a memory of such a fairy tale, it would help us to understand the dilemma of the two brothers, perhaps also why they cannot join forces and interests and establish a regime of the brothers against the father. Or perhaps they do establish a weaker, divided regime of the brothers, whereby one captures the materialism and the other the idealism of the father. One steals the father's material goods, the other steals the father's ideological attributes. The one develops the father's idle or latent material wealth; the other repeats the father's rodeo or useless achievements, the ritualized masculine contest with an animal, the rodeo being "the direct outgrowth of the cattle industry . . . [which] serves to reflect and preserve that heritage."³ The focus in *Junior Bonner* is upon the older son, the rodeo rider. As Michael Bliss rightly notes, the film's point of view "compels us to identify with Junior" rather than with any other character.⁴ The film carries, thus, a strong argument in favor of the rodeo-rider brother at the expense of the land-developer brother, a position intensified by the iconic differences between Steve McQueen and Joe Don Baker. But there is actually a strong argument in the narrative in favor of the younger brother's position. The story of the younger son is his attempt to get the older brother to join him in his economic enterprise. If the brothers have separated over the father, split the inheritance and gone their separate ways, the younger brother claims to want to bring the two paths back together again. Beyond the surface strategies of the film, the narrative acknowledges that "the two types of repetition relate to each other" in such a way "that one can no more 'separate' them from each other" than one can distinguish between "the medicine and the poison, the good from the evil, the true from the false, the inside from the outside, the vital from the mortal, the first from the second."⁵ In the Bonner family history, with its members always fleeing from each other, the spokesperson for the fantasy of family togetherness is the little brother, even as he is responsible for transforming the western land and landscape. A viewer is tempted to take sides, against the little brother, but the narrative as a whole is a melancholy acceptance of the different possibilities for thinking about the West, about the past's relations to the present and future.

As we can see, however, the younger brother, Curly, has usurped the role of the father, turning his father into a child, turning him into the proverbial younger brother, just as Curly has also, in his mind, turned his older brother into a younger brother. As throwbacks to an older vision of the West, JR and his father, Ace, are really powerless against the more up-to-date possibilities of the West. Curly's usurpation hints at the illegitimacy of this new sense of the West, but if JR and Ace represent a more authentic West, a contemporary West with visible links to the past, the past that they represent is an absolute past, ineffective, vulnerable to a charge of being irrelevant to the present. In a sense, the rodeo might be indefensible, at best merely entertaining symbolism. Rodeo riders are just competing athletes.

What is especially amazing is that the father, without losing anything of his raucous complexity, does not seem to care, does not even notice, the usurpations. As himself an avatar of a legendary and archaic West, he is narcissistically oblivious to the struggle between the sons in their claim to something in which he has no interest, oblivious to the very history his chaotic flesh remembers. Ace is at once the excessive and the deficient father who has dispersed himself into his different and competing sons and continues on his own path. If the sons have divided their heritage, Ace is also always trying to figure out some way to exploit the sons in order to reclaim his own inheritance of drift and chaos. In the simplicity and complexity of their affiliations, this family of father and sons, along with the self-effacing women —mothers, wives, mistresses, one-night stands—seems to comprehend the legend, if not exactly the history, of the West. Ace embodies the legend since he is, albeit embarrassingly, vaguely recognized as a composite figure, but the very energy of his atavistic view of the world must generate, in part, his ability to forget the past. When a young woman asks him, "Are you JR's dad?" Ace's response is, "I used to be, didn't I, Roy?" Even the past of his fatherhood seems caught in an absolute past, unapproachable from the present. He is still going strong, without looking back. He has no nostalgia for the good old days. It appears that every action or design of his past life lives again, coexistent with the present. What he holds on to is his repetition compulsion, a past as a kind of Western unconscious, which he now translates as a future in Australia.

According to Patricia Limerick, "If Hollywood wanted to capture the emotional center of Western history, its movies would be about real estate. . . . The showdowns would occur in the land office or the courtroom; weapons would be deeds and lawsuits, not six-guns."[6] Theodore Roosevelt and other ranching figures in the Gilded Age always referred to cowboying as a "business."[7] And the Westerns of popular culture, beginning with Owen Wister's novel *The Virginian* (1902), presented their narratives as conflicts between genuine cowboys who are capable of becoming businessmen and false cowboys who are incapable of any kind of business sense unless they become outlaws, an inversion of business principles. Larry McMurtry presents this binary of two characters, the cowboy and the rancher, in *Leaving Cheyenne* (1963) when it may have looked, in l963, as if the cowboy and the businessman were no longer compatible. In popular film culture, this structure of elementary binaries has been used to convey a sense of the ideological possibilities of Western experience and identity. Moreover, in Hollywood, from its beginnings, the use of the binary opposition was seen as the most economical way for a narrative to convey the intended message of a film narrative.[8]

Junior Bonner takes on both of these issues in a classical and brilliant economy by presenting what appear to be opposing values in the two brothers, the rodeo entertainer and older brother, Junior or JR, and the land developer and younger brother, Curly, who refers to himself as "a United States businessman, and I'm proud of it." But it also adds the rich and deeply ambiguous presence/absence of the father, who combines the values of the two sons in an archaic but still incarnate synthesis. Somehow, the meaning of the West has undergone diremption, a splitting apart into sets of values that appear to be incompatible and that can now be represented by the divergent brothers, the older and the younger. The two responses to the Western heritage must be tied together in such a way that their separation seems a violent decision made somewhere in the past in the silent mysteries of a family history. Despite the best efforts of Curly to bring the fragmented family together, to celebrate the family as a loving entity, the individuals disperse again at the end.

An imaginary patriarchal synthesis has come apart of its own (historical) impetus, perhaps because of some contradiction within patriarchy or within the history of the West or of the United States. The father's classic dream of instant wealth and instant consumption, the dream of minerals, is running out of the possibility of fulfillment in any actual world. Only Curly is hanging on to an aspect of this dream, tearing up the land not for the precious mineral wealth underneath but for a gravel pit and for the newly conceived wealth of vacation housing development on a flattened land, the enclosure of the West's legendary "wide open spaces."

The brothers in Peckinpah's film fight with each other over who is the true inheritor of the father, of the patriarch, which is to say that they struggle over the character of the culture of the West. The younger brother, Curly, thinks that he is acting against his father, who is an embarrassing and scandalous alcoholic and woman chaser, an irresponsible ne'er-do-well and dreamer. Thus, Junior and Curly are examples of the purity of the enemy-brother theme,[9] one for the father, the other against the father. They are in no danger of joining their forces. And the father, Ace Bonner, is still very much alive, a generator of archaic Western dreams and delusions, a spirit of disorder and instability, a gambler through and through.

"You and Ace are the lucky ones, drifting the way you do," says Ellie, the mother, to JR when he returns to his hometown of Prescott, Arizona. JR is identified with his father both by his mother and by Curly, who gets a vicious sock on the jaw when he says to JR, in what we could see as a gesture of brotherly or fatherly affection: "I just don't want you to turn out like the old man." Curly, like a younger brother, shows his revolt against his father by usurping the conventional role of the father, which, in the case of Ace, is no doubt easy enough to do. Ace, the absent father, a physical ghost of a father, is almost impossible to catch. Curly is the financial and stable and domestic center of the family, in a position to call the shots for both his mother and his father. In relation to Curly, Ace is truly some ancient juvenile delinquent whose "father" can both indulge his unpredictable and unreliable child and attempt to control him by putting him on a "weekly allowance." From this perspective, Curly is the "good" son, thinking about the future, getting a grip on the economic possibilities of a western "land boom." As Curly explains to Junior, concerning the land deal that Ace made with Curly, "He needed the money fast, and I got it for him. Me." Little brother has been able to answer the father's need for instant gratification. Junior, on the other hand, is unable even to pay back an apparent loan to his mother and seems to be perpetually "broke," and he cannot meet Ace's request to "grub-stake your dad." Instead, he imposes upon his dad a rodeo event, the wild-cow milking contest.[10] But like a true and powerful patriarch, Curly feels entitled to wield the disciplinary role over the members of the family. His actual mother and father have to bow to his regime, at least in his imagination, although holding Ace and JR within his imaginary system of constraints is difficult, if not impossible. Even though Curly enters enthusiastically into the barroom fracas of playful violence, joining in the spirit of this recreation of frontier disorder, his true impulses move toward constraint and convention. He is a responsible father, husband, businessman. He is an entrepreneur appealing to the public and to a public orderliness, promoting pride in the local community, selling a piece of the heritage of the West to all comers.

Ace Bonner, in his archaic dreaming and confidence games that lead him to chase after silver mines or gold mines or a pastoral dream of sheep ranching, is a figure who embodies something like the history of the stages of the dreams associated with the West. In his old age, he seems to have learned nothing from his experiences of success and failure. His life is constituted by repetition. As his exasperated wife says, "You are a broken record, Ace." His archaic dreaming has split, like a dubious inheritance, into his two sons, each taking a share of this Western heritage. JR's stubborn loyalty to the performance of the rodeo holds on to a Western past. Curly has found a way to exploit his inheritance by committing himself to a future that could, it seems, destroy many of the obvious vestiges of the Western past. The rodeo as repetition of the past in the present captures features of the two brothers' commitments. But the presence of the rodeo also brings up important questions about the past's relationship to the present (and to the future).

Ace's resolve to move to Australia implies an assessment of the future of the American West for his values. "What's a man to do?" he pleads to his wife as he informs her that he is going to Australia. "Silver all shot to hell, no more bounty on the lions." He feels that he needs "the wide open spaces" for his activities, "one hundred and fifty thousand square miles" in Australia available for prospecting. As a lifelong and indiscriminate seeker after hidden metals, he is clearly a throwback to an older West. He seems more committed to the hunt for hidden wealth than to the wealth itself. The contemporary West of Arizona and Nevada is closing down "opportunities" for the fulfillment or the perpetuation of such dreams and chaotic adventures. He still has the energy to imagine a new frontier, to fantasize a step beyond the closed-off opportunities, Australia and "gold for the taking." Curly is the son who sees the opportunities of the West in a new light, in a much more modern exploitation of the land. "You may not know it," he says to Junior, exhorting him to join him, "but the future is here and now." He is a repetition of his father's commitments to "an opportunity of a lifetime," with an important difference. The father cannot make this spiritual move with Curly, even though he may be able to grasp the family resemblance of Curly's ventures. Curly is committed to bringing his father's energies and dreams to material fulfillment, transforming a virtual wealth of the land into an actual wealth.

The two brothers or the enemy-brothers theme is an ancient one in Western civilization, and it is a prominent theme in the history of American popular culture, going back at least as far as Cooper. But it is not exactly clear which is the right inheritance for the two Bonner brothers. Viewers of other Peckinpah films are, perhaps, prepared to understand *Junior Bonner* as slanted on the side of JR and against Curly. JR refuses to compromise with modernity and to admit that he is past his prime. Curly has completely embraced modernity and its frenzy of development toward greater urbanization. The authentic West of the past is, for Curly, mainly a legend now in the service of a salesman's rhetoric for his multiple business ventures. "What a salesman you'd be for the rancheros," Curly tells his rodeo-rider brother, "big cowboy like you. Sincere. Why, you're as genuine as the sunrise." Curly is quite literally exploiting his father's land for his get-rich schemes and is willing to exploit his brother's commitment to the rodeo, whereas JR's rodeo riding seems to be a genuine homage to his father as a former rodeo champion and to a genuine Western past. JR lives in such a way that he can repeat a believable Western past; he can also repeat the legend of his father's rodeo victories. Repetition, in Junior, is a form of homage and not a usurpation. Implicit behind Curly's schemes seems to be a belief that the Old West is really dead and that what lives on is only the legend of the Old West, eminently exploitable. Legend is the ultimate idealization of history, and there are no checks within its make-up to control its use value.[11] History of one sort becomes eminently exploitable for history of another sort. On the other hand, the rodeo has little of the cash nexus within it. There is prize money, of course, but such money simply enhances slightly the aura of winning and losing, a pure competition of bodily competence, perhaps a competition in male masochism. The rodeo stars compete with each other in their athleticism and ability to endure pain.

Curly's economic exploitations also have a long American history, as Limerick and other historians have demonstrated, although Peckinpah in his own loyalty to Western archaisms might not wish to endorse such a history. These different histories turn out not to be actually incommensurable to each other. In promoting the heroic character of Daniel Boone as a founding father of the frontier explorer, "the man of the ax and the rifle," Theodore Roosevelt,[12] for example, overlooked the fact that Boone was also a land developer. This double consciousness generates the pathos for the Peckinpah/Rosebrook narrative. The two brothers are supposed to define the two values, as if they were irreconcilable, but they are not completely so, since both are embodied in the father. Both brothers represent what Pierre Nora calls a "repetition of the ancestral."[13] The rodeo life of Junior is a dead end for the individual, as athletic contests are for any professional athlete. Curly's future in land development is rich and open-ended. Why cannot tradition and trend become reconciled?

Can we assume that JR will be able to settle down and live a somewhat domesticated life after his rodeo days are really over? As someone whose life has been dedicated to the rodeo, rather than as someone like his father with divided loyalties, Junior cannot be seen as likely to take up the will-o-the-wisp life of chasing after various mines in the future. Such chasing has never been a part of Junior's life. Perhaps he will become a respected promoter, in some way, of rodeo in the future, an opportunity suggested by Buck Roan. It is equally possible that he will turn out like his father. He will hang on to an inheritance in whatever way possible. But the question can always be asked: just what is he hanging on to? How is it possible for this repetition of the past to live in the present? What is the need in the present for such a repetition? What does it mean to "stay cowboy?"[14]

It is Junior who reminds his father that "Someone has to hold the horses." The important notion of the rodeo seems to posit repetition as the sign of the past. Despite the fact that there is a common wisdom that warns us that we must remember history in order not to repeat it, the past, a certain version of the past, is accessible to repetition, and, because of its physicality and actuality, because this cowboy experience is visual, such a repetition is a strong version of the past. But is not the sense of repetition also a sense of the past as profoundly compromised, modernized, simulated? The hold on the past as repetition is easy as long as there appears to be little at stake, as in a rodeo. A rodeo is a display, a game, a theater, something that once existed alongside the ranching work of the West. As the announcer explains to the audience over a loudspeaker, a rodeo is "an exhibition of ranch activity and cowboy sports."[15] Roosevelt noted that the cowboys in the 1880s, for their leisure entertainment, engaged in ranching activity contests with each other, activities such as bucking broncos, horse racing, roping calves.[16]

What Peckinpah/Rosebrook seem also to value in the past is the chaos of the Western experience. The rodeo rider, the "hero of repetition," was scorned, in the early days of professional rodeos, for his "laxity in formal living," as a historian of the rodeo euphemistically noted.[17] The rodeo is a form of chaos, protected or ritualized chaos, chaos contained within a set of rules and spaces and regulations. Perhaps a barroom is also such a precinct for chaos, for violence as chaos, not as something that hurts people or endangers their lives. The unused (such as land or landscape) might also belong to such a syndrome of chaos. Exploitation will be of this frontier that we call chaos. *Junior Bonner* seems to argue in favor of these precincts of chaos, since order (civilization) has to feed on something, call it chaos or the wild. The rodeo, in being traceable to a highly recognizable Western past, in wearing a strong aura of this past, thus keeps serving a cultural function that Frederick Jackson Turner thought the frontier served. And, as Elizabeth Lawrence claims, the rodeo comprehends a whole set of attitudes and relationships, an "American frontier ethos."[18] It is committed to wildness, something unassimilable to any historical moment or trend of culture, and this wildness disseminates to personalities, subjectivities, institutions, rituals.

Rosebrook's/Peckinpah's West is profoundly contradictory or paradoxical. Junior would appear to be the most conserving of the old historic values of the West, whereas Curly would seem to be creating new values. But Junior's nomadic life, irresponsible to everything except riding in the show, maintains what is conceived to be a historic disorderliness. He is committed to the tradition of chaos, drift, the purposefulness of a purposelessness. The values that he upholds have no defense, no weight. The rodeo is always in need of defense and is always defenseless. Curly's wife, Ruth, is the first person to utter, "If you've seen one rodeo, you've seen them all." How can one defend such pure repetition? Curly interrupts his wife by reminding her that this denigration does not apply to Prescott's rodeo, because it is "a part of history."

When Ace and JR break out of the parade line, they point to this self-enclosure as they take a line of chaos against the somewhat orderly procedure (or ritual) of the parade. It is not so much that they are escaping convention, orderliness. It is not the case, also, that Ace is expected to engage in some kind of disruption, although he is a living monument to disruption. Acts of disruption are expected and tolerated within the conventionalities, but they cannot, of course, be planned in advance. There has to be a genuine sense of spontaneity and improvisation. And Ace is the likely figure to engage in something like breaking the informal protocols of a parade in the West called Frontier Days. The frontier is this chaos, in this view, a subversion of the normal habits of ordinary life. Even the parade has to incorporate its own chaos within its orderliness, with the clowns performing their little contained acts of chaos while scooping up horse manure. The parade cannot ignore the energies of nature and must incorporate them within its loose frame. The conventions seem to be established so that there can be clear examples of chaos or the breaking out of the frame. Who is it that can be depended upon to break out of the frame? Ace Bonner, of course. He could have ridden in an orderly fashion through the whole parade. But whenever Ace is orderly, his capacity for disruption will simply be in repose, always ready to break out in a way that is both anticipated and unanticipatable. For citizens of the West, this quasi-expectation of chaos must find a figure. The true West is this reservoir of chaos, the wild, that will never be conquered or suppressed as long as there are Ace or JR Bonners, as long as there are rodeo animals who can be depended upon to perform their own culturally induced, prostheticized chaos and physical energy, as long as they can be forced to simulate the wild. In fact, from Curly's entrepreneurial perspective, Ace's land, as a fragment of the wide open spaces, had been merely in repose, and Curly has now liberated a family-inherited chaos upon the land itself with the violence of unconstrained development.

Even the rodeo riders, as they enter the contest and get their draws for the events, all know in advance the animals who perform their parts in the play of wildness. What Peckinpah/Rosebrook are interested in is this repetitiveness, this hanging on to something that has always already been known in advance. The rodeo is an aura or relic of a past, but it is a kind of presence of the past, a past that has been capable of ritualization so that it can be maintained because it holds within it a set of values that may not even be clearly known any longer, may not be able to be stated or articulated in any other way than in the ritual. What does it mean to ritualize the unritualizable, chaos? The modern world is this super rationalization and excessive ordering of culture so that it can even ritualize chaos, but this ritual chaos of the rodeo is one of the few historical traces left from the heritage of the frontier experience. The rodeo cowboy, as the "hero of repetition,"[19] is committed to simulation, and this simulated entertainment is a direct link to the cattle ranching frontier of the past. The rodeo is, for the American West, what Pierre Nora refers to as a site of memory, "where memory crystallizes and secretes itself." "There are *lieux de memoire*, sites of memory," he says, "because there are no longer *milieux de memoire*, real environments of memory."[20] Curly's urban development plans are likely to eliminate Prescott, Arizona, as a distinctive environment of the Old West's cattle ranching frontier, placing the burden of the memory of the Old West on the rodeo.

And so a sense of subversion against conventionality itself becomes ritualized convention. The banner at Prescott's railroad station announcing Frontier Days with the motto "Stay cowboy" makes the commitment to cowboying as rodeo riding an official cultural imperative. Rodeo riders could not possibly be subversive of any conventions, since their role as the figures of the wild is officially proclaimed and endorsed. The official proclamation seems to understand, within the imperative, that there is a risk that cowboying will become lost to the world. Basically, the sign is exhorting some unknown and anonymous addressee to hold on to a legend from the past. The cowboy may be the saint of capitalism, but he is also the hero of a Western past. JR holds on to the role of rodeo rider, past his time. Such cowboys, like so many of Peckinpah's heroes, never know when to quit, as if there ever could be a clearly designated time to quit. Just as they hold on to a historical past, so they also hang compulsively on to their own past without recognizing it as past. They seem not to be able to assess time, their own time, their body's time. "Get a grip on your future," Curly exhorts JR. "You're still trying to beat eight seconds." "Might as well face it," Buck Roan advises him, "you're just not the rider you was a few years back." How can one face such fact? How can one turn a self-assessment upon oneself and arrive at a clear decision? Other people may be in a position to make such judgments, but it would be inauthentic for one, especially JR, to make this judgment of himself definitively. Holding on to the past is the same as holding on to performing in the rodeo. There is a valuable excess here, a surplus of energy that is all that the performer has to rely on.

Once their performance level has declined, rodeo riders might be put out to stud, metaphorically speaking. But, like Ace, who seems still to take the role of stud, they must also live within the erotics of their commitments to a past that is presented, in its legendary mode, as still more adventurous than anything in the present. JR's success with the young woman, Charmagne, his response to her interest, does not suggest that he is over the hill. It suggests, rather, the eroticism of his "line of work." Why is it that JR will not be tempted by all the offers of new jobs, since everyone seems to understand that JR's major rodeo achievements are also of the past? He is offered a range of possible business ventures, including staking his father in his Australia schemes. But JR will remain loyal to the official proclamation on the banner and stay cowboy. JR's commitment to the rodeo, past his time, and to all that it entails is a strong affirmation of the values of the legend of the West. Only the strong can be heroes of repetition.

Curly's ventures transform nature, conquer and master nature, bring the wide open spaces into the orbit of modern human culture. But the myth of conquering a wild nature is at the heart of the rodeo also. The difference is that the rodeo is capable of infinite repetition, whereas the capitalist development truly transforms nature, changes the terms of nature so that there can be no return. The rodeo rider can defeat the prostheticized wildness of the animal, and so the animal's wildness can be maintained in order to defeat the rider on another day. The culture of the American West no doubt needs this myth, an enlightenment myth, of mastering nature. The rodeo's starkly repetitive nature changes or transforms nothing; it simply affirms the past. In this way, the rodeo also holds on to history. Its repetition unfolds a severely reduced history, making it vulnerable to the denigration that "if you've seen one rodeo, you've seen them all." Curly may have exploited his father by getting so much land for so little money, and his business venture entails wiping out the vestiges of his father's presence by bulldozing Ace's house along with his mementoes. Perhaps the photographs and posters would be worth saving. But Junior is a living memento, a flesh-and-blood connection to an actual past, a presence of the past. Since rodeos are repetitions of the past, then, the dismissal implicit in the expression "If you've seen one rodeo, you've seen them all" is completely reversible. Any one rodeo contains any and all rodeos of the past, present, and future. Like a festival, such as the celebration of Frontier Days, rodeos "repeat the 'unrepeatable.' They do not add a second and a third time to the first, but carry the first time to the 'nth' power."[21]

The hard question is: what kind of game is the rodeo for the modern world? Is it a deep play, a model of life, as Elizabeth Lawrence understands it from her anthropological perspective, a loyalty not only to the father but to the past (one and the same thing)?[22] The rodeo is like an oral form of the transmission of a tradition. It is a ritual expression of values that the West feels it needs to hang on to, especially in the context of important historical change. Of course, the sons have to hold up the father now. The father cannot support the sons. The relations of power have become inverted. Or, in the case of JR, the loyalties of the father have simply been passed down to the son. The son has taken over from the father in a natural passing on of the ideological line. Curly would link up, in a commercial venture, with the son who is loyal to the father. He can truly appropriate the past only by joining with his older brother. Thus, for him, the father is mainly irrelevant and eminently dispensable. He has all of the father he needs in the brother. Curly wants to establish the regime of the brothers, not so much to displace the father as to fill a void, since for him as well as for his mother, the father is a void, even as he is an embarrassing presence.

Curly has been able to take advantage of his father's inattentiveness and peculiar need for money right now to cheat his father out of his property. We can still ask why Curly's economic ventures are any worse than his father's Australian schemes for getting rich. JR's orientation toward the world seems to be a "respect for something which has no market value."[23] The presence of JR and the rodeo shows that modern real-estate development ideology and capitalism have not been able to "compel men to indulge solely in purposeful behavior."[24] Such ritualistic game playing holds a society to its mythic origins. That these origins serve as a framework for the capitalist ideology may have been overlooked by Peckinpah. The rodeo is a game of humankind (mostly, but not exclusively, men) against the animated energies of nature, in which man is supposed to subdue the energies of nature. Of course, riding broncos and roping cattle did have an economic function at one time in history. Curly's activities in land development level out the difference of the West from the rest of the country. It would dispel eventually the myth of the

West, and thus the myth of America in general. In that respect, Curly is engaged in a true killing off of the past—a material, physical past—leaving only myths, which, without physical support, will be liable to disappear completely. The real-estate business can go on with a different ideology supporting it. It can eventually ignore the rodeo and the mythologies of the West. Curly may exploit these myths of wildness (with his caged animals and his family of famous rodeo performers) to launch himself into the high money stakes of real-estate development, but eventually he will be in a position to forgo such mythology, in which case he can forget about the West and think purely in the terms of liberal capitalism, of profit and loss. Curly's adventure is moving toward the extinction of the West even as he now is exploiting its historic and historical ideology.

One brother steals from his father while satisfying his father's desire. The other brother gives his father a gift, a ticket to Australia, in order to answer his father's desire. According to Deleuze, "If exchange is the criterion of generality, theft and gift are those of repetition."[25] Curly may believe that he is committed to exchange, but he lives somewhere between exchange and thievery. In this view, he is a chip off the old block. He is only half committed to an economic difference between generality (i.e., exchange) and repetition. The half may be enough to condemn him, but the half that condemns him is exchange, not thievery. In his thievery, he is merely committed to the logical inversion of his brother's gift. Curly, then, may be seen as a transitional figure into a future, rather than a total rejection of the Western past of his father. But if a viewer is inclined to condemn Curly, it is for stepping into a new sense of the West, into a future wherein the West will lose many of its distinctive and sectional features. In the typical bad faith of the businessman, Curly advertises the distinctive and seductive features of the West as clean air while promoting an urban sprawl that will soon bring about the end of clean air and the wide open spaces. "I've seen your wide-open spaces," JR says to his brother. If JR is responding to the regional Western imperative to "stay cowboy," Curly is also responding to a cultural imperative, the duty to commit oneself to the business of economic progress.

Junior's criticism of his brother is not merely that he is "selling the old man's land," but that he got the land so cheaply, that the fifteen thousand dollars he paid for four sections of undeveloped land was an unfair exchange. Junior's criticism, that is, has the richness of oppositional and incompatible values that we find at the heart of this narrative. Not even Junior, committed as he is to the rodeo, can protect himself from the split. Junior is trying to guard the father's interests, despite the fact that the father seems uninterested, just as Curly wants to take Junior into the business of developing "our land," again, despite the father's disinterest. Both of these positions could be said to honor their inheritances, the father's riches. Only Junior seems especially interested in protecting the father as a way of protecting the past, but no one in this drama has much of any concern with guarding or honoring the past. Only the rodeo protects the Western cowboy past, and rodeo riders participate in this past with their bodies. When the two brothers first meet, they exchange greetings by patting each other in their midriffs. Curly has put on a protective layer of fat; Junior has exposed and bruised ribs and winces at the gesture. The two bodies figure their respective commitments to the West and its heritage.

We could say that what the two brothers do is dramatize the father's actions. In such theatrical displays, the danger is that a certain surplus is produced; the dramatization brings out into the open the implicit presuppositions within the father's stance in the world. What might seem most damaging in the unfolding of the father in his sons is that Curly's schemes might be overlooked as coming from the riotous personality of Ace. Curly brings into the open the otherwise concealed truth of the father, an obscuring that even the rodeo and Junior participate in. What may seem especially damaging in this display or double display is the powerlessness of Junior and the effectiveness of Curly. Junior has no power to change anything in the world, whereas Curly has all the power to bring about substantial change. But the rodeo rider does not want change. There may be a stubborn militancy to the rodeo rider, but he cannot, and will not, compete against the land developer and mere exploiter of the legends of the West.

The rodeo is a synecdoche of the mythic frontier cowboy past. It repeats the past and does so without a memory of the past. Those who remember the past suffer from it, like Ellie, who slaps Ace when he asks her to go with him to Australia, reminding her of his past expressions of his dreams and promises. She recovers quickly from the painful memories, however, and joins Ace in what is intimated to be a last sexual encounter between a husband and wife who have been separated for a length of time. In a sense, the rodeo preserves the past by forgetting it, by enacting it. Throughout the film, Junior keeps remembering, in cinema flashbacks, his ride on Old Sunshine, a bull who had never been ridden for the full count of eight seconds by any rodeo rider. But it seems clear that Junior is remembering only for the purpose of evaluating his recent ride on the bull and of working out a strategy for a successful ride. In his thinking about the past, and a very short past it is, he is actually projecting his future ride, correcting his earlier performance.

Remembrance is in the service of anticipation. Junior claims to Hunsacker that he cannot remember back six years. It seems as if he cannot even remember back a few minutes, when he refuses to remember Hunsacker saying that Junior can have only one dance with Charmagne. The rodeo rider—like the rodeo itself, like Ace—has no memory. He is, like them, the past as present, a pure repetition of the frontier experience, a repetition perhaps of a past that has never been. According to Deleuze, "I forget because I repeat."[26]

The rodeo is an authentic spectacle, capturing the historic sense of original frontier cowboying. But it provides no bulwark against general historical change. It can defend itself against its own transformation in its compulsive repetitiveness, but it is also vulnerable to being used, invoked for the purposes of a rapacious commercialization. Ultimately, its only defense is the culture's need, conscious or unconscious, for tradition, for a link to its storied past. And the culture may feel the need all the more acutely now that the West is undergoing so many changes. As Buck Roan suggests to JR, the rodeo business is expanding. In such an expansion, there is the suggestion that, in the West, there is a call for just such sites of memory as the rodeo, an "embodiment of a memorial consciousness that has barely survived in a historical age that calls out for memory because it has abandoned it."[27]

What is especially significant is that Curly wants JR to join with him in his enterprise. If JR should join his brother, Curly would have captured both the material reality of the father and the mythic significance of the father (in his rodeo-rider brother). What I think is so powerful in this idea is that most of us in American society would believe Curly's motive in his offer to JR, that he is trying to look out for the long-term interests of the family. Curly claims to value the family, but this desire also disavows the explicit usurpation of the role of the father in the name of a fraternal order. He is also offering to take in his mother, to give her a chance to sell antiques (to sell off the traces of the past, to become a dealer in the material heritage of America). How could we possibly say that there is something wrong with this desire, this motive? He wants to hold the family together, to help it thrive and succeed. He is looking at the long term by looking at the future, at prospects. Why would we sympathize with JR, who seems to be merely the ghost of a nomadic, useless, irresponsible Western past? But this point is simply to argue for the fact that Peckinpah/Rosebrook have presented us with a genuine dilemma that we can say is a dilemma for citizens of the West or of the United States in general. History, the past, can become split, generating a schizo narrative. We may not like the outcome of such a historical development, but we understand that it arises out of the values that we love and respect. We understand that there is a deep background from which the contemporary West emerges even as the contemporary strives to dismiss or belittle the past that it exploits and needs in order to promote the legitimacy of the present.

The problem with Curly's desire to bring the family together is that it is impossible to separate such a little brother's fantasy from the imperialism of his businessman's point of view, a need to bring everything into his orbit of mastery, including the rodeo and its aura. Curly's quest for mastery comes out of a spirit of gravity, of historical transformation. The rodeo rider's quest for mastery is profoundly mythic and comes from the affirmative spirit of play.

Perhaps the appearance of a group or subgenre of rodeo films in the early seventies was Hollywood's way of coming to grips with the end of the Western as a film genre.[28] Either these films acknowledged the end, or they were designed as a hope for the rebirth of the Western. The great Westerns of the genre belong to the classic Cold War era, and the Vietnam War was able to keep the genre viable, as *The Wild Bunch* and other films such as *High Plains Drifter* or *McCabe and Mrs. Miller* would testify. But by the early 1970s, Americans had become profoundly disillusioned with the war and the popular film arguments for American militarism. Moreover, in the rodeo narrative, Peckinpah and others could conceal or at least tone down their reactions to the feminism of the late 1960s and early 1970s. The unimportance of women belongs to the rodeo phenomenon.[29] Hence, there was no need to be histrionic about women, as Peckinpah could be in other films. Maverick filmmakers like Nicholas Ray could offer a rodeo film in the early 1950s in which the men compete over a woman. But between 1952 and 1972, a lot had happened in the ideological make-up of the United States.

Junior Bonner is a film worth thinking seriously about. It is certainly one of Peckinpah's more gentle films, along with *Ride the High Country* and *The Ballad of Cable Hogue*, but it is as complexly resonant with ideas about the meaning of the West as anything Peckinpah ever did. Besides, it is eminently watchable yet today, in a period with less tolerance for Peckinpah's indulgences in racism and sexism. Stephen Prince has written extensively on Peckinpah's cinematic technical innovations in depicting violence that verges on a pathological pornography and clinical perversity.[30] Peckinpah's innovations have had an important and demonstrable influence on subsequent Hollywood filmmakers. But *Junior Bonner* provides one of the best dramas of a basic dilemma for Westerners (no doubt, for Americans in general): the contradictory impulses to hold unto an identifiable and identifying past and to join the accelerations of historical change.

Notes

1. *The Morphology of the Folk Tale*, translated by Laurence Scott, revised and edited by Louis A. Wagner (Austin and London: University of Texas Press, 1968), 95.

2. See David Weddle, *"If They Move . . . Kill 'Em!": The Life and Times of Sam Peckinpah* (New York: Grove Press, 1994), 429.

3. Elizabeth Atwood Lawrence, *Rodeo: An Anthropologist Looks at the Wild and the Tame* (Chicago and London: The University of Chicago Press, 1982), 5.

4. *Justified Lives: Morality and Narrative in the Films of Sam Peckinpah* (Carbondale: Southern Illinois University Press, 1993), 169.

5. Jacques Derrida, *Dissemination*, translated by Barbarah Johnson (Chicago: The University of Chicago Press, 1981), 169.

6. *The Legacy of Conquest* (New York and London: W. W. Norton & Co., 1987), 55.

7. Theodore Roosevelt, *Ranch Life and the Hunting Trail* (Lincoln and London: University of Nebraska Press, 1983), 7.

8. One might think of the 1929 film version of *The Virginian*, wherein a number of Wister's characters are synthesized in the character of Steve so that the two friends, the Virginian and Steve, carry the drama in the binary clarity of their oppositional differences.

9. Rene Girard, *Violence and the Sacred*, translated by Patrick Gregory (Baltimore and London: The Johns Hopkins University Press, 1977), 61 ff.

10. According to Danny Freeman, the historian of the Prescott, Arizona, rodeo, wild-cow milking "has always been a favorite with the crowd—almost anything can happen and usually does." It is a kind of chaos, a comic struggle to appropriate the wild for the domestic. See Freeman, *World's Oldest Rodeo: 100 Year History, 1888–1988* (Prescott: Prescott Frontier Days, Inc., 1989), 81.

11. Curly's willingness to turn the legend of the West into a capitalist commodity is a strong comment on the Western films of John Ford, whose films of the forties and fifties strongly endorsed the moral and political value of maintaining the legend of the West as against its much less edifying history.

12. *Ranch Life and the Hunting-Trail*, 15.

13. "Between Memory and History: *Les Lieux de Memoire*." *Representations* 26 (Spring 1989): 7.

14. One of the banners advertising Prescott's Frontier Days hanging at the railroad station has the expression: "Stay Cowboy."

15. In another rodeo film, *When the Legends Die* (1972), released the same year as *Junior Bonner*, a rodeo announcer says over a loudspeaker, "While times have changed, the pioneer spirit is still with us."

16. *Ranch Life and the Hunting-Trail*, 53, 54, 62. Danny Freeman, in *World's Oldest Rodeo* (53), quotes a proposal by the Arizona Cattle Grower's Association in 1924 to the state legislature to subsidize the Frontier Days rodeo as "a non-profit, educational contest devoted to the upbuilding of stock raising."

17. Clifford P. Westermeier, *Man, Beast, Dust: The Story of Rodeo* (Lincoln and London: University of Nebraska Press, 1987), 97.

18. *Rodeo*, 20.

19. Gilles Deleuze, *Difference and Repetition*, translated by Paul Patton (New York: Columbia University Press, 1994), 5.

20. "Between Memory and History," 7.

21. Deleuze, *Difference and Repetition*, 1.

22. Michael Allen refers to the rodeo cowboy as a "*contemporary ancestor*" in *Rodeo Cowboys in the North American Imagination* (Reno and Las Vegas: University of Nevada Press, 1998), 80.

23. Juliet Flower MacCannell, *The Regime of the Brother: After the Patriarchy* (London: Routledge, 1991), 19.

24. *The Regime of the Brother*, 19.

25. *Difference and Repetition*, 1.

26. Ibid., 18.

27. Pierre Nora, "Between Memory and History," 12.

28. In addition to *Junior Bonner* (1972) and *When the Legends Die* (1972), there is also *J. W. Coop* (1972), *The Honkers* (1972), *Black Rodeo* (1972), and the Disney studio's Academy-Award-winning documentary *The Great American Cowboy* (1973), which follows two young riders through the rodeo season to see who gets the prize as the top money and point winner of the year. For a brief account of these films and others, see Michael Allen, *Rodeo Cowboys in the North American Imagination*, chap. 2.

29. Michael Allen quotes a line of cowboy poetry: "'The rodeo life has no room for a wife'" (*Rodeo Cowboys in the North American Imagination*), 102.

30. *Savage Cinema: Sam Peckinpah and the Rise of Ultraviolent Movies* (Austin: University of Texas Press, 1998).

References

Allen, Michael. 1998. *Rodeo Cowboys in the North American Imagination*. Reno and Las Vegas: University of Nevada Press.

Bliss, Michael. 1993. *Justified Lives: Morality and Narrative in the Films of Sam Peckinpah*. Carbondale: Southern Illinois University Press.

Deleuze, Gilles. 1994. *Difference and Repetition*. Translated by Paul Patton. New York: Columbia University Press.

Derrida, Jacques. 1981. *Dissemination*. Translated by Barbarah Johnson. Chicago: The University of Chicago Press.

Freeman, Danny. 1989. *World's Oldest Rodeo: 100 Year History, 1888–1988*. Prescott: Prescott Frontier Days, Inc.

Girard, Rene. 1977. *Violence and the Sacred*. Translated by Patrick Gregory. Baltimore: The Johns Hopkins University Press.

Lawrence, Elizabeth Atwood. 1982. *Rodeo: An Anthropologist Looks at the Wild and the Tame*. Chicago: The University of Chicago Press.

Limerick, Patricia. 1987. *The Legacy of Conquest*. New York: W. W. Norton and Co.

MacCannell, Juliet Flower. 1991. *The Regime of the Brother: After the Patriarchy*. London: Routledge.

Nora, Pierre. 1989. "Between Memory and History: *Les Lieux de Memoire.*" *Representations* 26 (Spring).

Prince, Stephen. 1998. *Savage Cinema: Sam Peckinpah and the Rise of Ultraviolent Movies.* Austin: University of Texas Press.

Propp, Vladimir. 1968. *The Morphology of the Folk Tale.* Translated by Laurence Scott, revised and edited by Louis A. Wagner. Austin: University of Texas Press.

Roosevelt, Theodore. 1983. *Ranch Life and the Hunting Trail.* Lincoln: University of Nebraska Press.

Weddle, David. 1994. *"If They Move . . . Kill 'Em": The Life and Times of Sam Peckinpah.* New York: Grove Press.

Westermeier, Clifford P. 1987. *Man, Beast, Dust: The Story of Rodeo.* Lincoln: University of Nebraska Press.

EIGHT

STEPHEN TATUM

Don't *Mess* with Texas

RECUPERATING MASCULINITY IN *THE GETAWAY*

THE POSE OF ABJECTION

The rather long opening sequence of director Sam Peckinpah's *The Getaway* (1972) concludes with a medium profile shot of Doc McCoy (Steve Mc-Queen), sitting on the edge of his bed in a prison cell, elbows resting on his knees and hands covering his bowed head and ears, this abject pose occurring just moments after he has slung his eyeglasses in despair on top of the remains of a matchstick bridge he had been constructing. As we later discover when he talks with his wife, Carol (Ali McGraw), in her apartment, this pose of abjection occurs directly in the aftermath of the Texas prison parole board's refusal to release him after he had served four years for an armed-robbery conviction. In concert with the numbing monotony and isolation of prison life (brilliantly detailed by Peckinpah's trademark accelerated crosscutting of scenes and sounds), the parole board's decision reinforces McCoy's emergent feeling that he "couldn't handle it anymore in there." "It"—the life of constant surveillance and supervision inside prison—has done "something" to him, McCoy confesses to his wife, has now contaminated his consciousness as well as controlled his body's movements. With life "in there" thus having now finally gotten to McCoy, we see him in the movie's next sequence in the prison's visitation area, separated from Carol by a wire mesh screen, uttering to her, in clipped, staccato fashion, his first words of the movie: "Get to Beynon [Ben Johnson]. Tell him I'm for sale. His price. Do it now."

In this opening sequence, Peckinpah formally reinforces the accumulating evidence of McCoy's abjection to the system by using reaction shots instead of point-of-view shots; cameras either positioned above or, more typically, looking at Doc through bars or screens; freeze frames to interrupt any continuous, fluid motion (such as Doc's opening walk from his cell through the prison yard and into the prison board's hearing room); and close-up shots of prisoners' bare feet or their outstretched hands holding belts, or of McCoy's right hand on the lever of a mechanized textile loom—or of the power loom itself as it clatters on in the prison shop. Through these various cinematic techniques, Doc and the other prisoners in the film's *mis-en-scene* are made immobile, are objectified by the gazes of prison guards in surveillance towers and of shotgun-bearing guards atop their horses, and are fetishized by the camera as part-objects, not whole bodies. At one point a guard on horseback admonishes Doc and the prisoners detailed to clear an area of brush and stumps outside the prison's security fence to keep the pile of brush "tight" and the line of their bodies working with axes "straight," while another guard's directive to "rack 'em up"—that is, to close the long line of cell doors on the prisoners housed within them—serves to equate the prisoners with the brush and stumps being similarly policed. Peckinpah and cinematographer Lucien Ballard strategically produce linear, regimented, and cellular spaces to complement the carceral system's overweening desire for efficient, predictable, and docile labor. As the movie begins, for example, the Huntsville prison's buildings and grounds (much less its interiors) appear as a series of regular, symmetrical rectangular or square shapes, these blocks organized by clear perspectival lines that recede to a central vanishing point before then cutting to the first shot of McCoy as he moves from shadows into the light of an enclosed yard during his walk to the parole board hearing room.

At the outset of the movie, then, Peckinpah's editing and camera directives and the script's dialogue serve both to fragment spatial and temporal relations and to isolate human bodies. As a result, the viewer must reconstruct the logical sequence of various scenes in the opening credit sequence, and—as it turns out—the movie's sound montage provides the chief clue for solving the logical relationship between events in the movie's present and past. Significantly, the industrial clatter of the textile looms in the prison shop drowns out the bleating of sheep heard in the prison ground during the film's opening seconds, when the camera visually pans back from a shot of grazing deer to the fences, towers, and dormitories of the Huntsville prison. These industrial sounds grow in frequency and intensity as the opening sequence proceeds, eventually overpowering not only the overlapping sounds of human voices but also at one point disrupting McCoy's reverie of making love with Carol prior to his imprisonment. Repetitive, mindless work of the sort Doc performs in the prison shop theoretically frees his mind to daydream about just such intimate moments. But in this particular regimented space and place Peckinpah's tactical use of intrusive industrial sounds and repetitive close-up shots of different parts of the power loom overwhelm Doc's consciousness, producing both his pose of abjection before the broken matchstick bridge that ends this sequence and his command to Carol to make a deal with Beynon for his release.

From this perspective, *The Getaway* begins as a drama of framing and being framed, of looking and being looked at and over as the State clamps down on a human's physical and mental freedom. Doc's powerlessness and incoherence—figured here by his silence as well as by his being the object of the viewer's and the various authorities' gazes—allegorize an "it" or a "something" (to use his words) I want to explore and define somewhat against the critical grain of commentary on Peckinpah's work. To be sure, the imagery, dialogue, editing, and camera angles in this opening sequence reveal fairly standard thematic oppositions evident in several other Peckinpah film productions: "nature" (animals; sexual desire) versus "culture" (the carceral system; machines; the alienation of labor); the "authentic" (individual) versus the "inauthentic" (collective or bureaucracy); "active" (mobility and agency) versus "passive" (containment; obedience). A normative way of thinking about Peckinpah's films, given such predominant imagistic and thematic oppositions, is to stress how his various heroes discover or recover their authentic, true, or genuine selves (and along the way bond with like-minded sorts) in opposition to a dehumanizing and decorporealizing modern social and political order.

Yet with regard to *The Getaway*, we need to keep in mind how this particular movie's narrative motor starts in earnest when Doc orders Carol to tell the corrupt oilman-politician Jack Beynon that his criminal expertise can be bought and exchanged for a parole from prison. As a key member of the prison parole board, Beynon covertly arranges for Doc's release, reversing the board's earlier decision not to grant it, ostensibly in exchange for Doc orchestrating a bank robbery and then splitting the proceeds with him. What Doc doesn't know, and what moves the narrative forward beyond the basic robbery-escape-pursuit formula, is that Beynon's "price" for arranging the parole involves Carol's offering up her body to him and her further promise to betray Doc after the robbery so that she and Beynon will keep all the stolen loot. Furthermore, we need also to consider how Doc's reticence with language—for instance, his inability to articulate to Carol the effect of prison on his inner life in words other than the vague markers "it" and "something"—occurs as the couple sit on Carol's bed, both clearly anxious about matters of sexual performance and intimacy after four years of separation. Indeed, as the movie proceeds and the couple try to make their getaway in the aftermath of Doc's having learned about Carol's deception and sexual intimacy with Beynon, intermittent dialogue scenes reveal his obsessive anxiety about Carol's sexual activity during his stay in prison—and, as a result, his uncertainty about the viability of their marriage. In the movie's language, then, instead of Carol "getting to" Beynon, as Doc had ordered her to do, and instead of Doc paying the price by marketing his criminal expertise to Beynon, Doc eventually confronts the fact that Beynon instead "got to" Carol, that she perhaps liked "it" better with the older, more politically and financially powerful Beynon.

Midway through the film, as a series of betrayals come to light after the bank robbery goes "bad," Doc verbally wounds Carol by telling her that the only thing he *trusts* is the slogan "In God We Trust" printed on U.S. paper currency. With this comment Doc seemingly fetishizes both the tangible, material substance of the paper money he holds in his hands and can count and, further, the idea that it is possible there might be no gap between words (representations; promises) and things: so apparently he and "we" can trust in a "god" who is embodied in and exactly equivalent to words and images printed on paper currency. The problem with Carol's behavior, from Doc's perspective, centers exactly on the uncertainty about the relationship between Carol's words (of loyalty to Doc) and her actions (infidelity with Beynon). From Carol's perspective, though, she has given her body—but not her word—to Beynon; from Doc's perspective, though, her body, or what she has done with it during his prison term, is her true word, regardless of her verbal expressions of intention and meaning. And so he does not trust her words but apparently will trust the words inscribed on a twenty-dollar bill whose meaning and value or worth is guaranteed by the U.S. government. For Carol, by contrast, survival in this world means that one doesn't always or necessarily mean what one says or say what one means. Or do what one means or mean what one does. As a result, Carol's world contains both surfaces and depths. So she is inclined, as she tells Doc after their night buried in a garbage truck, to regard life as a "game." Doc's world of desire, by contrast, is or should be like an ideal contract—all surface transparency, as legible as the written guarantee on a twenty-dollar bill and as predictable in its outcomes. Is it any wonder he is shown losing at chess to another inmate during the film's opening sequence? ("Ah, man, it's just a game," the inmate tells him.)

And yet the fact is that whatever success Doc enjoys as a bank robber depends upon his own duplicity, in this case his posing as a respectable bourgeois businessperson in requisite dark suit and tie, glasses, and briefcase in hand in order to infiltrate a bank and gain "insider" knowledge of its operations. Yet of course paper money is not, linguistically speaking, a stable signified but rather a signifier whose value is not truly fixed and authenticated by God or by the U.S. government but rather by a fluctuating process of economic exchange in the marketplace. Yet of course neither the production nor the exchange of commodities constitutes a fully efficient economic process. Doc's and Carol's self-commodification in the film's opening sequences—their willed translation of their bodies and criminal expertise into "capital" that can be bought and sold—on one level illustrates Peckinpah's ongoing cinematic critique of alienated labor and commodity fetishism. But on another level their criminal labor produces *excess residue* along with the "tight" and "straight" bottom lines and profit margins desired by oilmen and prison guards. The movement of capital and labor force in the movie produces things that will not or cannot stay in their places and that, as a result, highlight the constructed, rather than God-given ("In God We Trust"), nature of things. Things like "trash" (human and nonhuman waste), things like women (Carol McCoy or, later, Fran Clinton), and things like paper money laundered through a bank and exchanged among several hands illustrate how this matter of policing borders and stabilizing boundaries remains highly problematic. Thus, even as Doc tries to sort out the "truth" of Carol's intentions with regard to her body's use and her stated love for him—while at the same time the couple try to elude the police, Beynon's men, and the surviving robbery accomplice (Rudy Butler, played by Al Lettieri)—*The Getaway* strives to recover and relocate power and authority in the competent male body laboring to rein in things that circulate (women, money) while simultaneously fending off threats from hypocritical paternal authorities like Jack Beynon or from working-class goons like Rudy Butler.

Though a different movie, generically and tonally speaking, from *Straw Dogs*, *The Getaway* discloses just as clearly as that movie Peckinpah's compulsive interest in displaying masculinity in crisis and under siege. Whether as a figure that has transgressed norms and defied vested authorities or as a cuckolded figure that occupies a submissive, and hence feminized, position while in prison, Doc McCoy constitutes a Peckinpah version of what Julia Kristeva has called "the abject." Kristeva's "abject" represents those things or actions or practices (such as sexual immorality; murder; bodily wastes; corpses) that transgress notions of purity, that disturb borders, positions, limits, and rules, and that—as a result—disclose the tenuous and contingent nature of normatively defined authority and identities.[1] The abject thing or person thus represents a type of polluting agent that threatens the security and stability, the coherence and the integrity, of an individual or social body or territory. And so regardless of its specific form the abject thing or person, like a ritual scapegoat figure, must be repulsed from the individual or social body whose survival is threatened. From this perspective, both horror films and police procedural dramas characteristically proceed as narratives of defilement and purification: representatives of society (police; detectives; scientists) are put into contact with and threatened by polluting agents (vampires; murderers) prior to the ritual performance of violent acts aiming to protect the individual, familial, or social body from the abject's contaminating presence.

As I have indicated above, in the opening sequences of *The Getaway*, the abject armed robber named Doc McCoy basically is abjected by the system: he is placed on the far side of the human/nonhuman binary, both literally framed behind bars and figuratively identified as an object without voice and agency, an object equated with or subservient to the tools, machines, and brush piles littering everyday life in the state's carceral system. Even so, his and Carol's eventual reconciliation and getaway across the border into Mexico at the end of the movie effectively recapitulate a ritual of defilement and purification from two opposing directions. From one direction, the transgressive outlaw couple, whose path to Mexico has littered the Texas landscape with bloody mayhem, has removed its polluting presence across the border, in the process recapitulating a staple conclusion of the Western film genre. However, since the camera's gaze and the Hollywood star system solicit our spectatorial identification with Doc and Carol McCoy, *The Getaway*, in contrast to horror movies, also inverts the standard ritual process of defilement and purification. That is, the romanticized outlaw couple, in their final getaway across the border into Mexico, at the same time free themselves from contact with polluted humans such as Jack Beynon and the dirty politics and violence of Nixon's America during the Vietnam War.

Thus one of the continually fascinating things about this Peckinpah movie since its initial release over twenty-five years ago is this: as disclosed by Doc's discourse on "trust," *The Getaway* somewhat anxiously *alibis* for a masculine subjectivity never in full control of itself, never sufficient unto itself, and anxious about its abilities and its status or authority. Whatever the level of its overt cynicism about traditional authorities and their symbols of power, the movie nevertheless must work hard at recuperating a normative masculine subjectivity. Under the force of tension-filled circumstances that always threaten to abject him once again, Doc McCoy must discover ways to produce "waste" (i.e., make others spill *their* blood and guts) and then to dispose of it without himself getting "wasted." Because waste disposal usually involves "taking out" the trash or "taking care" of the messes created by women, as well as by men with their dirty politics, *The Getaway* meditates at some length on what it means to become abjected and lose one's "manhood"—through contact with women and corrupt fathers—and then to recover it by successfully holding on to a black satchel of money stolen from an oil company's payroll. Moreover, the tension in the film between what I'm regarding as its true subject (the tenuous nature of masculine authority) and its official alibi (the male hero gets away with the money and the girl) provides a complicated address to the film's spectators. Just as the film repetitively dramatizes its male action hero trying to understand his subjectivity and legitimate his authority in relation to hygiene matters—that is, being clean or being soiled, wasting others or being wasted—so too the film's hypothetical male spectator must figure out whether or not it can be possible to consume the pleasures of a "trashy" action film without being himself soiled in the process.

McQueen's Body

The gait. The eyes. The hands. We first glimpse him walking through a tunnel and across the Huntsville prison yard, the camera's panning motion eventually stopping to freeze him in full stride in a medium profile shot just as the name "Steve McQueen" appears on the screen. His gait here and throughout the entire movie suggests a fluid but dangerously coiled grace. The crisp economy of his body's actions and the solidity of his torso (strong but not bulked up like more contemporary action heroes), along with the penetrating gaze of his blue eyes, combine to make McQueen's Doc McCoy a distinctive object of attention amid a sea of similarly white-clad inmates in the prison yard. McQueen's screen presence as Doc McCoy seems neither serene nor inviting, but rather coolly defiant, composed and self-possessed. Both Peckinpah's direction and the logic of the movie's editing highlight people looking at McQueen's Doc McCoy. But he basically refuses this solicitation. When the camera centers on his face while he works the power loom after hearing that his parole request has been turned down, McQueen looks through, past, or beyond the camera. This look, his coiled athletic walk, and an overall reticence with language constitute McQueen's hyperphallicized presence on the screen.

Although apparently impervious to the prying eyes of people and to the camera's gaze, McQueen's own measured looks and alert eyes disclose a cerebral dimension to his character. He is, after all, called "Doc": as he tells Rudy Butler, all the "fine stuff"—the planning; the working the lock on the bank vault; the delivery of the stolen money and the negotiations with Beynon— will be his (Doc's) responsibility. McQueen's two predominant ways of using his hands in the film suggest the organic "fit" between McCoy's thoughts and his bodily actions. His hands themselves are lethal weapons on occasion, and, unsurprisingly for a Peckinpah production, they also hold and operate lethal weapons such as revolvers and riot guns. When McQueen cradles a pump shotgun and stalks the Laughlin Hotel's corridors and stairways, or when he knocks out a small-time thief in an Amtrak train passenger car with a couple of focused elbow jabs to the face, he clearly displays a full being at "home" in his corporeality. In other scenes—I'm thinking specifically here of the scene when the McCoys hand out bulletproof vests and go over the plan for the bank heist with Beynon's hired help—McQueen, dressed in black, waves a pencil or points with his index finger or makes circular motions with his hand and wrist while lining out instructions to the other characters. Precisely because their timing and efficient motions perfectly accentuate McQueen's spoken words, and precisely because their flashing motion and flesh color contrast with his stationary torso clad in black, these simple, direct gestures speak to the streamlined unity of his mind and body.

Influenced by the convergence of feminist theory and psychoanalysis, several recent film theorists and critics, often in the process of elaborating and extending Laura Mulvey's theory of the gaze, have discussed how various film conventions and narrative structures work to captivate the film spectator through the psychic mechanisms of voyeurism, fetishism, and narcissism.[2] As my address to the appeal of McQueen's corporeal presence on the screen begins to suggest, part of the pleasure I for one certainly experienced while watching *The Getaway* centers on my projective identification with the fantasy of power, mastery, and control embodied in its leading star's compact yet kinetic screen presence. Such projective identification with McQueen as Doc McCoy perhaps can be said to represent a version of narcissistic identification, in that as a spectator I desire to "recognize" myself in the images on the screen, which itself functions as a kind of mirror fostering the process of projecting and introjecting idealized images. By fetishizing McQueen's screen performance at the outset of *The Getaway* as an ensemble of "parts"—hands; eye movements; walk—perhaps on another level I desire to suture over the gap between seer and seen and, as a result, become anything but a detached, voyeuristic looker, become instead a viewer enthralled as McQueen's body spectacularly returns—in action films, again and again—to proclaim its substantial reality, its power, finally, to shape the given world even as this world poses obstacles to it. More specifically, then, perhaps an identification with McQueen's embodied screen presence should be regarded as a compensatory, somewhat nostalgic response to the felt "loss" of corporeal power either attendant upon one's maturation and aging or entailed by one's conformity to buttoned-down behavior on behalf of the greater civic good.[3]

Glass

Consider the following: (1) Doc often, though not always, wears eyeglasses. (2) When Doc and Carol McCoy enter her apartment's bedroom after his parole is secured, he asks her if she has been with other men during his prison term. "Four years is a long time," Carol evasively replies, her facial reaction additionally suggesting her incredulity that Doc has never asked her this question before during her prison visitations. As Doc ponders her answer, he moves into the bathroom, where the camera shows him shirtless, facing a mirror but not really looking at it. As the couple reach a provisional peace while they sit on Carol's bed, Peckinpah shoots the scene from behind them, their backs and turned heads dominating the screen, framing them with a large mirror resting atop a chest of drawers behind them. (3) When Doc prepares to enter Beynon's ranch home, aware now that Beynon has already double-crossed him by hiring Rudy Butler to kill him after the robbery, Doc's full figure is briefly framed by and reflected in a sliding glass door. (4) Later, when Doc and Carol stop in a small town on their way to El Paso, Doc's picture flashes on television screens inside an appliance and hardware store. In order to make their getaway from a pair of local cops who soon arrive on the scene, Doc covers them with a shotgun he steals in the store and proceeds to shoot out the windows and the lights of their squad car. (5) Later still, when Doc and Carol stop for hamburgers at a drive-in restaurant, they are identified by the carhop as the "wanted" Beacon City bank robbers. Doc soon notices in their car's rearview mirror a police car sliding in behind them. Shots of shattered car windshields and windows punctuate the resulting chase and exchange of gunfire. (6) During the film's final shoot-out in the Laughlin Hotel, Doc at one point blasts his shotgun through one of the hotel's interior doors that has an upper panel of glass, exploding both the door's glass and the body of one of his pursuers who was hiding behind it.

The prominence of glass, windows, and screens in *The Getaway* confirms the movie's investment in the thematic and visual issues of framing, being framed, and escaping the frame(s). For me one of the film's pleasurable effects results from its visual (and noisy) destabilization of normative authority through images (and sounds) of material things exploding and shattering—in particular all the assorted police vehicles whose windows Doc demolishes in two different shoot-outs in two different small Texas towns. I suppose pleasure just might accrue in this world of multinational corporate capitalism where everything—whether oil in the ground or an armed robber serving hard time—has a price and can be put to work and exchanged, and where "productive" or "profitable" work means being (theoretically speaking) efficient, with putative little wasted effort and resources—because in just such a world shattered glass and chrome and wood and plastic, as well as vehicles exploding or swerving out of control during chase scenes, dramatize truly *extravagant* losses and expenditures. Doc McCoy finds himself laughing elatedly at the mayhem his shotgun creates with police cars, his childish glee emergent as material objects become entirely expendable in this theater of shattering.

Moreover, the abrupt transformation of heretofore solid forms into shattered glass and disparate fragments of metal and plastic and rubber thematically underlines the contingent, chance world presented in Peckinpah's films—where, for instance, an unexpected delay caused by a school crossing guard forces Doc to steer his car through the front porch of a house after it has been blown off the street by the concussions of explosives rigged to deflect the police attention away from the Beacon City bank. So perhaps my emergent identification with McQueen's "style" also involves not just his total look, so to speak, but how capably he responds to the sudden challenges posed by the volatile, unpredictable world through which his character moves. Literally and figuratively on the run, Doc McCoy displays his magical ability to shape material objects to his use. The fact is that Peckinpah's world is not, say, that televisual world of *Mission Impossible* or *CSI: Crime Scene Investigation* where things, so it seems, *always work*. All the successive violent explosions of glass and other material substances highlighted by Peckinpah's patented slow motion and crosscutting techniques complement the trajectory of McCoy's education under fire in this film. Thematically speaking, then, the movie's plot essentially educates McCoy to place his trust in his wife and companion—not in the paper money and the metal cars and the plastic radios that are just as volatile as any other material item in the film and that are indifferent or, better yet, entirely neutral with regard to personal commitments.

Repeated scenes involving reflecting surfaces and shattered glass also serve another important function in *The Getaway*. This is to deflect the male spectator's gaze from transforming a male action hero (such as McQueen) into an object of erotic looking. As Paul Smith and Steve Neale have argued, male spectatorial pleasures in traditionally "masculine" movie genres such as action-adventure films depend on the kind of narcissistic identification through which, as I summarized above, the male hero becomes an attractive object of desire. From this perspective, the challenge faced by Hollywood moviemakers is to solicit such identification with the male hero—but at the same time to prevent that looking at the male actor (and his body) by male viewers from crossing over into or becoming in the end a fully homoerotic look. For his part Smith discusses various cinematic techniques in Clint Eastwood's movies that function to prevent the male hero from becoming the object of male spectators' erotic gazes, while Neale discusses how wounding and scarifying the male hero's body presumably forestalls any transformation of homosocial attachment into the patently homoerotic gaze.[4] With such insights in mind, I would suggest that in *The Getaway* Peckinpah's obvious delight in shattering effects works in analogous fashion to keep a male spectator's narcissistic identification within normative bounds. We might recall in this context how in the wake of the bank robbery Rudy Butler shoots Frank Jackson (Bo Hopkins) in the groin and kicks his dying body out of their car just as the timed detonations of diversionary explosions go off around Beacon City.

In addition, Peckinpah's repeated use of mirrors and other reflecting screens self-reflexively reminds viewers how the very act of looking—not just the manifest act of getting away with the money and the woman—itself structures or determines the movie's narrative logic. Peckinpah does not adorn the movie's sets with reflecting surfaces so as to show Doc and Carol looking at themselves, but rather to foreground how a drama of surveillance and voyeuristic looking potentially implicates movie viewers as well as characters in the scenes. I watch McCoy wrap a towel around himself in front of a bathroom mirror in Carol's apartment, for instance, and it dawns on me that the spatial logic or perspectival optics of Peckinpah's shot means McCoy, or someone else reflected beyond the mirror's frame, could in fact be watching me watching the scene. Self-consciously aware both of my looking at McCoy in the bathroom and of my potentially being overlooked and looked over in this very scene of looking, my spectatorial identification gets eerily distanced from Doc McCoy, my erstwhile masculine *imago*. Thus, as McQueen beats on and gets beaten up by others before either whole or shattered reflecting surfaces and screens, Peckinpah creates a paradoxical visual space in which commingle both a distanced objectification of and narcissistic identification with McQueen's corporeal presence.

Carol Is Being Beaten

When Carol McCoy visits Jack Beynon in his office to "sell" Doc in exchange for Beynon's arranging his parole, Beynon asks if she would like a drink. In this moment the camera is centered on the seated Carol, looking toward the off-screen Beynon, who has moved from his desk to the bar, her face registering her acceptance of his invitation, to quote his words, to "come on over." After the robbery, when Doc tensely enters Beynon's home through the sliding glass porch door and converses with him while the money is being counted, Carol enters through another door and silently approaches Doc from behind with a raised pistol. Beynon believes Carol has in fact "come on over" to his side and will shoot Doc in the back, so successful has been her performance in convincing him of her desire to be free from Doc's authority. But Carol switches the direction of her aim from Doc's back and shoots the surprised Beynon several times in the chest, his dying body caught in slow motion flying backwards from his desk and chair. By continuing the slow motion effect when the scene cuts back to Doc and Carol as they turn and point their pistols at each other, Peckinpah intensifies the shock of this sudden outbreak of violent action and sound, and this technique further intensifies—by stretching out the moment's duration—the viewer's own uncertainty about whether Carol's killing of Beynon was premeditated and about whether Doc and Carol now will impulsively open fire on each other in the heat of the moment.

Beynon thinks he is the puppet master in charge of financing the whole "show," while Doc thinks he is in charge of the robbery caper's "fine stuff," which is to say both its planning of the job and the handling of the stolen money. Doc tells Rudy Butler and Frank Jackson that they are "strictly backup, backup all the way." Unsurprisingly, masculine authority and power get bound up with class and gender hierarchies, these facets of identity ostensibly grounded in relation to money, which is to say dependent upon how close or how distant characters are from its source and how much or how little they possess or are likely to possess in the future. Because money can be only a sign of value (in *The Getaway* the stolen money represents an oil company's earnings and investments), not the ground of value itself, and because money constantly circulates as an exchange item, men pursue it, struggle to possess it, and through its possession (or loss) authorize their masculine subjectivities (or their passive subjection or abjection to others). The linear narrative movement of *The Getaway* traces how a desire for money (and the power and freedom it signifies) brings men together (and ultimately divides them) in a series of transactions beginning with McCoy and Carol selling themselves to Beynon and ending with Doc and Carol purchasing an old Chevy pickup truck from a cowboy-junk dealer (Slim Pickens) whom they have commanded at gunpoint to drive them across the border into Mexico.

The detours, wrong turns, and backtracking Doc and Carol make on their way to El Paso and their final border crossing prolong the pleasure of the action movie's basic capture-escape-pursuit plot. Yet as much as I might prefer to linger on a male hero's ultimate mastery of the material world through a series of life-or-death tests, McCoy's obsessive approach to and courting of death, much less the disasters displayed during the couple's uneven progress toward their successful getaway across the border, suggests still another point: that my viewing pleasure just might depend as much on the male hero's *inability* to master the world—his being subject to unpredictable circumstances that constantly threaten to catch him, figuratively speaking, with his pants down. *The Getaway* officially locates this dialectic of power and powerlessness, mastery and dependency, as battles between men over possession of "money" that was, first, in the ground in the form of petroleum and natural gas, then in a bank vault in the form of paper currency, and eventually placed in a briefcase that changes hands more than once after the initial heist by McCoy and his crew. "Dirty" money, in short, brings "dirty" men together.

But as the scene in Beynon's home reveals, the struggle over possessing an attractive woman named Carol McCoy proves to be the real "price" the film's narrative exacts in order to progress from Huntsville through Beacon City and on to El Paso and across the border. Carol's actions behind the scenes—and her apparently spontaneous decision to shoot Beynon rather than Doc—produce Beynon's bloody corpse instead of a clean fiscal exchange between the two men, and so the narrative must detour away from the faster and smoother getaway signified by the nearby border crossing at Laredo. Moreover, the next major narrative detour on the McCoys' longer journey across west Texas to El Paso occurs in a train station when a small-time thief switches locker keys with Carol while Doc hides their car in a nearby parking garage. Although Doc eventually recovers the money after stalking the thief aboard an Amtrak train, he doesn't search the man he has knocked unconscious and, as a result, doesn't retrieve one sheaf of bills the thief has put in his coat pocket. Marked as the property of the Beacon City bank, this sheaf of bills get linked specifically to Doc when police later interrogate the thief, who, along with a couple of kids and their mother, identifies McCoy as the thief's assailant. The media broadcast of this news and the televisual display of Doc's booking photo further complicate Doc and Carol's escape and entangle them into two shoot-outs with police on their way to the Laughlin Hotel in El Paso.

In general, then, the successive displays of Doc's cool expertise in getting the couple out of tight spots on their way to the border always occur *in the wake of* Carol's movements and decisions. What seems to be the narrative center in *The Getaway*—the trust and betrayal among men struggling for control of a satchel of stolen money—is substantially eclipsed, then, by the film's unofficial narrative, its dirty little secret, so to speak. This narrative and its accompanying secret center on how women such as Carol McCoy (and, later, Fran Clinton) dangerously and somewhat unpredictably change allegiances, circulate across various legal and social borders, and in effect put masculine authority in crisis. The possibility of proving and (re)establishing normative masculine authority, much less achieving a "clean" narrative getaway, whether from Huntsville or Beacon City, thus depends at bottom on the access to and control of women, both their bodies and their possessions. But beginning with the bedroom scene in Carol's apartment and on through the scene of Beynon's death, Doc McCoy begins to learn what perhaps he always subliminally suspected: that access to Carol McCoy is not the same thing as possessing, much less controlling, her. Though cast as McCoy's messenger and assistant, and though fervent in voicing her loyalty to him in the aftermath of this confrontation in Beynon's home, Carol McCoy proceeds—as the camera frames her mouth open in shock and wonder while she points her weapon at Doc—to raise the specter of a woman acting as an independent contractor willing to wield her body and a gun to further her own desires.

Contemplating this specter of a woman who has traded places with a man and who has occupied the "active" position in the active/passive binary is apparently too much for Doc to handle, after he has already been abjected by the prison system and been forced to work for Beynon. *The Getaway* proceeds through disciplinary tactics and cynical mockery (rehashing the Jezebel type) to cover over the dirty little secret of women having their hands on and controlling guns, money, and men's sexual desires—and the consequences of this power for masculine subjectivity. On the one hand, the veterinarian's wife, Fran Clinton, does not stay in her place and sustain her loyalty to her husband. But the film codes both her complicity with Rudy Butler's plan to catch Doc and Carol and her sexual infidelity as a narcissistic, erotic preference for Butler's swarthy potency, this emblematized by the big pistol he asks her to fondle while the couple lies together in bed. On the other hand, Doc verbally humiliates and physically punishes the Carol McCoy who has transgressed her subordinate role as his messenger and helpmate. In the scene that directly follows Carol's shooting of Beynon, Doc drives their station wagon off the highway pavement, parks the car, and proceeds to slap Carol around as they stand beside the car, his rational "cool"—documented as being so crucial for his survival—now unable to keep up with and control the rage his ruthless, reckless hands act out.

Up to this point, Carol has beaten both Doc and Beynon to the punch, so to speak, but now she is being beaten as part of the movie's anxious recuperation of the patriarchal order. I say "anxious" here not only because of the emergent panic Doc experiences as he considers whether Carol can be trusted, which is to say "cleaned up" and restored to her subordinate place while he takes care of the caper's "fine stuff." Even as the movie's narrative trajectory displays Doc working from here on out to rein in Carol's past excesses as well as her present and ongoing amateurish mistakes regarding the handling of the stolen money, Doc's verbal and physical disciplinary tactics in this scene underline the movie's ambivalent visual address to its hypothetical male spectator. On the one hand, if the narcissist fantasy of mastery and control is grounded by the illusion that one finally has no need of another, then Doc's initial dependency on both Carol and Beynon contends against the character Doc McCoy's cool professionalism and the actor McQueen's image as an autonomous, self-sufficient, and private star. So any identification with Doc's panic as he slaps Carol around, a possibility clearly promoted by Peckinpah's successive point-of-view shots, involves on one level a male's *sadistic* pleasure in fending off the threat of a castrating woman and disciplining her for presuming to usurp masculine power.[5]

On the other hand, because Carol's shooting of Beynon confirms her preference for Doc over the older man, and because her instrumental use of her body as a means to an end clearly signifies to the viewer that possessing her body does not necessarily entail possessing "her," the movie simultaneously solicits the viewer's identification with the woman who in this scene has become the object of Doc's verbal and physical abuse. If it can further be said that Doc and Carol, in their careers as criminals, literally and figuratively have rebelled against a patriarchal society's laws and disciplinary authorities, then it is the case that Doc's beating Carol in this scene positions him structurally in the paternal function, fulfilling the role of patriarchal authority figure whom the viewer heretofore has been invited to challenge or at least to be cynical about since the movie's opening moments. The point here, then, is that this scene of Carol being beaten by Doc, although clearly sadistic in form and thus invoking a pleasurable fantasy of mastery connected with his recharged masculine competency, also hypothetically offers the "male" spectator a *masochistic* gratification through his identification with the symbolic victimized "child" who is being beaten by a sadistic parental patriarch. So in effect the scene proceeds in one direction as if its paradigm is "My father [Doc] is beating the child [Carol] that I hate/envy (and therefore [he] loves me)." Within this scene's overall sadistic form, though, the viewer's equally possible identification with the Carol McCoy who is being beaten fosters an alternative pathway for desire: "I am being beaten (and therefore loved) by my father."[6]

The additional point to make here is that the viewer's potential oscillation between sadistic and masochistic pleasures promoted by this scene underpins the movie's contradictory ambition *both* to challenge, at least temporarily, patriarchal authority *and* to reaffirm the dominant Law of the Father. "Here's your boy," says one of Beynon's men, gesturing toward Doc as he walks toward the meeting with the older man who has arranged his parole. As a corrupt father figure who represents Peckinpah's version of the state's bankrupt authority during the Vietnam-war era, Beynon, like the other figures of authority in the film, is displaced by a "boy" who in the end refuses to submit to his orders and directions. But as this "boy" beats Carol in his rage and frustrated panic, he begins to recuperate normative masculine authority and the paternal function at the same time his outlaw actions challenge it. Thus by means of this scene's restaging of a layered sadomasochistic scenario, the movie conceivably offers its hypothetical male views of the pleasurable experience of simultaneously inhabiting *both* strong-father *and* rebellious-son subject positions. One could argue that all of Peckinpah's major films—from *Ride the High Country* through *Pat Garrett and Billy the Kid* and on to *Convoy*—repeat and work through versions of this sadomasochistic scenario of filial relations so as to offer its spectators just this kind of pleasurable, though ambivalent, "gift."

The Excremental Gift

After switching storage locker keys with Carol and stealing the black satchel she has wanted to stow away until the train for El Paso leaves, the thief

(Richard Bright) hurriedly leaves the Amtrak station and boards another train preparing to depart. With Doc closely pursuing him, the thief quickly moves through each car while passengers are boarding. Reaching the end of the train, the thief backtracks through the passenger cars, picks a lock to a bathroom door, and hides inside the bathroom until the train leaves the station, the camera showing him looking out its window at McCoy, who has exited the train and scans the area, looking for signs of the thief's getaway. As the train picks up speed the thief leaves the cramped bathroom and stretches out in a nearby seat, finally having time to open the satchel and discover its contents. After discovering the stolen bank cash, he enjoys a few moments of happiness before McCoy, who we know has re-boarded the train, quietly slides into the adjacent seat. "When you're working a lock, don't leave any scratches," McCoy tells the thief—and then knocks him unconscious and covers his bloodied and soon-to-be bruised face with his cowboy hat. Doc buys two tickets from the conductor "to the end of the line," but he eventually gets off this train and returns to Carol, who is waiting for him in the train station where this surprising detour in their getaway has begun. The thief eventually wakes up in pain and asks two kids to call the conductor. As Carol and Doc resume their journey through the night on still another train heading west, Peckinpah's camera again framing them in front of a reflecting sheet of glass, police officers interview the thief, the conductor, and the kids. When asked where he got the bank money he had deposited in his inside suit pocket, the thief replies: "It was a gift."

Keys and gifts; bathrooms and closed doors—these spaces and things figure prominently in several other scenes in the film as well as this important sequence, which leads to Doc's identification as the Beacon City bank robber. Consider how, as Rudy Butler's pursuit of the McCoys begins to close the gap as everyone involved nears El Paso (Peckinpah shows their relative proximity by having them each listening to the same radio station in their respective cars), Rudy enters a motel bathroom in his underwear, notices the veterinarian Harold Clinton's corpse hanging from the shower rod, and—without much thought or any announcement of Harold's suicide to Fran Clinton in the bedroom—sits on the toilet and reads a newspaper while he smokes a cigarette. Later, at the Laughlin Hotel, Carol showers behind a closed bathroom door while Doc relaxes on the hotel room's bed, covering himself with some of the stolen bills and waiting his turn in the bathroom. After Carol exits the bathroom and joins Doc, their privacy is interrupted by Rudy's knock on the room's exterior door, followed by Fran's voice saying she has brought sandwiches for them. Instead of catching the McCoys by surprise and in various stages of undress, Doc picks the lock on the door connecting their room to a neighboring room and quietly opens its outer door. Masking his surprise at seeing Rudy's magical reappearance on the scene after having been shot several times, Doc drops him with a blow to the head just as he had earlier done with the thief on the train.

As is the case, according to Sharon Willis, for characters in director Quentin Tarantino's films, so in Peckinpah's *The Getaway* when characters enter or leave bathrooms, open or close doors, obtain and misplace keys, and pick locks and leave (or not leave) scratches, their worlds dramatically change for better or worse.[7] Both human and nonhuman objects of desire in this film exist literally and figuratively behind closed doors, so that a drama of breaking and entering receptacle-like spaces complements the cinematography's formal stress on framing and breaking the frame. In *The Getaway*, this sequence of "keys" creates openings, solves enigmas, or unearths hidden treasures: drilling bits bore through the earth's surface and tap into subterranean oil reserves; Jack Beynon literally "screws" Carol McCoy and figuratively tries to screw Doc by having Rudy Butler kill him after the robbery; bolt cutters wielded by an armed robber pry open a bank vault's steel gate protecting the cash reserves created by "black gold"; a key opens a storage locker holding a black satchel of money from the bank; a set of picks opens a locked bathroom on a train or a hotel room's connecting door. Beginning with the film's close-up shots of prison guards opening and closing a succession of cell doors and concluding with the drama of keys, locks, and doors during the Laughlin hotel shoot-out, the film indexes the possession of keys and the ability to open locked doors as a sign of power and authority just as necessary to survival as possessing Carol (the key to Doc's parole) and the satchel of money (the financial key to their future).

As the scenes with the thief on the train, with Rudy and the Clintons in the motel, and with the three-way shoot-out at the Laughlin Hotel indicate, this drama of breaking (by drilling bits, bolt-cutters, keys, picks) and entering (the earth; vaults; lockers; bodies) centers at key junctures on the space of bathrooms. As Willis points out, bathrooms constitute an important site for a certain kind of filmmaker exploring issues of gender and violence precisely because they define a paradoxical space where waste matter is produced (and disposed of) and where cleaning and hygiene occur. The thief enters a train car's bathroom and discovers that the storage locker and toilet receptacles have together produced a solid, countable "gift" in the form of "dirty" money; Rudy deposits his shit in a motel bathroom's toilet while being overseen by the lifeless eyes and limp hands of the dead vet who had earlier treated his bloody gunshot wounds in his animal clinic. As a site of both sanitation and contamination, bathrooms are places where matter gets transformed, where "gifts" are made, and where what could be called Peckinpah's abiding "excremental logic" linking anality, sadism, money, and feces comes into focus.

The movie's excremental logic—produced itself by the intersection of Jim Thompson's original novel, Walter Hill's screenplay adaptation, and Peckinpah's direction—defines all of its male characters' material objects of desire as forms of pollution or contaminating waste matter. "Playing the game" with deposits in the earth or in the bank or in a storage locker stains everyone and everything—as if the spreading pools of underground oil reserves have been transformed into the pools and streaks of blood draining or spouting out of bodies. This staining process theoretically envelops the movie's hypothetical spectator as well, whose pleasure as the plot proceeds in part depends on connecting with the movie's occasional infantile regression to anal sadistic pleasures—to the joint satisfaction of producing a gift (in the form of feces, blood, money, bodies; shattered glass) and subverting the social taboo on filth by smearing or playing with such gifts. Here we might recall the first instance of the color red the film presents: on the morning after his release from prison, Doc dollops a heavy load of ketchup on the scrambled eggs he is cooking for breakfast, his pleasure in the prospect of eating real food no greater than his boyish pleasure in mixing up these foods according to his own culinary vision ("Fantastic," he says aloud to himself). However, Carol enters the scene (if her wet hair and bathrobe are accurate signs, she has just come from the bathroom after another shower), and Doc responds as if he has been caught doing something he shouldn't be doing, say finger-painting with red and yellow, his mixing of foods in a visual disarray. Here we might recall of course Peckinpah's repetitive visual lingering over ribbons of blood sprayed on hotel walls, or pools of blood erupting and staining clothing, or faces purpling and discolored after being pummeled. Here we might recall Rudy's playing with his food while in the backseat of the Clintons' car as they make their way to El Paso, the way his taunting of Harold escalates from poking him with a barbecued rib into tossing the ribs at both him and Fran, also in the car's front seat, the sticky brick-red sauce eventually staining both her clothes and Rudy's white bandage that covers his wounded upper torso.

In concert with the motif of keys and the paradoxical space of bathrooms, such moments indicate how the movie's predominant conception of breaking and entering is that of phallic penetration. Frank Jackson's groin; Jack

Beynon's chest; Rudy Butler's collarbone; the thief's face—the solid male body is opened time and time again with penetrating violence, so that fluids leak out or flower forth as brilliantly as do the flames leaping out of police cars and flatbed trucks. The fluid matter in a Peckinpah film is typically blood red, but urine leaks out of penetrated bodies too, as when the vet Harold Clinton, after Rudy refuses to let him make a restroom stop, urinates on himself while driving his car. Wounds and trails of blood signify proof of one's penetration by others, one's body being broken into and entered and reduced to the level of polluted matter, to the corpse as abject body, as "dead shit" or trash in need of disposal. In this regard, Doc's question about whether Beynon "got to" Carol remains an open one because there is no visible evidence on her body in the form of wounds or blood that would allow Doc to confirm whether in fact she has been broken into and entered, possessed mentally as well as owned physically.

But there's more to be noted in this context. "Superior technology, my ass," says a Beacon City dentist whose lights and power drills are cut off at the same time McCoy disables the power to the bank by cutting through conduits covering electrical lines cached in an utility tunnel below the street. As Rudy forces the Clintons to take him to El Paso, Fran Clinton offers herself willingly to Rudy, and during their nights in the motels along the way Harold is bound to a chair and forced to watch his wife actively cavort with Rudy, whose sexual intercourse with Fran is at the same time an aggressive ocular penetration of Harold that cements his abjection and forecasts his suicide. "Stick 'im down a dry hole, if you can find one," says Beynon's accountant-brother in response to an accomplice's query about what they should do with Jack Beynon's corpse lying on the floor of his ranch home. Such a rejoinder explicitly links anality, sadistic pleasure, and death as clearly as does the scene with Rudy and the dead vet Harold in the motel bathroom, and such a rejoinder semantically links the "dry hole" to the ash pit Rudy falls into after being shot by Doc in the torso and collarbone outside the abandoned farmhouse where they have met immediately after the bank heist.

Given the movie's linkage of money and feces and the screenplay's various anal references (asses and dry holes), it becomes abundantly clear that penetration appears in this movie as not just any kind of aggressive phallic violation of a thing's or person's protective envelope—say, male and female bodies and orifices; a locked door; the earth's crust; a bank's vault. Such penetration of eyes and orifices and various closed receptacles by various "keys" gets conceptualized in this movie predominantly according to a model of *anal* penetration. Characters surprised by unexpected turns of events, by what happens when closed doors suddenly open, both literally and figuratively get it from behind (as do the thief and Rudy near film's end; as do Carol and Doc while they are eating hamburgers at the drive-in), have their "power" turned off (as does the dentist; as does the bank; as does the elevator in the Laughlin Hotel; as does anyone who dies), and get discarded down dry holes or in ash pits and in elevators, or over empty bathtubs, behind broken glass doors, and down flights of stairs.

Don't Mess with Texas

"If we're clean," Carol tells the group of robbers during a planning session, "we'll cross over at Laredo. If we're not, we'll try Laughlin's Hotel in El Paso." In the screenplay's logic, a "clean" series of transactions between men—that is, without blood or betrayals or "*foul*-ups"—would result in a "clean"—straightforward; uncomplicated—getaway across the border at Laredo. But of course such transactions as the film proceeds are *not* clean—bodies are jolted and spill blood; minds get polluted by various double crosses that breed suspicion and distrust. Instead of a straightforward escape by car at Laredo, Doc and Carol transact a circuitous and dangerous journey to El Paso by car, train, bus, and truck. As they near El Paso and stop for food at a drive-in restaurant, the McCoys are "made" by a carhop who has noticed the wanted flyers circulated by police in the wake of the thief's interrogation and Doc's earlier trashing of a police car in another small Texas town. Police officers in patrol cars try to capture them again, but this shoot-out sequence ends with Doc and Carol abandoning their damaged car and hiding in a garbage dumpster in an alley. As the lights of patrol cars pierce the darkness in vain attempts to locate the wanted couple, a garbage truck picks up the dumpster containing Doc and Carol, and they spend a tense night amid the smelly debris that accumulates as the truck completes its rounds—and that threatens to crush them as the truck's driver operates its hydraulic compactor during each stop.

After completing its rounds, the garbage truck drives with its full load of trash to an isolated, wind- and smoke-swept landfill, where Doc and Carol are ejected from the truck into a larger, debris-cluttered pit. They scramble to the cover afforded by the rusted shell of a car, and in the ensuing dialogue Doc admits the truth of Carol's earlier observation that their making a "clean" getaway wouldn't mean a thing if in the process they happened to lose each other. Whereas the dialogue scene at the train station after Doc has recovered the satchel from the thief revealed him proposing that the pair split the cash and separate, in this scene Doc, now admitting how difficult it is for him to express his "need" for Carol, must persuade Carol to continue their getaway together. When Doc accepts her demand that he say "no more" about Beynon, they mutually agree to "leave it there" in the landfill debris and then resume their journey together, the camera in a long-distance shot tracking them walking arm-in-arm up and out of the landfill, heading toward what will be a laundry where they are next shown waiting behind the doors of dressing stalls for their clothing to be cleaned and delivered to them.

The swimming hole into which the pair have jumped and emerged fully clothed after Doc's release from prison has been reconfigured near the movie's end as a garbage pit, which the couple enter and from which they similarly depart arm-in-arm; the cleansing motif that begins with their swim and their showers in Carol's apartment culminates in the El Paso laundry and then the Laughlin Hotel bathroom shower Carol takes (and Doc waits to take) while they wait to cross the border that night. As it turns out, after violently fending off the challenges to their getaway from Beynon's remaining men and from Rudy Butler, their emergency border crossing in daylight will be enabled by an old man in a cowboy hat driving an ancient Chevrolet pickup whose bed is loaded with assorted junk gleaned from the trash containers in an alley near the Laughlin Hotel. The movie's narrative trajectory thus displays how Doc and Carol's initial contact with water (Doc is also shown from the waist up showering in prison) documents merely an illusory cleansing, while it is only after their ritual contagion from society's waste and their passage through the "dry hole" of the landfill and the darkened corridors of the Laughlin Hotel that their border crossing at El Paso with a junk dealer can finally cleanse them of the polluting matter which has dirtied them since Doc's stint in Huntsville.

In his discussion of Clint Eastwood's films, Paul Smith argues that the male hero's sequential passage from objectification (as an ego ideal; as a potential object of erotic interest) through the testing of his powers (being beaten; given up for dead) and on to the recuperation of them at film's end through a destructive release of energy constitutes "the orthodox structuring code" for action movies.[8] For Smith, whose observations about Eastwood apply equally well to Peckinpah's films, the hero's ultimate reaffirmation of the male's status as the fully competent originator of action and meaning discloses how the "pleasure proffered in action movies can be regarded . . . not so much as the perverse pleasure of transgressing given norms, but as at bottom the pleasure of reinforcing them." Thus, the orthodox structuring code Smith deciphers in action movies reveals how the genre overdetermines its critique of traditional political, legal, juridical, and cultural authorities with an ending that reinforces its inherently conservative nature. Yet Smith also argues that the male hero's eventual resolution of the masochism trope (the pleasure of being tested and [momentarily] powerless) into mastery at film's end nevertheless exists "alongside a residual, of barely avowed male hysteria." Viewers glimpse this hysterical residue in moments where the male hero is incoherent or powerless and where he is vulnerable as a result of alliances he forges with, as is typically the case in this genre, women or homosexuals. Such moments and alliances together produce what Smith calls "an underside, a double edge, or residue" that threatens the stable (neat and clean) closures desired by even "the most conservative and rigid kind of cultural production" represented by male action movies.[9]

I refer to Smith's suggestive claims largely because they conceptually articulate what is at stake in Peckinpah's collection of visual images, dialogue references, and narrative progressions in *The Getaway*. As Doc travels from Huntsville to El Paso and across the border, he moves from the condition of abjection to that of mastery, in the process taking power back from Carol and Beynon and removing from a state of crisis both the marriage contract and his masculine agency and competency. As the cowboy junk-dealer (Slim Pickens) drives the couple toward the border after their getaway from the carnage at the Laughlin Hotel, he offers the opinion that the "trouble with the world nowadays" is that "there ain't no morals." His sense of contemporary immorality centers on the horror of "kids" living together and having sex without also undertaking the marriage commitment. His delight in hearing that the "kids" named Doc and Carol are married overpowers whatever reservations he might have about being forced at gunpoint to take them across the border—and the affectionate look between Carol and Doc riding beside him suggests that they are indeed getting away not only with murder and money, but also with their love and marriage renewed and strengthened. Normative heterosexuality, masculine subjectivity, and patriarchal authority get redeemed by the man Beynon calls at one point "the good doctor," all this sanctioned by an avuncular cowboy junk-dealer who gives the outlaw couple his blessing ("vaya con dios") as he begins his walk back to the U.S. side of the border with his pockets full of money offered by the McCoys. From this perspective, *The Getaway* is "just an old-fashioned love song," which is the lyric from the song of the same title that plays on their car radio as they approach their first roadblock in the wake of the Beacon City bank robbery.

Given the movie's overall narrative trajectory and the contrast it offers to novelist Jim Thompson's continuation of the story to the point where Doc and Carol eventually betray each other in Mexico, this closure surely seems not only sentimental, but also "conservative" precisely in the manner with which Smith characterizes Eastwood's action movies.

With this in mind, I think the key point about *The Getaway* would seem to be *not*, as at least one earlier critic of Hollywood masculinity argues, that Peckinpah's film violence represents displaced homosexual embraces by men who cannot communicate their true feelings for each other.[10] If anything, as I have tried to show by reflecting on the film's preoccupation with a verbal and visual discourse of hygiene and contamination, characters in *The Getaway* rather strain to avoid merger and fusing, avoid the embrace that would reduce a body with substantial integrity and coherence to indiscriminate, formless, or fluid matter, this dangerous condition epitomized by shattered glass and metal and landfill debris and, of course, by the numerous falling and fallen human bodies ripped apart by bullets. The movie's recuperation of masculine authority depends at bottom upon the preservation or restoration—in a dirty, violent, and morally ambiguous world—of solid borders and boundaries grounded by a fundamental principle of *difference and distinction*: the difference between letter and the spirit (of the law; of the body); the difference between masculine and feminine subjectivities (active/passive; penetrating/penetrated); the difference between genital heterosexual love and anal sadism; the difference between true marriage and casual sex; and the difference between life and death. Moreover, if things like marriages and money have value not for what they are or have been but for what they will be or become in the future, which is one way of defining the hopeful fantasy operating at this film's end when the McCoys agree to leave their resentments in the landfill, then we can understand the film's acute desire to establish also the difference between past and present as it proceeds to stabilize sexual, gender, and class differences.

But no matter how successful this effort might seem with the McCoys' getaway at the end, there still exists an "underside, double edge, or residue of hysteria" about possible contamination and abjection from being in contact with "dirty" things and people. In Peckinpah's movie the fundamental presence of surplus expenditures of desire means things like money, criminal men and women, and waste will not stay in place and, as a result, that the imagery of contamination and border crossing or blurring—blood leaking out and staining bodies; women getting to and being gotten to by various men; supposedly principled men who are yet criminals—cannot be eradicated. However "clean" their new start will seem to be in Mexico after their surviving an extended ritual of defilement, the McCoys of course have killed and robbed and have themselves been stained with the film's images of trash and waste matter. And however transgressive the film might be in its portrait of emasculated or corrupt official authorities, it yet moves to re-establish phallic law and the paternal function as the "kid" Doc usurps the position of the "father" Beynon. The real McCoys have to be considered clean and dirty, moral and immoral, rebellious children and reformed parents.

In the context of this movie's meditation on how one makes and what it might mean to make a "clean" getaway, another moment near the film's end deserves greater attention. After the McCoys' reconciliation in the landfill and before they check in at the Laughlin Hotel, a transition scene shows Doc eating a hot dog and drinking a soda while sitting on a bus bench and waiting for Carol, who is offscreen purchasing a new set of wheels to finish their journey. Carol arrives to pick him up, and after Doc joins her in the car and they drive away, a Latina woman still sitting on the bus bench picks up his soda bottle and drinks its remaining contents while she intently scans a newspaper. As this scene ends, Peckinpah positions the camera over the woman's shoulder, so the viewer also scans the newspaper with her—and thus sees a picture of Doc McCoy and the prominent headline about his being wanted for robbery and murder. Any tension present in the scene about Doc's being identified once again by the public dissipates into a quiet irony centering on the woman's obliviousness to the fact that the man who had just been sitting next to her is the same "wanted" man pictured in the newspaper she holds. So this relatively brief moment, besides providing Peckinpah with a transition between the McCoys waiting for their clean clothes and their arrival at the Laughlin Hotel, offers us another one of his sly jokes on normative mass society's blindness, its inability to recognize the danger in its midst posed by respectable-looking men like Doc McCoy (or Jack Beynon).

But this transition scene thematically links hygiene matters—the possibility of contamination and contagion—with the consumption by and of bodies. As evidence of the film's double-edged recognition about the futility of clearly fixing and stabilizing borders and boundaries once and for all, this scene's quiet humor also connects with an unquiet pleasure. It does this, first, as the woman on the bench obviously consumes the soda remaining in the bottle with Doc's germs on it. And she may not be aware of this man's notoriety because it's entirely possible she in fact is reading one of the other stories on the newspaper's page. The headline and story below the prominent attention given to Doc McCoy details news from Vietnam: "Naval Buildup Said Biggest of Viet War." Though the movie's capture-escape-pursuit format seems to exist outside of a specific historical moment, this is the second time in the movie that newspaper headlines subtly locate the story in a specific historical moment. As Doc sits next to the unconscious thief on the train and waits for its next stop so he can get off and backtrack to Carol, the front page of the newspaper he holds facing the camera displays this headline: "US Gunship Downed Over Laos, Killing 11." So stories of consumption of people and things bleed into each other just as easily as the soda moves from Doc's mouth to the woman stranger's mouth. The soda bottle circulates between two strangers; a newspaper reader consumes two different stories about similar violent actions; the film viewer consumes a headline about an illegal military incursion across the Vietnam border into Laos, which leads to higher body counts. On the train a young black male kid wearing a muddy green Army hat shoots Doc in the face with a water pistol, mimicking the adult actions of Doc and the training received by all those soldiers in uniform who are shown waiting back at the station for the trains to take them to their assigned postings.

As much as Doc's criminal activity transgresses norms, his destructively violent energy basically only allegorizes a privatized version of the larger social order's contagion. Against this contagious violence no one is immune or can be inoculated—including the movie viewer whose eyes take in the Peckinpah "effect," centering on the spectacle of ocular penetration. Consider, for instance, the Peckinpah signature slow-motion technique to depict violent action, and his crosscutting such scenes as they unfold from start to finish with reaction shots of various onlookers who have been called out to witness the action, usually as a result of their hearing explosive sounds (explosions; gunshots). In *The Getaway* this technique memorably occurs when Doc empties a shotgun into a parked police car, whose gasoline tank eventually explodes and starts a fire. Accelerated crosscutting intensifies the action by spreading out and registering its destructive effects on a variety of children's and adults' faces. Unlike the bound and gagged Harold Clinton forced to watch Fran and Rudy in bed together, these onlookers are shown shielding their faces or ducking out of sight and harm's way, as if responding instinctively to a hidden imperative to protect their eyes from visual soiling as well as their bodies from the flying shards of glass and bullets.

Since the camera positions the film's spectator so that he or she hypothetically continues to gaze at what the on-screen viewers cannot bear to look at, I reflect that my overall viewing experience inhabits an unstable zone of gratification produced by the gap between (1) an aggressive mode of looking ("show me everything—I can take it, Sam, even if they can't"), which parallels the male hero's aggressively phallic violence and distinctive individualism; and (2) an anxious fear of ocular penetration and soiling ("The spectacular excesses of this violence may spread like a contagion and infect me, as it did Harold Clinton, so I must needs avert my eyes and identify with those on-screen gazers scrambling for safety"). In the end, even as Doc McCoy resolves the masochism trope and recuperates masculine agency and authority, Peckinpah's various cinematic techniques work to prolong my irresolution and instability, my being caught in that borderland of ambivalence between identification with and objectification of McQueen's body, between the desire to be used up by what one takes in with the eyes, and the desire to protect oneself from ocular penetration so as not to become wasted by this film's own prolonged, anxious pleasure in playing with contagious waste.

Notes

1. See Julia Kristeva, *The Powers of Horror: An Essay on Abjection*, translated by Leon S. Roudiez (New York: Columbia University Press, 1982). My thinking about Kristeva's theorizing of the "abject" in relation to film and to gendered identity is also generally indebted to Barbara Creed, *The Monstrous-Feminine: Film. Feminism. Psychoanalysis* (London: Routledge, 1993), especially chapter 1, and Jonathan Rutherford, *Men's Silences: Predicaments in Masculinity* (New York: Routledge, 1992), 178–80.

2. Steve Neale, "Masculinity as Spectacle: Reflections on Men and Mainstream Cinema," in *Screening the Male: Exploring Masculinities in Hollywood Cinema*, edited by Steven Cohan and Ina Rae Hark (London: Routledge, 1993), 9–22. Also helpful in this regard is Anne Friedberg, "A Denial of Difference: Theories of Cinematic Identification," in *Psychoanalysis and Cinema*, edited by E. Ann Kaplan (New York: Routledge. 1990), 36–45.

3. With regard to the oscillating swing between objectification of and identification with the male body in relation to the increasingly abstract spaces of the modem era, see Gillian Swanson, "Burt's Neck: Masculine Corporeality and Estrangement," in *Me Jane: Masculinity. Movies, and Women*, edited by Pat Kirkham and Janet Thumin (New York: St. Martin's Press, 1995), 203–22.

4. Paul Smith, *Clint Eastwood: A Cultural Production* (Minneapolis: University of Minnesota Press, 1993); Neale, 15–18.

5. As Miriam Hansen has argued in another context, this pleasure of mastery and control constitutes the first phase of an overall sadomasochistic scenario predominant in certain films. See Miriam Hansen, "Pleasure, Ambivalence, Identification: Valentine and Female Spectatorship," *Cinema Journal* 25 (1986): 6–32.

6. Hansen, 19–20. My understanding of male masochism is also indebted to Kaja

Silverman's discussion in her *Male Subjectivity at the Margins* (New York: Routledge, 1992), 185–213.

7. Sharon Willis, *High Contrast: Race and Gender in Contemporary Hollywood Film* (Durham, N.C.: Duke University Press, 1997), 189–94.

8. Smith, 156.

9. Quoted material in this paragraph from Smith, 167.

10. See Joan Mellen, *Big Bad Wolves: Masculinity in the American Film* (New York: Pantheon, 1977), 322.

NINE

LEONARD ENGEL

"Who Are You?" "That's a Good Question"

SHIFTING IDENTITIES IN SAM PECKINPAH'S
PAT GARRETT AND BILLY THE KID

Much has been written on Sam Peckinpah's film *Pat Garrett and Billy the Kid*, on the characters, the themes, the differences in the three versions of the film, and, of course, on Peckinpah's usual battles with Hollywood executives. However, not much has appeared on the roles and relationships or the identities of the three major characters in the film: Pat, Billy, and Alias. The character of Alias is on the periphery of the action and is barely mentioned by some critics and reviewers, except to note that he is played by the folk/protest singer, very popular in the late 1960s, Bob Dylan. Reviewers have noted that Dylan's music is played and sung throughout the film and that the character of Billy is played by another popular singer of the time, Kris Kristofferson. Critics, of course, have discussed the relationship between Billy and Pat Garrett, played by James Coburn. But few have analyzed the roles of these characters or their interrelationships. This chapter will examine these principal players, paying particular attention to Alias's character as it relates to the theme of identity in the film.

Webster's Collegiate Dictionary defines alias as "otherwise known as" and "an assumed or additional name." In a text or film in which two major characters, like Billy and Garrett, have names that have been indelibly etched, not only in the consciousness of their own generation, but in the minds of many people in later generations, it seems odd to create a character with an "assumed or additional name," which is to say, a character with no name or an "anti-name." Using aliases is certainly not new to Western film; characters with several names, false names, and even no names have been prevalent; Clint Eastwood's "The Man with No Name" comes to mind. However, having a "nameless" character in a film where the identity of the two main characters is so emphatic invites further examination. One needs to ask what Peckinpah might be suggesting through the theme of identity, or lack thereof, in the film.

As many American writers and filmmakers have stressed the importance of identity in their characters, so does Peckinpah. From his earliest feature films to his latest, it is a major theme. Although many of his characters initially appear to have strong identities, these identities often change during the course of the film. Furthermore, characters whose identities do not change often experience an epiphany of sorts and discover they are not who they thought themselves to be. Examples would include Gil Westrum in *Ride the High Country*, Pike Bishop in *The Wild Bunch*, and David Sumner in *Straw Dogs*. In films where the main character seems to have a fairly fixed identity throughout (Junior in *Junior Bonner* or Cable in *The Ballad of Cable Hogue*), one can still see Peckinpah exploring identity, looking at what might cause it to change, and testing it against the identities of others.

In *Pat Garrett and Billy the Kid*, Peckinpah again emphasizes identity, particularly that of Alias, a term that ironically focuses the theme by announcing a no-name character. This namelessness and what it suggests about Alias's identity, however, also cause a reexamination of the two main characters, Billy and Pat, who have well-known names and seem to have fixed identities—at least in the beginning. Additionally, this theme also embraces larger issues, such as the changing times and changes in the nature of the Western itself. I base my argument on the 1973 film released in theaters by MGM, the shorter version, as it is commonly called, not the so-called Director's Cut, released on video in 1989. Though shorter, the theatrical version, as Paul Seydor has noted (1997, 300), reflects more accurately Peckinpah's cinematic artistry; it also, I believe, articulates more clearly the theme of identity.[1]

In Peckinpah's version of this well-known story, the identities of the two principals are established early. In a cantina in Fort Sumner, New Mexico, at their first meeting in the film, they have a last drink together while Pat states that he has been elected sheriff of Lincoln County and in five days he will start looking for Billy to force him out of the county. Surprised, Billy toasts Pat and asks how it feels to have sold out to the Santa Fe Ring. Not denying Billy's charge, Pat pauses, then slowly and deliberately says, "It feels like times have changed." Billy's retort is also very deliberate "Times, maybe; not me." While these remarks suggest change coming to the West, they also indicate that each of these characters knows who he is and what he is about. At the end of this short scene, one feels intensely the inevitability of the clash of these two characters, an intensity heightened by their seemingly fixed identities.

This clarity of identity is not evident in the early appearances of Alias. One sees him working in a newspaper office in Lincoln, carrying a pencil and pad, playing at being a reporter, but there is distinct uncertainty about him. When Garrett returns to town, after Billy's famous escape from the Lincoln jail, and sees Alias sitting in the barbershop, he asks "Who are you?" "Alias!" is the response. Later, when a posse is formed, Alias takes off his printer's apron, throws it on the floor, and rides off. Subsequently, he joins Billy's gang, but he's always hovering on the periphery, silent and watchful.

Paul Seydor points out that the role of the reporter in Westerns is a convention (1997, 288). One sees this character not only in other Westerns, but in the dime novels of the late nineteenth century. Interestingly, Peckinpah twists the convention a bit by casting Bob Dylan as the reporter. Dylan was a well-known singer and songwriter for a whole generation of 1960s young people. As Dylan's character becomes a sidekick to Billy, the audience hears Dylan singing of the Kid's exploits on the sound track. Thus, Peckinpah has Alias, the nameless character, help create the mythic identity of Billy the Kid, one of the West's most prominent and legendary names. However, Peckinpah will gradually undermine this identity as the film continues.

In point of fact, Billy's actions belie the mythmaking of Alias and the romanticizing music. "Virtually nothing Billy does is heroic, noble, or honorable. When he kills people, it is almost always from the back, out of ambush, or by surprise" (Seydor 1997, 288–89). In the earlier scene with Garrett, Billy's identity is revealed as stable and unchanging in the midst of change (times may change, but "not me"). One might even see a measure of heroism in his independent stand against the wealthy landowners of the Sante Fe Ring—with Dylan's music enhancing this heroic stance. But then Peckinpah undercuts this stance by showing the brutality of Billy's actions. They are depicted as thoroughly unheroic. Peckinpah cagily shifts perception, keeping the myth unsteady, so that viewers don't get too sure of or comfortable with Billy's identity.

If one has difficulty determining Billy's true nature and identity, one has even more trouble with the character of Alias, whom Barry Sarchett calls a "purposeful muddle." Peckinpah adds a clever touch to the complexity with the changing hats. In each of Alias's appearances, he is wearing a different hat (Sarchett 1992, 178), as though each were a different identity he is trying on for size.

In the shoot-out at Billy's outlaw camp, soon after Alias arrives, he is first seen awkwardly playing with his knife. When one of the bounty hunters asks him his name, he responds with "Alias." The hunter returns with "Alias what?" "Alias anything you please" is the reply, thus indicating he'll *be* anything you want. However, when the shooting starts, Alias, displaying bravura knife throwing, kills one of the bounty hunters cleanly through the neck and, from that point on, is accepted as one of Billy's gang. But he's always in the background, quietly observing, and he remains in this position until his appearance in Lemuel's saloon. This scene initially suggests Alias's importance to the gang, one of Billy's chosen, but that role is soon reduced to absurdity by Garrett.

Lemuel's place is a dirty hovel that passes for a frontier saloon and general store and appears to be a hangout for outlaws. Garrett is there, waiting, when Beaver, Holly, and Alias enter, and he draws his gun, quickly taking charge. Garrett commands Alias to knock Beaver out with the butt of a shotgun and pull a hat down over Lemuel's eyes. Then he tells Alias to read the labels of the canned goods on the shelves. While Alias reads, Garrett gets Holly so drunk that he pulls a knife, and Garrett shoots him. As Holly dies, Alias is still reading, haltingly, the labels "plums, beans, tomatoes...."

A brutal, ugly scene, it has been variously interpreted, especially by those who argue it is another instance of Garrett's cunning and cruelty as opposed to Billy's essential good nature and free spirit. Michael Bliss, for example, in an otherwise excellent series of readings of Peckinpah's films, argues that the entire scene "points up Garrett's . . . cruelty . . . in telling contrast to Billy, who kills only for retribution" (Bliss 1993, 244), which is not quite true. Undoubtedly, Garrett is cruel and manipulative, and, clearly, he wants to send Billy a deadly message. But it must be remembered that he is dealing with killers. Furthermore, he is certainly not enjoying what he does, especially when he shoots Holly, as his facial expressions indicate. The scene is also important in advancing the theme of identity.

As noted earlier, Alias is now a bona fide member of the gang, and although he's killed one of the bounty hunters, his role is still undefined, and he remains uncertain about who he is.[2] Garrett, in Lemuel's saloon, forces definition on him. Alias becomes, by Pat's direction, first, a man of action (or "Boy," as Garrett calls him), knocking out Beaver, pulling the hat over Lemuel's eyes, then becoming the sayer, the namer, that is to say, the chronicler of events, reminding one of Ralph Waldo Emerson's definition of the poet in his essay "The Poet." In short, Alias *does* become the poet of the Billy legend, but it's a legend that Garrett reduces to bathos, especially in this scene. In Alias's reading of the cans (the "airtights," Pat calls them), the legend becomes a joke, a ludicrous fantasy, perpetrated by wannabes and unreliable chroniclers.

On the other hand, the items Alias is naming defy legend; they are reality. The fruits and vegetables in the cans are basic, earthy commodities, whole and airtight, the simple truth, indestructible, unable to be denied or refuted, like airtight testimony. If Pat is giving Alias a message on how to chronicle the lives of so-called heroes of the wild West, like Billy the Kid, that lesson might be—beware the pitfalls of creating a legend about the "heroic" gunslingers. Beware creating a legend where reality will eventually disappear; it is better to stick to the basics. In Garrett's command to Alias to name the simple, unblemished fruits and vegetables, he is forcing Alias to state the unvarnished reality, confined within the can—the "airtight" truth.

Alias is still reading the labels, and Garrett, as he prepares to leave, says to him, "When you see Billy, tell him we had a drink together," which, although sounding simplistic, is another statement of reality—they *did* have a drink. When Alias relates this to Billy, Billy responds, "Maybe he'll have a drink with me," perhaps expressing his own desire for simple truth.

One other example of shifting identity occurs a little later, affirming, I believe, the direction in which Garrett has forced Alias's identity. Shortly after the character named Paco leaves Fort Sumner for Mexico, Billy says to Alias, "Mexico might not be bad for a couple of months." Alias replies "Depends on who you are." As Brad Stevens has noted, these lines are almost exactly repeated later, but the speakers are reversed. Alias says, "Mexico won't be so bad for a few months," and Billy responds, "I guess that depends on who you are." In his constant playing with identity and the nature of reality and myth, Peckinpah here reverses the roles of Billy and Alias, suggesting there may be little difference, ultimately, between myth and mythmaker; once the legend begins, they become, at times, interchangeable.

While concentrating on the shifting identity of Billy and Alias, Peckinpah has not neglected Garrett's identity; rather, he treats it with more subtlety. At the beginning, Garrett appears to know who and what he is, and what he wants. He is controlling and manipulative, forcing others, Billy and Alias most notably, to realize who they are. However, he seems not very satisfied with the new identity he has carved out for himself. Focusing on Coburn's world-weary face, Peckinpah vividly conveys the dramatic tension arising from Garrett's identity crisis. Thus, while the sheriff's actions are those of someone with a firm identity and in control, his face tells another story; it reveals his unhappiness and self-disgust.

In the first scene in Fort Sumner, at the beginning of the film, when Billy and his friends are target-practicing on the chickens, Garrett, approaching from behind with his deputy Bell, starts firing, sending Billy's crew momentarily flying for cover. His usurping the game by shooting at the chickens is an indication of his desire for control, and this dominance is evident in every scene in which he appears for the rest of the film—even those in which he is overshadowed by a more important character, for example, Governor Lew Wallace. However, in the cantina, when he tells Billy of his new role as sheriff and of his intention of growing old with the country, his face is tense and strained, revealing, I believe, the conflict of knowing he will eventually have to kill Billy.

In addition to the early scene with the chickens, another example of Garrett's desire for control is depicted when he is camping on the bank of a river. A slow-moving houseboat with a family aboard appears in the distance. Initially, the camera records this scene as an idyllic moment; the sun is setting, and a feeling of peace and tranquillity is evident. But this mood is quickly broken by the sound of shots. The father of the family on the boat is shooting at a target thrown into the water by one of his children. Garrett quietly observes this and then begins shooting at the target also. The father suddenly turns toward Garrett and fires, forcing Pat to seek cover behind a tree. Garrett aims at the man, as the man aims at Garrett, but neither shoots, and they remain locked in a silent stand-off, poised at the edge of violence, for several moments.

The mood is haunting, the atmosphere tense, but especially moving are the conflicting images. In depicting these family members floating down the river, apparently in harmony with their surroundings, Peckinpah juxtaposes the peace and beauty of the frontier with the disruption and dissonance of the father's shooting, first at the target in the water, then at Garrett. How low, the scene suggests, the threshold is for violence and sudden death on this beautiful, peaceful landscape. Implicit in the scene is another sentiment,[3] that of closure and death. When we first see him, Garrett is under a tree, which is stripped of leaves, sitting by a small fire that is nearly out. The day is almost over, the sun is setting; all is well, it seems, until the shooting starts.

Garrett has been lingering in his pursuit of Billy, not because he's undecided about whether to kill the Kid, but because he doesn't want to do it. This scene in all its tranquillity shows the imminence of death—its images are heavy in the air: the dying tree, the dying fire, the dying day, and the near death of either Garrett or the man on the boat. This imagery also anticipates not only Billy's death, but "the death of the vitality . . . associated with the frontier." By grounding the imagery in the scene on the four basic elements: earth, air, fire, and water (Stevens 1996, 270), Peckinpah enhances the melancholy mood and captures one of the truly profound moments in the film. In addition, he again implies his theme of the changing identity of the frontier landscape and, ultimately, of the West itself.

Furthering this theme of the shifting identity of the western landscape, Peckinpah frames Billy's return to Fort Sumner with a variety of camera shots featuring sunsets and barbed wire, both powerful images of closure and change. As Billy rides across what at first seems to be open land, the colors have a beautiful, autumnal glow, but barbed wire, displayed at odd angles, gradually appears, hemming him in. Clearly, Peckinpah is suggesting that change is coming to this landscape and to the supposedly free spirits who roam it.

Peckinpah saves the most effective sunset colors for the death of Sheriff Cullen Baker (played by Slim Pickens); this imagery, combined with Bob Dylan's song "Knocking on Heaven's Door," depicts an unforgettable, heart-rending moment. Garrett has asked Baker to help him clear out several members of Billy's gang who have been staying in a shack on the edge of town. Baker, a respected lawman in the past who now eschews gunfighting and has become a family man, is building a boat for his retirement. He doesn't want to join Garrett, telling him "the frontier is closing fast and there isn't much of the original spirit left in the old timers." Nevertheless, as though accommodating the new attitude and denying the "original spirit," he announces that if he agrees to go, it will cost Garrett "some change. I don't do nothin' no more lessen there's a piece of gold attached" (Wurlitzer, 1973, 32). Garrett tosses him a coin, which he at first pockets, but eventually tosses back to Garrett as he and his wife (Katy Jurado) prepare to leave.

The decision Sheriff Baker is faced with comes back to the question of identity; does he deny Garrett's request and remain fixed in his new, settled life, quietly awaiting retirement? Or does he accompany his old friend on this deadly mission, thus identifying himself with the "original spirit" of the old-timers? Trying to dissuade him from going, his wife says "You ain't that young no more. I say let 'em lie." Although he is not keen on going, his response indicates where his true identity lies: "Garrett'd git his ass shot off goin' up agin 'em alone. But I'll tell ya truth; I ain't got a shine fer it myself" (Wurlitzer 1973, 33).

The choice results in his being fatally shot in the ensuing gunfight. He haltingly walks toward the Pecos River, where he originally wanted to go with his boat. Then slowly he sits down by the bank "with a strikingly serene sunset and sublime mountains behind him in the distance, and his wife agonizingly crawling toward him" (Engel 1988, 27). In mythologizing Sheriff Baker's death, Peckinpah signifies the change coming—the end of the "original spirit" of the "old-timers," the death of the Old West.

Numerous other images of shifting identity appear in the film; I will mention only a few. When Billy and Alamosa Bill (recently deputized by Garrett) accidentally meet at the Horrell Trading Post and share a meal that will become, ironically, Alamosa's "Last Supper," Billy starts talking about how not so long ago *he* was the law riding for Chisum, while Pat was an outlaw. "The law's a funny thing, ain't it?" he says (Bliss 1993, 245). Before he was deputized, Alamosa Bill, also, lived outside the law. So the law, too, can change, depending on who has the power, money, and wherewithal to effect it.

A few moments after the meal, Billy shoots Alamosa in a confrontation neither wants but neither knows how to avoid. The role each plays at that moment, one a lawman, the other an outlaw, combined with the accidental circumstances throwing them together at the trading post, helps define their identities. In pacing the ten steps for the duel they must enact, they both cheat, but Billy cheats first and shoots, leaving Alamosa Bill lying dead in front of the Horrell family.

In two brief passing comments by minor characters, Peckinpah keeps the theme of identity present. The first is stated by Garrett's deputy, Bob Ollinger, just before Billy shoots him. Ollinger is returning to the Lincoln jail (where Billy is being held) and is in the street when someone off-camera yells that Billy has broken free and has killed Deputy Bell. Ollinger looks up at the second floor where Billy was in chains and sees Billy staring down at him, holding his (Ollinger's) shotgun. Announcing his new identity before it even happens, he states "Yeah, and he's killed me, too." Contributing to the irony is the fact that Ollinger has loaded the gun with dimes, and after he's shot, Billy sardonically quips "Keep the change, Bob." Ollinger is still lying in the dusty street with children and adults milling around him when Garrett returns to town. The scene resembles more of a party than a death. In a voice filled with contempt, Garrett says "Will some of you . . . people, get him off the ground and into it," finally putting closure to Bob's unlucky identity.

The second comment on identity is made by Sheriff Kip McKinney, who grudgingly has agreed to be one of Garrett's new deputies, none of whom approaches the task of hunting the Kid with much enthusiasm. After being coerced by Garrett, McKinney, anticipating his own death at Billy's hands, but desirous of having his identity clear, states "I just hope they spell my name right in the newspapers." Ironically, he is one who survives.

The climactic meeting between Garrett and the Kid at Fort Sumner is replete with images suggesting questions of identity also. When Billy gets up in the middle of the night looking for something to eat, he notices deputies Poe and McKinney outside in the yard and asks "¿Quién es?" ("Who is it?"). He then backs into Pete Maxwell's bedroom where Garrett is hiding in the dark, and asks Pete "who the hell's that outside?" (Wurlitzer 1973, 127, 128). Garrett, Wurlitzer tells us, "recognizes Billy," but pauses for an instant with his gun raised until Billy turns to face him. Then Garrett shoots and kills him and immediately turns to a full-length mirror on the wall and fires at his own image. The camera lingers over Garrett's shattered image, especially his strained, tight-lipped face, for several seconds.

This is Garrett's new identity, Peckinpah indicates, and he lets it slowly but inexorably sink into both Garrett's and our consciousnesses. This scene has been variously interpreted, but I read it within the context of the theme of identity Peckinpah has been emphasizing. In killing Billy, Garrett has symbolically killed part of himself. What Garrett shoots in the mirror is that part of himself he has symbolically killed—his heart, his feelings, his old identity.

Garrett's tragic recognition is borne out in the final scene, which depicts a subdued, almost lifeless, Garrett, early the following morning. The camera shows Billy's feet, his corpse on a pallet in one of Maxwell's rooms, and Garrett is reclining on a porch swing just outside, gently rocking and staring into space. He has been sitting there since the shooting, as though he were keeping a vigil. Finally gathering himself, he rides slowly and deliberately out of Fort Sumner. Most critics have interpreted this scene and the earlier one in which Billy is shot as Peckinpah's metaphor for the end of the free and independent spirit of the Old West. It *is* that, but it is also something more.

Garrett has just shot and killed his one-time friend and riding partner. In doing so, he has also killed part of himself—his old identity—an identity he has resisted relinquishing throughout the film; recall his delay in pursuing Billy. His new identity, which corresponds with the changing times and the changing country, the one he says he wants to grow old with, is hard for him to accept, and the imagery Peckinpah uses reveals Garrett's resistance. Depicted as having such a fixed identity, earlier in the film, and seeming so sure of it, Garrett, after Billy's death, is solemn and bereft, almost a tragic figure, an old Oedipus with blood on his hands. He slowly and dejectedly rides out of Fort Sumner without looking back, almost daring someone to shoot him. The only response is a boy throwing clumps of dirt at his back.

The images of Garrett's body, his stiff posture and slow, ponderous movements, and the slump of his shoulders in these scenes remind one of the feelings evoked by Emily Dickinson's poem "After great pain, a formal feeling comes." No words are spoken during the final moments of the film, but some of the lines from this poem correspond perfectly to the imagery Peckinpah presents: "The Nerves sit ceremonious, like Tombs— / The stiff Heart questions . . . / The Feet, mechanical, go round— / . . . A Wooden way / Regardless grown, / A Quartz contentment, like a stone— / This is the Hour of Lead . . ." (Dickinson 1994, 2454). The images of Garrett together with the brilliant lighting and color evoke the tragic drama of a human heart in conflict with itself, recalling William Faulkner's famous line from his Nobel Prize speech.

Clearly, times have changed, as Garrett indicated to Billy earlier, and now he has changed with them. However, it is anything but a happy or positive change, and his new identity reflects his tragic dilemma. The future, Peckinpah suggests, does not bode well for Garrett or for the country. Eliminating one killer like Billy the Kid will not change the essential nature or identity of the Old West or of America. The gang that hired Garrett to kill Billy will go on to other murders of those it identifies as hindering its path to wealth and power, including Garrett's own death—ironically dramatized in the opening and closing scenes of the longer, video version of *Pat Garrett and Billy the Kid*. However, the power brokers of the Sante Fe Ring, Peckinpah indicates, will now do their killing in a more sophisticated way, through hired killers, and will themselves remain far removed from the actual bloodletting. But their murderous nature is basically the same as Billy's.

D. H. Lawrence identifies this nature in his invaluable *Studies in Classic American Literature*. In speaking of James Fenimore Cooper's Natty Bumppo, he states, "The essential American soul is hard, isolate, stoic, and a killer. It has never yet melted" (Lawrence 1923, 62). As he has in films like *The Wild Bunch* and *The Ballad of Cable Hogue*, Peckinpah renders an updated version of Cooper's character by adding a modern consciousness. In those final moments of the film, Pat Garrett fully comprehends his new identity, which he hadn't acknowledged earlier. His *fatal* shot in Maxwell's bedroom is not the one that kills Billy; it is rather the one he fires at his own image in the mirror. Staring at his shattered reflection, he suddenly reaches his epiphany, his moment of truth, the moment that defines his new self—a shattered, lifeless self. It is a harsh identity to accept, and Garrett struggles with it for the rest of that night. The fact that he is unable to come to terms with it dramatizes, I believe, the tragic consequences resulting from an intellect that decides to move in one direction and a heart that resists and moves in another.

This inner conflict, of course, is not new; it is dramatized in our great literary characters from Sophocles' Oedipus and Creon to those of the present and is, perhaps, best articulated by William Faulkner in his Nobel Prize Address when he states that the only things worth writing about, "worth the agony and the sweat" are the problems "of the human heart in conflict with itself . . . love and honor and pity and pride and compassion and sacrifice" (Faulkner 1977, 723–24). Faulkner's words in 1950, not long after World War II, are still powerful today. Peckinpah captures this conflict of the heart by emphasizing the theme of identity in his 1973 film *Pat Garrett and Billy the Kid* in beautiful, poignant, and tragic images, especially those depicting Garrett in the final moments.

Notes

1. There are three known versions of this film: the theatrical version (106 minutes) released by MGM to theaters in 1973; the 1989 video (122 minutes), released by Turner Entertainment and advertised as the "Director's Cut"; and a "studio preview" (Seydor 1997, 299), 124 minutes, containing a scene between Garrett and his wife that was cut from the Turner version. (For further discussion of these versions, see my paper entitled "Which 'Cut' was Peckinpah's?: The Three Versions of *Pat Garrett and Billy the Kid*," 1999 Texas/Southwest PCA/ACA Conference [Albuquerque], published on CD as *Proceedings of the 1998 and 1999 Southwest/Texas Regional Conferences of the Popular Culture Association and the American Culture Association*.)

2. According to Garner Simmons, Dylan never knew how to portray the character, and Peckinpah never told him (Simmons 1982, 173).

3. This sentiment is diminished in the later, video version of the film because the image of the tree is absent.

References

Bliss, Michael. 1993. *Justified Lives: Morality and Narrative in the Films of Sam Peckinpah*. Carbondale: Southern Illinois University Press.

Combs, Richard. 1989. A Fabulous Melancholy & A Greater Design: *Pat Garrett & Billy the Kid*. *Monthly Film Bulletin* 56 (September): 262–65.

Dickinson, Emily. 1994. *The Norton Anthology of American Literature*. Vol. 1, 4th ed., edited by Nina Baym. New York: Norton.

Emerson, Ralph Waldo. 2001. "The Poet." In *Emerson's Prose and Poetry*, edited by Joel Porte, 183–98. New York: Norton.

Engel, Leonard. 1988. "Sam Peckinpah's Heroes: Natty Bumppo and The Myth of the Rugged Individual Still Reign." *Literature/Film Quarterly* 16.1: 22–30.

Faulkner, William. 1977. "Address Upon Receiving the Nobel Prize for Literature." In *The Portable Faulkner*, edited by Malcolm Cowley. New York: Penguin Books.

Hoberman, J. 1989. "Once Upon A Time in America." *Village Voice* (May 16): 63.

Jones, Allan. 1989. "Pat Garrett & Billy the Kid." *Melody Maker* 65:35 (September 2): 40.

Lawrence, D. H. 1923. "Fenimore Cooper's Leatherstocking Novels," in *Studies in Classic American Literature*, chap. 5. New York: Viking.

Merriam-Webster's Collegiate Dictionary. 1993. 10th ed. Springfield, Mass.: Merriam-Webster, Inc.

Sarchett, Barry W. 1992. "The Outlaw as Figure, the Figure as Outlaw: Narrativity and Interpretation in Sam Peckinpah's *Pat Garrett and Billy the Kid.*" *New Orleans Review* 19:3–4 (Fall-Winter): 174–81.

Seydor, Paul. 1997. *Peckinpah: The Western Films: A Reconsideration.* Urbana: University of Illinois Press.

Simmons, Garner. 1982. *Peckinpah: A Portrait in Montage.* Austin: University of Texas Press.

Stevens, Brad. 1996. *"Pat Garrett & Billy the Kid."* In *The Book of Westerns,* 269–76. New York: Continuum.

Wurlitzer, Rudolph. 1973. "Introduction by the Author." *Pat Garrett and Billy the Kid.* New York: Signet-New American Library.

TEN

ELAINE MARSHALL

"We're Always Moving"

SAM PECKINPAH'S MAKING OF *CONVOY*

Among the harsh criticism Sam Peckinpah received for *Convoy*, his 1979 trucker movie that took its title from the country-western song by C. W. McCall, probably the harshest came from his nephew David Peckinpah: "With *Convoy*, [Sam] forfeited his credentials as a serious director. . . . Important directors don't do movies based on CB songs."[1] Critics of the movie usually blame the director's personal demons for what most of them agree is the embarrassing nature of the movie, describing this period of his life as a haze of cocaine-induced paranoia, a continuing personal skid that one biographer designates a "convoy to oblivion."[2] Flawed as *Convoy* may be, however, the rush to categorically dismiss it was itself flawed, based, as much of the criticism has been, on criteria exterior to the movie. The view that this movie, Peckinpah's first Western since *Pat Garrett and Billy the Kid*, albeit a contemporary one, does not live up to his outstanding early work, is better founded. But even though it is not *Ride the High Country* or *The Wild Bunch*, *Convoy* is a great deal more than most critics have given it credit for.

That Peckinpah was thinking of *Convoy* as something more than a generic trucker movie based on a CB song is evident from documents contained in the Sam Peckinpah Collection housed at the Margaret Herrick Library in Los Angeles. For example, in the transcript of a meeting with Robert Hauser, a cinematographer who was joining the production, Peckinpah ponders the "story of a convoy": "what is a convoy?—where does it go? underneath, what is its meaning?" Several lines later, he announces to Hauser, "Welcome to *The Wild Bunch*."[3] Peckinpah's comments suggest he did not believe that with *Convoy* he was in the process of forfeiting his credentials as a director. To him, the movie he was making was as "provocative" and potentially as

❖ 211

important as what he knew he had done with the film most people consider his best.

Materials in the movie's production files also reveal that Peckinpah knew there were problems with *Convoy*. Discussions show that the story itself underwent many changes from the original script, and that often people working on the movie, Peckinpah included, were uncertain what it was really all about or where it was going. Several story-meetings were devoted to developing the main characters (Rubber Duck and Melissa, played by Kris Kristofferson and Ali McGraw, and Dirty Lyle, played by Ernest Borgnine), yet little of this character development comes through in the final film. Peckinpah also had difficulties with his principal actors, especially with Kristofferson, whose reputed switch from alcohol to marijuana made Peckinpah, still a drinker and now a user of cocaine, feel that he could not "communicate" or "get a performance with him, from him, around him, in spite of him."[4] The director's sense of the film's editing is summed up in a single phrase: "This picture does not match."[5] Whether he intended this as a criticism or a virtue is not clear. It is clear, though, that he often had serious, almost contemptuous, disagreement with others who were involved in story decisions. On a typed list of suggestions titled "*Convoy* Notes," Peckinpah scrawls comments in the margins like "disagree," "hardly," and "wrong."[6]

But despite the various difficulties he was facing, despite his recurring anxiety that "this picture" was suffering from "a sickness of the spirit," Peckinpah maintained hope that he could surpass the "rottenness" he felt the movie had started with and bring forth a picture "in the mother tongue,"[7] a phrase that seems to have meant making the most of what was available to him: trucks, images, the cinematic process itself. "Let's start making a film—a visual film," he told the incoming cinematographer. Clearly, something about this story of a convoy not only gave him intimations of the excitement he had felt on the set of *The Wild Bunch*, it also led him to feel that, with this movie, he was entering, or had the possibility of entering, new territory.

Although the statements in the production documents that stake out this territory are few and sometimes cryptic or garbled in transcription, they nevertheless reveal that, for Sam Peckinpah, the *Convoy* he was trying to make had importance for him. He had an "evolving" (his word) vision of the movie that led him toward seeing it as a story, not merely about truckers, but about the subject nearest to his heart—the movie-making process itself. And though this inclination is not explicit in the final film, its presence in what we see there makes of this much-maligned movie something more, and better, than has been allowed.

The Story of a Convoy

In a memo dated March 23, 1977, Peckinpah stated, "I feel that the trucks are as important as the actors."[8] When one looks to the movie, this attitude makes itself evident. Some of the most beautiful and energetic footage centers on the trucks, their movement in particular—the shimmering emergence from heat waves of Rubber Duck's truck in the opening shots of the movie; the lilting slow-motion dissolves in waltz tempo of vehicles and sand in the first escape sequence; the lyrical shots of 18-wheelers traveling in silhouette against a dying sunset. More important, the story itself proceeds through the growth of the convoy—its increasing size, activity, complexity, and power for evoking change within and outside itself.

Peckinpah was led to see the importance of the trucks as vehicles for his story in part because of the problems he was having with his main actors. Jim Silke, Peckinpah's longtime friend and collaborator, recalls watching hours of footage in which Sam tried patiently—but unsuccessfully—to coax a natural, spontaneous performance from Ali McGraw.[9] More difficult for Peckinpah was Kristofferson. In the memo to producer Michael Deeley cited earlier, Peckinpah complained that

> Kris has been a flat zero, and to take the story someplace else, I have to go with the truckers and the people.... [T]he focus must go upon the convoy, to move it forward, move the audience with it—becoming a part of the myriad reasons and lack of reasons they and we are on the move. The convoy and its people must take the place of the leading actor I don't have.[10]

In a conversation with Mort Sahl, who was then on the set to play the part of a Mike Wallace–type newscaster, Peckinpah said, "I don't know what the picture's going to be about yet—but I know it's about something."[11] The memo to Deeley shows that the "something" the movie was about was beginning to coalesce, in Sam's words, in "the movement and dynamics of the convoy itself rather than [in] the dialogue of some principal actors."[12]

In the conversations with Robert Hauser mentioned earlier, Peckinpah went even further in expressing his fascination with "the story of a convoy." After asking, "What is a convoy?" he continued: "Where does it go? Underneath, what is its meaning—what is its objective—a convoy—why do people want to join it—why was the song so popular—where is it going—where are we going?" "It is, I must say," he confessed, "the most provocative, the most exciting single thing I've ever come up against in my life."[13] So strong a statement shows that Peckinpah's imagination was fully engaged with his movie, with the narrative and creative problems and potential it was presenting him. The questions he asks imply that, for him, discovering the story of a convoy entailed working out its value as an action. How does it begin? How does it come together and go forward? What is its value for and beyond itself? They further imply that a convoy, in his mind, is more than a collection of trucks or of truckers worried about speed limits. It is a moral event in which people are coming together, "going somewhere on a road" (to borrow a line from *The Ballad of Cable Hogue*), and moving toward some vision of value out ahead.

Other documents give more specific insights into the way Peckinpah was seeing his convoy story. There was talk of the film being a protest picture, and this dimension comes into the movie when, after breaking through the roadblock near the New Mexico state line, the convoy enters Albuquerque to find itself celebrated as a populist phenomenon by marching bands and waving crowds. In fact, much of the criticism of the movie hinges on its being a muddled protest film. But while Peckinpah brings the protest story forward in the middle of the movie, the documentary record (as well as the last third of the movie) shows that political protest was only one phase in the life of the convoy, not its ultimate aim.

In a script meeting, for instance, the following statement is made: "It [the convoy] is the only thing in America that is moving—they can stop everything except theoretically the convoy."[14] While the speaker is not indicated, this sense of the convoy as "the only thing moving" corresponds with Peckinpah's emphasis on "the movement and dynamics of the convoy." It is also consistent with his views about what was called in those days "the military and industrial complex" (to which Peckinpah would have likely added the mainstream media). The sense of protest here is not aimed so much at identifiable political issues concerning truck drivers or others as it is suggestive of the convoy's power as a movement to evade and surpass vested authorities and cultural inertia.

In another conversation, Peckinpah clarifies further his view of what's wrong with America that the convoy is an antidote to. He has suggested that those present read Ayn Rand's *Atlas Shrugged*, then goes on to explain to them his idea of what the book is about. "It's the breakdown of maintenance," he says. "It's the breakdown of pride and achievement. It's the breakdown of the welfare state upon people's energies to create, to build, to the satisfaction of their own work."[15] In this comment, Peckinpah openly speaks to what he considered the bottom line of human endeavor: pride in achievement, creative energy, satisfaction with one's work, competence and professionalism—all of which, according to Jim Silke, Peckinpah included in his use of the term "maintenance."[16] It is the quality of maintenance that Peckinpah sees operating in his convoy that makes it a protest against forces opposing the kind of creative drive he values. For him, the convoy was emerging as the living image of a community of individuals whose dynamic movement, always outrunning formal constraints, is fueled by and advancing America's "energies to create."

Thinking Celluloid, Not Asphalt

When Peckinpah pondered the objective of a convoy, wondering what it revealed about where "we are going," he was already thinking beyond trucks. "We" implied an America he envisioned struggling to maintain its creative vigor—something he perhaps sensed as a factor in the CB song's popularity. But the collective pronoun could also have a more immediate and vital reference for Peckinpah the movie director—the communal "we" involved in the making of *Convoy*: the director and his cast and crew.

In a memo to screenwriter Bill Norton, Peckinpah made this correlation explicit. Responding to Norton's concerns about the production at that point, Peckinpah wrote, "We have got ourselves a convoy and nobody is going to fuck it up and that includes you and I [*sic*]."[17] The statement "We have got ourselves a convoy"— which is also a line in the movie—articulates Peckinpah's sense that the convoy's story was becoming a fusion of his art and his life. For him, the convoy whose story he was trying to narrate and the process of getting the movie made were the same enterprise. Both had the same creative objective: the cinematic "getting," or begetting, of a convoy.

On at least two occasions, the movie was actually discussed in metacinematic terms. Notes taken during a meeting with Peckinpah and key members of the crew reflect someone, almost certainly Peckinpah, saying, "But then you can understand the concept of a convoy within a convoy and the picture company making a convoy picture."[18] In another meeting, someone—again, most likely it is Peckinpah—says, "This is where you go into we're making a picture [*sic*]." The speaker goes on to describe some camera moves he imagines as conveying the sense of "the fantasyland of making a film."[19]

This notion of "a convoy within a convoy," in which one convoy is the motion picture company making a movie about the other convoy, shows up again in some post-production dialogue written by Jim Silke at Peckinpah's request. Conceived as CB conversations taking place out in the heartland as truckers unrelated to the convoy learn about it over their CB radios, this dialogue never made its way into the movie. Nevertheless, the scene between two of the CB voices, whose handles are "Tom Mix" and "The Bandit," shows that even this late in the making of the movie, the movie-as-convoy idea was still percolating.

Silke's description of The Bandit, for instance, is an outright portrait of Peckinpah the storytelling movie maker.

> He has more questions than answers and asks them in a deliberate whisper. He denies it's deliberate, and believes his denial, but some know better. He steals his dialogue from Dashiell Hammett, TS Elliot [sic], Raymond Chandler, Kipling, the Koran and an overworked liver . . . but with a sincerity he'll never admit to. Like most poets he is a skilled thief beguiled by his bandit heart. He claims to be a trucker new to the job, but is in fact a storyteller making a motion picture about truckers.[20]

In the dialogue, The Bandit presents himself to Tom Mix as a trucker "new to the asphalt, to this truck, and to this road." When Mix asks what he's doing "drivin' the night side," The Bandit, actually stealing many of his lines from Jack London's *Call of the Wild*, answers that he's seeking "that ecstasy that makes the summit of the trail," "that ecstasy that comes to the artist, caught up and out of himself in a sheet of flame." Amused by The Bandit's extravagant romanticism, Mix tells him, "You been seein' too many of them picture shows . . . you're thinkin' celluloid instead of asphalt."[21]

Silke's succinct phrase affirms that Peckinpah, in the making of *Convoy*, was indeed thinking "celluloid" at least as much as, if not more than, "asphalt." More than a story of truckers on the road, he was making a movie about what mattered to him most—the creative phenomenon he was engaged in, a phenomenon that he saw operating in the convoy that was becoming, as the hippie preacher in the movie says, "a spiritual event."

That Peckinpah would see a connection between movie-making and convoying should not be surprising, nor is it a self-reflexive contrivance. By the time of *Convoy*, Peckinpah had directed twelve major motion pictures, all of them on location, sometimes remote locations in Mexico and the American southwest. The trek to location entailed an assemblage of people and vehicles, such as that for *Major Dundee* described by David Weddle: "A production of this size would require hundreds of crew members, actors, extras, horses and mules, and trucks full of props, costumes, and equipment."[22] In other words, it would require a convoy—a convoy of creative individuals, all coming together for their myriad reasons with the objective of joining talents and energies in the creative "fantasyland of making a film." In that enterprise, the director, the one with the vision and the story, would lead, as Rubber Duck leads, because he is the narrator out in front of the story. The set of *Convoy*, with the dozens of 18-wheelers and their drivers in the movie commingling with the people and vehicles making up the cast and production crew, could only have heightened Peckinpah's sense of a correlation between the convoy *in* the movie and the convoy *of* the movie. Both were, in their own way, events of the creative spirit. Both were, for him, the same event.

Led into Images

With all the metaconvoy talk, however, not much was done explicitly with that idea in the movie. The only outright metamoment comes when Peckinpah appears briefly in the back of the newscaster's truck as a member of the television crew filming Rubber Duck as he leads the convoy toward Albuquerque. Peckinpah rides beside the video camera, wearing the headset of a sound man, as well as the bandanna, tied around his head, that had become his trademark. A bandanna would also appear on Rubber Duck in the final moments of the movie, strengthening the relation between the leader of the convoy and the director of *Convoy*. But the metaconcept of a motion picture company making a movie about a convoy never materialized in the final film. Moreover, in the same conversations in which this idea was discussed, Peckinpah himself would move away from making it overt in the movie. Instead, his thoughts drifted away from the metacinematic device toward the uninhibited action of the camera.

Excerpts from two separate meetings illustrate this movement in his thinking. In the first, when he says, "This is where you go into we're making a picture," he then continues:

> We only use a bit of it and then it might be a dissolve through a scene earlier and you see somebody walking out of a tree. You don't know what that is—but you don't really see it. . . . Drifting of the—that's very important. . . . The camera, somewhere, like a seven-year-old or three-year-old child walking around, looking. It's like a kid's point of view and the fantasyland of making a film, and we never see the actual making of the film but we do hear some of the sounds.[23]

In another meeting, a few days later, Peckinpah revisits this notion, this "drift" that is both a quality in his visualizing and a quality he wants in the movement of his camera:

I'd like to pull back and the camera's going on another road, go back and we think they're in the convoy and they're not, they're alone. The camera pans and we're now going on a third road and we're seeing the convoy. I'd really like to start working along those lines . . . without ever seeing a motion picture company working, but we're seeing a camera that's interested, completely on its own, and it has the mind, as I said before, of a very precocious four-year-old child.[24]

In this passage, the shift away from the self-consciously metacinematic concept becomes clearer as Peckinpah imagines detaching the motion picture company (the "they" in the statement) from the convoy, then eliminating it even as an image on the screen, evolving it into the drifting, interested camera ranging freely on its own. Further, the "camera" here would not be the image of a camera, but the camera freed of its own mechanical form to become the unencumbered action of vision itself—an eye opening with the curiosity and wonder of a child, drawn forward by and toward what is appearing out ahead.

Perhaps more than anything else in the *Convoy* transcripts, these two passages provide insight into the "something" Peckinpah saw that the movie could be about, and into the spirit he wanted for this film. One recalls the line from *The Wild Bunch*, when the old Mexican in Angel's village tells Pike, "We all dream of being a child again." No matter how jaded, how strung out, how paranoid Peckinpah may have become, he was still, before and after he was anything else, a creative man, a storyteller, a narrator, and one who, "at even his worst moments, knew what the bottom line was."[25] And in spite of, maybe because of, what he sensed as his own failings and "the rottenness" he felt about the making of *Convoy*, Peckinpah here dreams of making this a movie in which his camera, and his story, are born again with fresh, childlike vision.

In the long conversation with cinematographer Hauser, Peckinpah's romanticized vision of the camera as a precocious, childlike eye drops away to reveal an even more fundamental relation to his cinematic medium and its potential for visual narrating. Just as the lack of a leading man was forcing him to focus on the story of a convoy, here the lack of matching leads him to imagine a "nonlinear" mode of visualizing. In these statements, Peckinpah is, of course, trying to find a way to salvage his movie by making the most of the footage he has. But he also seems to be reaching beyond the practicalities of the moment toward a farther view of cinematic narrating, one in which "convoying" becomes a way of seeing how moving images come together and move forward on the screen.

The immediate problem that concerns him is continuity: "This picture," he tells Hauser, "does not match." Yet his solution is not to find a way to match the film, but to dispense with matching altogether:

> ... see the matching I can use aesthetically to work for the picture—I mean, the lack of it, because I can fade and dissolve into weather—get good images ... I want it to be done cinema verite, but I don't want it to be—I want you to be conscious after the fact that you've been hit by images—I mean the emotion in it. ... This whole picture is a montage. ... It is now a collage—we absolutely have texture and smell to it—and through that there is a line—it is fucking exciting—and we have the material to do it superbly well.[26]

A little further into the conversation he continues in this vein, describing a dream sequence that is "going to start breaking up":

> I'm going to break it apart because I have footage of things breaking apart and people breaking apart. ... There's no actors in the world I could get to get this kind of oblique, strange, marvelous combination of—coming together. ...[27]

Peckinpah imagines in these statements a movie beginning to be narrated not through conventional Hollywood continuities of character and matched editing, but through subtler, more "oblique" visual processes. He is describing montage itself as cinematic convoying in which discontinuous images move forward toward a "strange, marvelous combination" coming together in the story of the convoy. It is maybe this merging of cinematic process and story, and the sense that their "coming together" is now in the open and out in front of his narrating this movie that leads Peckinpah then to assert the statement cited earlier: that this "story of a convoy" constitutes "the most exciting single thing I have ever come up against in my life." In any event, it gives him the feeling that this movie that began so badly can go, is going, somewhere new, somewhere vital, and that it is now in "the mother tongue": "now we are evolving—we are making a picture now. We're making it photographically ... let's start making a film—a visual film."[28]

As this line of talk subsides, Peckinpah modulates his view slightly, imagining, finally, what he wants for the viewer of his movie. "I don't want to bust loose and do jangling things," he says; "I want people to be led into images—or have them lead us—camera images—pan—look—following the look—see somebody else. ... We're always moving."[29] In other words, he wants for his viewer what he, as a visual narrator, a maker of movies, experiences when he becomes caught up in the provocative excitement of his work: "to be led into images—to have them lead us." There is probably no better statement than that of what movie-making was for Sam Peckinpah, a man led by images to do the work he did, aware, as cinematic images in particular show us, that, like the convoy, "we're always moving."

The question remains to what extent Peckinpah's vision for *Convoy* appears in the movie we see. And even a cursory look reveals that it does, if the viewer, adopting Peckinpah's visual orientation, is open to being "led into images." When that shift in attention occurs, one looks beyond the movie's shortcomings as drama to the visual story of the convoy—or, more precisely, of convoying. For it is the action, the "dynamics" of convoying, that interests Peckinpah. (The movie's title, after all, is both noun and verb.) And the most visible fact about the convoying up on the screen is that it appears, grows, and evolves from the instant the movie's eye opens to brilliant white light emanating from the desert's sand.

Starkly elemental in color and form, the desert visualized here is no wasteland, but a fertile field of radiant energy out of which successive events of convoying will be born. Within this visual plenum, the camera moves, "interested, completely on its own," looking, in effect, for an image to convoy with. That image materializes out of the blacktop's shimmering heat waves—the powerful 18-wheeler driven by Rubber Duck, the man on the move led by vision, the human correlative of the camera's way of seeing. Almost instantaneously, Melissa's convertible XKE appears, and convoying passes from the camera's orientation toward what it sees into the visual "come on" she and Rubber Duck engage in at full speed down the highway. Viewed in long shot, moreover, their vehicles moving together constitute the movie's first image of a convoy. As will happen with each successive appearance of convoying, the law reacts to stop its momentum: here the trooper, forced off the road by the truck and sports car, gives chase and orders Rubber Duck to pull over.

Even in this momentary beginning, Peckinpah's visual and "evolving" sense of his story is apparent. Convoying appears initially as an inherent capability of the camera eye, leading it to see the "convoying" aspect of everything in its visual field. Active as a value in and of the movie's vision, convoying naturally begets further occasions of convoying—as it does next when Spider Mike and Love Machine come in behind Rubber Duck. This second proto-convoy, an intermediary stage between the convoying of the movie's opening and the convoy itself, brings forward the three men whose good-humored interaction will become a quality of the convoy. The correlation of values attaching to these three also begins to clarify the sense that three moral energies are involved in the appearance, growth, and evolving of the convoy.

Following the lead of the movie, these energies might be designated as birth, love, and convoying. Spider Mike, whose drive is always to get home to see his son born, centers the procreative energy of birth. When Lyle later questions Mike's paternity (setting off the truck-stop fight), his remarks are an assault on Mike's power for begetting life. Love Machine, particularly through his CB handle, crudely focuses the rational drive to transform the procreative in "love"; his truck, complete with its waterbed, is literally (and humorously) a machine for accomplishing this transformation. Rubber Duck provides the third, leading value. Appearing from the outset as the man in front, whose vision (like the camera's) draws him forward, the Duck's adaptability to emerging change and his ability to escape formal limits make him the moving center of the convoy's advance.

Mike, Love Machine, and the Duck are not mechanical representations of these three energies, but in their coming together as the core convoyers, they clarify the pervasiveness of this trinity of powers in the evolution of the convoy—a trinary discipline that will further elaborate its action in the three phases of the convoy's story. Within this discipline, convoying is the third power that sees ahead, making the evolutionary advance possible. But convoying cannot go it alone; it can lead only in co-relation with the other powers. Morally inclusive, convoying dispenses with formal division and hierarchy (the approach of "the law" in the movie) and involves all three energies in forward-relating action. When the convoy appears, it inherits all three creative potencies. Convoying, through vision, will lead it forward; "love" will characterize its cooperative human spirit; and "birth" will proceed through its ability to make new beginnings.

Given this inherent discipline, the convoy, with its birth out of the truck-stop brawl, is from its inception a creative event in the making. As Rubber Duck moves toward his truck announcing that he is heading "for the state line," the convoy happens spontaneously. Lyle's racist assault on Spider Mike, and the resulting fight, spark the conditions in which the convoy becomes a possibility, but Lyle does not cause it. Nor is it the Duck's intention to start and lead a convoy. He moves to escape, and the others move in behind him. As the movie's opening sequence has shown, convoying precedes the convoy, and the convoy itself occurs as an emergent phenomenon of individuals "coming on" together. Not even the convoyers know, initially, that they are creating a convoy. For them, it is the simple matter of making a getaway. But as the convoy-event begins to coalesce, it takes on a life of its own.

This becomes evident early in the off-road sequence when the truckers take the shortcut that will lead them to the Arizona/New Mexico line. Lyle and additional policemen are in hot pursuit, but once the truckers leave the main highway and enter the primitive back road, their attention begins to be focused less on what is behind them than on negotiating the road out ahead, with much more skill than the cops do. This sequence, moreover, shot as both comedy and a montage-dissolve dance of truck and police-car images, brings into view the growing good spirits of convoying. Through this sequence, the truckers are getting it together, increasing the self-generating coherence of the event they are creating. In effect, they are in the process of becoming not just a group of truckers, but convoyers. When they leave the back road, their capability for moving together has gelled—as Lyle and his companion discover when Love Machine (later called by his given name, Bobby) and Spider Mike make a "sandwich" of their police sedan.

As the truckers enter New Mexico, they have become a convoy both inherently (they now refer to themselves as such) and in the eyes of the law, for whom this means they are nothing more than a wild bunch of two-bit, runaway truckers. But their growth is already exceeding this characterization. New trucks appear, eager to join in behind an event they see as a different kind of phenomenon. Aerial long shots of the growing convoy, as well as the surprised reactions of the core convoyers, reveal the evolving dynamics of this new event. Melissa, for instance, asks the Duck in amazement, "Where are they all coming from?" and remarks that "they're all following you." His response—that he's just "runnin' for [his] life" and that he's not being followed, he's just "in front"—affirm the quality of the convoy as an event undergoing evolution on the move.[30] It is a "run *for* life" and *of* life toward its new possibility. That possibility is not known or designed in advance by its leader, but is an emergent value that draws the one "in front" ahead of the others.

For the evolving convoy, the new possibility as they smash through Chief Love's roadblock and drive on toward Albuquerque becomes their emergent value as a political phenomenon. This is not an eventuality they have prepared for, but another novel phase in their growth. In the beginning of the Albuquerque sequence, the mobile newscaster, Chuck Arnaldi, attempts to elicit the convoy's self-definition of its objectives, asking (as Peckinpah had), "What is the purpose of the convoy?" The "myriad reasons and lack of reasons" that he gets in response express the range of the common American's dissatisfactions with "big money," corrupt government, and racism. But the "myriad" nature of these reasons suggests that neither political causes, nor their verbal articulation, can definitively characterize convoying. Rubber Duck's response more accurately describes the action we see: "The purpose of the convoy is to keep moving."

The political, or "protest" phase of the convoy's life, however, threatens that view of it. Governor Haskins, who appears on the scene in this sequence as an authority from on high (he arrives in a helicopter), seeks to turn its vital "moving" into a formal "movement" that he can co-opt for his own political designs for reelection. Haskins accomplishes in Albuquerque what Lyle has so far been unable to do: he "arrests" the forward movement of the convoy, confining it within a holding area where he meets with Rubber Duck and the others in an effort to control and usurp the convoy's energy as a people's movement. In this formalized setting, drawn into the system's game of deal-making and compromise, the convoyers lose their forward momentum, the source of their coherence. They begin to fall apart in bickering and confusion over what the objective should be. Rubber Duck asks Melissa to tell him what she thinks she's involved in because, he says, "I'm beginning to think I have no idea." Then, with the news that Lyle is holding Spider Mike in the Alvarez jail, the efforts at formalizing the convoy as a political movement come unglued. The Duck heads for Alvarez, leaving Melissa and others angry and the protest in disarray.

But, of course, the protest has not defined the convoy any more than the initial getaway did; and while Haskins has temporarily diverted the convoy's movement, he has not stopped its evolving. It's at this juncture that the criticism of *Convoy* as a failed protest picture is aimed. And it would be a failed protest picture if it were a protest picture—but it's not. The protest is only the second phase in its story, and what *Convoy*, as the story of an evolving event, is "about," cannot fully appear until it enters its third phase in the Alvarez sequence.

This fact in itself, that the movie evolves a third story beyond the story of runaway truckers and beyond the story of protest, is crucial to *Convoy* and was alluded to, in an oblique way, by someone on the production who spoke of its "three endings":

> I had a feeling when I saw the picture that one other thing which is the three endings [*sic*]. The Alvarez ending which absolutely achieved their immediate goals as rescuing Mike, confronting Lyle and beating him. When they go to another ending which is the bridge, which is the cutting off the convoy from the leader and destroying the leader. Then we go to another ending which is the funeral. And we have to have all these sequences.[31]

Convoy "has to have" three endings to complete the three phases of its growth and to bring all the way into the open new value, and story, that begin to emerge in the Alvarez sequence.

At first, this sequence seems a reversion to the preprotest phase in that it again centers upon Lyle's vendetta against the Duck, played out by using Spider Mike as bait. The difference now is that the vendetta becomes clarified as a moral transition from the escalating forms of the law's old morality to the new, more open morality of convoying. A crucial aspect of this moral difference between the law and convoying has already been voiced by Haskins, who, as "governor," expresses the law's implicit inclination to bring life's energies within its control. When asked if he will use his connections to get Mike out of the Alvarez jail, he answers, "Sometimes you have to sacrifice the individual." Haskins's assertion that the abstract rationale takes precedence over individual life (and life occurs only in individuals), and over moral action, reveals the rigid, formalizing nature of causes—an attitude that surfaces with the protest phase of the convoy and threatens its ongoing life. In contrast, convoying happens, and can only happen, as a concretely moral phenomenon—through individuals converging beyond the governance of causes and coevolving an open vision of life's good.

The nine trucks that come together outside Alvarez, consequently, constitute a new convoy, morally invigorated by the capabilities it has evolved through its second phase, and poised to act in a new way. Rather than escape the law, it moves now to confront the law's formal morality head-on. As the trucks smash through the ramshackle buildings of the town, convoying is cinematically unleashed in this more violent montage as a moral potency whose objective is not only to save Spider Mike, but to dismantle for good the revenge that Lyle instigated and perpetuates. Spider Mike's release completes one aspect of the convoy's first story; he is free to go home for the birth of his son. It does not, however, resolve Lyle's revenge. Instead, Lyle's aim to get back at the Duck intensifies, enlarging the distance between the "moralities" of the two men, as their dialogue in this scene reflects. Rubber Duck speaks for the good in life ("What good are you, old man" he asks Lyle); Lyle asserts in response the cause of his action ("I am the law. I represent the law"), a rigidly rational ethic that will not allow him to "forget it" and move on. In his insistence on the law's reactive and reactionary prerogative, on anger rather than love, he proves himself to be what the Duck sees: "a broke down old piece of meanness" fixated on the past and incapable of morally advancing into the spirit of convoying.

The montage sequence in which the convoyers demolish the flimsy buildings in Alvarez shows visually that as the story's moral phase comes to the fore, physical structures and forms are giving way. But there are also narrative structures that must be effaced for the movie's convoying, like Spider Mike, to go free. Revenge is one such structure, and, to the extent that the Duck has become trapped in that story, and in his own persona as "leader" of the convoy, he, too, is a "form" that requires effacing. The bridge sequence narrates just that. It destroys the Duck as the convoy's formal leader, something he became as a consequence of the protest phase. This fiery scene, in which the amassed forces of law detonate Rubber Duck's explosive-laden tanker and send its detached cab, containing Rubber Duck, careening off the bridge, constitutes the movie's "shoot-out," the extreme moment when the moral tension between Lyle's way and the Duck's way reaches the breaking point and "finishes" (to use Lyle's word) not only the Duck as a formal persona, but the dramatic structure of Lyle's revenge.

That a death has occurred is evident from the reaction shots of Lyle, Melissa, and the convoyers now cut off from their leader. The quick edit from the destruction at the bridge to the funeral sequence further confirms that an end has been made. Governor Haskins's voice presides over the formal ceremony, laying claim to the virtues of the formally dead Duck (represented by the draped casket, an empty form that Haskins does not know is empty). Recalling the Duck, and the convoy, as an embodiment of the "native American" tradition of "controlled individualism" that "keeps this country alive," Haskins, a hold-over of the convoy's second story, here asserts himself as the official successor to its values and its life. But what is alive and what is finished and what is in succession are becoming apparent not in his words, but in the increasing activity of the camera eye to resurrect the life, spirit, and "appearing" of convoying.

From the first image of this sequence, when Melissa turns away from the camera to walk toward the Jesus-freaks' open bus, a kind of visual quickening occurs. The instances of physical birth that were active in the convoy's first story (the Duck's birthday, the birth of Mike's son) become, in this third phase of the movie's third story, cinematic "births," new appearings through which the moral succession from the old to the new spirit comes all the way in the open. In rapid, cross-cut convergence, three actions come together to give visual birth to the convoy's, and the movie's, new beginning. The Duck appears to Melissa in the bus, alive and anew—no longer the leader at the front of a line of trucks, but the moral center of its creative, open spirit. The beginning of a new convoy appears, led forward now by Bobby (formerly known as Love Machine). Fed up with the governor's speech, he leaves the formal platform, enters his truck, and moves out, drawing trucks and the crowd in behind him. With this new emergence of convoying, Haskins's words and control utterly give way, and the succession from old morality to new happens. Lyle, the man who "represents the law," sees all around him the complete disintegration of the law's hold on life. He sees the reborn Duck, the convoy beginning again—and he laughs, accomplishing his moral evolution into the lighter spirit of convoying. That spirit moves forward in the screen's light, passing seamlessly into the movie's final visual sequence as the credits appear—a cinematic reenfolding of the movie back through its action to seek out its beginnings in the opening shots. The final image, as well, suggests the convoy's power to evolve the old into the spirit of birth, love, and new beginnings. An elderly man and woman, forced off the road during the convoy's initial getaway, reappear, sitting in their ancient car. While in the earlier shot of them, the old woman turned to shake her fist at the passing trucks, now she turns to kiss the man beside her. In that kiss is born the movie's final act of convoying.

This admittedly quick rendering of the narrative "dynamics" of Peckinpah's "story of a convoy" cannot account for all its details, but can show how *Convoy* keeps moving to surpass the critical roadblocks that inhibit seeing it, as well as the limitations that arose within it—limitations Peckinpah knew were there. It also shows that his insights about where the picture was going are more accurate than perhaps even he recognized. The movie *was* "evolving," as he told Hauser. Not only does it evolve from the "straight-line action-adventure-funny picture based on a song"[32] to the protest story to the story of convoying, it evolves "convoying" as an action and story capable of revealing the process, the discipline of a creative moral advance. Peckinpah knew his movie was "not the well-made play"; it was instead "a Happening,"[33] an event in the making, generating its vision of its emergent possibility from the moment forward—a narrative of succession and surpassing, a creation story.

He also told Hauser, "Welcome to *The Wild Bunch*." It is probably heresy to even suggest that the two movies are comparable in value. And yet *Convoy* is not only a successor to *The Wild Bunch* in innumerable ways, but in at least one way surpasses it. Both are evolutionary narratives, since Peckinpah's story was always inherently a story of making the getaway to life's new beginning. But *Convoy* takes Peckinpah's story forward from the laughter *The Wild Bunch* ends with into the most open comedy he made. Dispensing with the hypermale histrionics the Bunch are prone to and the gut-tearing *agon* of their violence, "Bloody" Sam Peckinpah freely and fully gives us in *Convoy* his lighter spirit. What the movie loses in the way of dramatic depth of character it surpasses with the energy of moving images to "convoy" and visually evolve their story before our eyes. It narrates, moreover, a new kind of comedy—not the "well-made" literary version in which the formal social order is restored, but one in which the world goes beyond the old order and its encasing forms and opens out to see its new, exuberant, creative possibility.

A comedy of vision, *Convoy* celebrates the potential of the movies themselves as a medium for evolving the human spirit. Just as the literary arts in their way advance the moral possibilities inherent in the sound and language of the human voice, the movies advance the inherent potency of human vision to narrate, in their way, moral change. *Convoy*'s evolutionary story literally, visibly shows such a change happening. Peckinpah, moreover, even in his darker moments, always worked with this celebratory spirit of the movies as an instrument for furthering individual and collaborative creative advance: "You're not going to tell me the camera is a machine," he said; "it is the most marvelous piece of divinity ever created."[34]

There is really no reason other than elitism to assert that a movie about a CB song is not worth a serious director's attention. Peckinpah apparently did not share that elitism. He always worked from popular American genres and always made the most of what he had to work with—including the condition of his own capabilities at the time. He saw the possibility of something in *Convoy*, and the movie narrates the story of his eye always moving toward that possibility. If the production was plagued by a "sickness of the spirit," the movie is not. Through its good spirits, and its implicit vision of the movies as an instrument for evolving the good, *Convoy* surpasses even its own "rotten" beginnings. That so few critics have been moved by the movie to see this possibility is perhaps Peckinpah's failure; that it is there to be seen is his achievement.

Acknowledgments

I wish to thank the Special Collections department of the Margaret Herrick Library of the Academy of Motion Pictures Arts and Sciences in Beverly Hills, California, for granting me access to the Sam Peckinpah Collection and for the assistance of library staff while I was there. I am also grateful to Barton College for the sabbatical and funding that supported my research. Finally, I offer my gratitude to Paul Seydor, Jim Silke, and David Weddle for their time and encouragement.

Notes

1. Quoted in Marshall Fine, *Bloody Sam: The Life and Films of Sam Peckinpah* (New York: Donald I. Fine, Inc., 1991), 320.

2. "*Convoy* to Oblivion" is the title Fine gives to his chapter on this film. Michael Bliss's chapter title on *Convoy*, "Dead Truck Stop," advocates an equally dismal view of the movie. Bliss's book is *Justified Lives: Morality and Narrative in the Films of Sam Peckinpah* (Carbondale: Southern Illinois University Press, 1993).

3. Sam Peckinpah Collection (hereafter SPC), Folder 89, "Tapes (Transcriptions)," in the *Convoy* folders of the Sam Peckinpah Collection housed in the Margaret Herrick Library of the Academy of Motion Pictures Arts and Sciences, Los Angeles. Most of the source material for this essay comes from this collection. The quotations in this paragraph are all taken from Folder 89 and appear in a lengthy typed, undated transcription of two audiotapes presenting a conversation between Peckinpah and Robert Hauser. Hauser received credit in the film for additional photography. The comments quoted here come from the transcription of Tape 2.

4. SPC Folder 72, "Memos," containing the draft of a memo from Peckinpah to Executive Producer Michael Deeley regarding the difficulties of getting good dialogue from his principal actors, especially Kristofferson.

5. SPC Folder 89, transcription of Tape 2.

6. SPC Folder 77, "Notes," which contains several documents regarding scenes in *Convoy*. Some are records of conversations. One, dated 24 February 1978, and labeled "Convoy Notes," itemizes comments (probably written by one of the producers) about specific scenes in the movie. Peckinpah's critical responses, in his distinctive handwriting, appear in the margins of several of these comments.

7. SPC Folder 89. All quotations in this paragraph come from transcriptions of Tapes 1 and 2.

8. SPC Folder 71, "Memos," in a memo dated 23 March 1977 from Peckinpah to Tom Shaw, an assistant director.

9. Jim Silke. Telephone conversation with author, 22 June 1999.

10. SPC Folder 72. Several versions of this memo appear in the file, some marked "not sent." It may have eventually been sent as a cablegram.

11. Peckinpah's comment to Sahl occurs in SPC Folder 88, "Transcripts," in a transcript dated April 13.

12. From the Deeley memo in SPC Folder 72.

13. Both quotations come from SPC Folder 89, Tape 2 transcript.

14. SPC Folder 23, "Script Notes and Script." This comment appears in a document dated 30 March 1977 with the following heading: "The meeting started with a recapitulation of the meeting with Mort Sahl regarding the Convoy Script which was held on 3/28." The document does not state who attended the meeting, though marginal notes sometimes indicate who is speaking: for example, "SP" and "Jim."

15. Also from SPC Folder 23 in a document labeled "General Notes—Motor Home" and dated 21 September 1977. The document indicates "Sam, Tony, and Garth" were in attendance, and speakers are designated. Presumably these individuals would include

Peckinpah and Garth Craven, one of the film's principal editors. "Tony" is probably Tony Lawson, who was assisting Craven with the editing in September 1977. (See Weddle 1994, 517.)

16. Personal telephone conversation with Jim Silke, 22 June 1999.

17. SPC Folder 71, in a memo to screenwriter B. W. L. (Bill) Norton, dated 24 April 1977.

18. SPC Folder 23, "General Notes."

19. Quotations in the last two sentences come from SPC Folder 23, "General Notes."

20. SPC Folder 13, "CB dialog by Jim Silke," dated 17 December 1977.

21. Ibid. In a phone conversation (see note 16 above), Silke confirmed that The Bandit was Peckinpah. The relevant passages from London appear in chapter 3 of *Call of the Wild*. Other lines in the CB dialog are also taken from this chapter of London's novel.

22. David Weddle, *"If They Move... Kill 'Em!": The Life and Times of Sam Peckinpah* (New York: Grove Press, 1994), 231.

23. SPC Folder 23, "General Notes," dated 16 September 1977.

24. SPC Folder 23, "General Notes—Motor Home," dated 21 September 1977.

25. Jim Silke, telephone conversation with author, 22 June 1999.

26. SPC Folder 89, transcript of Tapes 1 and 2.

27. SPC Folder 89, transcript of Tape 2.

28. Ibid.

29. Ibid.

30. In the transcript of a discussion between "S," "G," and "T" (Peckinpah, Garth Craven, Tony Lawson) dated 14 September 1977 (SPC Folder 23), the following exchange appears:

> S: Where did they all come from?
> T: Why are they following you?
> S: Because I'm in front. That's the key line.

31. SPC Folder 77, "Notes." The transcribed text is not syntactically clear, nor is the speaker named.

32. SPC Folder 89, Tape 2 transcription.

33. Quoted in Stephen Prince, *Savage Cinema: Sam Peckinpah and the Rise of Ultraviolent Movies* (Austin: University of Texas Press, 1998), 216.

34. Quoted in Paul Seydor, *Peckinpah: The Western Films, A Reconsideration*, Foreword by David Weddle (Urbana and Chicago: University of Illinois Press, 1980, 1997), 330.

References

Bliss, Michael. 1993. *Justified Lives: Morality and Narrative in the Films of Sam Peckinpah*. Carbondale: Southern Illinois University Press.

Fine, Marshall. 1991. *Bloody Sam: The Life and Films of Sam Peckinpah*. New York: Donald I. Fine, Inc.

London, Jack. 1903, 1911. *The Call of the Wild*. New York: The Macmillan Company.

Prince, Stephen. 1998. *Savage Cinema: Sam Peckinpah and the Rise of Ultraviolent Movies*. Austin: University of Texas Press.

Seydor, Paul. 1997. *Peckinpah: The Western Films: A Reconsideration*. Urbana: University of Illinois Press.

Weddle, David. 1994. *"If They Move . . . Kill 'Em!": The Life and Times of Sam Peckinpah*. New York: Grove Press.

ELEVEN

ROBERT MERRILL

Ford, Peckinpah, and the Advantages of Making (Many) Westerns

In her review of Jane Tompkins's *West of Everything: The Inner Life of Westerns* (1992, 315), Sarah Markgraf notes that Tompkins's study is one of the few books about Westerns as a genre. Markgraf rightly points out that we prefer to study major artists, or crucial themes, or topics that interest us. *West of Everything* perhaps illustrates why we resist studying an entire genre, for Tompkins includes chapters on Owen Wister, Zane Grey, and Louis L'Amour (as well as the Buffalo Bill Historical Center!) as representative figures, and one must wonder how many of us would want to devote our days and hours to Grey and L'Amour. Indeed, the study of genres can be seen as hostile to the study of major works, as John G. Cawelti more or less admits when he writes, "The circumstances in which a Western is produced and consumed do not encourage the creation of unique individual works of art but lead to the production of particular realizations of a conventional formula" (Cawelti 1987, 52). Cawelti (1987, 13) describes films such as *The Godfather* and *Taxi Driver* as "very unlike Westerns in their moral ambiguity and tragic complexity." Those of us who would prefer to study moral ambiguity and tragic complexity are well advised to focus on those "unique individual works of art" that will probably work against the conventions of their genre rather than somehow define or embody it.

Students of Western films have estimated that the genre includes as many as eight thousand works (everything from serials to a few three-hour feature films). As Markgraf suggests, most critics prefer to focus on a small sample of the form. To do so is to engage those artistic strategies that mark the best examples of the form, even if one cannot claim to have defined the form itself. My own critical interest in Western films centers on thirty to forty films produced over the years by a handful of directors. A book-length study of these films and directors would "cover" the subject's artistic claims even as it would be radically selective and even, as Cawelti suggests, misleading about the form as a whole.

Here I want to explore a single observation that derives from reviewing the major Western films and their directors. Many of the best Western films have been made by a small group of directors who would identify with John Ford's famous introduction, "My name's John Ford. I make Westerns." Like Ford, Anthony Mann, Budd Boetticher, and Sam Peckinpah are identified with Westerns even though they also made other kinds of films.[1] I suspect that well over half the best Westerns have been made by these four directors, and it is possible that Ford and Peckinpah alone made seven or eight of the best fifteen to twenty Western films. It seems natural, then, to try to isolate what distinguishes the films of these directors and eventually to argue what these men got from their repeated practice of one form. Yet it is also true that some of the most respected Western films were the first Western made by their director or the only Western he made; primary examples would be Howard Hawks's *Red River* (1948), Fred Zinnemann's *High Noon* (1952), George Stevens's *Shane* (1953), and Robert Altman's *McCabe and Mrs. Miller* (1971). I would not want to argue that commitment to the form is necessary to produce excellent Westerns, for the examples just cited refute such a claim. Nonetheless, I do believe that directors such as Ford and Peckinpah benefited from the fact that they made numerous Western films and that we see the fruits of this commitment not only in their very best films, which are arguably superior to the best films made by directors who then abandoned the form, but also in films that for various reasons are either comparable to films such as *High Noon* and *McCabe and Mrs. Miller* or even inferior to them.

I am especially struck by the characterizations Ford and Peckinpah achieved precisely by emphasizing moral ambiguity and tragic complexity in their primary portraits. As I read it, the historical record suggests that it is far easier to achieve such characterizations in films that are not one's first venture into Western filmmaking. In the pages to follow I can only begin to outline the reasons why this is so, but I hope to offer a suggestive sketch of how the inveterate Western filmmakers differ from their counterparts who effectively poached on the form and then moved on as if it were an exhausted set of formulaic conventions.

I.

First or one-time Westerns tend to be either excessively reverential or excessively hostile. Films such as Lawrence Kasdan's *Silverado* (1985) lovingly recreate stock Western characters and situations, as if nostalgically resurrecting the form; films such as Arthur Penn's *Little Big Man* (1970), Frank Perry's *Doc* (1971), and Philip Kaufman's *The Great Northfield Minnesota Raid* (1972) subvert the conventions of the John Wayne–type Western so relentlessly as to inaugurate a new form, the so-called anti-Western. In either case, the first-time Western filmmaker seems to view his task (or opportunity) as the re-invention of the Western. Characters and scenes are handled with great self-consciousness, as well-known parts of the traditional form we know as the Western, and narrative interest seldom focuses on the particular story the film is supposedly developing.

Silverado is an extremely interesting example, for Kasdan is one of the most important recent directors, and films such as *Body Heat* (1980) prove that he is capable of reconceiving a genre (in this case, *film noir*) in ways that genuinely extend the form's appeal. In *Silverado*, however, Kasdan seems unable to present the Western as anything but a collection of implausible, all too familiar adventures. The film begins with a shoot-out in which Emmitt (Scott Glenn) kills several cowboys who attack him for no obvious reason, the first of several occasions where one of the four male leads overcomes odds of at least three to one. The film proceeds as a series of loosely related episodes drawn from Western archives: the sheriff (John Cleese) insisting that he alone dictates what constitutes the law; the young man (Kevin Costner) being rescued from jail by his relatives/friends before he can be hanged unjustly; the former outlaw (Kevin Kline) shooting one by one the men who robbed him and left him in the desert to die; the recovery of money stolen from a wagon train; the bloody conflict between homesteaders and ranchers; the showdown against a lawman (Brian Dennehy) who is conspiring with a local cattleman against the "people"; the inevitable final shoot-out in which the several good guys manage to kill their respective antagonists and to survive without serious injury. The film also echoes standard Western fare in its central (if underdeveloped) storyline. Paden, the Kevin Kline character, is made to choose between his friends, the homesteaders who are persecuted by the corrupt cattleman, and his financially rewarding connections with the crooked lawman. As this formulation would suggest, Paden's choice is pathetically easy to make, and the film's moral tension is therefore no more impressive than the plausibility of its individual exploits (as when Kevin Costner uses two guns to shoot enemies who are walking in different directions, perhaps the least-credible scene ever included in a presumably serious film).

As a first-time Western director who wants to honor the form's conventions, Kasdan falls into the hard-to-avoid trap of offering up as many Western tidbits and narrative situations as possible in a two-hour format, with no real commitment to telling a unique or at least significant story.[2] Many first-time directors come to bury rather than to praise, however, as the proliferation of modern anti-Westerns attests. Directors such as Peckinpah and Sergio Leone are sometimes included in this sub-genre, but any real analysis of their works suggests how misleading this label is as applied to their films. Indeed, how likely is it that a director would devote a *series* of films to exposing or ridiculing a filmic formula? Anti-Westerns tend to be one-shot efforts, whether offered by satirists such as Mel Brooks *(Blazing Saddles* [1974]) or Kasdan's peers such as Philip Kaufman.

The narrative voice at the beginning of Kaufman's film claims that he will tell "the true story of the Northfield raid" planned in 1876 by Cole Younger (Cliff Robertson) and somewhat erratically executed by Younger, Jesse James (Robert Duvall), and other assorted members and friends of the Younger and James families. This "true story" is obviously intended to counteract the benign treatment of these famous outlaws in films such as Henry King's *Jesse James* (1940) and Fritz Lang's *The Return of Frank James* (1940), in which the James brothers are played by actors such as Tyrone Power and Henry Fonda. *The Great Northfield Minnesota Raid* comes across as a kind of Western *film noir*, with its unrelieved darkness, rain, and squalor, its several scenes in which men are mistakenly hanged at a whorehouse, shot by our "heroes" inside a bank vault, or slaughtered by the ultra-Confederate Jesse James because they happen to be U.S. soldiers, and its general commitment to the least heroic interpretation of every event and character, the townspeople in Northfield as much as the outlaws. Most unforgettable, perhaps, is the scene near the end in which we see Frank and Jesse James driving away from Northfield in a wagon, the legendary Jesse James disguised as a woman in an outfit he has taken from an old woman after killing her.

The Great Northfield Minnesota Raid is a much more successful film than *Silverado*, but its revisionist energies are as distorting as Kasdan's loyalties to the time-honored conventions. Whether reviving the standard form of the Western or attacking its aggrandizement of historical figures taken to be squalid if not hateful, such films betray the literary/filmic interests of the outsider who is more interested in studying the genre or commenting on it than in making Western films. Even at their best, then, such films bespeak the limitations their directors faced in making their first (and often their only) Western.

Conclusions about one-time Westerns are more complicated if we turn to the best examples, films such as *High Noon* and *Shane*. In some ways these films recall the contrast between *The Great Northfield Minnesota Raid* and *Silverado*, for *High Noon* is sufficiently revisionist to strike John Wayne as "the most un-American thing I've ever seen in my whole life" (Lewis 1971, 90), and *Shane* has impressed many critics as continuing "the more traditional format of the heroic gunman saving the day for the decent but dependent settlers and thus redeeming himself—if necessary—through commitment to the good society" (Lenihan 1980, 121–22). *High Noon* and *Shane* are much better films, however, which perhaps makes their ultimate limitations both subtler and more revealing about the problems of working within the Western format for the first time.

High Noon provoked John Wayne and inspired Howard Hawks to "respond" by making *Rio Bravo* (1959) because Zinnemann's film casts a very cold eye on the western community of Hadleyville, which effectively abandons its marshal, Will Kane (Gary Cooper), to the revengeful Frank Miller (Ian MacDonald) and his three compatriots. The film has been unfairly treated as "an anti-McCarthyite tract," an "indictment of civic complacency" (Mitchell 1996, 191, 192), as if its controlling features were those of social allegory, and rather crude allegory at that. It seems to me that Zinnemann's handling of his Western materials is much shrewder than such readings imply. He is especially good at characterizing the people of Hadleyville, whether they attend church or the saloon this fateful Sunday, and he elicits from Gary Cooper one of the most intense and powerful performances by an American actor. The film's realism is especially useful in rendering credible the extremely dramatic, even melodramatic, events of this ninety-minute test of a town's moral character. The people of Hadleyville are all too believable, as opposed to the caricatures in Kasdan's and Kaufman's very different films. Its memorable but perhaps excessive music aside, *High Noon* is a brilliant first venture into the Western by one of the better directors of the 1950s.[3]

Nonetheless, *High Noon* illustrates the limitations of even the best one-time Westerns. As an experienced European director, Zinnemann did not bring to his task the ideological commitments, pro or con, of a Kasdan or a Kaufman, but he did harbor views about the Western that effectively restricted what he could do in the form. ". . . The characters have to be rather primitive types, not subtle or complex personalities," Zinnemann once said about the Western. "Once you grasp the form, it is fairly easy to fit the whole thing together" (Phillips 1998, 154). This comment from the film's director perhaps suggests why Cooper's Will Kane is not an even greater or more compelling character than he is. The film hints at but does not develop Kane as a man of tragic complexity. The fact that Kane has had an extended affair with Helen Ramirez (Katy Jurado), the ex-mistress of Frank Miller, the man Kane sent to prison five years before the events depicted in the film, is handled very cautiously. So far as we can tell, Zinnemann's hero organized the town's efforts to rid itself of Frank Miller and his gang for the most honorable reasons, then later became involved with the admirable Mrs. Ramirez, perhaps the film's most sympathetic character. How Helen Ramirez allowed herself to become involved with Frank Miller is not explored in a film that focuses on Kane, and in any case we are naturally much more interested in Kane's motives and complexities. Cooper admirably conveys Kane's mounting frustrations as he is rejected by one after another of his "friends," the very people who had helped him in the past, and even the woman he has married that very morning (Grace Kelly). Kane's very human fatigue is captured in a series of scenes that reveal his personal rather than his traditionally heroic qualities. Ultimately, however, Kane is not particularly subtle or complex, his moral worth is never in question, and while this is apparently what Zinnemann desired, it perhaps accounts for the fact that *High Noon* is a very good but not a truly great film.

Something like the same analysis applies to Stevens's *Shane*. Whereas *High Noon* humanizes the legendary Western hero while still insisting on his essential virtue, *Shane* offers what Lee Clark Mitchell (1996, 193) calls "a distillation of the Western itself" by retelling the classical story of the ex-gunfighter's decision to return to a life of violence on behalf of homesteaders who represent the future of civilization in their quarrel with western ranchers. The problem with this fine film is not, as so many allege, the unheroic presence of Alan Ladd in the title role. Indeed, the smallish Ladd seems very much the kind of gentle, soft-spoken figure Stevens wanted to include in this realistic incarnation of the classic homesteaders-versus-ranchers Western tale. Ladd as gunfighter is ultimately more believable than the extraordinary heroics of John Wayne or Clint Eastwood. What the film fails to do more than suggest is the depth of this character's commitment to the lawless life he is trying to put behind him. Shane's attraction to his new family, the Starretts, is nicely rendered in scene after scene, and one is tempted to forgive Stevens's sentimental excesses in depicting Shane's and Joe Starrett's (Van Heflin) fistfight against what seems a cast of hundreds (in reality, a dozen or so men). What the film needs is more of what we see for just a moment when Shane provokes the final gunfight by taunting his counterpart Wilson (Jack Palance) as a "Yankee liar," thus hinting at the sort of Confederate passion we will see again in the Ethan Edwards of Ford's *The Searchers*; what it especially needs is development of the insight into Shane's character that emerges when he twirls his guns proudly after shooting Wilson and his boss, Rufus Riker (Emile Meyer). Shane is the sort of man who knows how to provoke his enemies, just as Wilson does earlier in taunting Torrey (Elisha Cook Jr.) into drawing on him, and he obviously derives great personal satisfaction from his shooting skills, as we also see earlier when Shane delights in showing little Joey (Brandon De Wilde) how to shoot. The Shane captured in these brief moments is a man of tragic complexity, torn between love for the ways of his past and love for the Starretts and their friends. He is a man Stevens could have made the subject of his film had he been less concerned to "distill" the essence of the formulaic Western, or had he simply been more comfortable with the conventions and plotlines of a form he had never practiced before.[4]

Again, my claim is not that first-time Western directors are doomed to failure. None of the films treated above is simply a failure. *High Noon* and *Shane* are among the better Westerns ever made, and the inclusion in this brief discussion of Hawks's *Red River* and Altman's *McCabe and Mrs. Miller* would further acknowledge the successes possible for directors working in the form for the first time.[5] I do think these very films confirm how hard it is to create protagonists of real complexity, even tragic complexity, while one is feeling one's way with the conventions of the form or even addressing those conventions as one's primary purpose. For such protagonists we need to attend anew to the better films of John Ford and Sam Peckinpah, whose lifelong commitment to the Western allowed them to place characters of unusual complexity within situations they knew as intimately as their own clothes.

II.

"Things are always mixed," Peckinpah once said, a remark that would assist any critic who wanted to account for the distinctive character of the best films of Anthony Mann, Budd Boetticher, John Ford, and Peckinpah himself (Seydor 1997, 372, n. 21). Indeed, a thoroughgoing treatment of this theme would embrace all the Westerns by these four directors. Here I can only emphasize the pattern of development we see in Ford and Peckinpah, the most important Western directors. This pattern is much the same in each man's career and might be predicted from our review of the first-time Westerns. Relatively early we find films in which the protagonists are interesting, even fascinating, but still cast in the traditional mold that also produced Will Kane and Shane. Then, in a later, more mature period, we discover films of greater complexity, with heroes sufficiently morally ambiguous to elicit widespread critical controversy about their real nature. And finally, in films such as Ford's *The Searchers* (1956) and Peckinpah's *Pat Garrett and Billy the Kid* (1973), we get the kind of tragic complexity only the most ambitious artists would even aspire to depict. I think it is far from accidental that such films come relatively late in their directors' experience with Westerns.

Ford's many silent films complicate any account of his career, but his first talking Western, *Stagecoach* (1939), clearly represents the kind of film Ford felt he could make as he again took up his work with Western conventions, now in the new medium generated by speech. *Stagecoach* is in many ways a wonderful film, but Ford's handling of his hero, the Ringo Kid (John Wayne), is almost painfully conventional. Like many Western protagonists, the Kid traffics with those outside the law, but in his case imprisonment is unjust and at no time has he really violated the laws or moral standards of a just society. Indeed, the film seems based on a somewhat tidy inversion of conventional expectations, as our thoroughly well-meaning and good-hearted hero and heroine (Claire Trevor) are cast as escaped outlaw and prostitute, respectively. Ringo is too good to be true, just as he is miraculously efficient when he confronts his three antagonists with only three bullets. Ringo is so young we cannot reasonably ask that he be more self-reflective, and the film as a whole does not fail to achieve moral complexity so much as it declines to try for such effects. Interestingly, Ford's first great Western film, *My Darling Clementine* (1946), offers a protagonist rather closer in spirit to the Ringo Kid than to the later Ethan Edwards. Wyatt Earp (Henry Fonda) is older than the Kid, but his rather similar pursuit of revenge for the death of a brother seems unambiguously presented by his director as the only thing to do. The film's wonderfully ambiguous moments all concern the coming of civilized society to the once anarchic streets of Tombstone, not the moral character or cause of Ford's hero. It would be truly ungrateful to lament Ford's "failure" to discover the story of Wyatt Earp's tragic complexity amidst the legendary materials on which he drew, but his uncritical treatment of Earp does help to explain why the later and in some ways less artful *The Searchers* is the greater film.

Ten years separate *My Darling Clementine* from *The Searchers*. The most significant step toward the later film came only two years after *My Darling*

Clementine when Ford made the first of his so-called Cavalry films, *Fort Apache* (1948). He was not yet prepared to focus entirely on a morally ambiguous tragic hero, so the John Wayne character in this film, Captain York, remains an almost conventionally virtuous figure, albeit much older than the Ringo Kid. Captain York is a much more interesting study, however, for he is depicted as ultimately embracing the character with whom he is in conflict throughout the action, the notorious Colonel Owen Thursday (Henry Fonda), who leads his troops to a Custer-like disaster sometime before York assumes Thursday's command. For many viewers, Thursday is nothing but the "pompous egomaniac" Max Westbrook takes him to be in an essay that assaults *Fort Apache* as jingoistic blather, Ford's most lamentable venture into militaristic ideology (Westbrook 1990, 157). For York, Thursday is a fallen leader who offers the Regiment, as York thinks of it, a model devoutly to be wished—whatever the man's flaws prior to his fatal battle with Cochise. For Ford, I would suggest, Thursday is a complicated figure whose parts include both those Westbrook excoriates and those York memorializes.

The ambiguous nature of Colonel Thursday is the most striking thing about *Fort Apache* even though York remains the technical protagonist. That York ends up endorsing a man like Thursday, even if he does so for strategic reasons, suggests that Ford's typical hero is moving much closer to the realm of tragic complexity than in the earlier Westerns. Thursday is, as Westbrook and others have argued, a careerist who comes west only because he is ordered to do so and who sees his engagement with the Indians as an opportunity to win reassignment in the more civilized East once he has conquered the ignorant heathen. The contrast between York and Thursday could not be greater, as York is a valued friend of Cochise and extremely sensitive to the Indian's culture and ways of doing things, while Thursday all but prides himself on his ignorance of the Indian's habits and values. Thursday's insistence on his own superiority (essentially, the white man's superiority) clearly gets his men and himself killed unnecessarily. In this sense, it seems incredible that York should later praise Thursday to reporters and offer up Thursday as a model to the cavalry now charged with reigning in Geronimo. But the paradox here is more apparent than real. Thursday was wrong about Indians such as Cochise, but he was not wrong about Indians such as Geronimo, who presents the threat to civilized life Thursday mistakenly saw in all Indians and the younger York failed to see in Cochise's followers such as Geronimo. Nor was Thursday wrong about the Regiment's need for greater discipline and professionalism, even if York is the better man to advance these values humanely. Ford presents in *Fort Apache* a first version of that complex world he would later create in *The Searchers*, a world in which the simple human decencies are not denied by the presence of malign human behavior but instead are seen as fated to co-exist with such evil. If *Fort Apache* had focused more on York's education into this vision it would be a greater film than it is. This education—both York's and our own—is nonetheless crucial to an adequate appreciation of this key film in Ford's evolution as a Western filmmaker.

By the time he made *The Searchers*, Ford had done seven Western features, the many earlier silent films, and other pictures such as *Drums Along the Mohawk* (1939) that share a "western" concern with the frontier. He was accordingly well positioned to make the crucial change that transformed his source novel, Alan Lemay's *The Searchers* (1954), into one of our great films. This change is one of narrative focus, for Lemay's novel tells the story of Martin Pauley's and Amos Edwards's search for Debbie Edwards from Marty's point of view, and indeed the novel is essentially about Marty's wrenching five-year experience in seeking the safe return of his kidnapped "cousin." In Lemay's novel, the gruff, inarticulate Amos Edwards is seen only at some distance until he dies at the end trying to retrieve Debbie, whether to kill her or to save her we cannot say. It was Ford's genius to see that embedded in this undistinguished novel was a profound story about one of the least John Wayne–like characters Wayne was ever to play, a man all but defined by moral ambiguity and tragic complexity.

Ford's protagonist (rechristened Ethan Edwards) is a man of what seem commanding contradictions. At the beginning of the film we see Ethan return to his brother Aaron's (Walter Coy) home in a very dusty, very isolated section of Texas a few years after the end of the Civil War. His extremely courteous treatment of Aaron's wife, Martha (Dorothy Jordan), his playful exchanges with the young girls, Lucy (Pippa Scott) and Debbie (Natalie Wood), and his status as a returning war hero on the Confederate side accord with his imposing physical stature to suggest that Ethan is yet another version of the traditional Western hero. From the beginning, however, we see the darker side(s) to Ethan Edwards, a man who returns from Mexico with gold coins presumably won through theft and perhaps worse. This is the Ethan who taunts Marty (Jeffrey Hunter) because of his trace of Cherokee blood, the first sign of Ethan's virulent racism everywhere on display throughout the film; who rejects at once the legal and moral authority of Rev./Capt. Samuel Clayton (Ward Bond), who heads the local Texas Rangers; who shoots out the eyes of a dead Comanche so that the warrior will, according to his own beliefs, wander alone throughout eternity; who will fire randomly at buffalo so as to limit their use by Indians; and who scalps the Indian chief, Scar (Henry Brandon), who kidnapped Lucy and Debbie after murdering Aaron and the rest of his family. This is the Ethan Edwards who interrupts the funeral service for his family members, even as the congregation sings Ford's beloved "Shall We Gather at the River," in order to get a quicker start in pursuit of revenge. Indeed, this is the man who continues to search for Scar and Debbie for almost seven years rather than return to his home to rebuild the family ranch.

Who, then, is Ethan Edwards? The director/critic Lindsay Anderson sees Ethan as impossibly divided, two distinct characters Ford would force us to see as one: ". . . the Ethan who jovially bustles Mrs. Jorgensen back into the house as her daughter's suitors prepare to do battle . . . is not the same Ethan we have seen implacable to rescue Debbie from her shame by death" (Anderson 1981, 158–59). In truth, however, the engaging, humane Ethan who bustles Mrs. Jorgensen about has been with us throughout: when he suffers so palpably after finding Martha's ravaged body (thus confirming the film's hints that he has always loved Martha); when he covers Lucy's dead body with the war uniform he values so highly; when he thinks to send the Jorgensens (John Qualen, Olive Carey) a letter reporting the death of their son Brad (Harry Carey Jr.); when he jokes with Marty about Marty's new "wife" (an Indian maid attached to Marty by mistake); when he comes over time to call Martin Marty and to will him the Edwards property. The business with Look, Marty's "wife," is unmistakably racist as well as humorous, but Ford's Texas community is everywhere depicted as humane *and* racist; indeed, the most racist character in the film is Laurie Jorgensen (Vera Miles), who nonetheless functions as Marty's chosen mate and as one of the film's most sympathetic characters. In this world, more realistically imagined than any of Ford's other communities, Ethan is exemplary *both* in his brutality and his ultimate grasp of life's contradictions.

As I read the film, Ethan's divided but not irreconcilable features are essential to Ford's primary purpose: to chart Ethan's gradual acceptance of his role within the (flawed) human community. In this light, the film's real climax is Ethan's turning his gun over to Captain Clayton and agreeing to go to Austin for an inquiry concerning three men Ethan has been forced to kill. In the aftermath of this late moment, richly suggestive of Ethan's moral evolution, Ethan is able to joke with a Yankee soldier and to allow Marty to enter Scar's camp before the other men so as to give Debbie a chance to survive the rangers' attack. It is this Ethan, of course, who lifts Debbie from the ground, as he lifted her in the film's first moments seven years earlier, and brings her home to the Jorgensens rather than rescuing her from shame by killing her. He is still a man of strong feelings and a profound sense of alienation; thus his readiness to scalp Scar, who has been killed by Marty, and his famous refusal to enter into the Jorgensen home in the film's final scene as Debbie is enfolded within the community from which she was taken so many years before. Ford emphasizes Ethan's morally ambiguous nature and develops the man's tragic complexity beyond anything in his other films, Western or non-Western, in order to affirm in the end Ethan's severely tested decency. Toward this end, Ford made use of everything he had learned about human nature in a western setting to create the most memorable of his character studies.

III.

I assume that Ford learned over the course of his career that the characters in a Western do *not* have to be primitive types and that they *can* be subtle or complex personalities. In Ford's case, this shift toward complexity corresponded with his discovery, after watching Hawks's *Red River,* that John Wayne could play far more complicated figures than Ford had supposed. With Sam Peckinpah there is a somewhat different progression, for even in his earliest Western films, *The Deadly Companions* (1961) and *Ride the High Country* (1962), Peckinpah seems fully aware of the form's complex, even tragic possibilities. Nonetheless, as I remarked earlier, Peckinpah's major films do move somewhat similarly in the direction of greater moral ambiguity and tragic complexity, from *Ride the High Country* to *The Wild Bunch* (1969) to *Pat Garrett and Billy the Kid.* The progression here is not one of artistic excellence, for *Pat Garrett and Billy the Kid* is less successful than either of Peckinpah's earlier masterpieces, but Peckinpah's treatment of Pat Garrett (James Coburn) is the epitome of the complex characterization typical of the veteran Western filmmakers.

With his first Western features, after years of writing and directing Westerns for television, Peckinpah was already deeply suspicious of conventional Westerns. "I have never made a 'Western,'" he once said. "I have made a lot of films about men on horseback" (Schrader 1994, 28). Even a film such as *Ride the High Country*, with its exemplary hero, Steve Judd (Joel McCrea), does not offer the classical "Westerner" as defined by Robert Warshow. For Warshow, this conventional figure rides faultlessly and draws his gun faster than others, and exhibits as well "an apparent moral clarity which corresponds to the clarity of his physical image against his bare landscape"

(Warshow 1964, 139). Steve Judd approximates this type more than any other Peckinpah protagonist, but his physical powers are hardly "faultless" and his "moral clarity" is qualified somewhat by his stubbornness and his tendency to preach, his tinge of moral zealotry ("All I want is to enter my house justified," Judd says at one memorable moment). The aging Steve Judd is not very self-reflective, in fact, which both qualifies his status as paragon and suggests why he seems to lack the depth of Peckinpah's later protagonists, Pike Bishop (William Holden) and Pat Garrett.

In this relatively early film, it is Judd's old friend, Gil Westrum (Randolph Scott), who embodies a more complicated (though not tragic) mixture of good and evil qualities. It is Gil and not Steve who recalls that the good old days were hard, even unyielding, as well as the occasion for Gil's and Steve's most impressive performances as lawmen (very poorly paid lawmen, as Gil reminds his nostalgic friend). It is Gil who feels acutely the embarrassment of working in Western shows as a kind of relic from the past. And so it is Gil who crosses all moral lines by plotting to steal the money Steve has hired him to help guard. The film deals very effectively with this unmistakable transgression on the part of a "good" man, someone Steve Judd thinks of as an equal. Ultimately, Gil recaptures his former sense of moral obligation and is rewarded with Steve's assurance that he always knew Gil was the honorable man of their common past. The film thus develops fairly fully the story of a good but vulnerable man's inner conflict, but Gil is not the protagonist and his choices are not as severe as those we associate with genuine tragedy. This is perhaps appropriate in a film filled with realistic elements masterfully orchestrated by an important new director, but a film that does not aspire to the tragic dimensions of Peckinpah's later works. Indeed, the viewer who is familiar with Peckinpah's later films may well wonder if Steve Judd is not handled a little too reverentially in this slightly nostalgic reconception of the traditional Western.

No such reservations arise with Peckinpah's treatment of Pike Bishop in his finest film, *The Wild Bunch*. Seven years separate *Ride the High Country* from *The Wild Bunch*, and in this period Peckinpah—rather like Ford as he moved toward the creation of Ethan Edwards—apparently came to believe that the most powerful Western film would offer as protagonist a man who combines Steve's and Gil's more crucial features. The aging Pike Bishop is not as pious as Steve, but he is also inclined to lecture or preach, as when he warns his men that they are nothing but animals if they don't stick together. It is crucial to the film's ultimate effect that we appreciate Pike's commitment to the values of loyalty, comradeship, and professionalism, precisely the values Steve Judd espoused and more or less embodied. But we cannot help but see the darker, Gil Westrum–like side to Pike, as when he abandons the unreliable Crazy Lee (Bo Hopkins) to simplify the Bunch's retreat from the embattled town of Starbuck, or when he shoots the blinded Buck because the Bunch cannot afford to stop and take care of their friend, or when he joins sides—however briefly—with the monstrous Mexican "general," Mapache (Emilio Fernandez), attracted by the prospect of challenging work but also the fee of $10,000 ("Ten thousand dollars cuts a lot of family ties," as Pike proclaims). Pike's moral failures litter the film, in fact, from his overconfident decisions that lead to the imprisonment of his friend Deke Thornton (Robert Ryan), to his carelessness in protecting—or failing to protect—the one great love of his life, Aurora, who is killed by her estranged husband even as Pike is wounded for life in his thigh, to his late decision to let his longtime friend Freddy Sykes (Edmond O'Brien) fend for himself against an attacking posse while Pike leads his men back to Agua Verde, Mapache's town. In short, Pike Bishop is a real outlaw, not an older Ringo Kid, and his moral failures are of the essence in Peckinpah's tragic story.

Pike's troubled character has been splendidly reviewed by several critics, most notably Paul Seydor, John L. Simons, and Michael Bliss (see the relevant entries in my References section). Seydor's lengthy chapter on *The Wild Bunch* includes extended discussion of Pike's strengths and flaws, his recurring failures but finally his personal redemption when he takes himself and his men to certain death in order to reassert their commitment to one of their own, the young Mexican, Angel (Jaime Sanchez), whom Mapache has taken prisoner. Seydor meticulously traces the steps by which Pike comes to reverse his lifelong inability to live up to the stirring words about animals and real men he has preached to his gang (Seydor 1997, 137–212). Simons (1985) offers a complementary discussion of Pike's relations with women, a topic that adds immensely to our understanding of what motivates Peckinpah's protagonist. I think it is worth emphasizing that Peckinpah's film and especially his development of Pike Bishop are rich enough to warrant Seydor's 76-page chapter and Simons's shorter but no less highly detailed treatment. Almost everything in this film rewards such attention, and especially the tortured, remarkably complex character of Pike Bishop, the most tragic of Western protagonists from the Western director whose vision is itself best described as tragic.

Later, in 1973, Peckinpah returned to the subject of outlaw-as-hero with his controversial treatment of the Billy the Kid saga, *Pat Garrett and Billy the Kid*. Despite its flaws and the unforgivable interference of Peckinpah's masters at MGM, who cut sixteen minutes from the film and refused to let Peckinpah edit the released version, this difficult film amply confirms the notion that only veteran Western filmmakers are in position to incorporate highly complex protagonists within the structures and conventions of the Western. I am thinking especially of Peckinpah's Pat Garrett, though his Billy the Kid (Kris Kristofferson) is a much more complicated figure than we are used to in the many reinventions of this legendary figure. It is Garrett who makes this imperfect film a memorable experience, as Peckinpah slowly (too slowly, many would say) traces Garrett's conflicted efforts to survive in the new, post-outlaw West by becoming a lawman himself and purging New Mexico of its worst renegade, Garrett's friend and former colleague William Bonney. The best moments of this film capture Garrett's intense self- hatred as he doggedly works out his new commitment to the established order by tracking down the Kid and finally killing him. The portrait that emerges, that of a "hero" who violates his real values and inner self by surviving at any cost, is stunningly rendered by Peckinpah and his lead actor, James Coburn, and I can only suggest that anyone interested in the many details through which Peckinpah realizes this portrait should read Seydor's remarkable chapter on the film (1997, 255–306).

Pat Garrett and Billy the Kid is an extraordinarily bleak film that in some ways takes us back (or, in some cases, forward) to the anti-Western spirit of *The Great Northfield Minnesota Raid*. The film is very hard to cuddle up to, or even to give a fair chance to arouse our active involvement. Perhaps the complex Pat Garrett is ultimately too unlikable, too deeply encased in his mid-life crisis. Certainly he achieves nothing like the cathartic reassertion of self—moral self—embodied in Pike Bishop's final moments. Even at its best, *Pat Garrett and Billy the Kid* may be a film for Western aficionados who appreciate its uncompromising portrait of moral ambiguity (perhaps tragic, perhaps not) no matter how painfully dark the product. In any case, we are reminded that great filmmaking involves more than complex protagonists, though I think we should also recognize in this final example that only a dedicated maker of Western films could have conceived and largely achieved Peckinpah's dark portrait of Pat Garrett. As I have tried to show, this means that *Pat Garrett and Billy the Kid* could have been made only by one of several directors, those largely responsible for the Western film as an art form.

I suppose my point may seem a touch self-evident: experience helps. I think it specifically helps in allowing the veteran maker of Westerns to build on his previous efforts by focusing on what really counts. This does not mean he will ignore the accurate, often economical presentation of Western situations and settings; indeed, his experience will allow him to present these things, preeminently in *The Searchers* and *The Wild Bunch*, more thoroughly than other directors have been able to do. In addition, however, he will find himself focusing on protagonists of the greatest complexity and telling stories that engage us with this complexity as only the greatest works of art can do. In this sense experience not only helps but also is indispensable to the creation of the form's masterpieces. The more one studies the films of Ford and Peckinpah the more one appreciates the *careers* their films represent, in particular the films that climax those careers by embodying the Western's richest artistic possibilities.

Notes

1. Students of the Western film will recall that Mann, Boetticher, and Peckinpah were the subject of Jim Kitses's pioneering study *Horizons West* in 1969. It seems appropriate that the frontispiece is taken from a key scene in Ford's *My Darling Clementine*. Other useful treatments of the Western film include John G. Cawelti's chapter on the Western in his *Adventure, Mystery, and Romance* (1976), Philip French's *Westerns: Aspects of a Movie Genre* (1977), and Lee Clark Mitchell's *Westerns: Making the Man in Fiction and Film* (1996). It seems to me, however, that the best discussions of the Western film are to be found in Paul Seydor's book on Peckinpah (1997) and his more recent essay on the film script of *The Wild Bunch* (1999).

2. The superficiality of Kasdan's homage to the Western may have been as apparent to him as it was to others, for his second Western, *Wyatt Earp* (1994), is almost studiously different in its calculated attention to authentic details and its painfully slow narrative pace. Need one add that *Silverado* was a box-office winner and *Wyatt Earp* attracted few customers?

3. After making *High Noon*, Zinnemann went on to direct *From Here to Eternity* (1953), *Oklahoma!* (1955), *The Sundowners* (1960), and *The Day of the Jackal* (1973), among other films.

4. Edward Countryman and Evonne von Heussen-Countryman (1999) reach more positive conclusions about Shane by reading the film in the rich context of Stevens's other films, especially those he directed just before and after *Shane*. Much as I admire their analysis, easily the most extensive discussion to date, I think that the film's limitations emerge if one considers its place within the Western film genre.

5. Elsewhere I have discussed *McCabe and Mrs. Miller* as a classical Western, indeed one of the finest Westerns ever made; see Merrill 1990. In this context, however, McCabe's (Warren Beatty) limitations as a character seem to me as relevant as his considerable appeal. Hawks's Tom Dunston (John Wayne) is perhaps the protagonist in this category who most approaches the complexity of Ford's and Peckinpah's finest creations, and it is perhaps no accident that Hawks is the one director discussed so far who ended up returning to the Western several times in his later years.

References

Anderson, Lindsay. 1981. *About John Ford*. London: Plexus Publishing.

Bliss, Michael, ed. 1994. Introduction to *Doing It Right: The Best Criticism on Sam Peckinpah's* The Wild Bunch, edited by Michael Bliss, xv–xxiii. Carbondale: Southern Illinois University Press.

Cawelti, John G. 1976. "The Western: A Look at the Evolution of a Formula." In *Adventure, Mystery, and Romance: Formula Stories as Art and Popular Culture*, 192–259. Chicago: University of Chicago Press.

———. 1984. *The Six-Gun Mystique*. 2nd ed. Bowling Green, Ohio: Bowling Green State University Popular Press.

Countryman, Edward, and Evonne von-Heussen Countryman. 1999. *Shane*. London: British Film Institute.

French, Philip. 1977. *Westerns: Aspects of a Movie Genre*. Rev. ed. New York: Oxford University Press.

Kitses, Jim. 1969. *Horizons West—Anthony Mann, Budd Boetticher, Sam Peckinpah: Studies of Authorship within the Western*. Bloomington: Indiana University Press.

Lemay, Alan. 1954. *The Searchers*. New York: Harper and Row.

Lenihan, John L. 1980. *Showdown: Confronting Modern America in Western Film*. Urbana: University of Illinois Press.

Lewis, Richard Warren. 1971. "*Playboy* Interview: John Wayne." *Playboy* 18.5 (May): 75–92.

Markgraf, Sarah. 1992. Review of Jane Tompkins's *West of Everything: The Inner Life of Westerns*. *Genre* 25 (Summer/Fall): 315–19.

Merrill, Robert. 1990. "Altman's *McCabe and Mrs. Miller* as a Classic Western." *New Orleans Review* 17 (Summer): 79–86.

Mitchell, Lee Clark. 1996. *Westerns: Making the Man in Fiction and Film*. Chicago: University of Chicago Press.

Phillips, Gene D. 1998. *Exiles in Hollywood: Major European Film Directors in America*. Bethlehem, Pa.: Lehigh University Press.

Schrader, Paul. 1994. "Sam Peckinpah Going to Mexico." In *Doing It Right: The Best Criticism on Sam Peckinpah's* The Wild Bunch, edited by Michael Bliss, 17–30. Carbondale: Southern Illinois University Press.

Seydor, Paul. 1997. *Peckinpah: The Western Films—A Reconsideration*. Urbana: University of Illinois Press.

———. 1999. "*The Wild Bunch:* The Screenplay." In *Sam Peckinpah's* The Wild Bunch, edited by Stephen Prince, 37–78. Cambridge: Cambridge University Press.

Simons, John L. 1985. "The Tragedy of Love in *The Wild Bunch*." *Western Humanities Review* 39 (Spring): 1–19.

Tompkins, Jane. 1992. *West of Everything: The Inner Life of Westerns*. New York: Oxford University Press.

Warshow, Robert. 1964. "Movie Chronicle: The Westerner." In *The Immediate Experience*, 135–54. Garden City, N.Y.: Doubleday Anchor.

Westbrook, Max. 1990. "The Night John Wayne Danced with Shirley Temple." *Western American Literature* 25 (August): 157–69.

TWELVE

LEONARD ENGEL

The Killer Elite and the Critics

A NOTE ON THE ART OF INTERPRETATION

Most of Peckinpah's films have received a variety of critical, often sharply conflicting, commentary, but none has elicited more diverse criticism than *The Killer Elite* (1975). When it first came out in 1975, many reviewers and critics seemed not to know what to make of the film or how to deal with it, dismissing it as either a conventional thriller or as another indication of Peckinpah's fall from the directorial height he had reached in *The Wild Bunch*. Unlike *Bring Me the Head of Alfredo Garcia*, which Peckinpah had made the previous year and which received mostly unfavorable reviews, *The Killer Elite* led critics to find something to praise while attacking it, sometimes savagely, or something to attack while praising it. William Pechter, for example, states that however well made the film is, "it remains junk." Peckinpah has given himself "over to total perversion" (Pechter 1976, 61). Another reviewer, Tom Milne, writes that the script is "a mixture of opportunism and joke—craftily marrying the martial arts fad to the anti-CIA craze to produce a sort of *Enter the Dragon* meets *Three Days of the Condor*." Milne concludes his humorous piece with another conflicting comment, claiming the film is "a commercial chore, but one that is infinitely less faceless than *The Getaway*" (Milne 1976, 55–56). In yet another review emphasizing the conflicted thoughts of the writer, Richard Combs states that the film is "a strangely dissonant and compelling entertainment, an unsettling criss-cross of Chinatown Nights' fantasy and dyspeptic meditation on figures set firmly in their contemporary landscape"; at times, Combs writes, "the film slips . . . smoothly . . . into self parody" (1976, 121–22).

Two critical commentaries that take *The Killer Elite* seriously enough to get beneath its surface story and attempt to understand what Peckinpah is doing are written by Pauline Kael in a review for *The New Yorker* (Kael 1976), and by Michael Bliss, "Cold Killers" (Bliss 1993, chap. 11). Although separated by seventeen years, these two pieces, especially Kael's, are crucial for any student of Peckinpah interested in his life and work in relation to Hollywood filmmaking. Examining the comments of Bliss and Kael will give insights not only into Peckinpah's artistry but also into the amazing diversity of interpretation his films have received.

Early in his chapter "Cold Killers," Bliss notes the film's major theme, which has been one of Peckinpah's main concerns in most of his films, that of "the dehumanizing aspects of progress," the effects of deception and betrayal—selling out one's self and one's friends. "No film," Bliss writes, "is more concerned with cold, calculating, duplicitous behavior than is *The Killer Elite*," and one of Peckinpah's great achievements is "economy of plot, action, and characterization; the film is as lean and direct as its main characters" (Bliss 1993, 263). Furthermore, the film continually alternates between seriousness and comedy, compelling viewers "to experience the dual states of the characters. Thus, the film's serious beginning, which shows the laying of explosives, is followed by the seriocomic interplay between Mike and George in the escape car" (Bliss 1993, 272). This alternation between seriousness and comedy is, I believe, what puzzled many of the early critics and reviewers of the film and caused them to write such conflicting comments.

Bliss is right on target with his perceptions, and he does note some of the ironic scenes and conversations, but he misses, or fails to emphasize, the overwhelming importance of irony in the film. This is especially true when he analyzes the concluding scenes of the film that show the protagonist Mike Locken (James Caan) and his sidekick Mac (Burt Young) sailing away in an idyllic sunrise setting, leaving behind their loyalty to their former company, the corrupt ComTeg, and all their previous ties and relationships. Figuratively, Bliss writes, they head "for that special Peckinpah realm of wish fulfillment, where, as in traditional American myth . . . they will supposedly become innocent."[1] The "last act," Bliss continues, "makes it plain how death-oriented and pointless their escape really is . . . [and] it points up the weakness of the film's conclusion" (Bliss 1993, 273). Reading the film without an overall interpretation and without a sense of its biting irony, as Bliss seems to read it, the film does not merely have a weak ending, it has problems with character motivation and narrative cohesion as well.

Writing almost eighteen years earlier, Pauline Kael offers an interpretation of *The Killer Elite*, especially of the ending, that sharply contrasts with other views of the film, especially Bliss's. Kael raises the issue of the confusing elements in the film. "There's no way to make sense of what has been going on in Peckinpah's recent films," she writes, "if one looks only at their surface stories. Whether consciously or not . . . he's been destroying the surface content."[2] "In [*The Killer Elite*]," Kael continues, "there aren't any of the ordinary kinds of introductions to the characters, and the events aren't prepared for. The political purposes of the double-crosses are shrouded in a dark fog, and the company itself makes no economic sense. There are remnants of a plot . . . but that fog covers all the specific plot points" (Kael 1976, 72).

Kael, who had severely criticized Peckinpah's earlier film *Straw Dogs*, which she called "the first American film that is a fascist work of art" (Kael 1972, 74), renders an extended analysis and interpretation of *The Killer Elite*. Surprisingly, at the time, the film, as well as the review, did not create much of a stir among New Yorkers; ironically, outside of New York, the film was a hit (Pechter 1976, 62). Read today, Kael's review strikes one as amazingly insightful in its interpretation of Peckinpah's relations with Hollywood.

In an earlier interview, in reference to movie producers, Peckinpah had stated, "The woods are full of killers, all sizes, all colors. . . . A director has to deal with a whole world . . . teeming with mediocrities, jackals, hangers-on, and just plain killers. . . . The saying is that they can kill you but not eat you. That's nonsense. I've had them eating on me while I was still walking around" (Murray 1972, 74). Referring to this interview, Kael remarks, "Peckinpah looks and behaves as if he were never free of their gnawing. He carries it with him, fantasizes it, provokes it. . . . He romanticizes himself as one of the walking wounded" (Kael 1976, 72). The plot of *The Killer Elite*, she emphasizes, has "so many elisions . . . that it hardly exists on a narrative level, but its poetic vision is all of a piece." Thus, the story "is used as a mere framework for a compressed, almost abstract fantasy on the subject of selling yourself yet trying to hang on to a piece of yourself . . ." (Kael 1976, 70).

Kael sees Peckinpah as "the elite killer hero played by James Caan in this hallucinatory thriller, in which the hirelings turn against their employers." Yet, while Caan plays the hero who acts out Peckinpah's dream of redemption, it is "Gig Young's face that haunts the film" (Kael 1976, 72–73). Young symbolizes what Peckinpah believes he will become if he doesn't avenge himself and sail away. "Joel McCrea, with his humane strength, may have been Peckinpah's idealized hero in *Ride the High Country*, and William Holden may have represented his flawed, tragic hero in *The Wild Bunch*, but Gig Young, who represents what taking orders from the bosses—being used—does to a *man of feeling*"—Gig Young is the one Peckinah identifies with now. Young plays "the top whore in *The Killer Elite*," claims Kael, because "his sad eyes suggest that he has no expectations and no illusions left about anything" (Kael 1976, 73), and this is the character Peckinah has become in his movie-making.

The film is "intensely, claustrophobically exciting," continues Kael, and Peckinpah's "technique is dazzling." Similar to the bloody afternoon ballet of death at the conclusion of *The Wild Bunch*, the violent finale of *The Killer Elite* is a nightmare ballet of killers swarming over the antique fleet of World War II naval ships in obscure Suisun Bay, north of San Francisco. The darting figures, indistinguishable in their cult garb, "seen in slow motion fast cuts are exactly like Peckinpah's descriptions of the teeming mediocrities, jackals, hangers-on, and just plain killers that Hollywood is full of." When Mike Locken (Caan) rejects the offers of his former boss, at the end, it is Peckinpah rejecting the "teeming mediocrities" and crowing "'no matter what you do to me, look at the way I can make a movie.' The bedevilled bastard has a right to crow," (Kael 1976, 75).

I am not trying to canonize Pauline Kael's critical acumen here, but her insistence on an interpretation encompassing Peckinpah's art and life and Hollywood's executives makes a lot of sense in this film. One need not necessarily adopt *her* particular reading, but without some kind of extended interpretation, the surface story of the film does lack coherence.

Kael concludes her piece on a hopeful note: "The film is so cleanly made that Peckinpah may have wrapped up this obsession. When James Caan and Burt Young sail away at the end, it's Sam Peckinpah turning his back on Hollywood. He has gone to Europe, with commitments that will keep him there for at least two years" (Kael 1976, 75). Alas, that this would have been true, but it's unlikely now that anyone would argue Peckinpah's obsessions were "wrapped up"; rather, the opposite is probably closer to the truth.

After *The Killer Elite*, Peckinpah made three more feature films: *Cross of Iron* (1977), *Convoy* (1978), and *Osterman Weekend* (1983)—all of which reveal his obsessions, and, in the opinion of most critics, are inferior to his earlier films. Whether one agrees with Kael or not, her critique performs a valuable service for the Peckinpah scholar. First, it presents an incisive reading of character and theme; and, second, it presents a remarkable interpretation of the film in relation to Peckinpah's own life and art, especially in relationship to Hollywood filmmaking. Kael's insights suggest new realms of possibility for biographers of Peckinpah and reveal new approaches to the amazing art of this truly gifted film director.

Notes

1. Bliss's comments remind one of R. W. B Lewis's thesis in *The American Adam* (1955) where Lewis writes extensively about a concept of American innocence that preoccupied a number of thinkers and writers in the middle and latter half of the nineteenth century.

2. In literature, we would say Peckinpah is deconstructing his own themes in order, perhaps, to tell a more personal, underlying story.

References

Bliss, Michael. 1993. *Justified Lives: Morality and Narrative in the Films of Sam Peckinpah.* Carbondale: Southern Illinois University Press.

Combs, Richard. 1976. "The Killer Elite." *Sight and Sound* 45:2 (Spring): 121–22.

Kael, Pauline. 1972. "The Current Cinema: Peckinpah's Obsession." *The New Yorker* 47:50 (January 29): 80–85.

———. 1976. "The Current Cinema: Notes on the Nihilistic Poetry of Sam Peckinpah." *The New Yorker* 51:47 (January 12): 70–75.

Lewis, R. W. B. 1955. *The American Adam: Innocence, Tragedy, and Tradition in the Nineteenth Century.* Chicago: University of Chicago Press.

Milne, Tom. 1976. "The Killer Elite." *Monthly Film Bulletin* (British Film Institute) 43 (March): 55–56.

Murray, William. 1972. "*Playboy* Interview: Sam Peckinpah." *Playboy* 19.8 (August): 65–74, 192.

Pechter, William S. 1976. "Kubrick and Peckinpah Revisited." *Commentary* 61 (March), 60–62.

SAM PECKINPAH FILMOGRAPHY

1. *The Deadly Companions* (1961). A Carousel production, released by Pathe-America. Producer: Charles B. Fitzsimmons. Screenplay by A. S. Fleischman, based on his novel *Yellowleg.*
2. *Ride the High Country* (1962). Metro-Goldwyn-Mayer. Producer: Richard Lyons. Screenplay by N. B. Stone Jr.
3. *Major Dundee* (1965). Jerry Bresler Productions, released by Columbia Pictures. Producer: Jerry Bresler. Screenplay by Harry Julian Fink, Oscar Saul, and Sam Peckinpah.
4. *The Wild Bunch* (1969). A Phil Feldman production, released by Warner Bros. Seven Arts. Producer: Phil Feldman. Screenplay by Walon Green and Sam Peckinpah, from a story by Green and Roy Sickner.
5. *The Ballad of Cable Hogue* (1970). Latigo–Phil Feldman Production. Producer: Sam Peckinpah. Executive Producer: Phil Feldman. Screenplay by John Crawford and Edmund Penney.
6. *Straw Dogs* (1971). Co-production of Talent Associates Films and Amerbroco Films. Producer: David Melnick. Screenplay by David Z. Goodman and Sam Peckinpah from the novel *The Siege of Trencher Farm* by Gordon Williams.
7. *Junior Bonner* (1972). A Joe Wizan–Booth Gardner production. Producer: Joe Wizan. Screenplay by Jeb Rosebrook.
8. *The Getaway* (1972). A Solar/Foster-Brower production for First Artists Production Co. Producers: David Foster and Mitchell Brower. Screenplay by Walter Hill, from the novel by Jim Thompson.
9. *Pat Garrett and Billy The Kid* (1973). A Gordon Carroll–Sam Peckinpah production for MGM. Producer: Gordon Carroll. Screenplay by Rudolph Wurlitzer.
10. *Bring Me the Head of Alfredo Garcia* (1974). An Optimus-Latigo-Esudios Churubusco Co. production for United Artists. Producer: Martin Baum. Screenplay by Gordon Dawson and Sam Peckinpah from a story by Peckinpah and Frank Kowalski.

11. *The Killer Elite* (1975). An Arthur Lewis–Baum/Dantine production, distributed by United Artists. Producers: Martin Baum and Arthur Lewis. Screenplay by Mark Norman and Stirling Silliphant, based on a novel by Robert Rostand.
12. *Cross of Iron* (1977). A co-production of Anglo-EMI Productions, London, distributed by Avco-Embassy. Producers: Alex Winitsky and Arlene Sellers. Screenplay by Julius Epstein, Walter Kelley, and James Hamilton, based on the novel by Willi Heinrich.
13. *Convoy* (1978). EMI Films, distributed by United Artists. Producer: Robert Sherman. Screenplay by B. W. L. Norton, based on the song by C. W. McCall.
14. *The Osterman Weekend* (1983). A 20th Century–Fox release of a Michael Timothy Murphy and Guy Collins presentation of a Davis-Panzer production. Producers: William Panzer and Peter Davis. Screenplay by Alan Sharp, adapted by Ian Masters, and based on the novel by Robert Ludlum.

Editor's Note

I am indebted to Marshall Fine's *Bloody Sam: The Life and Films of Sam Peckinpah* (New York: Donald I. Fine, 1991) for the information in this filmography. See pp. 387–93 for a complete description of Peckinpah's films. For information on Peckinpah's television work and on films that have been released on video, see Paul Seydor, *Peckinpah: The Western Films: A Reconsideration* (Urbana: University of Illinois Press, 1997), 391–98.

CONTRIBUTORS

FRANK BURKE has taught at the University of Kentucky, the University of Manitoba, and Queen's University (Canada). He has worked on Italian, American, and Italian-American cinema and has produced two books on the Italian director Federico Fellini: *From Variety Lights to La Dolce Vita* (New York: G. K. Hall, 1983) and *Fellini's Films: From Postwar to Postmodern* (New York: Macmillan/Twayne, 1995). He is the co-editor (with Marguerite Waller, University of California, Riverside) of *Federico Fellini: Contemporary Perspectives*, currently in press at the University of Toronto Press. He has also authored or edited approximately forty other publications related to all three of his areas of interest.

LEONARD ENGEL, Professor and Chair of English at Quinnipiac University, Hamden, Connecticut, was selected "Outstanding Faculty of the Year" in 1989. He edited *The Big Empty: Essays on the Land as Narrative* (University of New Mexico Press, 1994) and has published numerous articles on American literature, Western fiction and film, and detective fiction and film.

JOHN M. GOURLIE, Professor of Communications at Quinnipiac University, co-wrote (with Leonard Engel) the Introduction to *The Big Empty* and wrote the chapter entitled "Cactus Eden: Sam Peckinpah's *The Ballad of Cable Hogue*." He has written on a variety of topics in American literature and film and is currently at work on a project on literature and the environment.

RICHARD HUTSON teaches English and American Studies at the University of California, Berkeley. He has contributed a chapter on John Ford's *The Searchers* to *The Big Empty*, and his essay on Owen Wister appears in a collection of essays published during the Wister centennial. His recent article, an essay on Teddy Blue Abbott's *We Pointed Them North*, appeared in *Western American Literature* in the summer of 2002. His current interests are in various writings from the cattle trade after the Civil War.

ELAINE MARSHALL teaches courses in American literature, film, and composition at Barton College in Wilson, North Carolina. She has published essays on Stephen Crane and Harriet Jacobs. Recently, she conducted research in the Peckinpah Collection of the Margaret Herrick Library in Los Angeles and is writing a book on the role of women in Peckinpah's films.

ROBERT MERRILL is Foundation Professor of English at the University of Nevada, Reno. He is the author or editor of books on Norman Mailer, Joseph Heller, Kurt Vonnegut, and Raymond Chandler. His essays on a variety of American writers have appeared in such journals as *American Literature, Modern Fiction Studies, Studies in American Fiction, Texas Studies in Literature and Language, Modern Philology,* and *Narrative.* With John L. Simons, he is currently writing a book on Sam Peckinpah's tragic films.

ARMANDO JOSÉ PRATS was born in Havana, Cuba and came to the United States as a political exile at the age of thirteen. An associate professor of film and American literature at the University of Kentucky, he is the author of *Invisible Natives: Myth and Identity in the American Western* (Cornell University Press, 2002).

JOHN L. SIMONS, Professor of English and Film Studies at The Colorado College, specializes in modern American literature and film, with particular focus on the Western. He has published essays on William Carlos Williams, Nathanael West, John Berryman, Philip K. Dick, Thomas Pyncheon, Kurt Vonnegut, Mike Nichols's *Catch-22* (with Robert Merrill), Sam Peckinpah's *The Wild Bunch,* Billy Wilder's *Double Indemnity,* and the entries on "Plains Westerns" and "Gary Cooper" for the *Encyclopedia of the Great Plains* (University of Nebraska Press, forthcoming). He is currently co-authoring a book on Sam Peckinpah with Robert Merrill.

PHILIP J. SKERRY is Professor of English and Film at Lakeland Community College in Mentor, Ohio. He has published several articles on Westerns in *The New Orleans Review* and *The Journal of Popular Film and Television.* He is also a contributing author to the books *Beyond the Stars* (Bowling Green, Ohio: Bowling Green State University Press, 1993 and 1996) and *Superman at Fifty* (New York: Macmillan-Collier, 1988). Currently, he is working on a book on the film *Psycho* to be published by Edwin Mellen Press.

STEPHEN TATUM is the author of *Inventing Billy the Kid: Visions of the Outlaw in America, 1881–1981* (University of Arizona Press, 1982/1997), as well as numerous essays and articles on western American literary and cultural studies. He has written the volume on Cormac McCarthy's *All the Pretty Horses* for the Continuum Contemporaries Series and coedited (with Melody Graulich) a collection of new essays on *The Virginian*, marking the centennial of Owen Wister's *The Virginian*. He is currently completing a book manuscript entitled *The Remington Moment: Dwelling In/With the Late Paintings*. He teaches American literary and cultural studies at the University of Utah.

MATT WANAT is an assistant professor of English at Denison University in Ohio, where he teaches U.S. literature, composition, and courses on the formal and cultural conventions of the Western. He earned a Ph.D. from Ohio State University for his dissertation "'Feels Like Times Have Changed': Sixties Western Heroes," which reads transformations in the Western through sociopolitical contexts and argues for a better understanding of the Western as allegory through an attention to issues of authorship.

INDEX

Achilleus *(The Iliad),* 116, 121
Adorf, Mario, 95, 109
Adventure, Mystery, and Romance: Formula Stories as Art and Popular Culture, 246n
Adventures of Huckleberry Finn, The, 59
African Queen, The, 104
"After great pain, a formal feeling comes," 208
Allen, Michael, 168n
Allied Artists, 6
Altman, Robert, 14, 232, 237
Alvarez, Juan, 134
American Adam, The, 253n
American Bicentennial (1976), 133
Anatomy of Criticism, 58, 64
Anderson, John, 28
Anderson, Lindsay, 241
AndersonMichael, Jr., 89
Anderson, Quentin, 145, 148n
Apocalypse Now, 104
Aristotle, 64, 65
Armstrong, R. G., 16n, 66, 97
Arrowhead, 95, 98, 108
Asad, Talal, 24
Atlas Shrugged, 214
Auden, W. H., 65
Australia, 153, 156, 162, 163

Baker, Joe Don, 11, 152
Ballad of Cable Hogue, The: cinematic technique in, 10–11; and *Convoy,* 130–31, 140–41, 143–47 *passim,* 214; criticism of, 115–17, 122–26, 130–31, 138–47; as epic, 10, 115–17, 122–23, 125–26; mentioned, 10, 22, 56, 118–21 *passim,* 129, 147n, 166, 200, 208, 214; and *The Wild Bunch,* 10, 115–26; themes in: religious, 10, 124–25, 130–31, 138–43, 146–47, 148n; revenge, 138–41, 148n
Ballard, Lucien, 7, 84n, 172
Bassman, George, 77
Battleship Potemkin, The, 122
Beatty, Warren, 246n
Bercovitch, Sacvan, 148n
Berger, Senta, 90, 113n
Bible: The Garden of Eden in, 66, 71, 76, 83n; The Gospel According to St. John, 63, 71–72, 74–75, 77, 79, 85n; — St. Luke, 83n; — St. Mark, 77; — St. Matthew, 82n; Leviticus, 29; mentioned, 7, 10, 39, 64, 69, 75, 80, 83n, 130, 131, 135, 141–42, 145–46; Proverbs, 29; St. Paul in, 137–38
Birdsall, Diane, 113n
Black Rodeo, 168n
Blazing Saddles, 234
Bliss, Michael, 5, 9, 16, 71, 105, 110, 112n, 144, 147n, 148n, 152, 202, 206, 228n, 244, 250–51
Body Heat, 233
Boetticher, Budd, 112n, 232, 237, 246n
Bonanza, 106
Bond, Ward, 240
Bonnie and Clyde, 8
Boone, Daniel, 157
Borgnine, Ernest, 212
Brandon, Henry, 241
Braudy, Leo, 71
Bredahl, A. Carl, 51n
Bresler, Jerry, 88, 104, 105, 110
Breughel, Pieter, 71

Bright, Richard, 187
Bring Me the Head of Alfredo Garcia, 13, 113n, 132, 147n 249
Broken Arrow, 6, 56, 95
Brooks, Mel, 234
"Brown," 55, 59–60
Buell, Lawrence, 83n
Buffalo Bill (William Cody), 32, 68
Buffalo Bill Historical Center, 231
Bunyan, John, 77
Burden of Dreams, 113n
Burke, Frank, 10, 129
Butler, Terence, 13, 143
"Butterfly Mornings," 124

Caan, James, 250, 251, 252
Cagin, Seth, 79
Call of the Wild, The, 216, 229n
Calvinism, 43, 53n
Camus, Albert, 63
Canfield, J. Douglas, 40, 52n, 53n
Carey, Harry, Jr., 241
Carey, Olive, 241
Casablanca, 90
Cawelti, John, 22, 51n, 231–32, 246n
CBS, 6
Chandler, John Davis, 91
Chandler, Raymond, 216
Cheyenne Autumn, 95
Chinatown Nights, 249
Christian Tragedy, 64–66 *passim*, 70–72, 77–80, 81n, 82n, 83n, 84n, 85n
Church, Denver, 6
CIA, 249
Cincinnati Kid, The, 8
cinema verité, 219
Civil War, 240
Clark, David Anthony Tyeeme, 112n
Cleese, John, 233
Coburn, James, 12, 13, 93, 199, 203, 242, 245
Cochise, 95, 108, 239
Cody, William. *See* Buffalo Bill
Cold War era, 166
Columbia Pictures, 104
Combs, Richard, 249
Comic Mind: Comedy and the Movies, The, 58
Confidence Man, The, 59

Conrad, Joseph, 40, 52n
Convoy: background, 132, 211–20; and *The Ballad of Cable Hogue*, 130–31, 140–41, 143–47 *passim*, 214; criticism of, 13–14, 129–38, 140–47, 148n, 211–27; mentioned, 252; religious themes in, 131, 135–38, 141, 145–46, 225; style (narration/point of view), 214–27; and *The Wild Bunch*, 130, 147, 211, 212, 218, 226
Cook, Elisha, Jr., 237
Cooper, Gary, 235, 236
Cooper, James Fenimore, 22, 35, 156, 208
Coppola, Francis Ford, 104, 113n
Corrigan, Robert, 65
Costner, Kevin, 233
Countryman, Edward, and Evonne von Heussen-Countryman, 246n
"Courting of Libby, The," 55, 59–60
Coy, Walter, 240
Craven, Garth, 228–29n
Creed, Barbara, 197n
Crime in the Streets, 6
Cross of Iron, 13, 252
CSI: Crime Scene Investigation, 180
Custer, George Armstrong, 94

Daves, Delmer, 95
Day of the Jackal, 246n
De Wilde, Brandon, 237
Deadly Companions, The, 7, 22, 242
Deeley, Michael, 213, 228n
Dehner, John, 59
Deleuze, Gilles, 163, 165, 168n
Deloria, Philip J., 94, 112n
Democratic Vistas, 148n
Dennehy, Brian, 233
Destry Rides Again, 35
Dickinson, Emily, 208
Difference and Repetition, 168n
Doc, 233
"Dos Pinos," 59
Dray, Robert, 79
Drums Along the Mohawk, 240
Duvall, Robert, 234
Dylan, Bob, 199, 201, 205, 209n

Eastwood, Clint, 52n, 192, 194, 197n, 199, 236

Eisenstein, Sergei, 122
Eliade, Mircea, 23–24, 52n
Eliot, T. S. 216
Emerson, Ralph Waldo, 133, 145, 146, 202
Engel, Leonard, 3, 199, 249
Enter the Dragon, 249
Environmental Imagination, The, 83n

Farber, Stephen, 9
Faulkner, William, 5, 208, 209
Fernandez, Emilio, 244
Film Heritage, 55
film noir (Western), 234
films. *See individual titles*
Fine, Marshall, 112n, 228n
Fink, Harry Julian, 89, 105
first-time western directors, 14, 231–38, 245–46
Fisher, Philip, 148n
Fitzcarraldo, 104
Fitzgerald, F. Scott, 66
Fitzgerald, Robert, 127n
Flintstones, The, 60
Fonda, Henry, 94, 234, 238, 239
Ford, John, 14, 26, 35, 66, 75, 81n, 87, 94–95, 108, 231, 232, 237–42, 243, 246n
formulaic Western, 231, 237, 238
Fort Apache, 94–95, 108, 110, 112n, 239–40
Four Star (Dick Powell's studio), 57
Franklin, Benjamin, 75, 76
Freeman, Danny, 167n
French, Philip, 246n
Fresno State College, 6
Friedberg, Anne, 197n
From Here to Eternity, 246n
Frontier Days, (Prescott, Arizona), 159, 160, 161, 167n
Frye, Northrop, 58, 60, 64, 66, 80, 81n

Geller, Bruce, 60
Gentnen, Richard, 113n
Geronimo, 95, 108, 239
Getaway, The: cinematic techniques and narration in, 11, 84n, 171–73, 176–77, 180–82, 187–91, 194, 196–97; criticism of, 171–97;
themes in: abjection, 171, 175–76, 190; crossing borders, 175–76, 183, 191, 193;

defilement and waste, 175–77 186–91, 194–97; masculinity, 175–86, 193; violence in, 176, 179–86, 194, 196–97
Gilded Age, 153
Glenn, Scott, 233
Godfather, The, 231
"Going Home," 57, 58
Gourlie, John, 3, 10, 115
Great American Cowboy, The, 168n
Great Northfield Minnesota Raid, The, 233–35, 245
Grey, Zane, 231
Guns in the Afternoon. See Ride the High Country
Gunsmoke, 6, 56

Hammett, Dashiell, 216
Hansen, Miriam, 197n
Hardy, Phil, 94, 113n
Harper's Bible Commentary, 73
Harris, Richard, 89
Hartley, Mariette, 63
Hauser, Robert, 211, 213, 218, 219, 226, 228n
Have Gun—Will Travel, 56
Hawks, Howard, 14, 35, 112n, 232, 235, 237, 242, 246n
Hawthorne, Nathaniel, 5
Heart of Darkness, 40, 52n, 97
Hearts of Darkness: A Filmmaker's Apocalypse, 113n
Hector, (*The Iliad*), 45, 121
Heflin, Van, 236
Hemingway, Ernest, 5, 49, 140
Hepburn, Katherine, 104
Herzog, Werner, 104, 113n
Heston, Charlton, 88, 89, 113n
High Noon, 20, 27–29, 232, 235–36, 237, 246n
High Plains Drifter, 166
Hill, Walter, 189
Hitchcock, Alfred, 105
Hobbes, Thomas, 4, 13
Holden, William, 121, 243, 251
Hollywood, 4, 8, 121, 129, 145, 166, 176, 194, 199, 250, 251, 252
Homer, 10, 121, 125, 126, 127n
Honkers, The, 168n

Hopkins, Bo, 244
Horizons West, 246n
Hunter, Jeffrey, 240
Huston, John, 104, 113n
Hutson, Richard, 11, 151
Hutton, Jim, 89

Iliad, The, 10, 115, 116, 126n, 127n
Invasion of the Body Snatchers, 6
Isherwood, Christopher, 63

J. W. Coop, 168n
James, Henry, 145
James, Jesse, 234
Jameson, Richard, 10
"Jeff," 59
Jefferson, Thomas, 25, 26, 39, 52n
Jehlen, Myra, 148n
Jesse James (1940), 234
Johnson, Ben, 11, 111, 171, 120
Jordan, Dorothy, 240
Junior Bonner, background, 11; criticism of, 151–66; themes in: enemy brother, 11, 154, 156, 162–65; rodeo cowboy (hero of repetition), 11, 158, 160, 161–62, 165
Jurado, Katy, 205, 236

Kael, Pauline, 11, 13, 250–53
Kane, Bruce, 84n
Kasdan, Lawrence, 233, 234, 235, 246n
Katz, Ephraim, 113n
Kaufman, Philip, 233, 234, 235
Keats, John, 3, 13
Keith, Brian, 60
Kelley, Grace, 236
Kent State University, 133, 145
Kermode, Frank, 81
Killer Elite, The, 13; criticism of, 249–52; cinematic techniques and narration in, 250–52, 253n
King, Henry, 234
Kintner, Robert, 60
Kipling, Rudyard, 216
Kitses, Jim, 4, 80, 96, 97, 112n, 113n, 246n
Kline, Kevin, 233
"Knife Fighter, The," 6
"Knocking on Heaven's Door," 205

Kolodny, Annette, 82n
Kristeva, Julia, 175, 197n
Kristofferson, Kris, 12, 199, 212, 213, 245
Kurosawa, Akira, 122

L'Amour, Louis, 231
"La Golondrina" ("The Swallow"), 34, 51, 120, 125
Ladd, Alan, 236
Lang, Fritz, 234
Laos, 196
Lawrence, D. H., 208
Lawrence, Elizabeth, 158, 162
Lawson, Tony, 228–29n
Lay of the Land, 82n
Leatherstocking Tales, 35
Leaves of Grass, 133
Leaving Cheyenne, 154
Lemay, Alan, 240
Lenihan, John, 235
Leone, Sergio, 234
Lettieri, Al, 175
Lewis, R. W. B., 26, 29, 52n, 253n
Lewis, Richard Warren, 235
Limerick, Patricia, 153
Lincoln, New Mexico, 201, 206
Little Big Man, 233
London, Jack, 216, 229n
Lonely Are The Brave, 66
Lou Lombardo, 116, 121–22
Ludlum, Robert, 14
Lupino, Ida, 11

McCabe and Mrs. Miller, 166, 232, 237, 246n
McCall, C. W., 211
MacCannell, Juliet Flower, *The Regime of the Brother: After the Patriarchy*, 168n
McCarthy, Joe (Senator), 235
McCrea, Joel, 7, 63, 242, 251
MacDonald, Ian, 235
MacDonald, J. Fred, 56
MacGraw, Ali, 171, 212, 213
McKinney, Doug, 88, 98, 99, 112n
McMurtry, Larry, 153
McQueen, Steve, 11, 152; in *The Getaway*, 171, 177–82
Magnificent Seven, The, 52n

Major Dundee: background, 7–8, 16n, 87–89, 111–12; criticism of, 87–112; mentioned, 22, 85n, 216; themes in: crossing cultural borders, 87–88, 91–93, 95–100, 103, 109–12 *passim*; playing Indian, 94–98, 112n; style (narration and point of view), 88–89, 103, 104–112 *passim*; and *The Wild Bunch*, 8, 16n, 112;
Malcolm, Derek, 13
Man Who Shot Liberty Valance, The, 66, 81n, 95
Man, Beast, Dust: The Story of Rodeo, 167n
Manifest Destiny, 26
Mann, Anthony, 14, 35, 112n, 232, 237, 246n
Mardi, 16n
Markgraf, Sarah, 231
Marsden, Michael, 82
Marshall, Elaine, 14, 211
Marshall, George, 35
Marx, Leo, 25, 52n, 67, 83n
Mason, James, 13
Mast, Gerald, 58
Mellen, Joan, 198n
Melville, Herman, 5, 16n, 23, 52n, 59, 84, 249
Merrill, Robert, 14, 231
Mesce, Bill, 9, 14
Mexico, 12, 22, 53n, 87, 88, 89, 99, 100, 103, 118–19, 123, 134, 176, 183, 194–95, 216
Meyer, Emile, 237
MGM, 7, 12, 200, 209n, 245
Miles, Vera, 241
Miller, Perry, 83n
Milne, Tom, 249
Misfits, The, 66
Mission Impossible, 180
Mitchell, Lee Clark, 235, 236, 246n
Mitchell, Mitch, 107, 108, 109, 111
Moby Dick, 16n
Monte Walsh, 66
"Mrs. Kennedy," 59
Mulvey, Laura, 178
Murphy, Kathleen, 5, 73
Murray, William, 65, 144, 251
My Darling Clementine, 35, 238–39, 246n
Nagel, Joane, 112n

NBC, 7, 60
Neale, Steve, 181, 197n
Nevada, 156
New Yorker, The, 11, 55, 250
Newsweek, 7
Nichols, Bill, 147n
Nietzsche, Friedrich, 21, 51n
Nixon, Richard, 145, 176
Noon Wine, 8
Nora, Pierre, 157, 160, 168n
Norton, B. W. L. (Bill), 215, 229n

O'Brien, Edmond, 244
Oates, Warren, 13, 73, 90, 92, 109
Odyssey, The, 10, 115, 116, 125, 126n, 127n
Oklahoma, 246n
Osterman Weekend, 5, 14, 252

"Painting, The," 55, 59–60
Palacios, Begonia, 100
Palance, Jack, 237
Pat Garrett and Billy the Kid: artistic vision in, 13,14; cuts in, 12, 245, 209n; criticism of, 199–209, 244–46; mentioned, 22, 78, 85n, 186, 211, 238, 242, 244; release of, 12, 245, 200; themes in: changing times and aging, 12, 200–1, 204, 205–9; identity, 12, 199–209; versions of, 12, 200, 209n; western legend of, 12–13, 244–46; and *The Wild Bunch*, 78, 200, 208, 242, 244–46
Pate, Michael, 89, 106
Pechter, William, 249
Peckinpah Collection, The Sam, (at the Margaret Herrick Library, Los Angeles), 211, 228n
Peckinpah, David, 77, 211
Peckinpah, Sam: and American literary tradition, 5–6, 11, 129, 130, 132–34, 135–36, 144, 146–47, 148n, 200, 209; and American history, 6, 8–9, 11–13, 19–20, 21–29 passim, 30–33, 37, 53n, 85n, 133, 144–46; and conventions of the Western, 4–6, 13–15, 19–25 (classic Western), 223–27, 242, 245–46; and Hollywood, 4, 8, 121, 129, 145, 166, 176, 194, 199, 250, 251, 252; and revisionist Western, 5–7,

15–16, 21–22, 25, 39, 60–61, 87, 111, 245–46; artistic vision and expression, 3–6, 13, 14, 15–16, 80–81, 84n, 115–19, 122–23, 125–26, 201, 203, 207–9, 211–18 *passim*, 220, 223, 226–27, 232–33, 237, 245–46, 250–53; comic elements, 7, 55–61 *passim*, 122–23, 143, 202–3, 226–27, 250; family, 6, 64, 65, 77, 83n; films of. *See individual titles*; interviews, meetings, and memos (statements from), 4, 9, 10, 13, 58–59, 64, 65, 78, 121, 132, 147n, 212–15 *passim*, 217–18, 219, 237, 242, 251; life and career, 4–5, 6–16, 55–61 *passim*, 64–65, 71, 85n, 87, 111–12, 125, 132, 242, 245–46, 251–52; major themes of: American Adam (edenic America), 20, 25–26, 28–29, 31, 32, 39, 76, 102, 141–42; Appearance and reality, 7, 29, 32; changing times and aging, 3–5, 12, 13, 22, 32, 35, 80–81n, 120, 158–66 *passim*, 175–86 *passim*, 193–94, 200–1, 204, 205–8, 242–43; code of masculinity, 11, 15, 40–45 *passim*, 50–51, 87, 112n, 117–20, 122, 129, 144, 147, 200, 244; crossing borders, 8, 87–88, 91–93, 95–100, 103, 109–12, 175–76, 183, 191–93; identity, 12, 34, 48, 199–209 *passim*; revenge, 7, 138–41, 224–25; self-sacrifice and redemption, 10, 19–20, 36–37, 45–51 *passim*, 63–64, 77–81, 82n, 84n, 115–17, 119–20, 134–38 *passim*, 140, 142–43, 145–46, 195, 225–27 250, 253n; violence, 4–5, 8–9, 11–12, 13, 15–16, 30, 45–46, 49–50, 78–79, 117, 119, 121, 123, 125, 142, 176, 179–86 *passim*, 194, 196–97, 202, 204, 205–6, 207, 208, 225, 252; western legend (heroic identity), 3–5, 7, 12–13, 33, 35, 40, 48, 58–59, 80–81, 135, 145, 153, 157, 161, 164, 201, 203, 205–6, 245–46; women and feminism, 11, 14–15, 44, 46–47, 69, 82n, 83n, 101, 102, 116, 122–23, 129, 139–40, 143–44, 166, 175, 177, 178, 182–86 *passim*, 194, 244;
style of: editing and cinematic technique, 3–6, 8, 10–11, 12, 46, 49–50, 70, 76–78 *passim*, 80, 81n, 121, 123, 171–73, 176, 177, 181–82, 188–91, 196–97, 251–52; narration/point of view, 3–6, 8–9, 10–16 *passim*, 49–50, 80–81, 84n, 88–89, 103, 104–12, 115–19, 121–23, 125–26, 151, 171–73, 176–77, 180, 187–91, 194, 196–97, 200, 204–5, 207–9, 214–21 *passim*, 244, 250–53;
television work of, 6–8, 55–61 *passim*, 242. See also *The Westerner*, and *individual titles*

Penn, Arthur, 8, 233
Perry, Frank, 233
Peters, Brock, 90, 109
Phillips, Gene D., 236
Picaresque hero, 58
Pickens, Slim, 11, 183, 205
Poe, Edgar Allan, 69
"Poet, The," 202
Porter, Katherine Anne, 8
Powell, Dick, 57
Power, Tyrone, 234
Prats, Armando, 6, 19
Prescott, Arizona, 11, 155, 160: Frontier Days in, 159, 160, 161, 167n
Preston, Robert, 11
Prince, Stephen, 5, 9, 16, 53n, 166, 229n
Propp, Vladimir, 151

Qualen, John, 241

Rafferty, Terrence, 55
Ranch Life and the Hunting-Trail, 167n
Rand, Ayn, 214
Raphael, D. D., 81n
Ray, Nicholas, 166
Red River, 35, 112n,, 232, 237, 242
Reisner, Joel, 84n
Return of Frank James, The (1940), 234
Reyguaera, Francisco, 95
Ride the High Country: criticism of, 3–4, 32–33, 35–39, 242–44; criticism and religious themes (Christian), 7, 63–85; mentioned, 19, 22, 29, 34, 87, 131, 166, 186, 200, 211, 251; release of, 7; and *The Wild Bunch*, 4–5, 19, 22, 29, 32–33, 34–37, 78, 81n, 85n, 242–44
Riding the Video Range: the Rise and Fall of the Western on Television, 56

INDEX ❖ 267

Rifleman, The, 6, 57
Rio Bravo, 235
Rio Grande, 87, 98
Riot in Cell Block 6, 11
Robertson, Cliff, 234
Rodeo Cowboys in the North American Imagination, 168n
Roosevelt, Theodore, 153, 157, 158
Rosebrook, Jeb, 152, 157–60 *passim*, 165
Ruiz, Jose Carlos, 93
Rutherford, Jonathan, 197n
Ryan, Robert, 244

Sahl, Mort, 213, 228n
Said, Edward, 24, 52n
San Rafael Military Academy, 6
Sanchez, Jaime, 244
Sante Fe Ring, 12, 200, 201, 208
Sarchette, Barry, 201
Savage Cinema: Sam Peckinpah and the Rise of the Ultraviolent Movies, 9, 168n
Schell, Maximilian, 13
Schrader, Paul, 242
Scott, Nathan, 81n
Scott, Pippa, 240
Scott, Randolph, 7, 63, 243
Searchers, The (film), 20, 26–27, 51n, 52n, 95, 98, 237, 238, 240–42, 246
Searchers, The (novel), 240
Sense of an Ending, The, 81
Seydor, Paul, 4, 5, 6, 10, 16, 22, 50, 51n, 52n, 56, 68, 82n, 126n, 133, 148n, 200, 201, 229n, 237, 244, 245, 246n
Shakespeare, William, 64
"Shall We Gather at the River," 241
Shane, 20, 25–26, 27, 35, 51n, 57, 232, 235, 236–37, 246n
Sharp, Alan, 14
"Sharpshooter, The," 6
Shaw, Tom, 228n
Siegel, Don, 6
Silke, Jim, 213, 215, 216, 228n, 229n
Silverado, 233–34, 235, 246n
Silverman, Kaja, 197–98n
Simmons, Garner, 4, 13, 14, 56, 60, 76–77, 147n, 209n
Simons, John, 7, 63, 244
Skerry, Philip, 7, 55, 61n, 78, 81n

Slotkin, Richard, 23, 52n, 98, 113n
Smith, Henry Nash, 26, 52n
Smith, Paul, 181, 192–93, 197n, 198n
"Song of the Open Road," 131
Sophocles, 209
Stagecoach, 19, 26, 39, 238
Starr, Ron, 63
Stephen, St. (Christian martyr), 83n
Stevens, Brad, 203, 204–5
Stevens, George, 14, 175, 200, 232, 236, 237, 246n, 251
Straw Dogs, 11, 125, 144–45, 251
Studies in Classic American Literature, 208
Sundowners, The, 246n
Swanson, Gillian, 197n

Tales of Wells Fargo, 56
Tarantino, Quentin, 188
Tatum, Stephen, 11, 171
Taxi Driver, 231
television Western, the, 6–7, 55–61, 242–43. *See also individual titles*
Ten Commandments, The, 91
Thompson, Jim, 189
Thoreau, Henry David, 20, 21, 51n, 73, 133
Three Days of the Condor, 249
Tin Star, The, 35
Tombstone Territory, 56
Tompkins, Jane, 82n, 231,
Touch of Evil, 113n
Transcendentalism, 133, 135, 145–47n
Trevor, Claire, 238
Troy, 121
Turner, Frederick Jackson, 158
Turner, Ted, 209n
Twain, Mark, 5, 59

Unforgiven, 52n
U.S. Constitution, 75
University of Southern California, 6

Vietnam War, 8, 9, 49, 53n, 133, 145, 166, 176, 196
Virginian, The, 153
Virginian, The, (1929 film version), 167n

Wakeman, John, 14, 16n
Wallace, Mike, 213

Wanat, Matt, 8, 87
Warren, Charles Marquis, 95
Warshow, Robert, 242–43
Watergate, 133
Wayne, John, 81n, 94–95, 112n, 233, 235, 236, 238–40, 242, 246n
Webster's Collegiate Dictionary, 199
Weddle, David, 5, 9, 16, 56, 66, 104, 105, 113n, 119, 126n, 168n, 216, 229n
Welles, Orson, 113n
West of Everything: The Inner Life of Westerns, 82n, 231
Westbrook, Max, 239
Westermeier, Clifford P., 167n
Western, the: conventions of, 4–6, 13–15, 19–25 (classic Western), 223–27, 231–32, 245–46; revisionist, 5–7, 15–16, 20–23, 25, 39, 60–61, 233
Westerner, The, 7, 55–61, 242–43. See also individual titles
Westerns: Aspects of a Movie Genre, 246n
Westerns: Making the Man in Fiction and Film, 246n
When the Legends Die, 168n
Whitehall, Richard, 65
White Hunter, Black Heart, 113n
White Jacket, 23, 52n
Whitman, Walt, 26, 131, 133–34, 145, 146, 147n, 148n
Who Shot the Sheriff?: The Rise and Fall of the Television Western, 56
Wild Bunch, The, background, 4–5, 8; and *The Ballad of Cable Hogue*, 10, 115–17, 122–26; and *Convoy*, 130, 147, 211, 212, 218, 226; criticism of, 29–31, 40–51, 52–53n, 115–26, 243–44; as epic, 10, 31–32, 33–34, 47–48, 115–17, 121–22, 125–26; and *Major Dun*dee, 8, 16n, 112; mentioned, 13, 14, 19, 56, 78, 85n, 130, 147, 148n, 166, 200, 208, 211, 212, 218, 226, 245, 246, 249, 251; release of, 5, 8–9; and *Pat Garrett and Billy the Kid*, 78, 200, 208, 242, 244–46; and *Ride the High Country*, 19, 22, 29, 32–33, 34–37, 78, 85n, 242–43; violence in, 4, 8–10, 14–15, 30, 46, 49–50, 53n, 117, 252
Williams, Tennessee, 6
Willis, Sharon, 188, 198n
Wister, Owen, 82n, 153, 231
Wolfe, Thomas, 11
Wood, Natalie, 240
World War II, 209
Wurlitzer, Rudy, 205, 207
Wyatt Earp, 246n

Yoggy, Gary, 56
You Can't Go Home Again, 11
Young, Burt, 250, 252
Young, Gig, 251–52
Young Mr. Lincoln, 84n
Younger, Cole, 234

Zane Grey Theater, 57
Zinneman, Fred, 14, 232, 235, 236, 246n